The Costa Rica Reader

THE

COSTA RICA

READER

HISTORY, CULTURE, POLITICS

Edited by Steven Palmer and Iván Molina

DUKE UNIVERSITY PRESS   *Durham and London*   2004

2nd printing, 2006
© 2004 Duke University Press
All rights reserved
Printed in the United States of America on acid-free paper ∞
Designed by Amy Ruth Buchanan
Typeset in Dante by Tseng Information Systems, Inc.
Library of Congress Cataloging-in-Publication Data appear
on the last printed page of this book.

To Lubín
in loving memory

Contents

VI. *Other Cultures and Outer Reaches* 229

VII. *Working Paradise* 275

VIII. *Tropical Soundings* 319

Acknowledgments

Creating this anthology proved a pleasure because of the goodwill shown to the project by virtually everyone we approached. We would like to thank the authors of the texts and illustrations included in this work, or their heirs or other copyright holders, for authorizing reproduction of the material. Many authors wrote original pieces for this collection, or gave their time to rework previously published material: special thanks are due to Eulalia Bernard, Kirk Bowman, Marc Edelman, Steve Marquardt, Manrique Mata-Montero, Carmelo Mesa-Lago, Eugenia Rodríguez, and two writers who wish to remain anonymous. We are grateful to Paula Palmer, whose generosity with her time and materials was truly extraordinary given that we had never been in contact prior to undertaking this collection. Much of Steven Palmer's translation and thinking about this reader was done under the roof of Don Narciso, Nena, and Eylem Rodríguez, and Doña Blasa Barrantes, and he thanks them for that and so much more. The book would not have been possible without the cooperation of the Museo de Arte Costarricense, the Museo Nacional de Costa Rica, the Museo Histórico Cultural Juan Santamaría, the Archivo Nacional de Costa Rica, the University of Costa Rica newspaper *Semanario Universidad*, and the Centro de Investigación en Identidad y Cultura Latinoamericanas (CIICLA) of the University of Costa Rica. Our thanks also to Verónica Ríos, who helped make contact with some authors, and Ericka Lippi, who assisted with the collection of sources. At Duke University Press, we wish to extend our thanks to Miriam Angress for her editorial assistance, and especially to Valerie Millholland for encouraging us to pursue the project, providing excellent advice throughout, and keeping us going with her enthusiasm.

A Note on Style and Sources

Many of the selections in this anthology are abridged, and some have had footnotes and other scholarly armature removed. Readers interested in the full versions should refer to the Acknowledgment of Copyrights section.

The occasional term that may have an odd or pejorative ring for readers (for example, the repeated use of the word *Indian* in selections on the colonial period) have been retained because they are the accepted norm in Latin American scholarship.

Translations in this anthology were done by Steven Palmer.

Introduction

In 1999, the Costa Rican Tourism Institute officially declared Costa Rica "a land of marvels," their marketing campaign only the latest in a long line of celebrations of Costa Rican exceptionalism. The country has been imagined as the Switzerland of Central America and, in one *Time* magazine report, as a tropical Shangri-la. It has been hailed as a democratic oasis on a continent scorched by dictatorship and revolution; the ecological Mecca of a biosphere laid waste by deforestation and urban blight; and an egalitarian, middle-class society blissfully immune to the violent class and racial conflicts haunting most Latin American countries. As John and Mavis Biesanz put it a half-century ago in *Costa Rican Life*, the "little country of the Ticos" has been characterized "by one writer after another" as a land of "peace, hard work, and progress."

Costa Ricans themselves have been only too happy to concur that they are exceptional—to the point of finding evidence of their blessed distinction in the oddest places. In 1909, the great man of letters Ricardo Fernández Guardia declared that the terrible poverty and isolation suffered by the society during the colonial period had been a positive thing, since "such great and prolonged misfortune served to inculcate habits of work and sobriety in the Costa Rican people." Two decades later, another brilliant intellectual, Carlos Monge, would take this statement a step further, finding in the equally shared misery of the colonial era the origin of a supposed "rural democracy" that made Costa Rica different from every other Latin American country and explained its tendency toward peaceful politics. Indeed, Costa Rica has never been consumed by the civil strife, militarism, and race-based oppression characteristic of its neighbors. Perhaps most strikingly, it is the only country in Latin America to have enjoyed uninterrupted political democracy over the past fifty years, a time when even bastions of democracy like Chile and Uruguay suffered bloody military coups and long dictatorships that replaced civil liberties with state terror. It is above all this democratic heritage that makes the exceptionalist proposition so compelling.

The mantra of Costa Rican exceptionalism can also prove disconcerting, however. For one thing, it provides the centerpiece of a dubious mythology

Costa Rica

that equates Costa Rican national identity with an alleged white racial heritage, setting it apart from other Latin American countries. This generates xenophobia and promotes discrimination against the vast majority of visibly nonwhite Costa Ricans, especially those from Guanacaste and Limón, who have marked mestizo and African ancestries. A deep-seated racist strain remains alive and well in Costa Rica. In a recent cyberspace chat, one Costa Rican mused, "Sometimes I wish they'd leave us alone like in the colonial era. Thanks to God, Costa Rica is a marvelous country protected by the Virgin of Los Angeles. . . . Costa Rica has been genetically privileged, this is understood around the world, so why do we want to ruin this inheritance?"[1] On the more formal end of the intellectual spectrum, the notion that Costa Rica is a historical freak, or "outlier," allows social scientists to dismiss the country's relevance for understanding patterns of development in Latin America and elsewhere.

If we adjust our lens a bit, the exceptionalist picture of Costa Rica blurs very quickly. The country's coffee economy offers a classic example of development based on a single export commodity — and of the pitfalls of this so-called monocrop route into the emerging global economy. From the colonial period to the present, the northwestern part of the country has hosted a ranching economy of vast haciendas that bears a strong resemblance to other Central American countries. After 1880, Costa Rica also became the original "banana republic": it was the crucible of the United Fruit Company, a transnational giant long linked to U.S. power in Latin America. From William Walker's attempt to take over Central America in the 1850s, to Teddy Roosevelt's canal project in early twentieth-century Panama, to Ronald Reagan's obsession with destroying Nicaragua's revolution, U.S. policy has exerted as much pressure on Costa Rica as it has on any other country in the area. More recently, while Costa Rica received international laurels for its peace and ecological initiatives, the government has tried to implement structural adjustment programs as comprehensive as any others on the continent. The logging of the rain forest assumed feverish rates equivalent to those in the Brazilian Amazon. All the while a new super-elite associated with drug trafficking and other forms of transnational corruption have gained a new foothold in Costa Rica's national society.

We resist the temptation to see the country as an exception, yet we do insist on the distinctiveness of its past and present. We understand Costa Rica as one recognizably Latin American outcome, its history a network of Latin American paths tracing a particular journey. These paths may be most visible here, but to one degree or another, they have been blazed everywhere in the region, and we think they are worth rediscovering and exploring. Its size and geographical location mean that Costa Rica is, and will continue to be, a highly vulnerable country, and the peoples of Costa Rica have met the challenge of this vulnerability in a variety of ways. This book shows Costa Rica as a place of alternatives and possibilities that undermine stereotypes about the region's history and call into question the idea that current dilemmas facing Latin America are inevitable or insoluble.

During the colonial era, Costa Ricans suffered a relatively miserable lot, and they have depended on two agricultural exports for most of the modern era. Yet they have built a democratic political system and achieved a healthy measure of social justice in a region where dictatorship and grotesque inequality have been the sad norm. Contemporary Costa Rican society struggles to maintain ecological dignity against the tide of expanding nontraditional export agriculture and a booming tourist economy, and tries to preserve high levels of social services and social cohesion in the face of the antistatist pressures of global free trade. Many pundits are telling us that globalization has stripped individual countries of their capacity to shape their own destinies. If this is said about the large, powerful metropolitan countries, how much more true must it be for the tiny ones on the periphery? Yet Costa Ricans have been able to fashion an uncommonly democratic and equitable society within the small spaces left them in the grand construction of a global political economy. This confirms that Third World people do make their own history, though they may not make it just as they choose.

★ ★ ★

It is less than 300 miles from Costa Rica's southern frontier with Panama to its northern border with Nicaragua, and the country's Pacific-to-Caribbean width never exceeds 161 miles. Off the Pacific side are two small but notable islands: San Lucas, once a dreaded penal colony, and the Isla de Coco, famous for its stories of pirates and buried loot and today a National Park branded "treasure island" by the tourism marketers. Costa Rica is a tiny country, then, of about 20,000 square miles, and at roughly 4 million inhabitants, relatively small in population as well. The greatest share of that population lives in the Central Valley, an area accounting for only 6.4 percent of national territory which stretches from the cities of San Ramón in the west to Turrialba in the east. Justly famous for its extraordinary range of microclimates, flora, and fauna, Costa Rica is not known for its cultural diversity. This was certainly different prior to the Spanish conquest. At that time, as many as twenty distinct indigenous societies numbering in the hundreds of thousands and speaking many different languages inhabited the area. The disaster of conquest reduced the numbers of indigenous people under Spanish control to a mere 10,000 at the beginning of the 1600s. This had important consequences for the area's subsequent development. The scarcity of labor made the province unattractive to most settlers, and given the weak colonial economy, Spanish settlers could not afford to import large numbers of African slaves. The failure to build a colonial society on indigenous or slave labor led to a peasant economy in the Central Valley during the 1700s. The continuing migrations of families of free mestizo peasants outside the Central Valley, especially during the twentieth century, along with the extension of a government presence to all parts of the country, provided the basis for a relatively coherent nation.

Still, modern Costa Rica has been shaped by geographical, social, and cultural diversity. Already during the colonial period, cattle estates and a peasantry of pervasive mulatto and indigenous origins characterized the north and central Pacific areas. The Caribbean, with its cocoa plantations and African slaves, also offered landscapes quite distinct from that taking shape in the Central Valley. During the nineteenth and twentieth centuries, ranching activity on the Pacific side, as well as the development of the banana economy first on the Caribbean lowlands and later in the Pacific south, shaped the social and economic characteristics of these areas and, in the case of the banana industry, brought a large immigration wave of people of Afro-Antillean descent. Nevertheless, the populations of the Central Valley provided the institutional and cultural bases of national society, not those of the Pacific or the Caribbean. The former was a society characterized by small and medium producers in both city and countryside, and market relations prevailed here, rather than coercion based on factors such as ethnic difference.

One of Costa Rica's clearest traits has been to resolve conflict by channeling it in a legal and institutionalized fashion. This tendency had become apparent by the end of the colonial period, especially in the Central Valley, and it was consolidated in the nineteenth and twentieth centuries. Forces favoring social, ethnic, and cultural integration have tended to outweigh those favoring discrimination. The most important of these integrative forces have been the public education system and an electoral dynamic that by the end of the nineteenth century was already promoting the electoral registry of all adult Costa Ricans independent of ethnicity, education, or class. In Costa Rica, the state has played—and continues to play—a central role in the management and resolution of differences and conflicts, and this dynamic has favored the strengthening of the institutional bases of national life.

During the crisis years of the 1980s, it often appeared that these deep continuities in Costa Rican life were being scrambled or erased altogether. Yet as a new century gets underway, some familiar patterns have reasserted themselves. Perhaps most important, the popular protests against the structural adjustment program begun in the 1980s—protests shaped and made possible due to a long-established democratic dynamic—imposed a gradual rhythm on reforms intended to cut back the state's role in guaranteeing the welfare of all Costa Ricans. This has meant that economic restructuring, some of it drastic in scope, has taken place without a radical jump in poverty or unemployment rates. And these are unemployment rates that have remained low despite the immigration of tens of thousands of Nicaraguans since the mid-1980s. The newcomers are remaking Costa Rican culture in ways that, while still far from determined, appear much less dramatic than the xenophobic panic of the 1990s predicted. The advent of large-scale tourism and the installation of high-technology manufacturing plants, led by INTEL, have also ensured economic stability for the moment. The pressures of public opinion, meanwhile, have propelled a new struggle against the corruption and impunity of the elites in all areas of national life, including the much-vaunted but ill-treated environment.

As the twenty-first century takes flight, public accountability has become a focus of Costa Rican social and political life.

* * *

Instead of succumbing to the notion that Costa Rica is a happy anomaly, our reader is designed to provide windows onto the country's extraordinary past and present, ones that offer unique perspectives on some of the continent's most pressing issues. The anthology features a diverse cast of characters: eloquent working-class raconteurs from San José's poorest barrios; English-speaking Afro-Antilleans of Limón Province; Nicaraguan immigrants; factory workers; dissident members of the intelligentsia; indigenous people struggling against ethnocide; and children living through civil war, to name but a few. They tell of themselves and their country in ways that brush against the grain of ethnic and middle-class homogeneity. We have also included an eclectic and lively selection of travel writing, essays, literature, scholarship, and visual "takes." Over the years, the country has been blessed with original thinkers from different social classes, and it has attracted perceptive visitors. Many of the finer exponents of this broad intellectual tradition are anthologized here, translated into English for the first time.

The anthology has eight parts. We begin with the period from the initial Native American encounter with the Spanish through to the early era of statehood in the 1830s. The reader's second part concentrates on the nineteenth century, when the coffee boom and the rise of the Liberal republic cemented Costa Rica's national identity. Part 3 is dedicated to charting the emergence of the social question and the radical politics of the first half of the twentieth century. The subsequent section complements these ideas with a focus on the evolution of the country's unique democratic institutions and fresh perspectives on the civil war of 1948, which temporarily broke apart the machine of Costa Rican democracy in revealing ways. The fifth part of the reader provides vignettes of the incredible "Costa Rican Dream" of social democratic consensus and middle-class prosperity the country lived from the 1950s until the crash of the early 1980s, when Central America descended into revolution and much of the world into economic slump. The final three parts are thematic and oriented toward understanding this small nation-state's complex present. "Other Cultures and Outer Reaches" explores the real diversity of the country's peoples and regions, as well as their past and present confrontations with discrimination and assimilation. This section is followed by "Working Paradise," which provides a selection of texts that see the country's ecology not as pristine, virgin Nature being ravaged, threatened, and rolled back but as a rich natural environment worked continuously and often brutally in order to sustain human and corporate life. Finally, "Tropical Soundings" offers a sampler pack of contemporary Costa Ricans negotiating the exhilarating—if treacherous and contaminated—waters of globalization as the mall supplants the town plaza, a spectacular tourism boom transforms the social as well as the natural topography, and the foundations of the national economy are turned upside down. Yet—to the surprise of almost everybody—Costa Ricans have never persisted more firmly in their defense of social democracy.

Note

1. Cited in Carlos Sandoval, *Otros amenazantes: Los nicaragüenses y la formación de identidades nacionales en Costa Rica* (San José: Editorial de la Universidad de Costa Rica, 2003), 270.

I

Birth of an Exception?

The exceptional attributes of contemporary Costa Rica are commonly assumed to have pre-Columbian or colonial origins. In the century after 1880, nationalist historians forged three myths in particular about these origins, ones frequently repeated uncritically by visitors and American scholars. One is that when the Spanish arrived, they found but a tiny indigenous population in Costa Rica. The second holds that the Spanish conquest of the area was essentially peaceful. The third, more complex, myth of Costa Rican exceptionalism claims that the lack of indigenous people to serve as laborers and the scarcity of precious metals made Costa Rica a poor and marginal colony, a condition from which a society of homogeneous yeoman farmers without any meaningful class or racial divisions emerged and flowered in the eighteenth century. This, then, constituted the humble but sound origin of the "rural democracy" that remains the core of the nation-state to the present day.

The first two of these myths are nonsense. Historical demographers have shown that prior to the arrival of Columbus in Cariari (today Puerto Limón) in 1502, the territory of Costa Rica was home to about 400,000 indigenous people. They were organized into small and politically fragmented chieftainships, not comparable in complexity to the Mayan groups in the north of Central America. Some of the largest and most organized indigenous societies in Costa Rica were located in the Nicoya region. They were influenced by Mesoamerican culture, and the cultivation of corn predominated. In the Caribbean lowlands and the Pacific south, by contrast, populations were more dispersed, the consumption of *pejibaye* (the rich, pulpy fruit of a palm tree) and yucca was the norm, and the influence of Chibcha culture from northern South America prevailed. Both poles influenced the Central Valley, which was divided into two confederations of chieftainships, Garabito and Guarco. The Spanish conquest of Costa Rica lasted for more than half a century after efforts got underway in 1510. The genocidal enslavement of the indigenous societies of Nicoya on the Pacific north coast was the conquest's first stage. Its second phase began with fruitless attempts to consolidate a Spanish settlement on the country's Caribbean side. In the process, the Spaniards reduced the indigenous population to the point of extinction through disease, war, reprisals, relocation, and brutal exploitation. The Native American population stood at about 120,000 in 1569, and had fallen to 10,000 by 1611. By 1675, a mere 500 "Indios" paid tribute. One can hardly call any of this a peaceful conquest of a virtually uninhabited area.

Addressing the myth of rural democracy requires a more nuanced look at the way colonial Costa Rica was configured into three different zones—a basic division established by about 1650. In the Central Valley *encomenderos* (Spaniards with special rights to indigenous labor and tribute), colonial functionaries, and ecclesiastics took control of the agricultural and craft wealth produced by the indigenous populations. In the Pacific center and north, cows, mules, and horses were raised on great estates. This area's economy experienced its greatest growth after 1750, when the displacement of pasturage by export crops in El Salvador opened a market for cattle on the hoof from Nicaragua and Costa Rica. Finally, on the Caribbean side, some cacao production developed and enjoyed a brief boom, but waned in the face of competition from Caracas, Maracaibo and Guayaquil. Although the cacao boom was based on the labor of imported African slaves, the slave trade was limited in Costa Rica and did not become an alternative to compensate for the collapse of the indigenous population. Beyond these spaces dominated by Spanish culture, in the coastal plains of Talamanca and near the current border with Nicaragua, so-called *indios bravos* (wild Indians) took refuge and resisted Spanish conquest until the second half of the nineteenth century.

Costa Rica found itself on the margins of the colonial Central American world due to a lack of mines and the scarcity of indigenous survivors. The Spaniards who settled in Costa Rica failed to construct a society similar to that of their neighbors, that is, one based on the exploitation of indigenous and slave labor. The development of a peasant economy in the Central Valley indeed proved the fundamental outcome of this failure. The families of small and medium agriculturalists constituted a free peasantry with a strong mercantile vocation, and they did become the principal social group of the Central Valley during the eighteenth century. In contrast to the myth of rural democracy, however, an unequal access to land and significant differences in wealth marked their reality, and in their majority, they had mixed-race (mestizo and mulatto) ancestry. Agricultural colonization begun by this peasantry extended the primary area of settlement from Cartago and environs to the west, leading to the founding of the towns of Heredia (1706), San José (1736), and Alajuela (1782). These tiny urban milieus, where the more specialized artisans lived, also bred a clear colonial elite made up of small groups of merchants, owners of large estates, and military, civil, and ecclesiastical functionaries. Their wealth came from unequal exchange with the peasantry: they bought the agricultural surplus at low prices and sold imported articles at high ones. The so-called rural democracy of the eighteenth century was a society of peasants and merchants in which the exploitation of the former by the latter was not based on physical coercion, but rather on the different position each enjoyed in market relations.

Ethnic and class differences did divide and separate the population of the Central Valley, but the people experienced four important processes of integration. First, social hierarchies depended increasingly on economic wealth rather than ethnic origin, a phenomenon aided by the process of race mixture. According to figures from 1777–78, the province was ethnically comprised of 60 percent mestizos, 18 percent mulattoes and blacks, 12 percent Indians, and only 10 percent Spanish (both peninsular and American-born, the latter of whom claimed pure racial lineage back to Spain). Second, in contrast to other parts of Hispanic America, where a deep cultural division existed between Indian and Hispanic societies, in the Central Valley of Costa Rica, a Hispanic and Catholic culture took shape and was shared — if unequally — by most groups. The third factor favoring social cohesion was the size and location of the mass of the population. In 1824, the province had only about sixty thousand inhabitants, and four out of every five of them lived in the Central Valley, in small urban and rural communities strongly endogamic. As a result, the spread of family ties helped to compensate for social and ethnic divisions and promoted cohesion at a time when colonization of the agricultural frontier tended to remove emigrants from their hometowns. Finally, as some of the following selections will reveal, Costa Ricans tended to channel individual and collective conflicts along legal and institutional avenues even in the colonial period.

When Costa Rica became independent in 1821, it was the society of the Central Valley — not that of the Caribbean with its cacao plantations and slaves, and not that of the Pacific center and north with its vast haciendas — that provided the foundations of Costa Rica's national experience and institutional character. That is, the basis of Costa Rica's so-called exceptionalism was a certain regional development whose agrarian structure resembled that of other parts of Latin America, such as Antioquia in Colombia, Boconó in Venezuela, Santa Fe in Argentina, the Bajío in Mexico, and the Cordillera in Puerto Rico. In contrast to these areas, which developed as local or regional peculiarities, the ever more differentiated yet integrated world of Costa Rica's Central Valley became the foundation of the nation-state. Moreover, distance from the fractious centers of Central American political and economic power in Guatemala and El Salvador allowed the province to evade the protracted civil wars of the postindependence era — wars that also consumed the imperial pretensions of Costa Rica's more powerful neighbors to the north, who might otherwise have conquered and annexed the province.

Warriors and Sacred Struggle

Pre-Columbian Distinctions

The pre-Columbian indigenous societies of the Pacific north displayed a greater Meso-american influence, especially in religion and art, than those of the Caribbean, where a greater Chibcha influence prevailed. The tendencies are evident in these two works, one realized in ceramic, the other in stone.

(left) Jug with anular base; Pacific north, 800–1350 C.E. (Museo Nacional de Costa Rica)
(right) Male figure; Caribbean, 500–1000 C.E. (Museo Nacional de Costa Rica)

A Conqueror Looks on the Bright Side

Town Council of Castillo de Garci-Muñoz

In 1560, the colonial administrators of Guatemala gave Juan de Cavallón the right to conquer and settle the territory then known as New Cartago and Costa Rica. His expedition left Nicaragua in two groups: the first tried to establish a settlement on the Caribbean, but was thwarted by indigenous resistance. The second, under Cavallón, penetrated into Costa Rica via Nicoya, and in March 1561 founded Castillo de Garci-Muñoz, the first settlement in the Central Valley. But the Audiencia then recalled Cavallón and allowed Juan Vázquez de Coronado to take his place. In 1562, the new leader had his town council write the following letter, a representative of a classic genre. These letters underlined the sacrifices the conquistadors had made in the name of God and king, while they also solicited favors from the Crown and speculated wildly about the economic possibilities of the territory they had subdued (often by making spurious comparisons with the spectacular conquests of the Aztecs and Incas). Ironically, this letter was one of the sources used to forge the myth of Costa Rica's peaceful conquest.

Catholic Royal Majesty,

By other letters that we have written Your Majesty we have given a lengthy account of how, in your royal name, we are engaged in the pacification and discovery of the provinces of New Cartago and Costa Rica, and of how, because of the rebellion and stubborn disobedience of the natives who are set in their many ancient rites and sacrifices, we have suffered trying to attract them to the knowledge of our Lord and the dominion of Your Majesty by peaceful means because they have done everything possible, with riots and treachery, to defend against the settlement of this city. . . .

On the second of November of this year, Juan Vázquez de Coronado entered this city of Castillo, where the Spanish people of the province are gathered, and he was received with much love and goodwill by everyone. The colors were presented and all the customary formalities were extended him. Realizing the urgent needs of all who were there, the said Juan Vázquez gave and supplied to almost everyone linens, sheets, cloths, shirts, dresses, arms, horses, and shoes and many other things of which he came well provided, and so took care of the said needs. He spent his goods liberally and with great generosity on everyone, inspiring them to serve Your Majesty with greater zeal and willingness in the campaign. The said Juan Vázquez, besides spending a vast sum in gold pesos, put himself deeply in debt in order to provide the aforementioned relief.

And afterwards he immediately dispatched his master at arms and other captains to the lands of Garabito and Coyoche, leading chieftains who were rebelling against us, so that they might be made to understand how he had come to these provinces sent by Your Majesty to pacify them and settle the place and bring the natives to a knowledge of God our Lord and under the dominion of Your Majesty. By peaceful means and with much love and many gifts he persuaded them, sending them ransoms and presents and getting them to agree that the gospel might be preached among them. And our Lord has willed that through the determined zeal with which the said Juan Vázquez serves Your Majesty, eight chieftains have arrived and are now in this city. They have consigned themselves to the dominion of Your Majesty, recognizing you as their sovereign lord. We believe that, God willing, in this way they will attract and subdue the rest.

According to what has been seen so far, this province offers great wealth, with fertile soil and abounding with good and delicate airs and waters, good sky and land, with temperatures more cool than hot. It has oaks, alfalfa and plantain and verbena and other trees of Spain, and oranges and lemons, and we believe it will produce other fruits. The people are rich, of a good disposition; they closely resemble those of Peru in their clothes, customs, and service; their faces are lovely, sharp and wise, and they can have our Spanish language introduced to them and, through God, our law and Christian faith. All wear gold lockets, and it is believed that they have among them a great quantity of very rich mines of this metal, although up to now we have not searched for them due to the demanding tasks that have presented themselves.

We greatly need Your Majesty's royal favor and require that those who govern in these parts understand that Your Majesty is served by the continuation of the said pacification and settlement. It is going ahead in peace and with Christian virtue as Your Majesty has wished it, and the said Juan Vázquez is carrying it out with integrity. And we ask that Your Majesty favor us with his royal treasury for the purpose of this mission, since up to now this has not been done. For such an important thing it will be necessary, and the fortune of any one individual will not be enough because the costs involved are large.

Hunting Indians

Claudia Quirós

The Central Valley was subdued beginning in 1561, but in the northern plains and the southern Talamanca region, important refuges of so-called wild Indians consolidated themselves and survived throughout the colonial period despite constant harassment from the Spanish. Unlike the Chichimecs in northern Mexico and the Araucanians in the south of Chile, who carried out guerrilla wars against the Spanish, the indios bravos *of Costa Rica relied on their ability to survive and defend themselves in inaccessible areas. Cartago, the colonial capital, relied on the exaction of tribute and labor from local indigenous groups, and so there was constant demand for more Indians, especially as the population of those under Spanish rule declined through disease and other factors. The recent work of the noted historian Claudia Quirós describes the* correrías *organized by Spaniards—expeditions to hunt and extract Indians, principally from the Talamanca region.*

The juridical concept of *just war* began to take shape in Spanish law with a royal edict of 1500 that condemned the slaving activities undertaken by Columbus in each of the islands that he had "discovered." This proclamation established that all Indians had to be considered free vassals of the Crown of Castile, but the same document included a contradictory caveat saying that the aboriginals captured in "just war" could be kept as slaves, since this was the message contained in the notorious *requerimiento* (literally, the giving of notice; a text read aloud by the Spaniards prior to conquering an area, which exhorted the Indians to accept Catholicism and a new king without acting aggressively or suffer the consequences). It was undoubtedly under cover of this legal exception that the abuses against the antislaving law were committed, and which indeed allowed an increase in Indian slavery. The monarchy tried to rectify the situation in a royal decree of August 1530, in which it ordered that Indians should not suffer enslavement, even in cases of just war. Nevertheless, due to the strong pressure of conquerors and discoverers, the same exception was definitively reestablished four years later in the New Laws of 1542 and became ratified later in the New Code of 1680.

In my view, the concept of *just war*, understood in light of these juridical dispositions and based on the real practices that developed in Costa Rica, was characterized first and foremost by permanent violence and aggression by the Hispanic population against the irredentist indigenous communities or against those indigenous communities whose rebelliousness, or geographical inaccessibility (this held especially true in Talamanca and the Pacific south), had thwarted effective and permanently established domination. The objective of this aggression was to assure a labor force that, given the juridical conditions of its recruitment, took on the character of a semi–slave labor force. The indigenous people captured in so-called just war did not fall under any of the categories of Indian workers or tributaries in the Law of the Indies, which might have eventually afforded them some protection.

The arguments used to legitimize the assaults against the Indian communities of Talamanca and the Pacific south were many and varied, but three stand out. One was to punish the "crimes" committed against missionary priests and Spaniards. Another was to repopulate Indian communities within the orbit of Spanish tribute, whose populations were suffering a constant decline. The third argument held that these communities needed to be resituated in more accessible areas. These arguments became jumbled up with dogmatic religious rhetoric about the necessity to bring the unhappy and rebellious infidels the "gentle yoke of the gospel."

The campaigns of just war in seventeenth-century Costa Rica began with the visit of the oidor (a high court judge with powers of a governor), doctor Pedro Sánchez de Araque. From the moment he arrived in the province, he participated in activities that took on the character of just war. Passing through the villages of Chome and Abangares, he issued orders to imprison Indian "vagrants" from these communities, recruiting them for the conquest of Talamanca he was proposing to undertake. When he entered Cartago, in April 1611, the city received him with all the honors befitting a person of his rank, as it was the first time that such a notable authority of colonial justice had visited there (he represented the tribunal of the *Audiencia*, the highest political and judicial organism in the jurisdiction). The governor, the members of the town council, and representatives of the royal treasury and the church greeted the oidor. Following the ceremonies held in his honor, Sánchez de Araque told all soldiers present that they were not to leave the city "on pain of death." He immediately decreed that all the principal residents of Cartago should go with him to the "Talamancan war." He also issued orders that reduced the availability of Indian laborers to the colonists, both in terms of numbers and of the amount of time they might be used. Obviously, the disposition was not fully respected, but it functioned as an argument to justify violence against Indians who had yet to be subdued, since the principal residents of Cartago alleged that with such a reduced number of *alquilones* (indigenous laborers rented out by an encomendero), it would be impossible to satisfy their labor needs. Despite Sánchez de Araque's acute interest in the conquest of Talamanca, he was unable to undertake it personally during his visit and so delegated the governor and a certain Captain Diego de Sojo to carry it out after his departure. They made various attempts to reactivate the conquest of Talamanca, but repeatedly failed. . . .

According to the official records, the Indians of Chirripó rebelled in 1614. A detachment of soldiers sent to the area easily put down the rebellion, in the process capturing twelve *piezas* (as healthy male slaves were called during the colonial era; the term denied them human status, while also suggesting their use as dynamic "parts" of the machinery of colonial labor systems). A year later, arguing that the Indians of Tierra Adentro and Talamanca had allied with those of the Valley of Duy, the new governor Juan de Mendoza y Medrano proceeded to punish them, "taking 80 piezas," along with the chieftain, don Lorenzo, in order to resettle them in a village he named San Juan de Auyaque. Immediately afterward, and citing new uprisings, the governor himself went to the village of Quepo where he captured thirty Indians and the chieftain, Sebastián Jarú. Later he went to the region of the Votos, who had rebelled, and took twenty Indians, "achieving this by incursions and other military stratagems." In a report to the Audiencia, this governor summed up the results of his "three incursions," boasting that he had taken more than four hundred Indians.

In 1620, Mendoza's successor, Alonso del Castillo y Guzmán, wrote to the Audiencia to report on the measures he had taken with respect to the "uprising" of the Auyaque, Curero, and Hebena Indians, who four years earlier had murdered their missionary priest and other people. He explained in his letter that he had rounded up more than four hundred piezas along with their chiefs. Trying to outdo the deeds of his predecessor and to improve his position with the Audiencia, he added: "I put all the prisoners in this city where I brought to bear exemplary punishments on the heads and captains, which will assure the security of this province." Note that the new authority punished crimes that his predecessor had already addressed.

A later review of his tenure in Costa Rica revealed that in order to establish legal justification for his actions, Castillo y Guzmán had convened an "extraordinary war junta" in June 1619, alleging that given the high cost to all of maintaining a fort in Tierra Adentro, it was necessary for the "peace and security of the province to proceed with the punishment and conquest of the Auyaque, Cacero, and Hebeno Indians." He said that he would go in person and that all those who accompanied him would receive Indians in service for building houses and for agricultural work. Near the village of Auyaque, having taken 220 Indian prisoners, he one morning ordered raiding parties in every direction with the objective of hunting more Indians, and in this way obtaining the 400 "piezas." These Indians were taken to Cartago, where they were subjected to a military trial, whose sentence, without any right of appeal, was decreed on 24 December 1619 in the following terms: first, all the Indians, including the caciques and leaders of the Curero, were condemned as instigators of the crimes of rebellion, sacrilege, and homicide. All were sentenced to expulsion from their villages, whose lands would be ploughed and sown with salt. Under pain of death, neither these Indians nor their descendents unto the third generation could go within ten leagues (fifty kilometers) of Curero.

Second, the following special sentences were handed down to the Indian leadership:

The caciques don Juan Serrabá, Francisco Cagji, and Diego Hebena, were taken from the church of La Soledad—which served as a prison—on horseback, their feet and hands tied and nooses hung around their necks, paraded through the streets of Cartago in the company of the town crier denouncing their crimes, and taken to the outskirts of the city, where they were hanged. Afterward, they were decapitated and their heads put on pikes—Serrabá's in the plaza of the village of Guicucí and Hebena's in the village of Hameas. The headless corpses were dragged to a bonfire and reduced to ashes.

Francisco Muchú, Yiriquirá, Mateo Catebá, Diego Areucará, Lucas Noariz, Duará, Quirodujara, and Juan Ibaczará y Bicara were hanged and decapitated. Their bodies were buried in the cemeteries of the city churches. Two of the heads were sent to the village of Quepo, another to Co, and others were left on the road to Ujarrás, in Auyaque, in Pejibay, in Catapas, and in Abangares. Two other heads were placed at the site of the execution as a warning against the frequent Indian uprisings. Pablo Zuré, Quirigrama, Baltazar Cruz, and Chirobujiburú were paraded through the streets of Cartago to the plaza, where each had the tendon of his right foot cut.

Other minor sentences included Jeca having to serve ten years for the vicar Baltazar de Grado; Luis Querisocá, after being paraded through the streets, receiving one hundred lashes; Pedro Gómez Quiquirá having to work in the convent of San Francisco for four years; and Alonso Jiménez Quiñore, Juan Díaz Cacaricará, Pedro Yaramá, and Diego Garito being condemned to perpetual exile from the village of Auyaque, on pain of death.

* * *

The sentences were decreed and carried out by judicial means on 8 January 1620. The surviving Indians were shared out, as promised by the governor, among the soldiers who had accompanied him in this campaign of just war in Costa Rica. After committing such horrible crimes, Castillo y Guzmán wrote to the king to tell him of the "services" he had rendered in his favor, and for which he asked to be rewarded with 3,000 pesos or in Indians from vacant *encomiendas* (a grant to a Spanish colonist of the tribute of a number of Indians), as he did not have the resources necessary to provide adequate dowries for his daughters.

In the face of the atrocities committed against them by this governor and his predecessors, it is obvious that the Indians' capacity to respond to Spanish domination was much reduced, and with it the possibility of rebelling against or successfully confronting their aggressors. The massacre of Indian caciques, chiefs, and other leaders, particularly those of Tierra Adentro and Talamanca, undoubtedly dismantled Indians' sociopolitical structures. Nevertheless, the political and socioeconomic organization of the Talamanca Indians, combined with their geographic inaccessibility, allowed them to remain irredentist.

Although no documentation exists on any new campaigns of just war in Talamanca for the four decades between 1620 and 1662, this does not necessarily suggest that they stopped. After 1662, the governor Rodrigo Arias Maldonado began the conquest of Talamanca and Tierra Adentro anew. With this objective, he penetrated into the region and established an encampment on the banks of the Tarure River (Sixaola). From there, and with the intention of founding a new indigenous settlement, he, together with the cacique Cabsi, proceeded to take away Indians from Ciruro, Uruscara, Duqueiba, Moyagua, and Jicagua. In this fashion they succeeded in gathering 1,200 men of productive age, who together with women and children populated a settlement named San Bartolomé de Duqueiba. This new campaign, and especially the siting of a new village of such impressive size, gives evidence to the qualitative change that began taking place in Costa Rica with the emergence of cacao growing, which had begun with great success in the Atlantic littoral in the middle of the seventeenth century.

In 1665, the governor Juan López de la Flor took ninety Voto Indians and resettled them in Atirro, and in the town of Tariaca he captured sixty-three Indians, executing seven by crossbow and taking the rest to Cartago to share among his colleagues. From this point on, no more evidence exists pertaining to the incursions in search of rebellious and "infidel" Indians. Without a doubt, the resources traditionally destined for the just war had to be directed toward meeting the threat of pirate incursions. This becomes apparent in a document from 1677, in which the treasurer refused to give the governor 161 pesos "to embark on a campaign to take out Indians," saying that these funds should go toward a war with the English and the French and not be used against the natives. Three years later, an attempt was made to reduce the Caribes and Abubaes, who lived between Quepo and Boruca and whose population was estimated at five hundred families, but the campaign could not be undertaken because the "South sea was infested by the English enemy."

The Execution of Pablo Presbere

José María Figueroa

Album de Figueroa (Archivo Nacional de Costa Rica)

Starting in the mid 1800s, José María Figueroa, from an important Cartago family, began to put together an eclectic "album" of maps, drawings, lists, and other textual bits and pieces cataloguing life in Cartago and Costa Rica. The country had little in the way of a historical record when he began his work, so his depiction of the execution of rebel Indian chief Pablo Presbere suggests that the great indigenous rebellion of 1709 was still alive in the old colonial capital's collective memory.

The Trial of Pablo Presbere,

Cacique of Suinse

Lorenzo Antonio de Granda y Balbín

After the disastrous attempt to dominate the Indians by force, a new stage in the conquest of Talamanca began in 1689, this time assuming a missionary character. This phase lasted some twenty years and ended in 1709, when the indigenous peoples of the area rebelled and destroyed the churches built in their territory. Pablo Presbere led what became the most important indigenous uprising in colonial Costa Rica. Although effective in the sense that it put an end to Spanish efforts at colonizing the area, the rebellion was quelled, and Presbere was captured and subjected to Spanish justice.

In the city of Cartago of the Province of Costa Rica, the twentieth day of the month of June, 1710, don Lorenzo Antonio de Granda y Balbín, Governor and Captain General of this Province for His Majesty, records that in fulfilment of my orders, I went to the room where I have a man prisoner with the intention of hearing his confession. I made him appear before me. Also present was Christóbal de Chavarría, a free black and interpreter named by me because the prisoner is not fluent in our Spanish tongue. I asked the prisoner to swear an oath by God our Lord and the sign of the cross, and the said man did swear it and promised to tell the truth in all that he was asked. He was then subjected to the following questioning and cross-examination:

Asked his name and his place of birth, his age and his profession, he replied that his name was Pablo Presbere and that he was from the nation that in the Province of Talamanca they call Suinse, and that he was cacique of the said nation. He was unable to give his age; he looks more than forty years old.

He was asked if he knows that the King our Lord (God protect him) has in all his cities, villages, and places established his royal justice to punish that which is evil and reward that which is good.

He replied that he had heard it said.

He was asked how, knowing what had just been asked, he committed the grave and awful crime of conspiring with the Indians of the nations that were reduced to the yoke of our saintly Catholic faith by way of evangelist ministers. And why together with them he went through with murdering the Reverend Fathers Pablo de Rebullida, Juan Antonio de Zamora, ten soldiers, and the wife of one of them in the villages of Chirripó, Urinama, and Cavécar. And why he had burned churches and taken sacred ornaments that were then smashed to smithereens and subjected to degrading practices.

He said that it was because the Indians of Tuiná, Cavécar, and San Buena-ventura, as well as those of San Juan and Santo Domingo, saw the Reverend Fathers and also Father Antonio de Andrade and the soldiers who were in his company write letters to this city [Cartago]. They judged that it was so that the Spaniards could go and take them from their villages [to Cartago, according to the rumor that spread among the indigenous people]: these were the ones who united and committed the crime of which he was asked.

He was asked how it is that he denies in part or in whole that which is re-ferred to in the previous question when the Master at Arms don José Casasola y Córdova and other leaders went to the mountains and the nations and as-certained that he was the leader of the conspiracy and that he was guilty of the murders, for which he was brought in shackles to this city. He said that he says the same as that which he has already said.

Asked where exactly he was at the time of the conspiracy and murders, the prisoner replied that on that occasion he was in Taires.

He was asked if he knows or saw that Balthasar, Pedro Bocrí, Antonio Iruscara, Pedro Bettuquí, and Melchor Daparí, who the said Master at Arms brought as prisoners to this city, the last of them this very day, cooperated in the uprising and killings. He said that he does not know that any of those mentioned committed such a crime.

He was asked if he has knowledge of any other Indians among those brought to this city by our Master at Arms who were accomplices in the uprising and murders. The prisoner said that he does not know nor has he heard it said that any of those Indians were involved in any such thing.

We subjected him to further questioning and cross-examination regarding the conspiracy and the deaths of the Reverend Fathers and the soldiers, but he replied that he had nothing more to say than that which he had already testified, since the statement we had before us was the whole truth. This he affirmed and ratified after his confession was read back to him. Neither he nor the interpreter signed saying that they did not know how; I the said Governor and Captain General do hereby sign. . . .

The Sentence

In the criminal proceedings brought by Royal Justice over the conspiracy and uprising of the infidel and subject Indians of the mountains of Talamanca and the deaths thereby inflicted on the Reverend Fathers Friar Pablo de Rebullida and Friar Juan Antonio de Zamora, ten soldiers who were members of the guard, and the wife of one of them, against Pablo Presbere, Balthasar Siruru, Pedro Bocrí, Antonio Uruscara, Pedro Bettuquí and Melchor Daparí, prisoners, and the rest who appear to be accomplices:

Given the testimony and the other evidence relating to the case, it is imperative to condemn, and I do hereby condemn, the said Pablo Presbere for that which has been proven against him despite the denials contained in his confession, to be taken from the room where I have him prisoner and placed on a pack mule and led through the streets of this city while a crier declares and describes his crimes. Outside the walls of this city, he shall be tied to a post and have his eyes gouged out, *ad modum beli* [in military mode] and then shot by crossbow, since we are without an executioner who knows how to apply the garrote. Upon his death, he shall have his head cut off and placed high upon the post so that all might see it. As for the rest of the accused, given that it is not fully proven whether or not they were accomplices in the said uprising and deaths due to the variable depositions against them, I order them retained in prison until more exact investigation can take place, leaving the case open against them and the others who appear to be accomplices. . . . Don Lorenzo Antonio de Granda y Balbín, 23 June 1710.

A Slave's Story

José Cubero

The colonial elite also turned to slavery to fill some of their labor requirements. Local demand for African slaves was stimulated in the seventeenth century by a small cacao boom in Matina on the Caribbean coast. Costa Rica did not become a slave society, but the population of African origin had an important impact on the ethnic composition of the province. Most slaves worked as servants or artisans within the patrimonial house-holds of their owners. José Cubero was one such man, born a slave in the household of an elite Cartago family in the early 1700s and given as a young man to his mistress's son, Father Manuel Cubero. By 1749, when Manuel Cubero died, José Cubero enjoyed the status of so-called free mulatto. He laid claim to a portion of his former master's estate because, José claimed, Manuel Cubero had charged him more than he should have for his liberty. In order to establish his entitlement, the former slave narrated a life story that provides an extraordinary window onto the world of a "household slave"—a world with a surprising range of movement and opportunity. The document was discovered by the historian Franklin Alvarado.

Soon after becoming part of Manuel Cubero's household, I started to work with his mule team, and he dispatched me to Nicoya to deliver some goods to his supplier and bring back some others. I spent about eight years going back and forth like this for my master, to Nicoya and Bagaces and Landecho. Later, with the same team (which I had now succeeded in enlarging), he sent me to the province of Nicaragua with loads of tobacco and flour and other produce, and with me as lead mule driver. I delivered goods to his associates and brought back to my master what they gave me. My master occupied me six or seven years in these journeys to Nicaragua. Then, removing me from this task, he brought me with him to "San Juan," a cacao plantation in Matina owned by my former master, don Joseph de Mier Sevallos. There I lived with my master and the other slaves and servants for about two months, after which we re-turned to Cartago. . . . Then my master sent me to Nicaragua again. When I returned with a herd of about forty mules, my master Cubero dispatched me to the Kingdom of Panama with twenty-five loads of leaf tobacco to deliver to don Martín de Icasi. This I did and returned with the money don Martín had given me, along with a rosary and rings of gold, as well as other merchandise bought by don Martín in Santiago de Veragua and Panama. I surrendered all of this to my master. And I made another four journeys to that kingdom with my master's mules. . . .

And serving him as I had so honestly, three months or thereabouts prior to undertaking the first of these journeys to Tierra Firme [Panama], I married the woman who today is my wife. She did not want to marry me if I were to remain a slave. So in order to get her to agree to it, my master promised to give me my freedom. My wife married me only because she knew this, a fact that is known by the Vicar Ecclesiastical Judge of this city, don Joseph Miguel de Gusmán y Chabaría. . . . And for these reasons and others related to my good service, my master Father Manuel Cubero granted me license to trade and enter into contracts. From that moment, I began to do business, taking advantage of the means that I could to buy anis, coriander, garlic, onions, and potatoes from the residents of these valleys, as well as other [products] and other trifles that they sold me. I saw this as a way of proceeding, and I also traded in bales of tobacco, and socks that my wife made, and pounds of blue thread that she put together with her women friends and which they gave me so that I could get ahead and earn a living. My master Father Cubero was aware of all this, and he knew that I took this with me and transported it on his mules to the Kingdom of Panama.

This was how I was able to double my reserve in coin and pay off my creditors and with what was left over buy mules and horses for a number of other people. All of this was done with my master Father's permission, as the following people can corroborate: Captain don Juan Manuel de Alvarado, and [Cubero lists four other men from around the Central Valley with whom he had done business, including two other priests]. This can be certified by the Reverend Father Friar Joseph de San Antonio Seballos; being the brother of my master he knows how he acted, and he knows what good service I gave my master in all things relating to the management of his wealth over which he gave me responsibility without me taking anything whatsoever from him. . . .

On my last journey to the Kingdom of Panama with my master's mules and others that I had searched out and purchased with his license, I managed to take in some 380 pesos, which I brought back to this city. My master Cubero took them from me and kept them for himself. I asked him why he had taken my money after I had served him with such legality and seeing as I owed him nothing, but he failed to respond. The same day, Manuel Brenes came to collect payment for the mules that he had advanced me. I said to him, friend, my master has just taken my money from me, let's go and see if he'll pay you directly. Manuel Brenes, hearing this, said let's go and get what's mine, and together we went to see my master . . . who said "I'm busy now, come back tomorrow." [Brenes] turned to me and said, friend, I don't want to go back to your master because I know his game, and so you should do your tasks and try to pay me. And with that he bid me farewell.

What came of all this was that my master Father Cubero held onto my 380 pesos. Then, a few days after taking them from me he decided to journey to his cattle estate in Santana, and he took me and my wife with him without considering that she was within days of giving birth. Arriving at the hacienda and seeing that he was treating me rudely, I decided one night to take my wife from the service of my master and with great difficulty managed to get her to a country house in the jurisdiction of this city. After letting her master in on the secret so that my master Cubero would not be able to find her, I went to the city of Leon [Nicaragua] to present my grievances to the Illustrious Bishop don Isidro Marín, now passed away. Having heard my story, he wrote a letter on my behalf to the Vicar and Ecclesiastical Judge of this city, saying that he should attend to my concerns, and so I returned to Cartago. The Vicar told me [to stay in his house while] he went to speak with my master, and what I later understood was that the Vicar and other priests went to see my master Father Cubero.

Three or four days later, His Grace called me to his room, and after entering, I saw that my master Cubero was there. I greeted him and knelt before him, and he told me to stand up. He said to me, "In order for me to grant you your freedom, you will have to pay me 150 pesos." To this I replied that he should treat me with charity since I had served him well and honestly, but that I had not a single real, because the money that I had managed to get together, the 380 pesos, he had taken from me. He responded that if I didn't give him the 150 pesos or find someone who would provide them for me, then I would have to serve him for a period of two more years, after which he would grant me my certificate of freedom. To this the Vicar intervened on my behalf, supplicating him to reduce the sum. [We finally agreed] that I would give to my master Cubero 100 pesos in pieces of eight within a period of two years — conditions that I satisfied for my master in the presence of the Vicar before the two years were up.

Free Blacks, Mulattoes, and

Mestizos Seek Legitimacy

Cabildo of Cartago

By the late seventeenth century, Cartago and its environs were ethnically diverse. Groups of free blacks, mulattoes, and mestizos had established themselves on the margins of white society, many living in a barrio known as La Puebla. In 1676, apparently taking advantage of the goodwill won by their decisive help in defending Cartago against pirate attack, these black and mixed-race groups sought to gain official recognition of their community in terms of political stature and property. The governor and the town council of Cartago issued a favorable response, one also motivated by the desire of colonial authorities to concentrate and control an increasingly dispersed population.

Having considered the various points of the petition, we see that it is in the interests of the Crown that the mulattoes, free coloreds, and lower-class mestizos come together and settle so that their lives might be overseen by regular justice and they might live in Christian discipline. Until today, they have lived freely in the valleys and mountains without the justices being able to control them. So we determine it to be useful and convenient to concede that a settlement be established in this city with the name of Arrabal, and its residents shall join the residents of this city. It is the desire of the governor and captain general in the service of God our Lord that they avoid the serious sins that are committed in the *chácaras* [farms] and mountains where these people have been living and continue to live. And it is also the desire of the king our lord (may God protect him), and in the interests of the security of these provinces, to have them together and ready with arms in hand, as they are today, for the defense of this province against the hostilities that our enemies intend to inflict upon us and for whose great benefit this city in its mercy thanks them. We therefore concede them the right to settle in the place called La Puebla de Nuestra Señora de los Ángeles, which was the site of their first settlement . . . and the right to name and develop a town council consisting of three councilors, a mayor and a bailiff. . . .

Brotherhood of the Virgin

Ricardo Fernández Guardia

One of the most important events in the cultural history of Costa Rica was the early development of the cult of the Virgin of los Ángeles (Costa Rica's black Madonna, similar to the Virgin of Guadalupe). Like many such cults, this one probably contributed to the attenuation of social tensions between distinct ethnic groups. Ricardo Fernández Guardia's "colonial chronicles" are tales of great literary quality and historical rigor that, in their time, were compared to those of the Peruvian Ricardo Palma. The following chronicle reveals the manner in which the cult of the Virgin of los Ángeles, evolving over the seventeenth and eighteenth centuries, became the basis of "scandalous celebrations" by religious brotherhoods, in which Cartago's self-styled aristocracy played a preponderant role. Fernández Guardia rediscovers the carnivalesque moment in which the lowly origins of the cult attracted the Cartago elites to the dark depths of the lower orders' sanctuary for a pagan feast replete with bulls, drunkenness, dances of African origin, fornication, and miscegenation.

As the tradition has it, the second of August of a year not registered in any known document, but which is apparently 1635, an Indian woman went to wash clothes on the outskirts of the city of Cartago, at a spring whose waters issued from beneath a stone upon which she found an image of the Virgin. The figure was the size of the palm of a hand, and crudely sculpted in black granite. Finishing her work, she took the figure with her, placing it in a central spot in her poor hut. But the next morning, the image had disappeared. Quite worried about this inexplicable event, the Indian woman again went to the fountain, and imagine her surprise at again finding the figure of the Virgin in the exact same place that she had first found it. She quickly alerted other people, and it was deduced from the date of the appearance that the image was that of Our Lady of los Ángeles, and also, from her mysterious return to the site, that it was her wish that a temple be built there. Neither the name of the Indian woman who discovered the miraculous image nor any other details of the event have been preserved. The documents from the era tell us only that in 1639, an hermitage was already being built on the site today occupied by the Virgin's sanctuary, and that in the month of January 1653, Friar Alonso Briceño, Bishop of Nicaragua and Costa Rica, approved the statutes of the Brotherhood of the Virgin of los Ángeles, formed with canonical formality the year before by the colored people.

At the outset and for quite some time afterward, only the lower classes—the Indians and especially the blacks and mulattoes of the Puebla de Los Ángeles—practiced devotion to the image that the *chola* [Hispanized Indian woman] discovered. They lived separated from the whites of Cartago, with a border between each community formed by a Caravaca cross [a cross with four arms]. The Spaniards remained faithful to the ancient and also miraculous image of Our Lady of the Conception, which had its shrine in the village of Ujarrás. This was made clear in 1666, when they appealed to her and not to the Virgin of Los Ángeles during the great invasion of pirates. But with time, the whites also became followers of the little black image, and so we see in 1669 that the Master at Arms don Juan Fernández de Salinas y de la Cerda, the fourth Adelantado [colonial governor] of Costa Rica, donated a cacao plantation in Matina to Our Lady of los Ángeles. Following this, there were other donations from the nobility, and in 1675, a church, made of limestone, was begun to replace the primitive hermitage. . . . In 1722, the year the work was completed, the brotherhood of los Ángeles was mixed Spanish and black. The Governor, don Diego de la Haya Fernández, agreed to be its sponsor, and he spent a good part of his fortune on the new church, also building at his expense and contiguous to the sacristy a room of grand dimensions for the congregation.

Like the other confraternities of Cartago, each year the Brotherhood of los Ángeles celebrated its patron with religious and profane functions. For this reason, Bishop Benito Garret y Arlovi prohibited, on pain of excommunication, the spending of brotherhood funds on stage props for comedies, towers, sarabands, and other dances in 1711. He ordered also that the festivities be limited to the strictly religious; nevertheless, his edict was not rigorously obeyed, at least not by the Brotherhood of los Ángeles. The very governor, don Diego de la Haya, paid for a room in the depths of the shrine where the female followers could prepare the customary refreshment during the festivities. The devotion to the local image grew day by day. Good proof of this was the solemn offering made to Our Lady of los Ángeles by the clergy of Cartago during the plague that hit the city in 1737. By the mid-eighteenth century, the sanctuary of modest origins had become famous and received the visits of pilgrims and sojourners from throughout the province and beyond. New rooms were added to the first ones built by don Diego de la Haya, forming the great house known as the Congregation, which had a great variety of uses. Here, the board meetings and gatherings of the brotherhood were held, pilgrims and the infirm were given lodging, and the portable altars, retables, and old furniture were stored, along with anything that was in the way or for which there was no room in the church.

And in the month of August, great festivities were held that degenerated to the point of taking on a truly scandalous character. Over the course of more than twenty days, and under the pretext of devotion, Cartago gave itself up to a shocking licentiousness. For each day of the festive cycle, a female patron and a male sponsor were named, chosen from among the most distinguished people of the city (who believed in the obligation to throw money away). On the first of August, after vespers, ladies and gentlemen parading on horseback in a lively fashion and drinking to excess brought the bulls to the atrium of the sanctuary. The program of festivities changed little over the following days: in the morning, the religious functions were celebrated, followed by a succulent luncheon; in the afternoon, a bullfight, refreshment and a substantial meal, comedies, and main courses; in the nighttime, a splendid supper and a dance that generally lasted until dawn. All this was accompanied by a great deal of *rosoli* [spirit scented with cinnamon and anise] and other liquor that made men and women lose their head.

An investigation into the scandalous festivities of the Brotherhood of los Ángeles was undertaken in 1782 by Bishop Esteban Lorenzo de Tristán. The witnesses made surprising revelations. Father Juan José de la Madriz Linares said that the place where these celebrations took place deserved the name "House of the Congregation of Iniquity and Lodging of Everything in Hell," because "being so large and with so many rooms, people closed themselves in during the nights of fandangos and committed unheard of evils." A priest from Cartago, don Ramón de Azofeifa, declared that "in these splendid banquets excessive amounts of liquor flow, resulting in a huge number of disputes, and the worst of this is that once they have gorged themselves and imbibed excessively, they unleash a dance or saraband that lasts the entire night, because the greatest distinction for all the sponsors is that their fandangos last until dawn." He added that since the house was so large and had a variety of rooms, the devil provided there the facilities that the married women and the young ladies did not have in their own homes. He also mentioned that the place was turned into a public kitchen due to the great gathering of strangers from afar, who gave themselves over to coquetry and lewdness, "mixing them among the blessings and prayers that are said every day"—a scandal unseen in any shrine in the world.

Father don José Francisco de Alvarado lamented that "in this province of Costa Rica, dissolution and lechery was very widely and publicly notorious, since in every class of family one can find sins and the fallen at every turn . . . because God created the women of this province lovely and of fragile morality." He added that the priests retired when night fell, for fear of falling out with the authorities and eminent residents who attended the dances, and so left the house without any moral care, "and without much light," since only the great hall where the dancing took place was illuminated. Don Francisco Juan de Pazos, the public prosecutor, wrote that "The house of Our Lady of los Ángeles has become a school for learning how to dance, love and. . . . But the prosecutor does not dare to say that which thirty, forty, or a hundred imprudent souls dare to carry out in that sacred house under cover of devotion and feasting." We will imitate the discretion of the prosecutor, suppressing here more than one word pronounced by the witnesses that might make the reader blush. . . .

The scandals of the Brotherhood of los Ángeles continued until 1782, when Bishop Esteban Lorenzo de Tristán put an end to them—though with great difficulty. Understanding that he would not be obeyed if he simply prohibited the fiestas, as a number of visiting officials had tried to do, he resolved to allow them to go on, but without the scandalous practices that went with them. This objective could not be obtained while the festivities continued to be celebrated in the house of the Congregation, and so . . . the bishop came to an agreement with the governor, Juan Flores, the town council, and the Brotherhood of los Ángeles. The sacred image should be brought each year in a procession to the main church of Cartago where the celebrations would be held, and with the women patrons and the sponsors having to hold the feasts and dances in their houses. Once the celebrations were over, the image would be returned to its sanctuary. This was the origin of the ceremony that is known as "La Pasada," done for the first time in 1782. And on the fourteenth of August of the same year, Bishop Tristán, on the urging of the authorities and residents of Cartago, declared Our Lady of los Ángeles the patron saint of the city. Finally, with the intention of "forever shutting the door of that shrine to the dances, feasts, and scandals," the bishop established a grammar school in the house of the Congregation under the tutelage of Father José Antonio Bonilla. And to consolidate his work, he had all of this voted on with great solemnity on the eighteenth of August, the last day of the feasts. In the presence of the Saintly Sacrament, seated on his throne on the main altar and dressed pontifically, the bishop received the votes of the regular and secular clergy, the governor, the canons, and the principal residents of the city.

Life and Labor in the Central

Valley, circa 1821

Iván Molina

What was everyday life like as Costa Rica's colonial era drew to a close? An earlier generation of historians proposed that prior to the takeoff in coffee capitalism, the Costa Ricans of the Central Valley constituted a homogeneous group of yeoman farmers who lived in a world effectively without class distinctions and exploitation, vile things that came later with coffee and the country's links to the world market. Starting in the 1970s, Costa Rica's so-called New Historians began a systematic examination of unexplored records, such as notarial estate inventories made at the time of people's death. The following study provides an example of the resulting work, one that offers a more dynamic picture of social divisions and material conditions in the important transitional period between the decline of Spanish colonialism and the advent of an independent state with a ruling class of cafetaleros *(large coffee producers).*

At the beginning of the nineteenth century, the average farmer of the Central Valley planted beans, plantains, coriander, and garlic, but the basic grain, and the key to the peasant diet, was corn. Tomás de Acosta, one of the last colonial governors, noted in 1802 that "few eat bread here. . . . Flour is not a commercial option, due to its poor quality and the costs of its transport to other provinces, so that harvests of that grain are not abundant, merely sufficient to supply the country and a little bit extra that goes to Nicaragua more on consignment than in the course of regular trade." Bread was only served on the tables of the elite because wheat had a yield of ten to one, and it was a delicate, risky, and expensive crop that required constant attention, thereby absorbing a good deal of labor, especially at harvest (the same could be said for vegetable farming). Wheat also required the use of a particular tool, the scythe. Corn had none of these disadvantages. It yielded a hundred to one and was easily harvested. Moreover, while wheat had to be taken to a mill, corn could be ground in the house.

The work of subsistence, destined to satisfy peasant family consumption, coexisted with the openly commercial production of sugarcane and tobacco. Cane had been cultivated since the seventeenth century, and its success resulted from a local taste for brown sugar and sugar loafs (only the indigenous people consumed honey). The constant export of large quantities of brown sugar to Guanacaste, Nicaragua, and, above all, Panama sometimes threatened the province's own supply. The scarcity worried late colonial bureaucrats like José Antonio Oreamuno, assistant to the governor, who claimed in 1788 that "sugar was being taken to Bagaces, Nicoya, and Villa de Rivas in Nicaragua by the people who traffic with those areas." It was further aggravated by the rise in liquor production, since the manufacturers used sugar produced by the local peasantry. The sale of liquor, so important to the royal treasury, became strictly regulated by the colonial state starting in 1753, when the Royal Alcohol Board was established in the Kingdom of Guatemala with monopoly control.

Control over derivatives of sugarcane did not interfere with the economic independence of those who cultivated it, but this did not hold true for producers of tobacco—to their great chagrin. Tobacco farming flowered after 1760, and from 1782 onward, the Factoría de Tabaco, the colonial state agency designated to oversee the monopoly, controlled the crop. A faithful servant to the Spanish Crown and desperate to eliminate contraband, the Factoría strictly controlled the growing and marketing of the aromatic weed, even to the point of damaging the product and the producer's interests. The Factoría determined the number of growers allowed to plant each year, the number of plants each of these could cultivate, the organization of the workforce, the land where cultivation would take place, the price at which it was to be bought, and other such measures, and the agency did not hesitate to prohibit planting whenever it saw fit (1793–95, 1814, and 1820–21). The Factoría, not the market, was the decisive element in tobacco farming. Difficult ecological and social conditions deprived the valley around Cartago of the kind of dynamic commercial agriculture evident in the area around San José. Sugarcane was grown mainly around Ujarrás, east of Cartago, while the Factoría ordered that no more tobacco be grown in Cartago and Ujarrás in 1784; in 1795, tobacco's planting was prohibited in Curridabat (an area between San José and Cartago), and in 1814, Heredia was excluded from production as well. Cultivation was restricted to certain common lands around San José near the Factoría itself, and this concentration provoked conflicts between corn farmers and tobacco planters in 1809 and 1815.

Agricultural production—both subsistence and commercial—essentially took place on the *chácara*, the family farm. These smallholdings dominated the landscape of the Central Valley. In 1783, the chácara of Alejandro Méndez, a comfortable farmer from around San José, was valued at five hundred pesos, and it consisted of "living quarters and a kitchen with tile roof and log walls, a sugar milling shed with two rooms made of cedar . . . with tile roof and a regular mill inside with all its parts . . . ditches, fences of sugarcane, and a plantain tree." The most typical buildings were granaries, sheds, barns, and mills for sugar and wheat. These were simple constructions made of wood or adobe and covered with straw and sometimes with clay tiles. The most highly developed technology, that devoted to milling, was unevenly distributed throughout society due to the equipment's high cost. Only merchants and prosperous farmers owned the kind of mill worked by oxen (the *trapiche*). Possession of a hydraulic mill was a privilege exclusive to the merchant who enjoyed a comfortable income from milling the grain of others. The state of the equipment found in such rigs might vary greatly depending on the wealth and the interests of the owner.

The form of the chácara varied considerably. Land was valued above all for the crop that grew on it, for the buildings it contained, and for the fencing that defined its borders and protected plantings against the voracious appetites of cattle. A peasant sometimes had a pasture, but even so, the cattle generally grazed on the commons, whose forest cover provided a precious source of lumber for building houses and furniture, firewood, and reeds to make baskets. Arable land sometimes surrounded the house, but cultivation also took place on scattered plots devoted to specific produce. Of course, this lowered the farmer's productivity by obliging him or her to move from one to the other. Agriculture normally took place on private property, but some plots were located on the village commons. Whatever its size and structure, the chácara shared space with the hacienda. A large landowner exploiting his—rarely her—property could get a labor force of smallholders, although this was unusual. The owner of a large tract of land, usually a merchant, was not always willing to incur the costs and risks involved in agriculture. He frequently opted to rent the land to a worker who, short of land and with the spirit of a sharecropper, agreed to cancel his debt in kind with a portion of the harvest.

Agricultural technology was not overly complex. It included the use of trenching and fences of bushes, wood, and stone, whose value was far from negligible. The case of Joaquín Chavarría, a resident of Cartago who died in November 1823, proves illuminating. The deceased had invested 187 pesos in the enclosure of his father's land, located in El Potrero. The basic technique was to fence the plot so that the cattle would not destroy the crop. Work on the land was done with crude and simple instruments: axes, machetes, hoes, rakes, shovels, clubs, and picks. The tools were mainly made of wood, although starting around 1750, the use of metal tools became more frequent. Agriculture did not rely solely on manual labor: oxen provided indispensable energy for working the land. Processing instruments were likewise quite simple. The peasant family, a consumer of tortillas and chocolate, had mortars to grind the corn and the cacao, as well as pans and troughs to make cheese, butter, and sugar. The more expensive implements, and therefore less widespread, were saucepans and pots, often of copper, used to make brown sugar and liquor. Leather pouches and bags served to bale tobacco and cacao, while the corn and sugar were packed in wooden crates.

The products of farming, however, did not usually require further processing; the fruits of the harvest traveled without delay to the table and the market. A few exceptions to this rule existed: wheat, which required milling to make flour; cacao and tobacco, which were carefully treated to give them an agreeable flavor and an attractive aroma; and sugarcane, which was passed through the mill to extract brown sugar, liquor, foamy rum, and stalks used to give body to adobe. This meager list of derivatives hardly surprises in an economy with little in the way of value-added.

The long rainy season favored agriculture, but the latter did not depend entirely on the rain. A rudimentary form of irrigation was also practiced. Water was brought by way of channels from the nearest river to the growing area and was used to irrigate during planting, to water the animals, to fulfill domestic needs, and to drown out ant infestations. The magnitude of the labor required meant that the work had to be undertaken collectively. The village took charge of the project, organizing the labor and issuing a set of rules strictly enforced to insure the fluid's proper use and the waterway's maintenance. Individual effort did not always suffice to achieve technological improvements. Just as in the case of irrigation, harvesting wheat, exterminating locusts, and raising a mill required close collaboration among neighbors. It is true that enclosure promoted privatization of the land and possessive individualism. But putting up fences did not seriously threaten communal land. The commons provided firewood, lumber, and vines for rope, and it served for some planting and for pasturage, making it vital to many farmers and fomenting the type of mutual assistance forged in the hustle and bustle of everyday life in the heart of the village. This provided the foundation of improvement beyond the individual farm.

The chácara combined the raising of crops with the rearing of animals: chickens, pigs, and, above all, oxen, cows, steers, bulls, stallions, mares, burros, and mules. Livestock almost always figured in property appraisals. The valuation of the fortune of Estanislao Hidalgo, a resident of Heredia who passed on in October 1822, was typical: one third of the family wealth (which reached the modest sum of 355 pesos) was made up of livestock, and of this portion, three-quarters of the value were made up of cattle. The herd comprised "two mares at four pesos, four reals each; a young mule at nine pesos and an unbroken horse at twelve pesos; a team of oxen at sixteen pesos and another young team at nine pesos; two cows at four pesos and four reals each and five milk cows at seven pesos each and seven calves at three pesos each."

Ranching tools were simple and made of leather, iron, and wood: yokes, lances, and rigging for the teams; irons for branding; and riding gear (adorned with silver if belonging to a wealthy rider) that included a saddle, a sheepskin saddle cushion, spurs, a hub, a bridle, a bit, and stirrups. The gear was mostly employed for using the livestock, rather than for raising it, since, with the exception of mules, the latter activity did not demand a significant investment of labor, coin, or food. Livestock reproduced itself naturally, without requiring any intensive or vigilant intervention from the peasant farmer.

The local animals, though not noted for their toughness, made agricultural work a great deal easier. A team of oxen provided the essential strength for pulling the plough, moving the drums of the trapiche, and hauling the cart loaded with corn or cane. Cows contributed milk, cheese, fat, butter, and meat to the family diet and promoted the development of commerce in such goods as soap, tallow, leather, and jerked beef. Traffic in cattle on the hoof was also known. The peasant might acquire or sell cattle, and the merchant might export them to Nicaragua, a market that fetched higher prices.

The help obtained from beasts was not exhausted by the energy and the food that it offered. Animals also fulfilled another key task: at harvest's end, the farmer introduced the livestock into the field to clean the plot by eating the stubble and to fertilize the ground with its manure. Natural fertilizer, the only one available around 1800, was very valuable since it allowed the producer to use the soil more intensively, shortening and even eliminating the fallow period and combating the exhaustion of the land, both of which proved favorable for agricultural productivity. The town council of Cartago knew this, decreeing in July of 1813 that "the excrement of the cows sacrificed for public consumption shall be spread in a pit in the furthest reaches of the lots, since after they decay, they will be useful for sowing the lands used for vegetables."

Personal transportation was almost always entrusted to stallions and mares, though mules were also used. The beast of burden, whose endurance made it the preferred mode for transporting merchandise over long distances and stimulated those who possessed it to get involved in the lucrative life of commerce, proved a veritable treasure to those who did not have easy access to it. This expensive and high-strung animal, just like the purebred horse, demanded constant attention and had to be fed with corn. Those who raised it as a commercial venture had to rent or buy an ass—a rare and expensive animal indeed. Infinitely less care was required for keeping cows, bulls, stallions, and mares. The farmer simply had to brand them and then leave them—in open defiance of rustlers—to pasture and reproduce themselves naturally, straying out in the open on common lands. Livestock did not constitute a major cost for the farmer since it did not eat up labor, compete for land, or consume cultivated food. Cattle were faithful servants of farmwork.

Of course, human coexistence did not always prove peaceful. Disputes over how much land to dedicate to planting and how much to give over to pasture were common between farmers and ranchers. The argument might become serious if it occurred after animals had destroyed crops. This kind of conflict was particularly severe in the Valle del Guarco, where the peasant farmers of the commons suffered constant discrimination from the town council of Cartago. The council prohibited farmers from fencing their plots and charged a lower tribute to the large landowners—masters of abundant, privately owned land—who pastured their animals on the commons. In 1813, Manuel García Escalante and José Santos Lombardo, officials from Cartago, did not hesitate to charge that "many individuals from the barrios are without grounds on which to live and build houses, because the little land of the *ejido* [the commons] of this city is enclosed by various individuals who are using this land as pasture. Thus the poorest residents do not have a place to raise animals or to plant, and so they have to emigrate to other places."

Farmers who also dedicated themselves to crafts frequently had spools, looms, and racks to make clothing and carpentry tools essential for erecting buildings—houses, sheds, sugar and wheat mills—and fences, for providing some rustic furniture for the home—tables, stools, benches, chairs, bedsteads—and for making basic agricultural implements—yokes, wheels, conduits, troughs, boxes, lances, and farming hand tools. Domestic industry sometimes involved making cheeses, butter, soap, tallow, and a variety of sugarcane derivatives, but this was not only for subsistence. Occasionally a family might also spin and weave, urged on by a merchant who provided the cotton and marketed the finished work.

Specialized craftwork, of the kind that might distinguish a household or even a neighborhood, was concentrated in larger centers. Crafts involved a number of activities associated with "luxury" spending: sculpting, shoemaking, tailoring, chair making, hatting, cabinetmaking, and silversmithing. They also emerged out of construction needs: carpentry, stonecutting, masonry, bricklaying, and the making of tiles, bricks, and adobe. And of course there were specialists in crafts associated with farming and ranching: blacksmithing, carpentry, and tanning. Finally, there was some activity in spinning, weaving, and the making of candles, lime, plaster, charcoal, cigarettes, and perhaps gunpowder. Specialization *within* each trade remained quite rudimentary. The norm was, for example, the carpenter who built houses and churches and made furniture and agricultural tools.

Tile and brick making flourished in El Tejar del Guarco on the outskirts of Cartago, while another barrio, La Puebla was noted for its forges; Villa Vieja (Heredia) was the leader in hat and cigar making, while Villa Nueva (Alajuela) had the advantage in spinning and Patarrá was known for making lime. The deft artisan opted to live in Cartago or San José, the richer and more "urban" population centers with a better clientele, though there were one or two specialists in Heredia and Alajuela. The limited division of labor among artisans was logical, given that most also engaged in agriculture and stock raising to complement their income. The tools of Sebastián Acosta, a Cartago blacksmith, were valued in 1822 at 45 pesos—a mere 13 percent of a household worth 338 pesos. Acosta's experience was not exceptional: the Alajuela carpenter Juan José Morera, who died in 1823, invested 16 percent of his net worth of 265 pesos in land, 21 percent in livestock, 17 percent in his house, and only 8 percent in the tools of his trade.

Success in a trade, far from promoting specialization, induced artisans to try their luck in agriculture, ranching, or commerce. One extreme example of this trend comes in the form of Francisco Javier Mayorga, a Cartago silversmith, who died in 1824 with an estate worth almost 2,500 pesos. The deceased owned cattle, horses, mules, a house, and three lots in the center of the then capital, a loom, thread and textiles, jewels, gold, silver, mercury, iron, copper, books, furniture, ornaments, tableware, and a variety of implements. He was engaged in commerce, rented land for planting corn, and apparently rented or sold large pans distributed to kitchens throughout the Central Valley.

Was the economic distance separating Mayorga from Acosta and Morera unusual? The distribution of wealth and prestige among artisans was not equitable at all, with spinning, weaving, basket making, and pottery making at the base, shoemaking and silversmithing at the apex, and carpentry, blacksmithing, masonry, and other activities in between. The differentiation certainly depended on the artisan's skill and effort, but also on the demand for each trade and the instruments, materials, and specialization each trade demanded.

The external market usually provided the artisan with his or her tools: scissors, thimbles, and needles for the tailor; bellows, anvils, and files for the smith; ball bearings, anvils, moulds, drills, and hammers for inlay for the silversmith; saws, hammers, lathes, planes, chisels, and adzes for the carpenter. The outside world also sometimes provided him or her with the raw material. Cotton from Nicaragua kept the spinners and the looms working. Tailoring required fabric, thread, lace, and buttons. Shoemaking, which was not always done with locally produced leather, demanded frills and buckles. Blacksmithing, although making use of old tools and other materials, demanded the constant import of iron, copper, and steel. And silversmithing could not do without precious metals and fine stones.

Raw material, however, did not always come from afar. Agriculture provided cane, wicker, and tobacco, and stock raising provided leather and tallow. The quarry pit provided stone. Clay was used to make bricks, tiles, and pots. Adobe was made of earth and leftover cane stalks. The forests also proved vitally important for providing wood—cedar, caoba, cocobolo and others—used in construction, cabinetmaking, and carpentry, and the firewood sometimes converted into charcoal was the key fuel of artisanal work, since it fired the blacksmith's forge and the oven of the lime, brick, and tile maker.

The craftspeople of the Central Valley may have lacked a guild tradition, but they did not lack a hierarchy that went from the master down to the journeyman and the apprentice. Still, this hierarchy was not generalized. The master who worked on his own coexisted with those who employed a salaried labor force (and sometimes even a slave labor force) and those who had apprentices whom he had promised to instruct in the secrets of the trade. The tailor Agustín Núñez of Cartago figured in the latter category: in 1801, he received Santiago Otárola for six years and Jesús Arcia for five, committing himself to "teaching them the trade perfectly without hiding anything from them whatsoever, either theoretical or practical, so that applying themselves, at the end of the years indicated, they shall be capable of being examined and approved and of exercising the trade on their own, without the intervention, license, or direction of anyone else."

Age had a decisive influence in the hierarchy among artisans. The apprentice, agitated and without discipline, was usually a child; the journeyman traveled the difficult and tricky road of adolescence, almost on the threshold of manhood; and the master, sage and severe, watched over them as a mature adult. The weight of sex and ethnicity also proved significant. The artisans of the Central Valley were basically criollo or mestizo, and male. Women were prevalent only in spinning and weaving; the slave (so significant in trades elsewhere) was visible only occasionally; and the indigenous person, who had figured in the majority of trades in the seventeenth century, was limited to working in basket weaving and pottery between 1800 and 1821. Merchants undermined the craft spirit without second thought; they preferred peasant industry and contracted a salaried labor force to spin and weave, especially from women in Cartago and San José. Male rural laborers who had no land, possessed few cattle, and had insufficient resources to make it on their own found a complement to their subsistence in the income earned through spinning and weaving. As a result, they resembled women in that they put up with a meager daily wage that reduced the cost of thread and clothing to the benefit of the merchant, who often not only owned the raw material but also the loom and the spinner.

The Central Valley was notable for a certain link between agriculture, ranching, and crafts—a link that simply did not exist in other regions of the country such as Matina, Orotina, Esparza, or Guanacaste. The axis of this production structure was, of course, farming. Craft specialization was fed by the agricultural surplus, just as it favored the growth of herds, and the agricultural surplus was achieved using the wood and metal tools forged by the virtuous artisan and grown with the energy and manure of the cattle.

The Fall of Morazán

Unknown

Independence came to Costa Rica in 1821 without much strife. Spanish rule was over-thrown in Mexico, but the new Mexican state failed to incorporate Central America. Many of the elites throughout Central America dreamed of uniting into a single nation-state. A tenuous federal republic of Central America did come into existence in 1824, but differing motivations for union and popular resistance to the project plunged the region into civil strife over the following fifteen years, so that the project collapsed in 1839. Costa Rica fortunately remained distant from most of the theaters of war. In 1842, however, the Honduran-born Francisco Morazán used Costa Rica as a staging ground for an attempt to reunite the federation by force of arms. The official version of the fall of Morazán has always been that the military elite of San José led the movement, but this document reveals the spontaneous and popular nature of an uprising in which women played a particularly important role. The author was probably Francisco de Paula Gutiérrez, a member of a prominent San José family. The letter was published in the Redactor Oficial de Honduras *on 30 December 1842.*

Cartago, October 4, 1842

About public affairs I am sure you are anxious to hear, and do not doubt that I will inform you of the great events that have taken place here. . . . On the thirteenth of April, Morazán entered San José, and the entire State army was disarmed. He made his triumphal tour of every city in the State and was received with arcs of triumph, hails, and artillery salutes. He wasted little time in bringing together an Assembly of timid deputies who in a certain sense de-creed the Reconquest of the Central American Republic, authorizing Morazán to take from Costa Rica the necessary men and resources. The forcible contri-butions began under the name of "contracts" or "loans," but ended with the name "mandatory contributions." They began the recruitment, taking land-owners (which basically included every inhabitant of the State) and heads of family and requiring many soldiers and officers to contribute with more people and more purses. The people became so exasperated that in May and June there were two attempts to wrest from Morazán the power that the people had confided in him. . . . Morazán began to hurry the recruitment and the monthly contributions, which were raised to twenty thousand pesos, all of which left the entire State in great consternation and made the people so desperate that they began to say in private to their officer friends that they would not go to fight enemies who had never done anything to offend them, but that for the homeland they would willingly die. . . .

On Sunday, the eleventh of September, the cries of "long live sacred liberty, Our Father San José, Our Lady of los Ángeles" could be heard everywhere, and "long live the united towns [of Costa Rica]." The cries were coming from the soldiers and recruits who Morazán was counting on to begin the reconquest of Central America. The first of these, from San José, showed up on the edge of their central plaza, and though they were few in number because they were quartered in Alajuela, six leagues distant, they had heard from a messenger that on that day at three in the afternoon there would be 800 men in San José, including 150 from Cartago on their way to join the quixotic expedition. Morazán had prior knowledge of the conspiracy and had gathered thirty or forty officers on horseback, but he did not understand that the uprising was general, assuming that it was a conspiracy of four men from San José.

Firing broke out that day at eight in the morning, small parties left the plaza, and later, when they met with the people, they withdrew to the plaza after some shots that killed or wounded officers and soldiers in the surrounding area. . . . [Morazán's] force was made up of 40 officers and 80 soldiers from El Salvador, and about 150 from Costa Rica, who had been convinced to stay in a thousand ways. The force of the towns would be difficult to estimate, but I can deduce with certainty that, between those armed with sticks, machetes, rifles, and rocks, including women, the number exceeded 5,000. There were very few officers, and they were almost unnecessary, of little use even though some served with distinction. All those who had been in the plaza fought admirably. They tried to reach verbal and written agreements on a few occasions, but none came into effect due to the obstinacy on both sides. The towns offered guarantees in the first treaty, on the condition that all on the other side left the country, while Morazán replied that he would pardon the four from San José who were in mutiny, and that he would not leave the State, thinking that the mutineers were on their own. He sent three orders to his lieutenant, Sajet, who was in Puntarenas with forty or fifty officers and about two hundred men, thinking he would disperse the rebels, but his orders were intercepted in the tight circle of the siege. He thought then that Sajet and some from Alajuela and even from Cartago would come to his aid. The latter in fact did come, sixty in number . . . but those from Alajuela who came to join forces were met by a mighty charge that left four dead and twenty-two injured, and they arrived completely defeated.

On the Monday, the principal residents of San José, seeing that Morazán's cause was lost there and hearing the news from elsewhere, were encouraged by the Commandant of the city, Mayorga, to pronounce in favor of the towns. After a meeting of a small number of eminent residents, since some of us were absent due to our work while others had fled the fighting, we pronounced our adherence to the popular cause on Tuesday. That day the firing on the plaza intensified, and since Morazán's force had dwindled, he ceased his fire and the popular insurgents were able to take the house of don Alejandro Escalante where Morazán's family was holed up (they were treated with all consideration). At dawn, Morazán broke the line of the siege and withdrew to Cartago, but received a poor reception in the city, which was also in rebellion against him, and was arrested, along with his Minister, General Saravia, Villaseñor, and many other soldiers and officers, the upshot being that many of them remain prisoners.

After Morazán and his companions were taken prisoner, men from Alajuela and San José, 550 in number, arrived and took him on the fifteenth, and by the time they reached the outskirts of San José, another 3,000 men from the four principal cities had joined them. On his arrival in San José, there were about five or six thousand men in the plaza and the streets, but the people kept such silence that not a single insult was directed toward him, nor a single shout, nor anything of the sort.

Well guarded on arrival, after being charged with very few but quite terrible crimes — Why did he trick the people of the State and not fulfill the promises in his proclamations? Why did he treat them so harshly? Why had he offered Costa Rica to the State of Nicaragua, telling them that there was no one here who could direct public affairs? — he replied only that they were tricks required by war. He had his confession heard by the Vicar General of the State, and his son Chico wrote his will and sealed it. Villaseñor had his confession heard and reconciled himself, and they were taken to the plaza, Morazán on foot, as if out for a stroll, Villaseñor in a chair because he was in bad shape with a stab wound in his left side that he had received the day before and somewhat groggy from draughts of laudanum and ether that he had taken two or three hours before he was to be shot.

Arriving in the plaza, Morazán asked to take charge of the firing squad, without seating himself on the stool. He opened his shirt to the riflemen and said, "Aim well, my sons." He bade farewell to the officers and priests who were nearby, then turned to Villaseñor: "Farewell, friend. Until we meet in death."

When he saw that one soldier was not aiming, he asked him why, and the man told him his shot was to be held in reserve, whereupon Morazán announced, "Good then, FIRE!" After falling, he said, "Kill me, kill me," and in effect the coup de grace finished him off.

The two corpses were placed together, some soldiers saying, "That's right, let them go together making the same old plans and intrigues," and another, "Cover them with the same blanket, since the two of them always did the same." Three or four days after the burials, some of the people, doubting that Morazán had really died, went and exhumed the cadavers, and the corrupt state they found him in removed any doubts. In sum, in the sentencing there was only one judge, victim, accuser, witness, and executioner—the people. And so, their war having no other object, the people all retired to their houses, as if the events had never occurred, without trying anything with any of the other prisoners, some of whom were walking the streets in total liberty within a few days while they found ways to disappear.

Libelous Pornography from 1841

José María Figueroa

(Archivo Nacional
de Costa Rica)

In at least one instance, the new legal system that expanded after independence was used by a respectable family from Cartago to defend its honor when the young rake and social rebel José María Figueroa drew and distributed libelous pornographic drawings of the clan's young women. The drawing was discovered by the historian Ana Paulina Malavassi.

Civilizing Domestic Life in the

Central Valley, 1750–1850

Eugenia Rodríguez

Some claim that domestic violence was unknown in Costa Rica's past, or that domestic violence existed but remained confined to the lower classes. Others imagine that wives were passive victims of male domination. An exhaustive study of charges brought in hundreds of marital dispute suits filed by wives and husbands between 1732 and 1850 suggests a more complex picture of marital power relations in an age when new understandings of matrimony began developing.

Prior to independence, the church played the key role in the policing of marriage. This can be seen in the following communication sent by the bishop of Nicaragua, José Antonio de la Huerta, to the Costa Rican clergy on 19 August 1797. He declared that "there are many [married couples] in this bishopric, as well as from other distant provinces, who, causing a great hurt to their souls, live separate for long periods, without any legitimate cause which is approved by sacred canons." He ordered all priests to investigate married couples in their parishes "who live separated and divided and who do not cohabit as husband and wife . . . and to persuade and admonish them jointly to live in conjugal consortium; and if you do not succeed by subtle methods, require the Royal justices of your respective districts to compel them to follow such require-ment[s]." The growing intervention by civil authorities in the first half of the nineteenth century was part of a gradual process of separating the roles of the church and the state in the area of domestic morality and in the normalization of the gender order. The doctrinal regulation of marriage and the registration of vital statistics were left to the church, while the state began to take on a more active role in regulating the domestic life of the popular classes and in transforming it according to the values of the dominant class.

Between 1750 and 1850, an upper-class family ideal gained in appeal: the self-sufficient, male breadwinner and the dependent, homemaking wife subjected to domestic space. In tandem with this came a heightened appreciation of the ideal of marital relations as intimate, harmonious, and affectionate. The development of the civil judicial apparatus played a key role in these changes, by means of the centralization of the state. This expansion of the civil courts stimulated the authorities and the community to play a more active part in the regulation of domestic morality and in the promotion of upper-class ideals of family and marriage. It is particularly interesting that wives from the middle and popular classes had greater access to the legal process and used this process as an arena for airing marital discord. Their access encouraged greater public influence on marriage relationships, principally in cases of men's tyrannical abuse of their familial power, and contributed to a wider belief in the benefits of marital companionship.

Certain conditions allowed marital dispute suits to become an accessible resource for wives in the first half of the nineteenth century. During the colonial period, this type of claim was filed before the local priest, the only person authorized to deal with it. After 1821, the main change came in the ecclesiastical authorities' gradual loss of exclusive power in the resolution of marriage conflicts, except in cases of divorce. This change was fostered by the centralization of the liberal state, which brought with it the expansion of the judicial apparatus and a greater coverage of the population, especially for the popular sectors in provincial capitals. After 1830, the civil courts became the best option for couples in conflict, and for women of the middle class in particular. Moreover, the development of the judicial apparatus was reinforced by state politics, which normalized the gender order through the enactment of the General Code of 1841 and the Police Code of 1849; both endorsed the legal prerogative of civil authorities to regulate domestic morality and suggested the type of penalties that should apply. The expansion of the civil judicial apparatus and its power to regulate domestic morality can be seen in the fact that in the 1822–50 period, 78 percent of the cases came before civil tribunals, rather than ecclesiastical ones.

The procedures to set and resolve marital disputes before the courts were simple and brief. After hearing an accusation in the civil courts, the judge would name two *hombres buenos* (good men or partners) to speak on behalf of the involved parties. Together with the judge who heard the case, they acted as mediators in the judicial process, attempting to establish the facts, to reconcile the couple, and to propose some sort of settlement. As for the process of reconciliation, the secular response did not differ markedly from the ecclesiastical one—both stressed the upper-class ideal of marriage. The hombres buenos, with the judge, tended to insist that the couple restore harmonious relations and attempt to fulfill the Christian upper-class model of marriage. But this model was interpreted differently according to gender. Whereas wives stressed the companionate, affective, and self-sufficient breadwinner as ideal partner, husbands stressed the submissive and domestic woman as ideal partner. This differentiated emphasis in the upper-class marriage ideal was incorporated into the General Code of 1841, which established that "spouses mutually owe each other fidelity, aid, and assistance. . . . The husband must protect his wife, and she will be obedient to her husband. . . . The wife is obliged to live with her husband, and follow him to wherever he deems convenient to reside. [The] husband is obliged to . . . give her everything necessary to live, according to his abilities and status."

Marital dispute denunciation emerged primarily as a female resource. Wives accused their husbands before the courts twice as often as husbands accused their wives: 166 of the 252 cases in which the accuser is known were filed by the woman partner, only 86 by the male. A sharp contrast existed between the number of suits filed by those from *familias principales* (the elite ranks of society) and those from *familias del común* (the commoners); just over 80 percent of suits were filed by couples of the familias del común. Both elite and common wives, however, tended to take the initiative to accuse their husbands. However, among the couples of the familias del común, there was a sharper contrast in the proportion of accusations made by wives and husbands (68 percent by wives, 32 percent by husbands). For their part, elite husbands filed accusations against their wives (43 percent) on more occasions than did their commoner counterparts.

Fourteen main types of charges were filed by wives against their husbands. Of the 166 complaints in which the causes are known, the most frequent on the list is physical abuse. Taken together, physical and verbal abuse account for 34 percent of the charges. Furthermore, wives frequently claimed abandonment and lack of food and necessary clothing, saying that their husbands had squandered their assets (22 percent), or they claimed that husbands had been unfaithful or were living with other women (20 percent). Other women accused their husbands of constantly threatening to kill them (5 percent) or of being "friends to vice and alcohol" (5 percent). Finally, women sometimes claimed that their husbands made them live in places they did not like (4 percent) and did not allow them to visit their families (2 percent), or that his relatives interfered in their affairs, thus provoking conflicts (7 percent). In addition, the type of charges varied according to the wives' social origin. It is evident that domestic violence was not a practice exclusive of popular sectors. However, common wives tended to place more emphasis on charges associated with physical and verbal abuse and with death threats perpetrated by their husbands (40 percent) than the affluent wives (33 percent).

Among the cruel methods employed by husbands against their wives, the following stand out: yanking or cutting off their braids, tearing their clothes, slapping, lashing with twigs and horsewhips, and threatening their lives with knives, rocks, machetes, and other weapons. According to the General Code of 1841, the penalty for this type of abuse varied according to whether the consequences of violence (wounds, hits, and bad treatment) impeded the victim from working temporarily or permanently, reflecting the fact that in a predominantly agrarian society centered on coffee production and characterized by a shortage of labor, the ability to do physical work was taken seriously. The greater tendency among common wives to file for abandonment and lack of economic support underlines the importance of a husband's economic contribution. It became particularly serious if he did not fulfill the ideal of the self-sufficient breadwinner. It is likely that material conditions of the familias del común made it more difficult for husbands to adjust to the upper-class ideal of the self-sufficient breadwinner and of the caring and respectful husband.

The following case illustrates both the difficulty experienced by the popular and middle sectors in adjusting to the upper-class marriage model and the role of drunkenness as a cause of domestic violence and lack of financial support. José Segura, a tailor, was sued by his wife for always being drunk, provoking public scandals, punishing her, and not fulfilling his duties as a provider. In April 1844, the judge sentenced Segura to jail for habitual drunkenness, saying that "because of this vice, he scandalizes the neighborhood where he lives. . . . he does not fulfill his marital duties in that he does not provide the necessaries for his wife, and wants to kill her when he is drunk. . . . [He] sets a bad example and abuses Jesús Herrera, an orphan in his care, who being so young does not talk, and is a little deaf and cannot manage alone. . . . Even though said Segura is a tailor, he does not work because of this accustomed vice." The husband defended himself against these charges by arguing that even though drunkenness often prevented him from working, "when he is sober he works to support his obligations." The judge ruled that the husband had to fulfill two months of public service, and once the sentence was completed, he would be "turned over to his brother Francisco until he be redeemed." Mr. José María Aguilar, "second-degree relative and good man trusted by this Court," was appointed "to administer his goods and with them provide for the mentioned orphan." Presumably the wife's reward was an orderly household and a chastened husband.

Although marital dispute suits constituted a predominantly female resource, husbands' accusations against their wives increased in the 1830–50 period. Husbands of both groups tended to charge their spouses most often with infidelity (38 percent), abandonment (20 percent), and disobedience and failure to accomplish duties (23 percent), followed by in-laws' interference in marital affairs (8 percent), verbal abuse (6 percent), and threats to life (2 percent). The main grounds alluded to by husbands were adultery, abandonment, insubordination, and lack of fulfillment of domestic duties. In other words, husbands measured their wives' shortcomings in terms of those patriarchal elements that fit the model of the ideal upper-class wife: submissiveness, obedience, faithfulness, and dedication to domestic chores.

In spite of husbands' shared perspective regarding the patriarchal marital ideal, certain differences existed in the emphasis placed on accusations according to social origin, although these differences were less marked than among wives. Elite husbands tended to question their wives' faithfulness more than commoners. Whereas 69 percent of elite husbands accused their wives of adultery or abandonment, common husbands reported this complaint only in 58 percent of the cases. Common husbands tended to focus on disobedience and lack of compliance with the obligation to serve them and the family (25 percent), but upper-class husbands complained of this problem in only 14 percent of the cases. The greater fears of elite husbands about their wives' infidelity may stem, in part, from the weightier influence of social and familial considerations and from the seclusion of elite wives in the domestic sphere. In this context, contact with the opposite sex was taken much more seriously. Moreover, among the dominant class, honor was conceived of in corporatist rather than individual terms and was related to social and familial considerations. Thus an elite husband was inclined to pressure the authorities to "reestablish" the honor and reputation of his wife and, therefore, of himself and of his family.

The third ground for accusation listed by husbands — that wives did not submit to their authority or fulfill their domestic duties — is an interesting one. Only 14 percent of elite husbands made these charges, while 25 percent of common husbands made them. Probably submission was associated with a husband's limitations in exercising the role of main household authority. Wives of familias del común made complementary contributions to the maintenance of the home, they had greater freedom to mobilize and work out of the home (which increased their contact with other people), and husbands had their own financial difficulties in providing adequate living space, food, and clothing for the family, especially in the first years of marriage.

That husbands (well-to-do and commoner alike) would resort to the courts reveals a certain level of frustration at not being able to resolve the contradiction between ideals and everyday realities using their own, private resources. This frustration was particularly associated with the sensation of loss of authority in the home. Masculine impotence before the expected ideal of self-sufficient breadwinner and main authority in the nuclear family is demonstrated in the case of Domingo Arce. In 1843, Arce accused his wife, Mercedes Chacón, before the court of Heredia "of having ignored his authority that he rightfully has over her and his house. [Thus] he lives an insufferable life because he is not the owner of anything in his house, nor does he govern [his house]." He asked the court "to establish his right to govern his wife in his house, according to his rights granted him by law, as husband."

Mercedes Chacón granted power of attorney to Mr. Cayetano Morales, who stated on her behalf that "the charges made by her husband seem to be nothing more than whims. . . . [He] himself has confessed that his wife is hardworking, as can be seen by the articles in their home that were acquired by her. . . . she [also] plants corn and beans, makes clothes for herself and her children, and even for her husband. . . . and, although he works, she has no idea what he does with the money because, as can be proved, having been absent from the house for one year and eight months, he had not brought any food or clothing for his family. . . . Finally, so as not to discredit him, she declines to make other declarations, and . . . asks the Court to sentence him as deemed convenient so that in the future he fulfill his obligations."

After hearing the depositions of the two spouses, the judge emphasized feminine subjugation in explaining the sentence.

> A woman is obligated to respect, and be submissive and obedient to her husband, as well as observe the duties imposed on her by Article 133 of the civil code, which gives the husband the right to govern her and what concerns his home. . . . a husband's duty is to feed her, keep his job, and love her amorously. . . . therefore, based on Articles 132 and 135 of the same code, I find that the accused should observe in the future the obligations placed on her by the cited articles, and the husband should also comply with the parts that correspond to him which I have made known to both parties.

In conclusion, a redefinition in the ideals of marriage and gender roles occurred, but in the end, the discourse of upper-class companionate and affective marriage both hid and legitimated patriarchal dominance. Nevertheless, the ideal marriage based on companionship and affection was more than an attenuated version of the patriarchal ideal. It is in this light that we have to view the growing criticisms of masculine and feminine conduct and the legal reforms, which civilized rather than eliminated the husband's patriarchal power.

II

Coffee Nation

In the mid-1840s, the Economic Society of the Friends of Guatemala, interested in finding new export products, commissioned Manuel Aguilar, a Costa Rican lawyer, to prepare a booklet on coffee growing in Costa Rica, where the bean was already king of exports. Aguilar sent back a detailed report to the merchants of the north, setting out in elaborate detail how coffee could be cultivated, harvested, processed, and exported with dramatic benefit for those willing to take the risk. Coffee, he said, had transformed Costa Rica from poor and miserable to "rich and prosperous in the space of fifteen years, bringing it trade, civilization, population, and tax revenues with such increasing rapidity that it can be said without reservation that relative to the rest of the Central American Republics, Costa Rica is the one that exports most and so is richest."

Aguilar was not exaggerating. Costa Rica entered the modern era in the 1840s with an abrupt takeoff in coffee cultivation for export to Europe. Between 1850 and 1890, the sale of coffee accounted for almost 90 percent of the country's export earnings, stimulated by the high prices that prevailed throughout the nineteenth century and interrupted only by a few sharp but relatively brief crises. Cultivation of "the berry," as it was called, was initially concentrated around San José, but it rapidly extended to other areas of the Central Valley and ultimately bent the entire country to its will. In 1890, the poet Carlos Gagini would quip:

> Who's the one who built the Theater?
> Who do they call the golden bean?
> Who's the one who fills the Treasury
> And pays you profits swift and clean?
> Coffee!

A new system of government took shape as well because the export economy required a more active public power to improve roads to the port of Puntarenas and to oversee a legal system that regulated business life. After 1880, like many Liberal regimes throughout Latin America, the Costa Rican state undertook to "civilize" the common people of town and countryside through education and a stricter supervision of their supposedly barbaric customs. The creation of a national identity emerged as one important result. The bud of Tico consciousness became visible in 1856, when Costa Ricans went to war against the American mercenary William Walker, who had taken over Nicaragua and was threatening a Central American conquest. National identity was finally consolidated in the 1880s, alongside an ambitious reform of public education and a flurry of monument building promoted by a bold, young political vanguard carrying the banner of liberalism, positivism, and modernity.

The common people from urban and rural areas also made their presence felt, however. They helped to decide critical moments of political life despite the autocratic system that prevailed through most of the nineteenth century. And they struggled to benefit from—or at least to avoid losing out in—the privatization of the land and the colonization of the agricultural frontier. The clearest winners in the agroexport boom were the *cafetaleros*—the better-connected and better-financed coffee barons who danced their dance of the millions, mostly through controlling credit, purchase prices, and processing facilities. Most coffee barons owned significant tracts of coffee land, but unlike in some other countries, production was not confined to their large estates in Costa Rica. Many small and medium-sized growers made a successful transition to the commercial farming of coffee, and this led to some measure of prosperity for them. The indigenous communities of the highlands, who saw their common lands stripped and their traditional rights trampled by encroaching colonists and state alike, emerged as the clearest losers in this transitional phase. The country's monocrop export economy became "duocrop" after 1880, when bananas were planted on the Caribbean lowlands for export to the United States. This move quickly turned the province of Limón into an enclave of foreign agribusiness. The two so-called motor products, coffee and bananas, sustained and shaped the expansion of Costa Rica's Liberal state, even after 1914, when the agroexport model started showing signs of stress.

Privatization of the Land

and Agrarian Conflict

Silvia Castro

The presidency of Juan Rafael Mora (1849–59) proved key in consolidating the social and political changes that had taken place during the boom in coffee capitalism. The new capital, San José, was graced with a presidential palace, a theater, and a hospital. An important stage in consolidating patriotism was also reached in 1856–57, when Mora was able to muster a citizen army to fight against the threat posed by the American mercenary William Walker, who had seized control of Nicaragua. Mora was an exemplary coffee baron who used his power to facilitate further expansion of coffee agriculture, all the while making sure that he and his family and allies benefited. As historian Silvia Castro shows, Mora and the coffee barons found allies in prosperous peasants at the local level. The poorest peasants, on the other hand, suffered the most significant loss in the game of privatizing common lands. Yet although they could not stop the process, their struggles won them better terms and more time to adapt.

Even before coffee appeared as an export product with great promise, governments of the young country of Costa Rica promoted colonization and the private appropriation of public land. Starting in 1824, dispositions were passed to facilitate the purchase of *baldíos*, technically idle land owned by the state, and rewards were offered to those colonists who established themselves in sparsely populated areas. As the allure of coffee became more apparent, the lands close to the principal population centers were transformed into a vital resource for increasing production of the bean. The governors of the day, some of them important *cafetaleros* [coffee producers], turned their gaze not only to state lands on the periphery but also to the fertile fields around San José, Heredia, Alajuela, and Cartago. Around 1850, desirable "state lands" still existed around the capital and other cities of the Central Valley. In legal terms, they were state lands, but they were often occupied by farmers who did not have property

titles. These were peasants established on the land, perhaps for over a generation, who enjoyed customary usufruct rights. How could access be gained to
these lands to turn them into productive coffee groves? How could some security be offered to the people in possession of the land in order to get them to
substitute the planting of corn and beans with a more permanent crop like
coffee? It became urgent to define the legal condition of these lands, but they
would have to be defined in a way that established who their owners were,
and not simply who possessed them in usufruct. This is where state intervention became indispensable—the "ordering" of something that did not have
the legal character required by the most dynamic sector of agricultural producers. This new order involved the dismantling of communally held property,
as well as lands in collective usufruct, which were usually administered by the
municipalities.

It has been noted that between 1842 and 1870, the executive power was
the agency with the most influence over public administration. Due to a very
simple division of labor, the regime was characterized by an extreme presiden-
tialism. Essentially, two or three ministers and a few offices were responsible
for organizing public services. In agrarian terms, the executive held an important quota of power over the entire process of privatizing common resources.
The periodic dissolution of congress and the influence of the executive in the
legislature tended to neutralize opposition that might have sprung up in the
congress. Nevertheless, the making of decisions about putting up lands for sale,
distributing them among interested parties, and charging the corresponding
fees for the properties required the intervention of both the executive and the
municipalities.

A kind of coordinated division of tasks existed. The issuing of decrees authorizing the sale of municipally administered lands known as *leguas* was the
job of the president of the republic. The request to sell the leguas, however,
was generally presented to the president by the town councils of the areas in
question. Once the sale had been decided and the legal paperwork issued, the
responsibility for executing a decree or resolution was handed over to the municipalities or to agencies named especially for the task, sometimes created just
for overseeing all the decrees regarding land tenure. This coordinated division
of political labor became a chain of pressures and decision making difficult for
opponents of privatization to break. Movements against the approval of a land
sale, or petitions to have it delayed, could be brought to bear on any link in the
chain. But even when negotiations were undertaken, or when the municipalities began consultations, the adjudication and sale of lots would inevitably take
place in short order anyway. To understand this dynamic, one must analyze
the play of interests among the groups involved.

For almost the entire period under scrutiny here, Juan Rafael Mora occupied the presidency, and he was the signatory of all the decrees in question. Fed on liberal ideals and very conscious of the conditions necessary for stimulating the national economy through coffee production, he understood the urgency of transforming an agrarian world that combined distinct forms of land tenure. Although some authors claim that there was no concerted action among the powerful groups of the country at this time, the various fractions of the coffee bourgeoisie agreed that the Central Valley would be converted into a region of landowners. That none of these groups ever acted as an opposition during the conflicts arising over the privatization of public lands offers proof of such a mutual understanding.

The privatization of the lands of Pavas, which belonged to the city of San José, began in the 1840s. The case illustrates how the bourgeoisie, sheltered by the state, took possession of valuable lands. The following petition from poor peasants tells the story:

> In agreement no. 100 of 2 March 1858 of the Ministry of the Interior, the Government decreed that twenty-five plots of that land should be remeasured, and enclosed, appraised and put in the hands of the Intendent General for auction, with the goal of investing the proceeds in the piping system that currently provides water to the capital. On these plots today you will find the best coffee haciendas of señores Montealegre, Le Lacheur, Hubbe, etc., etc. and previously don Juan Rafael Mora, under whose administration the matter of these lands was decided. As in all things relating to the public good, despite the beneficent desires that generally animate the Head of State, these kinds of machinations leading to private benefit can always be seen. This is what has happened in the matter which we bring before you today, since . . . San José with the immense benefit of piped water, and the landowners with their valuable haciendas on the outskirts of the most important population center of the Republic, have acquired uncommon advantages, but the people of Pavas have been reduced to indigence for they have nowhere to provide for themselves, and have no access even to firewood. What an adverse effect has come of reducing to private domain the common lands upon which we live.

If such cases showed clearly how the coffee bourgeoisie expanded its land base under the cloak of the state's privatizing action, they do not encompass the full panorama of the era, nor do they explain the dynamic of social forces surrounding public power. An interest in creating conditions for the transition from tenant to landowner was not exclusive to the dominant class. There also existed a sector of the populace, one that might be called a middle peasantry, that in many cases did not oppose the privatization process. Indeed, such peasants may even have advocated the process because the acquisition of such lands might allow them to begin planting coffee and to expand their cultivation of grains and cattle-raising activities. It is possible that the voice of this peasantry made itself heard through the municipalities, in petitions to privatize certain lands. Once the sale was decided, they would purchase the lot that they had formerly possessed in usufruct. Sometimes they would have to join with other peasants if the land in question was expensive, as was the case in Pavas, but at other times the responsibility might be assumed singly, especially when the sale was covered by a particular decree (number 39) that established favorable conditions for payment of the sale price.

Precisely the representatives of this latter group began having problems paying off their debts around 1856. The demand for men and material contributions from the Costa Rican people to fight the National Campaign created agonizing circumstances for and concern among peasants. Many families lost fathers, sons, and brothers, and many contributed generously, to the point of upsetting their own economic stability. The decrease in labor resulting from the war and the ensuing cholera epidemic made agricultural production very difficult. It left some families incapable of paying their debts. Their anxiety became manifest in congress when deputy Nazario Toledo intervened to avoid a strict application of the decree concerning the sale of the commons of Cartago and so saved many indebted peasants from losing their lands.

It is possible that some of these middling peasants, perhaps the most comfortably off, held public office as municipal aldermen or receivers. To do so, they had to fulfill certain requirements—residency in the canton and full citizenship. The latter required that they be at least twenty-one years old, own real estate worth at least 300 pesos or have an annual income of 150 pesos, be in good standing with taxes, and know how to read and write. The capacity to purchase lands, and the possibility of participating in political life, made for conditions that promised a bright future for some of these middling peasants. It was the alliance between the large landowners and this peasantry—or rather the coincidence of certain expectations that these two actors had for the future—that likely provided the backing for state intervention in the privatization of land resources.

In the 1850s, the rising agrarian bourgeoisie found a certain amount of help among middling peasants for carrying out the task of privatizing public lands in distinct locales around the Central Valley. With the protection of the government, these groups took possession of valuable terrain. Coordinated action among the municipalities and the upper echelon of the executive power made it possible to start the process of land privatization and to find ways of silencing the protests of disgruntled peasants. The very poor feared losing access to the lands in common usufruct but found little positive response to their appeals. Other peasants who had ventured to transform themselves into landowners, but who due to circumstances beyond their control could not pay their debts, received certain concessions, such as extended repayment terms. This privatizing thrust channeled by certain groups via the state was undertaken in different parts of the Central Valley throughout the decade. Even though functions were delegated to different public agencies, the executive level of government in the figure of the president of the republic retained an important quota of power over the process. There were two reasons for this: he had the authority to issue decrees and held responsibility for making the ultimate decisions in conflicts. The fact that there were officials in midlevel public posts who were politically connected to him, and the fact that the members of the town councils were at least prosperous peasants, created a certain homogeneity in the various links of the chain of people who had to make decisions about the sale of public lands.

Tico Sweepstakes

Pío Joaquín Fernández

A good idea of an average coffee estate from the boom period of the mid-nineteenth century, and of the relative value of each of its components, comes from the following curious source. It appeared as a newspaper advertisement urging readers to partici-pate in a raffle for a coffee estate that had gone into receivership during the serious economic downturn of the late 1850s.

Having obtained the necessary permission to raffle a coffee hacienda located in Hatillo, half a league from the plaza of the capital, the undersigned is making the lottery conditions known to the public.

The estate in question has been legally valued by the appraisers don Alonso Gutiérrez, named by the receiver's lawyer, and don Nicolás Sáenz, named by the seller. According to the appraisal, the hacienda with all its adjunct parts is worth the sum of twelve thousand six hundred and fifty-seven pesos and four reals; but the undersigned would like to hold a raffle for ten thousand nine hundred and ninety-nine pesos, divided into six hundred and forty-seven tick-ets at seventeen pesos each, with the winner having to pay the corresponding sales tax. People who would like to acquire one or a number of tickets can pur-chase them in the Capital at the store of don José Esquivel, where the tickets are for sale. Don José will also hold onto the money collected in order to re-turn it to the ticket holders in the event that sufficient tickets are not sold by the last day of this month. Those who have already purchased their tickets can get a return up to the fifteenth of the month.

★ ★ ★

The hacienda is comprised of:

Forty-five manzanas [1 manzana = 1.75 acres] of land corresponding to the map offered, consisting of fifteen manzanas of pasture and the rest in coffee, at one hundred and fifty pesos the manzana

The Labyrinth Coffee Estate in 1859 (Artist: Ramón Páez)

One cane field of a third of a manzana at 60 pesos

About four thousand plantain trees planted along the roads of the estate at
40 pesos

About eight yards of corridors five yards wide, floored with cedar wood, and
with walls of lime and stone, with good roofing, and along the corridors
three rooms enclosed by wood and one by a wall at 350 pesos

About half a manzana of tiled courtyard surrounded almost entirely by a
stone wall of two and a half yards in height at 800 pesos

One basin for washing and rinsing coffee, situated on the river bank at
20 pesos

One mill of foreign manufacture with its steam engine at 300 pesos

One first-class fanner, used, at 85 pesos

One ox-driven threshing machine inside of thirteen yards in diameter with
wooden wheels of nine and ten hands in height at 100 pesos

About ten thousand coffee plants of premier class at one and a half reals
per plant

About eight thousand coffee plants of second class at one real

About twelve thousand coffee plants of third class at three-quarters of a real

One large iron plough, at 34 pesos

One cutting blade for an iron plough of about 150 pounds weight at 25 pesos
One cutting blade for a wooden plough with iron teeth at 84 pesos
Two wooden ploughs at 6 pesos each
Twelve iron shovels in good condition at 12 pesos
Two axes at 1 peso
Two iron bars at 3 pesos
Six hoes for weeding at 3 pesos
Two ox carts with wheels and hitchings at 24 pesos
One dismantled ox cart at 8 pesos
Four crates for transporting coffee at 20 pesos, 4 reals apiece
Two pannier crates at 1 peso each
Two wire sifters at 3 pesos
Seven whetstones at 3 pesos, 4 reals

Total 12,657 pesos, 4 reals

San José, 2 October 1858

Witness to Heroism

Gerónimo Segura

Most visitors to Costa Rica will arrive at the Juan Santamaría International Airport, and many will notice other monuments bearing his name. Santamaría was a humble day laborer from Alajuela celebrated for a heroic act at the battle of Rivas that allegedly snatched victory from the jaws of defeat for the Costa Rican troops in their fight with William Walker's mercenaries in 1856. Thirty-five years later, in 1891, with the official recuperation of the figure of Santamaría in full swing but the veracity of his heroic act coming under question, Francisco Montagné, an employee at the Ministry of War, sought out veterans who had been present at the battle of Rivas. The most vivid of the testimonies he heard was that of Gerónimo Segura, who was interviewed under oath in his house, making the following an unusual mix of witness statement for the defense of a new national mythology somehow on trial and an early oral history project. The testimony was rediscovered by the historian Rafael Méndez.

On the eleventh of March, 1856, I left the city of Heredia for San José to get fitted out and incorporate into the expeditionary army, which left for Puntarenas on the twelfth. There I embarked with part of the troop for Bolsón and then went overland to Santa Rosa, though I didn't take part in any of the fighting there in which our army triumphed. I then went on to Nicaragua as part of an advance guard, leaving for Sapoá, where I stayed for three days, and then on to Sapuasito, where I took part in the fighting that was going on there. After the victory I continued on to Rivas, arriving in the city on about the seventh or eighth of April. By order of Colonel Alejandro Escalante, I was made an aide to the Nicaraguan General don Francisco Argüello and posted to his house.

At the crack of dawn on the eleventh, General Argüello ordered me to go and get him some coffee. While I was out doing this, a youngster went running past and told me that the enemy was coming, and sure enough I looked and saw them coming from the north. I hurried back to notify the General, who was still barely dressed, and he and I left at full tilt for the barracks of the General Staff, which was about four hundred yards from his house, and from there to the barracks of General Cañas, about another three hundred yards. But I had to leave the General on the way to go and call various soldiers who were at the corner of the *mesón* [inn], looking after the harnessing of the army mules. They came with me full speed, and when we got to about fifty yards from General Cañas's barracks, the enemy's fire was very heavy, and since we didn't have at that time any weapons in hand to defend ourselves, we had to hole up in an abandoned house. The enemy soldiers spotted us, and one part of them moved to attack us through the yard of the house we were in—Simón Delgado was there, Jesús Chavarría, Bernardo Rodríguez, Vicente Zamora, a guy Soto from Alajuela, yours truly, and others whose names I don't remember.

General Cañas's troops, seeing that we were under attack, kept up fire on the enemy for ten full minutes and succeeded in getting them to retreat some twenty-five yards. Taking advantage of the opportunity, we escaped out of there and joined up with the troops of General Cañas, Jesús Chavarría being wounded in the arm before getting there. There we were armed with flint rifles and joined the ranks in the street who were raining fire on the enemy. The barracks of the General Staff and of Cañas (where we were) were under simultaneous attack by the enemy. There was a moment in which the enemy got very close to the barracks of the General Staff after taking over one of our army's artillery pieces, which had been placed far down the street. So one group from our army went around the block to come to the aid of the General Staff. . . . We came together and forced the enemy to retreat. In their confusion, most took shelter in the mesón, the others having occupied the Town Hall and the Church. We were keeping up our fire on the mesón, when don Juan Alfaro Ruiz ordered me to Cañas's barracks to get more ammunition; I incurred great danger by following that order.

Once inside the barracks, General Cañas said to me, "What are you doing here?" "I've come to get more ammunition," I replied. Then he said to me, "Don't leave yet, wait here a second."

And he promptly grabbed a cloth, gave it to me, brought over a bottle of varsol and drained it over the rag that I was holding and said, "Wring this out." Once this was done, he brought over a stalk of sugarcane about two yards long and made me tie the cloth securely to one end of the cane. He handed me a box of matches and said, "Do you know what you are going to do?"

"No idea, Sir," I replied.

He went on: "I am going to open that corner door for you, and straightway you go out on all fours as fast as you can; then get on your feet and run like hell to the mesón. Any one of those doors recessed in the wall, fly past it because that's where the danger lies. When you've gotten past two doors, stop and lean well back against the wall, put a match to the cane and put the eaves to the torch. When the fire's well started, come back at full speed and let me know."

I replied to the General, "How is it going to be possible to exit that door? You can hear the bullets raining like hail." The General replied, "Don't be a coward. This is a lottery; if you don't want to die, you might save yourself by doing this despite the bullets; if you stay here, you'll just die eventually."

This all took place in the presence of Juan Santamaría, who was the only soldier accompanying the General at that moment, since all the other soldiers were firing from the high ground of the cuartel (the Garita). The General hadn't quite finished pumping up my courage, when Santamaría spoke to me in the following terms: "Why are you being so chicken? I already went out once to light the place on fire, and I didn't put up any resistance to the idea." And I said to him, "This is not cowardice, I'm just saying that it's dangerous."

And the expression on Santamaría's face so bothered me that I said at once to the General, "Open the door, I'm going to put the place to the torch."

The General opened the door, and I ran out at full speed with the cane and the matches. But in my state of confusion, I had taken an extremely dangerous route and don Juan Alfaro Ruiz, who saw me, screamed to warn me of the danger, which I was able to spot and avoid in time. I finally arrived at the mesón and carried out my mission. When I saw that the fire was well established in the eaves, I ran back as fast as I'd come. The General greeted me with a lot of praise and he said, "Now that you are back here all right, go out one more time to light afire the other corner so that the fire spreads." He gave me another cloth well soaked with varsol, and tied it to the end of the cane.

"I'm ready," I said to the General. "But don't you think it would be better for two of us to go?" He answered me, "But who is there here?" And I said, "How about this guy who says he's so brave," pointing to Santamaría (who he liked a great deal and had little interest in sending).

Santamaría shot back, "Yes, I'll go. I'm a man. I've already been and come back. I won't resist the idea."

It was agreed. Each one of us prepared our respective cane, the General opened the door for us, and out we went at full gallop, me first and Santamaría immediately behind. We got to the spot that had been pointed out to us, with me having gone past one door, and Santamaría stopping before getting to it, the door between us. We simultaneously undertook our operation to light the fire when I looked over at Santamaría and saw that he gave a half turn from the point where he was leaning against the wall and immediately sat down and fell to one side, closing his eyes at the same time; I also noticed that the fire he had started in the eaves was falling and had set his hair alight. I saw blood running toward his neck, and I realized that he was dead. As I retreated, I tried to pull him with me, but Alfaro shouted at me to get out of there, and I was able to arrive at the corner where he was taking cover with his soldiers. He wouldn't let me undertake any more missions to return to the mesón; I wasn't the only man here who had to undertake such missions. The blaze grew in size, and the combat grew ever more fierce and bloody, until the enemy in great confusion had to retire at about three in the morning of the twelfth of April.

That same day at about seven or eight in the morning, the rest of the enemy who had holed up in the Church and the Town Hall were dislodged and defeated at bayonet-point. I carried on as aide to General Argüello until the beginning of the month of May, when I returned to Costa Rica.

Holidays in Costa Rica, 1858

Thomas Francis Meagher

(illustrated by Ramón Páez)

Thomas Francis Meagher had an extraordinary nineteenth-century career by any standards. Recipient of a classical Jesuit education in Ireland and England, he became de facto leader of the Young Ireland revolutionaries of 1848 (and was responsible for introducing the Irish tricolor), was captured by the British and transported to Australia. Meagher later fled to the United States and became a renowned lawyer in New York City. His fierce republicanism led him to support the Union cause in the Civil War, where he rose to the rank of brigadier general. His career ended in the 1870s, when he slipped from the deck of a steamboat and drowned while serving as governor of Montana. Meagher was one of many men contracted in the mid-nineteenth century to do feasibility studies on an interoceanic canal along the San Juan River and Lake Nicaragua. This brought him to Costa Rica in 1858 in the company of the artist, Ramón Páez, son of the Venezuelan president. Meagher's account, originally published in Harper's New Monthly *magazine, is the most compelling nineteenth-century traveler's view of Costa Rica, and indeed among the very best of its genre.*

Straggling up and down a long low bank of sand which gleamed across the Gulf, there was Punta Arenas, with its red-tiled roofs, whitewashed frame houses, church towers, flagstaffs, and dusky huts thatched with plantain leaves. Dotting the glaring picture at different points, and shading it a little, there was the indigo tree, the poisonous *manzanilla*, and the palm. Right before us on the beach was a wooden lighthouse, built and daubed in the fashion of a pagoda. Off there, in the roadstead, was the French flag drooping at the mizenpeak of a brig, from the quarterdeck of which a shining telescope had been leveled at us. Nearer to us a Dutch barque, with an awning stretched from stem to stern, and her broadside hung with matting to keep the timbers from the sun, lay

Puntarenas—the Inner Harbor

dead upon the tide. All about us were swarms of smaller craft—boats, *pira-guas*, scows, *bongos*—taking freight to the ships, or taking it away. All round us were the mountains and the forest, girdling the eager and glowing scene with solid grandeur and overlooking it in silence. . . .

Beautiful as Punta Arenas looks from the glowing Gulf of Nicoya, it is some-what behind the age: it has no pier, no wharf, no new or old slip—nothing of the kind. You go ashore in a boat, a bongo or a scow, just as the fancy strikes you or your purse permits. A boat will cost a dollar. Should the tide be out, the last fifty yards or so of the journey to the town, being through the slimiest mud, have to be got over on the back of a native, whose knees, as I can vouch, are none of the steadiest when put to the test of two hundred pounds of Irish flesh and blood, a double-barreled fowling piece and riding boots included.

The marketplace lies a little off the main street, a short distance from the Plaza. It was a bustling place the evening we visited it. The coffee was coming down from the interior—several carts laden with it had already reached the Port—and all the booths and stores were crowded. . . . All about—lying down or patiently bearing their ponderous yokes erect—were the ox teams that had supplied the market with its choicest goods. At every point—wherever it seemed a stake could be driven home—a fighting cock was held to bail, and, spite of it, kept the public peace disturbed. The bells of San Rafael, where the good Jesuit was to preach at sundown, rattled their shrill tongues all the while. Every now and then the trumpet at the gate of the *cuartel* flourished in and swelled the riot, while, at steady intervals, the thunders of the Dutch barque in the roadstead opened, for the Consul-General of the Hanseatic Towns was paying her an official visit, and in his honor fireworks and bunting were the order of the day. In the midst of all this dust, glare, and uproar, in the back-room of a *posada*, close to the market-place, a blind man sat, and, with his dark eyes vaguely following his busy hands, played on the marimba, to the delight of a breathless circle that had deepened round him. Shrouded in the *mantilla*, there was in that quiet circle more than one bright face bent on Miguel Cruz, of Nicaragua, as he touched the keys of his rude instrument, and made them vocal with his memories of Indian and Spanish song. He was accompanied on the guitar by a speckled native of Massaya. . . .

The evening of the day following our arrival from Panama we set out for the mountains. An hour of brisk galloping, along the beach which connects the town of Punta Arenas with the main land, brought us to Chacarita, an out-post of the Custom house at the Garita. . . . In the smoky interior of the hut, as we rode up to it, an Inspector of Customs, with the stump of a *puro* between his placid lips, serenely oscillated in his shirt-sleeves in his hammock of *agave* straw. Having satisfied him that the blue California blankets strapped to our saddles contained a change of linen only, the calm Inspector, without rising from his hammock, with a gentle wave of his discolored hand, signified that we were at liberty to proceed. A moment after we were in the heart of the forest. . . .

Winding through the mazes of this superb labyrinth, hundreds of carts, in the months of February and March, move down. The noble oxen have their foreheads shaded with the broad shining leaves of the *pavel*. They come from Cartago, from San José, from the great plantation of Pacifica, in the valley of the Tiribi, in the shadow of the mountains of San Miguel—from the plateaux beyond the ruins of Ujarrás, and overlooking the cataracts of the wild Berbis—descend four thousand feet into this forest, and so wend their way to Punta Arenas, at which port—with the exception of a few bags which find their way to the Sarapiqui, and thence to the Atlantic—the entire coffee crop of Costa Rica is shipped to Europe and the United States.

The carts are clumsy structures. A pole projects from an oblong frame, to which an axle is bolted underneath. The ends of the axle protrude through discs or solid wheels of cedar, the latter being four inches across the tire, and from four to five feet diameter. Within the wheels we have some open cane-work, and this supports an awning of untanned ox hide. A cart got up in this style costs from $25 to $30. The team itself generally costs from $75 to $80. The coffee lies upon the platform or bottom of the cart, sown up in bags of coarse white cotton. One of these carts will carry from eight hundred to one thousand pounds of coffee. The freight is a trifle less than 75 cents for every one hundred pounds. Over the bags another hide is fastened with leather thongs, while an iron pot, a calabash for holding water, and other utensils of use along the road, dangle on the outside. Peering out from underneath the ox hide covering, one may oftentimes surprise the black lustrous eyes and ruby lips of some bronzed daughter of the mountains. For the wives and children of the *carreteros*, in most instances, attend the coffee to the port. In the long journey — it is a journey of six days at least — they are companionable and most useful. They grind the corn for the tortillas, boil the frijoles, slice and fry plantains, ply the thread and needle, tend the oxen with water and *sacate*, and in various other ways prove themselves the kindliest handmaids and ministers of comfort to the honest fellows who trudge along on foot, and with the *chuzo* — their slender steel-piked wand — direct the docile teams. . . .

The yelping of dogs — the crowing of cocks — small panes of glass glimmering through the blackness of the night — the tinkling of a guitar at an open door-way, and a row of greenish bottles shining along a shelf against the white-washed wall opposite the door-way — the coarse round pavement, full of holes and hillocks, all dry and hard, over which, smartly striking it as though they felt their footing sure, the muscles went nimbly, though with an occasional jerk and slide — women, with bare heads, bare necks and arms, seated on door-steps, mildly fumigating the narrow street with their cigarrillos, and ejaculating their surprise and surmises as we rode by them — a belfry, for all the world like a water-tank on a double pair of gawky stilts, flanking a capacious church, the face of which, whitewashed as all the houses were, looked corpse-like in the sickly smiling of the moon — and then a shelterless broad space, fringed with orange-trees, which our guide, Anselmo, told us was the Plaza — these were the sounds and sights which pleasantly assured us we had reached our encampment for the night [in Esparza]. . . .

★ ★ ★

Two leagues and a half from San José we stopped to breakfast at the posada of La Asuncion. With its broad white face shining through the clouds of yellow

The Belles of Esparza

dust which the coffee carts still continued to roll up, we found this posada a sweet retreat. The windows, the walls, the floor were clean and bright as those of a Yorkshire dairy. The atmosphere was fresh and richly scented. The furniture — quaintly shaped, curiously and lavishly carved, all of black mahogany — looked as though it were assiduously polished. And so it was. The three plump, black-diamond-eyed, sprightly girls — daughters of the healthy widowed lady of the house . . . — were living assurances of that, as they glided round the table with overflowing cups of delicious chocolate, the milkiest eggs conceivable, and oranges from the trees which shaded and perfumed the house. In every respect the breakfast at La Asuncion had the advantage of the breakfast at San Mateo, though the garlic, with which the stewed beef was stuffed to suffocation, might have been dispensed with. The Chili peppers more than sufficed to heighten the flavor of the feast. They drew tears even from the eyes of don Ramon, who, from infancy, had been accustomed to them.

From La Asuncion into San José the road was in the best condition. It was broad, compact, and level. Gangs of laborers, moreover, were busy at different points, filling up ruts, breaking stones, clearing out trenches, strewing gravel, or over some fresh patch of rubbish, grit and mortar, hauling a monstrous roller after them. Then came the coffee plantations, laid out in squares and avenues with strictest regularity, the delicate dark-green foliage glistening with the sunshine—glistening as though it were suffused with gold—and the fragrance of the blossoms, white and soft as snowflakes, exhaling in the hazy heat—blending the mildest sweetness of the earth with the fiercest glory of the sky.

[Arriving in San José,] we dismounted at the door of the Hotel de Costa Rica. Ascending the staircase as leisurely and gracefully as our big boots and spurs would permit, we leaned over the banister at the first landing . . . the houses are so prudently low. It was a Liliputian city, it seemed to us, and we, the Gullivers in red flannel shirts, riding it down. For the most part built of adobe—the brick dried in the sun—and whitewashed from head to foot, San José looks clean and bright. If it has none of the sombre picturesqueness peculiar to most of the Spanish cities of Central America and South America, neither has it any of their peculiar odor, and little of the refuse with which they teem. . . .

* * *

Being one of the Institutions of the country, it would have never done for don Ramon and don Francisco to have overlooked or shunned the Cockpit. It was Whitsunday. The place was crowded. All classes of Society were represented there. The merchant and the peddler—Colonels with blazing epaulets and half-naked privates—doctors, lawyers, Government clerks, fathers of families, genteel gentlemen with ample waistcoats and gray heads, youths of eighteen and less—the latter peppered with the spiciest pertness, and boiling all over with a maddening avidity for pesos and *cuartas*. The benches of the theatre rise one above another, forming a square, within which, on the moist clay floor, enclosed by a slight wooden barrier eighteen inches high, is the fatal ring. In a nook, to the right of the pink calico curtain, stands a small table, upon which the knives, the twine for fastening them, the stone and oil for sharpening them, the fine-toothed saw for cutting the gaffs, and all the other exquisite odds and ends, devised for the deadly equipment of the gladiators, are laid out. The knives used in this butchery are sharp as lancets and curved like cimeters [*sic*]. While the lists are being arranged, and the armorers are busy lacing on the gyves and weapons of the combatants, and many an ounce of precious metal is risked on their chances of life and death, the gladiators pertinaciously keep crowing with all their might, and in the glossiest feather saucily strut about the ring as far as their hempen garters will permit them. A ruthless, senseless, ignoble game, it is fast going out of fashion. There was a time, and that not more than five or six years ago, when the President and the whole of his Cabinet were to be seen in the Cockpit. . . .

* * *

Hubo un revoloteo de alas recortadas, una sacudida de crestas rojas, un cambio de miradas asesinas, un arranque súbito, un encuentro encarnizado, ruido y plumas en el aire, una charca de sangre, y el puñado de oro, todo lo que sobre la tierra poseía el mozo de la cara cetrina cubierta de espinas, desapareció.

The Cock Fight

The next day — Good Friday. . . . When evening came, the procession which commemorates the interment of Christ, moved slowly and darkly from the great door-way of the Cathedral, and, descending into the Plaza, entered and passed through the adjoining streets. The *aceras* or side-walks of these streets were planted with wild canes, round which the leaves of the palm and wreaths of flowers were woven, the carriage-way being strewn with the *seimpreviva* [*sic*; *siempreviva*], the finer branches of the *uruca*, and the wondrous and beauteous *manitas* of the *guarumo*. Curtains of white muslin, festooned with crape or ribbons of black silk and satin, overhung the balconies of the houses along the line of the procession, and at the intersection of the streets were *catafalques* covered with black embroidered cloth, strewn with flowers, laden with fruit, and luminous with colored lamps and cups of silver. . . .

Close behind the candlesticks and crucifix there walked four priests abreast, each one in *soutaine*, black cap surplice. There was a black hood drawn over the black cap, while a black train, the dorsal development of the hood, streamed along the leaf-strewn pavement a yard or two behind. They were the heralds of a large black silk banner which had a red cross blazoned on it, and was borne erect by a sickly gentleman in deep mourning. Then came another swarm of

Procesión del Viernes Santo en 1858. Cañas silvestres en torno a las cuales se entrelazaban palmas y coronas de flores, adornaban las aceras; el pavimento de las calles estaba sembrado de siemprevivas, bellas ramas de uruca y extrañas y lindas manitas de guarumo. Cortinas de muselina blanca con festones de cintas negras de seda y raso colgaban de los balcones de las casas; a lo largo del camino que seguía la procesión y en las intersecciones de las calles, había catafalcos cubiertos de paño negro bordado, salpicados de flores y cargados de frutas, en que brillaban lámparas de colores y jarrones de plata.

The Easter Procession

boys, clearing the road for a full-length figure of Saint John, the Evangelist, which, in a complete suit of variegated vestments, and with the right hand pressed upon the region of the heart, was shouldered along by four young gentlemen, all bareheaded and in full evening-dress. A figure of Mary Magdalene followed that of the Evangelist. It was radiant with robes of white satin and luxuriant tresses of black hair, and the noble beauty of the face was heightened by an expression of intense contrition. As works of art, these figures are more than admirable. They are exquisite and wonderful. Guatemala, where they have been wrought, has reason to be proud of them. . . .

But one, loftier far and statelier than those preceding it, approached. Lifted bayonets were gleaming to the right and the left of it, thuribles [*sic*] were rolling up their fragrant clouds around it, pretty children in white frocks, and fresh as rosebuds, were throwing flowers in front of it all over the leafy pavement. It was the Mater Dolorosa. Sumptuously robed, the costliest lace and purple velvet, pearls of the largest size, opals and other precious stones, were lavished on it. From the queenly head there issued rays of silver which flashed as though they were spears of crystal. The black velvet train, descending from the figure, was borne by a priest. Behind him, carrying long wax candles, were many of the first ladies of the city, all dressed in black silk or satin, their heads concealed in rich mantillas, and these, too, black as funeral palls could be.

★ ★ ★

Every Sunday evening . . . the Band plays in front of the President's private residence. Situated in the Calle del Presidente, a little off the Plaza, this house is a model of Republican modesty. The narrow street darkened with listening groups—the lanterns at the music-desks piercing the shadows with the thinnest rays—groups of *señoritas* whispering at the door-ways, the faint smoke of their *cigarettos* gliding dreamily from their lips—a lean sentinel leaning against the door-post of the President's house, no. 12, rubbing one bare foot against the other—the whitewashed hall behind him, with a yellow candle in a glass case, suspended from the ceiling, winking at the brown balusters of the staircase—an officer in white trowsers [*sic*] and gold-lanced cap lifting his spurred heels up the steps of the door-way, and slipping into the street again, having satisfied himself that all was right—these were the incidents I noticed the first Sunday evening I loitered in the Calle del Presidenté [*sic*], arm in arm with don Ramon, listening to the Band. . . .

The Theatre, too, is open on Sunday evening. Adorned with a Grecian front, this pretty edifice occupies an area sixty or seventy feet square. The street-door opens into a vestibule lighted by a large Chinese lantern, underneath which, on the nights of the performance, half a dozen barefooted soldiers are seated on a bench. There are two tiers of boxes. Under the lower tier are three rows of benches, and these are shut off from the parquette [*sic*] by horizontal bars of iron, which give the enclosure the appearance of a semi-subterranean cage for wild curiosities. The object of this arrangement I was unable to ascertain. Probably it is owing to an apprehension that the poorer people might grow savage if brought into contact with the civilization of the parquette. The night we were there the house was crowded. The boxes rustled with silk. There was a profusion of pearls, and clusters of teeth which rivaled them in whiteness, and masses of luxuriant black hair, and a plump array of arms laden with chains and bands of gold, and eyes of sparkling jet, and coronals and festoons of luscious flowers, and the airiest network floating about the daintiest heads. It was a Gala night. The play was *El poeta y la beneficiada*. In a box decorated with the National colors, directly facing the stage, sat President Mora. To the right and left of his Excellency sat the Minister of Foreign Affairs, General Joaquin Mora, Señor Escalante, the Vice-President of the Republic, and M. Felix Belly, the champion, upon paper, of the Latin Race generally.

The performers, hailing from Cadiz and other parts of Spain, rendered the humor of don Manuel Breton de los Herreros with a graceful vivacity. But the orchestra was fearful. Eight fiddlers, a drummer, and two trumpeters, all in a row, tortured us mercilessly whenever the curtain went down. The scenery was just as unpleasant. No two wings were alike, and fully one half the performance passed off in a parlor, upon which the skylight and stairs of a garret obtruded. The drop-scene, however, representing Minerva instructing the Muses, displayed considerable taste, effectiveness of touch, and brilliant coloring. Between the acts, the occupants of the boxes promenaded the *galinero* [*sic*; *gallinero*] or lobby of the Theatre, smoking their puros and cigarettos. The Ladies indulged in this refreshment as well as the Gentlemen. Lemonades, also, were handed round, and the cigarettos gave way to almond cakes, ices, and other delicacies. The President, mingling unaffectedly with the crowd, was voluble and radiant. M. Felix Belly, exquisitely booted and gloved, bowed himself constantly into profuse perspirations. . . .

* * *

In the Lunatic department of the Hospital there were two women and two men. The two women were crazy on the subject of religion. One of them had covered the walls of the room, in which they were confined, with the strangest hieroglyphics—with death heads and crossbones—with skeletons—with horned devils and instruments of torture. These disordered fancies were portrayed in charcoal, and, as we entered, the bewildered artist was absorbed in the contemplation of her performances. The other woman was sitting upon a table—her feet bent under her—the stormiest picture of desolation. She had the one story for every ear that hearkened to her. It was that of a beautiful pure child, who, on passing through a dark street one evening, was presented by two abandoned women with an ear of corn. This she took from them and brought home. The child, the frenzied creature said, had ever since been under the spell of these bad women, and it was this which worried her. As she repeated the story to us—she tells it every day and every hour—the tears started from her bloodshot eyes, the clasped hands dropped with the weight of death upon her knees, her head fell upon her breast, and, shaking it from side to side in the vehemence of her grief, the long, black, disordered hair swept over her shoulders to her naked feet.

Leaving her, the Keeper opened the door of another room. It was a wilderness of a room. There was no ceiling to it. The cobwebbed rafters were exposed. The tiles, with which it has been floored, were torn up. Many of them were broken. The clay underneath the tiles was, also, torn up. The plastering on the walls was all in flakes. The window-panes had been smashed. Large splinters of glass lay strewn about the plowed-up floor. Every thing within there was defaced. Every thing bore the stamp of exhausted riotousness and irreparable ruin. Crouching in a corner—naked to the waist—the paltry covering he had suffered to remain upon his wasted limbs flapping in frowsy rags about him—eying us with the timidity of a worried rabbit—eying us stealthily from behind a heap of earth and broken tiles—was a boy with sunken jaws, shuddering from head to foot, jabbering violently, and frothing at the mouth. This poor wretch was little more than eighteen years of age. He had been one of the garrison of Fort Castillo. On the approach of Colonel Frank Anderson, December, 1858, he was seized with spasms, and from that day to this he has been a ghastly lunatic. The shouts of the Filibusters ring incessantly in his ears. Armed to the teeth—gliding like panthers through the *chaparral*—they are ever making toward him. He leaps from them, shrieks, writhes, foams, tears his tangled hair, harrows the walls and floor with his nails, digs up the earth, as through he were a hyena tugging at buried carrion, and so hacks and wastes himself to death. . . .

★ ★ ★

[We] set out, one Sunday evening, from San José to the ancient city of Cartago. The drive was pleasantly exciting all the way through. There was the landscape, both sides of the road. There were the coffee-plantations, all in full blossom, looking as though there had been a fall of snow during the forenoon. There were banana patches, fields of corn and sugarcane, church towers and Indian villages. There was the funeral procession of a child, the little corpse prettily dressed and decked with flowers, violins and flutes preceding it, women strewing the dusty road with violets, lilies, and green branches, an old priest, in white embroidered stole and surplice, enveloped in the smoke of swinging censers, with closed eyes and bare head, borne along in a gilt sedan-chair behind the bier, and with his shriveled hand blessing it at times. There were bright green meadows veined with flashing streams—wavelike wooded hills seamed with red cart-roads—steep bridges built of lavastone, the causeways roofed with burned tiles—bulky farmhouses half-buried in sweet rich foliage—the great lonely mountains of the Central Range dissolving in the mellowed sunlight miles away.

As for the city of Cartago—the city itself—it is a dismal wreck. The streets are broader than those of San José, but they are lonelier, drowsier, colder.

Plaza of Cartago

Scarcely a soul is seen in them any hour of the day. Now and then one meets an Egyptian figure lithely balancing a plenteous *tinaja* on a dauntless head — gliding noiselessly along — but that, for hours perhaps, is the only living object which relieves the sepulchral vacuity of the place. Hurled about in every direction, monstrous boulders and masses of lavastone, monuments of the terrible eruptions of the volcano that overlooks it, heighten the forlorn aspect it presents. Upward of three hundred years old, it has seen better days. It was the Royal Capital under the Spanish Crown, and Thomas Gage — a Great Briton who visited Central America in 1636, and who, in the quaint book he published of his travels, describes himself as the first Protestant who ever penetrated these parts — mentions that it had in his time many opulent citizens who traded directly with the Peninsula. The recollection of what it was in those days renders it haughty and sullen. Cartago is, in truth, a stupid aristocrat, out at the elbows and gone to the dogs. How the aristocrat lives, it is difficult to say. . . .

But the Thursdays are livelier, though, in the absence of the Band and the Bells, a native might say they were somewhat less musical. Thursdays are market days in Cartago. The Plaza — the massive white towers of the Parochial Church on one side — substantial one-storied houses, with projecting roofs and bowed windows, on the other — the Cuartel and Governor's Audience-Hall in front, all glistening with whitewash, and close behind them, the volcano of Irazu, the sun flashing from its cloven forehead, and the snowy clouds gathering round it, as the Sicilian flocks crowded to the Cyclops—these are the outlines of the picture. It is a vivid blending of most of the contrasts of Tropical life with the majesty of nature. The streets leading into the Plaza are thronged—thronged with the carts and oxen, with mules and muleteers, with soldiers and wandering minstrels—thronged with the booths and beggars, and with cripples who imploringly work out a fortune with their distorted bones. In the Plaza we have innumerable articles for sale, and pictorially viewed, the gayest of groups. We have rainbow colored silk-woven shawls from Guatemala, blankets, and brigand-like jackets with superfluous bright buttons and fringes. We have the cacao nut in ox hide bags, which barelegged sinewy fellows have carried up all the way from Matina, and drinking cups, carved out of the Calabash fruit with an exquisite nicety of touch and an elaborate richness of design. At other stalls we have English printed calicoes, *barèges*, pen-knives, crockeryware, scissors, smoothing irons, scythes, and razors. From the United States, I'm sorry to say, we have little or nothing. There are, to be sure, some American drillings. But that, for the present, with a few coils or sticks of Virginia tobacco, is all we have in the market. Cartago herself contributes hats—soft hats made of the fibre of the Century-plant—and goldwork, such as chains and armlets, Love-knots and votive baskets, the latter with the most tempting delicacy constructed and redundant with pearls—roseate, plump, lustrous pearls—from the Gulf of Nicoya. Then, of course, we have oranges, cocoa-nuts, sweet corn, bananas, *zapotes*, sweet lemons and *granadillas*, the most liquid and refreshing of fruits, edible palm tops, which make the most piquant and delicious of salads, blackberries, the blackest and juiciest that ever purpled one's lips, and potatoes as mealy and toothsome as any Irish mouth could desire.

As for the groups and detached figures—filling up, though dispersed, through the picture—there are Señoras richly dressed, cooling their bare and glossy heads with the airiest sun-shades, accompanied by their *criadas*, who carry on their plump shining arms baskets for the purchases their mistresses make. At times you come across a German housewife, with leg-of-mutton sleeves and Leghorn bonnet. The mestizas—the women of the country—in very loose low-necked dresses of white or colored calico, with bare arms and feet, sit behind their *serones* of fruit and vegetables, behind their blocks of cheese and *chancaca*, the coarse brown sugar of the country, or behind a double row of bottles choked with *guarapo*, the fermented juice of the sugarcane, and with accents as liquid and refreshing as the guarapo, and with a shy gracefulness if the passer-by happens to be a stranger, expatiate upon the merits of their merchandise, and press their varied commodities for sale. . . .

* * *

With the water up to our saddle-girths, having forded the Naranjo and spurred into a thicket, we suddenly pulled up, for an Indian, the color of new copper, thrusting his shaggy head through a fence of *piti* plant, saluted us warmly. The son of a deceased King, his father was an extensive landed proprietor in this part of the country, a few years ago, and owned several hundred head of cattle. His offspring is a reduced gentleman, however, and lays claim to a few bananas and sugarcanes only. His name is Pedro. Notwithstanding the two-and-sixty years he has served on earth, Pedro is active. In this respect not one of his brethren, kindred aristocracy or tribe, is comparable to him. As brown as a slab of old mahogany, he is just as well seasoned, and almost as durable. The sinews of his bare legs — visible in blue through the tanned skin — are hard and flexible as whipcord. . . . But Pedro has for antiquity an immutable reserve, and his poverty, disowning these innovations, inspires him with the dignity of labor, while it restricts him to its muscular exploits. We took him for our guide, for his knowledge of the forests and mountains in the neighborhood of Orosi was keen and serviceable, from the fact that, for little less than half a century, he has hunted the wild hog through them, and from boyhood has lived like a prince on fried bananas and pork. . . .

We were told [the Indians] were meanly cunning, and toward profane things, of every description, were thievishly disposed. The Padre Acuña, and other reliable gentleman, told us all this. A glance convinced us they were slovenly, ugly, and woeful, did little or nothing for their living, while they knew and cared as much about Costa Rica as they did about Lapland. When, for instance, we asked Pedro, the son of the deceased King, if he remembered the time the Spaniards were there, he opened his mouth, gaped, stared, and scratched his sudoriferous old sconce, as through we propounded him a problem in Euclid. "What Spaniards?" he laughed out at last. We endeavored to explain. But Pedro knew nothing about them — not an iota — never knew there had been such people as Spaniards in the country. Now this was rather unpardonable, for the Spaniards "vamosed [*sic*] the ranch" in 1821 only, and Pedro, as I have already divulged, was two-and-sixty years old when the question was put to him. . . .

Pedro had one peculiar fault. He professed a knowledge of Botany, Geology, Natural History, and various other sciences and subjects, a moderate proficiency in any two or three of which would have rendered him a priceless companion to the philosophers, who, treading in his footsteps, day after day continued their search after the Sublime, the Curious, and the Beautiful.

Don Ramon would say to him, "What palm is this, Pedro?"

"I know it," Pedro would instantly answer. "I know it — 'tis a palm."

Glossary

agave	agave
bongo	punt
carreteros	carters
chaparral	thicket
cigarettos	small and slim cigarettes
criadas	servants
cuartel	barracks
gallinero	the gods, incorrectly attributed here to the lobby
granadillas	granadilla
guarumo	*Cecropia,* a shrub
manitas	bunch
mantilla	shawl
manzanilla	chamomile
piraguas	canoe
piti	agave
posada	lodge
puro	cigar
sacate	straw
serones	big baskets
siempreviva	*Jacquinia angustifolia,* a shrub common to the area
soutaine	cassock
tinaja	jar
uruca	*Trichilia havanensis,* a small tree
zapotes	fruit of the large tree, *Calocarpum mammosum*

Denunciation of the Lazarene Brothers

Diego Quesada

In 1884, in the Seminary (which also served as a secondary school), a group of students began to publish a newspaper called The Circumstance *with the approval of the school authorities. Shortly afterward, another student periodical,* The Seminarist, *began to circulate, and this one had radical tendencies. The confrontation between each student group and its respective papers took place in the context of a bitter feud between the Catholic Church and an anticlerical Liberal regime. Such was the background to this following denunciation of homosexual practices by the Lazarene Brothers. The seminarian's letter to the authorities served as the basis for an investigation, as a result of which the religious order was expelled from the country and the Seminary closed in 1885 "for reasons of public morality." The student's letter registers how important newspapers were to the Liberal cause, and how young the vanguard of the Liberal government was (Bernardo Soto, president during the most radical phase of Liberal reform from 1885–89, was thirty-one years of age when he took office).*

San José, 21 November 1884

To the Honorable Minister of Public Education,

Because I am a lover of progress, I have been the victim of serious punishment and have even been in danger of expulsion from the college that, without good reason, has the title of a Seminary. I will detail without exaggeration the reason that I was victimized along with two schoolmates who are also lovers of science. On the basis of the principle that "theory without practice goes nowhere," we began to write a newspaper with the objective of putting into practice some of what we knew in theory; we published six issues, and almost all the students read them; but the seventh issue, which was ready to come out, was never published because one of the Fathers' darlings, to get in good with them, gave them a copy of the paper. The Fathers read it, and since the issue discussed something about the filth that the priests do with their pricks, and since they saw that we were true Costa Ricans and that we stood up in the paper for what has been going on between the eighteenth of July (the day when the Bishop and the Jesuit priests were expelled from the country) to the present, and insisted that it was well done, all these things disgust them and they mistreat us most cruelly. I can show you the newspaper so that you can judge for yourself whether or not we have deserved what they have done to us. Our intention was to ensure that the children of our Republic progress, and that we could one day occupy the place of those who today govern our country with such dignity. But there are many who are opposed to such progress. What the Fathers of the Seminary want is for us to be perpetually praying, but they do nothing to make us useful for the country. The Fathers now speak very badly of you and the President of the Republic and say that the government should not involve itself in their affairs, but I tell them that they should be silent because we are all subject to the laws of the nation. I beg of you now not to turn me in but instead to judge honestly the things that go on in the Seminary, because it would be better if the place did not exist.

I am the Minister's faithful servant,

Diego Quesada

Building Civilization

Fernando Zamora

The Penitentiary

Fernando Zamora was the country's leading turn-of-the-century photographer. In 1909, he trained his lens on the monuments to Costa Rican civilization that appeared during the self-conscious nation-building period of the Liberal state (1890–1909): the panoptic penitentiary; the sumptuous National Theater; Costa Rica's "Crystal Palace," the Edificio Metálico, a prefabricated metal building serving as public school and community center; and the Italianate Colegio de Señoritas (the normal school). Zamora's photographic album of Costa Rica in 1909 also captured the world of labor in the coffee and banana sectors that drove the export boom.

The National Theater (above) and the Edificio Metálico

Colegio de Señoritas

Coffee pickers (above) and banana workers

Getting to Know the Unknown Soldier

Steven Palmer

Costa Ricans of all social classes, ethnicities, and regions are notably patriotic. While many observers think this dates back to the colonial era and is the product of a small and close-knit society, the following study proposes that modern Costa Rican nationalism crystallized in the Liberal period of the 1880s and 1890s, when the war against Walker and the figure of Juan Santamaría were rescued from relative obscurity and turned into the cornerstones of national mythology. These and other historical events and characters were reshaped to square with liberal ideology by a group of intellectuals self-consciously engaged in the elaboration of an "official" nationalism for the new cultural machinery of state: an expanded public school system and a proliferating network of national monuments venerated according to a crowded calendar of official celebrations.

Guatemala's president and military dictator, Justo Rufino Barrios, declared the Union of Central America on 28 February 1885 and made it plain that its establishment would be achieved through force of arms if the four other Central American republics did not consent to his decree. During the following days, as the Costa Rican state scrambled to mobilize the people for war, an article with the title "An Anonymous Hero" appeared in the pages of the *Diario de Costa Rica*. Curiously, the hero of the piece did not remain anonymous at all, for his name was soon revealed: Juan Santamaría, a humble foot soldier whose act of heroism turned the tide of battle at Rivas in favor of the Costa Rican army during the war against William Walker in 1856–57. The invention of Costa Rica's "Unknown" Soldier had begun. The secular beatification of this forgotten warrior continued to pick up momentum. Within two weeks, the *Diario de Costa Rica* would spice up its call to arms against the Guatemalan threat by referring to an earlier occasion when, as "a party of filibusters tried to take over our territory, the heroic valor of the sons of this soil manifested itself; the names of Juan Santamaría, Captain Rojas and Mercedes Guillén are announcing it out loud." Santamaría was now placed beside two officer heroes of the war; he would soon outstrip them all.

On 11 April, the anniversary of the battle of Rivas, both daily newspapers published an article on the defeat of Walker. But celebration of the heroic event and the patriotic war would soon shift from 11 April or 1 May (the anniversaries of the battle of Rivas and the surrender of Walker, respectively) to 15 September—the anniversary of Costa Rica's independence from Spain in 1821. Prior to 1885, Costa Rica's independence day remained a rather muted affair. This was because 15 September actually commemorated the day in 1821 that Guatemalan elites, fearful of what might happen if independence was declared after a popular rebellion, agreed with local Spanish officials to break Central America's ties with Spain; by the time the messenger on muleback arrived in Costa Rica with the news, Costa Ricans had been independent for almost a full month without knowing it. As late as 1882, an independence day editorial in the official newspaper declared that "we cannot fill ourselves with pride over the remembrance of heroic feats, because our independence was not the result of patriotic and bloody efforts, nor the achievement of incomparable and redeeming martyrs . . . ; rather it was a corollary detached from the logic of historical events." Mathematicians aside, corollaries are hardly the stuff to fire nationalist spirits.

Now, however, the campaign of 1856–57 would be resurrected as Costa Rica's surrogate war of national independence. This is why the statue commemorating Juan Santamaría was erected in Alajuela, his birthplace, on 15 September 1891 during an enormous popular celebration of Costa Rica's independence *from Spain*. Four years later, again on 15 September, the National Monument commemorating the defeat of Walker would be unveiled during a mass public ceremony in the newly renamed Parque Nacional. Between 1885 and 1895, the Liberal state and its intellectuals resolved the problem of the nation's "imagined origins" and developed Santamaría into a prototypical patriotic hero the lower classes were encouraged to emulate. This formed the symbolic, cultural complement to the Liberal reforms carried out by the state during this period in education, the law, and church-state relations.

This is not to say that the war against William Walker was not a patriotic war in 1856–57. But the horizons of that patriotism were more flexible than we might imagine, and certain events that followed hard on the heels of the glorious victory over Walker impeded the war experience becoming the immediate basis of a national mythology. In the 1850s, the hope for Central American Union was still alive and well, and, in fact, the National Campaign against William Walker was often called the Central American National Campaign because all of the armies of Central America were mustered to expel the filibuster. Their very ability to cooperate made it seem that a federal Central American nation-state might now become possible. Furthermore, the mounting of a costly expeditionary force helped to plunge Costa Rica into pronounced recession, while the country was devastated by a cholera epidemic, introduced into the country by troops returning from Rivas in 1856, that killed 8 percent of the population. Finally, President Juan Rafael Mora, the great hero of the campaign, was ousted from the presidency in a coup of 1859, sent into exile, and subsequently shot in 1860 following a hapless attempt to regain power at the head of an invading army. For all these reasons, the campaign of 1856–57 left many bitter memories to vie with those of patriotic glory.

The 1885 publication of "An Anonymous Hero" was not the first time Juan Santamaría had received public mention. In 1857, Manuela Carvajal, the hero's illiterate mother, solicited a pension from the government on the basis of her son's death in battle. The minister of war accepted her account of the heroic manner in which she claimed her son had died, and she was granted a pension. In 1864, during a wide-ranging independence day address, the exiled Colombian liberal, José de Obaldía, extolled a number of valorous acts from the recent war, including Santamaría's. It is possible that the government had asked Obaldía to recuperate a new group of heroes to replace the now awkward figure of Mora. He might also have found the pension request of Carvajal, or possibly Santamaría's heroic act was circulating as part of local legend. Three months after his speech, Carvajal solicited an increase in her pension, this time under the name Santamaría and referring to herself as an *hija del pueblo* (daughter of the people) who was honored to call herself the hero's mother. She was no doubt trading on the public recognition of her son by state officials—and to good effect, for the government tripled the meager allowance. She may also have acted for fear that the recognition would be fleeting; if so, she acted wisely, for Santamaría would not appear again in official discourse for over twenty years.

There are two reasons to suppose that the figure of Santamaría remained alive in the oral popular culture of Alajuela. One is that his nickname, el Erizo (hedgehog), though it does not appear in the article "An Anonymous Hero," survived even after his conversion into an official hero in 1885. Because the word connotes mulatto characteristics, it constituted an uncomfortable anomaly for state intellectuals, who maintained the official line that Costa Ricans were a homogeneous, essentially white race. The second is that the newspaper piece had actually appeared first in 1883 in a local Alajuela paper, *El Tambor*. If the recuperation of Santamaría indeed indicated the transformation of a local popular culture figure into a national one, it formed part of a general process observable during the 1880s. According to the historian José Daniel Gil, the cult of the Virgin of los Ángeles also experienced a metamorphosis during that decade, transforming from a marker of Cartago identity to a national one. In the case of Santamaría, however, this transition was not organic at all. The Guatemalan president, Barrios, may have declared the Union of Central America on 28 February 1885, but the Costa Rican government kept this a secret until 8 March, when the state issued its call to arms and declared the emergency measures act. So the reprinting of "An Anonymous Hero" on 5 and 6 March clearly resulted from a conscious search, in the context of a mass conscription campaign, for a popular military hero who the lower classes could identify with.

Indeed, the Liberal regime had good reason to wonder how responsive the people would be to this patriotic appeal. For one thing, the country was only just emerging from a serious economic recession. For another, only a year earlier, in 1884, the government had signed the notorious Soto-Keith contract, which transferred control of the national railway — the central symbol of national identity during the dictatorship of its principal promoter, General Tomás Guardia (1870–82) — to the American entrepreneur Minor C. Keith, future founder of the United Fruit Company. Perhaps most seriously, the secular liberals were involved in a bitter fight with the Catholic Church over cultural and political influence in the modern state. In mid-1884, the archbishop and religious orders had been expelled on the justified grounds that they were fomenting popular resistance to the liberal reforms. The government thus needed a secular national symbol with popular appeal, and Santamaría fit the bill. Events would prove that the intelligentsia had chosen wisely.

The appearance of Santamaría can be understood as the creation of a Costa Rican Unknown Soldier (an "anonymous hero"). In the case of Costa Rica, however, the anonymous hero had to have a name — an identity, if only of the sketchiest kind — for a very good ideological reason. The rules for representing Santamaría, established by the author of the article, Álvaro Contreras, would be followed throughout the Liberal era: "There is nothing of interest that we can refer to concerning the life of Santamaría . . . because everything about it is confused within those dark and silent depths of the passive and dispossessed class of society. . . . *However it makes no difference that we cannot present here the biography of our hero, since the object which we propose is simply to outline . . . a beautiful victory for the patria.*" Santamaría only has an identity to the extent that he can be linked to the popular classes. Conveniently, he has no voice that might be reclaimed.

The process of Santamaría's rapid "beatification" culminated in 1891 with the erection of the statue in Alajuela. This elaborate inaugural ceremony and the national holiday were clearly designed to encourage the lower classes to identify with Santamaría and his alleged selfless sacrifice to the principles of liberal republicanism — to urge the lower classes to adopt as their own the values that liberal intellectuals made Santamaría speak. Again and again, the connection of Santamaría with the popular classes was made, as was the insistence that he and they shared the same principles as the oligarchy. The editorial in *La Prensa Libre* declared that "people who even in the inferior social classes produce men of the moral mettle of Juan Santamaría, the hero of Rivas, have an awareness of their dignity and make of their principles a cult, immolating themselves for their liberties: they march toward sacrifice with their heads high, eyes front, as if toward a festival through which a glimpse can be had of the apotheosis of immortality." A speaker at a celebration in Cartago called Santamaría "a lay saint" who should be immitated because "all the great institutions, all the great triumphs of law and liberty; the progress of science, of art and of the beautiful; the advance of light and freedom of education, the emancipation of women, human culture and material progress — all is the work of patriotism." The editorial in the official paper was more direct about the moral lesson to be learned by the popular classes: "Juan Santamaría! Here is the name of the humble child of the people. . . . The hero came from the lowest social strata, illegitimate child of a poor woman . . . [but] History rescued the name of Juan Santamaría from obscurity, and presents if before the eyes of the Costa Rican people as a model of patriotism that must always be followed." Associating him with Simón Bolivar and other titans of the age of Latin American independence, the editorial dubbed Santamaría "the Liberator of the Republic."

The great modernist poet, Ruben Darío, working at *La Prensa Libre* during a short visit to the country, described the unveiling ceremonies. The dignitaries arrived by train to find the city elaborately decorated with nationalist symbols. The central event of the ceremony was the veterans of 1856–57 marching past the statue and then into the Municipal Palace to be received by the president and offered food and drink. "They laughed and conversed amongst themselves, with their expansive rustic manners," wrote Darío. "And they drank to the memory of the brave 'Erizo'!" The commoners of 1891, all now symbolically "Santamarías," received sanction by the paternal president. The sacrifice of these veterans and the ultimate sacrifice of Santamaría to the patrimonial state of 1856–57 was symbolically replayed in the Liberal state of 1891. The loyalty of the "humble folk" was rewarded by an audience with the president and the adulation of the state intellectuals. But the significance of this loyalty became transposed to conform to the present circumstances. Ricardo Jiménez, who had been one of the lawyers in charge of the Liberal legal reform of the 1880s and was then president of the supreme court, made this explicit in his address to the assembled masses.

> May this statue come to be a monument to the humble people, to the un-
> known of Santa Rosa and Rivas, to the anonymous heroism that saved the
> Nation. . . . [With] the rifle in one hand to preserve the integrity of our land
> and that of its genuine republican institutions, and the torch in the other;
> but may it never be the torch of discord or civil war, rather may it be at times
> the flame lit in the defense of the Patria, and at other times the torch of
> Liberty, before whose light are dispersed in the national consciousness, like
> shadows before the night, any spirit incompatible with our institutions. . . .

The speech by Jiménez also underlines one of the most crucial aspects of Santamaría as a national figure. The myth of Santamaría does not constitute one of national liberation, but rather one of national preservation — the preservation of already established liberal institutions and an already established social hierarchy. As a result, this figure has far less popular possibilities than the more common myths of revolutionary independence. Santamaría's act is not symbolic of that apocalyptic moment of liberation in which all is possible. Santamaría dies on foreign soil to preserve the Costa Rican order of things. With Santamaría, then, the oligarchy received the best of both liberal worlds. They harnessed a symbol of authentic popular will informing their polity, but they were able to do so with a nationalist figure not easily reworked to articulate class antagonisms.

A larger scale repetition of the 1891 ceremony took place four years later with the erection of the National Monument in San José (ironically, this monument to the war of 1856–57, whose real origins lay in the call to arms against Barrios's unionist threat of 1885, was cast by Louis Carrier-Beleuze, the same French sculptor who created the monument to Barrios erected two years later in Guatemala City). The unveiling succeeded a street parade of government officials, followed by religious and municipal officials. After all gathered about the national monument and the army formed around the park, "the invalids of the war, those venerable old men who were about to witness their own apotheosis after thirty years of indifference and obscurity, entered and occupied their places." A throng of public school children congregated to sing the national anthem. Educator and state functionary Juan Fernández Ferraz described the scene with approving liberal eyes. "Beside the aristocratic woman in her silks, the humble woman of the lower classes who shines in her one outfit in a percale skirt and a shawl of lively colors. Thousands of faces, all distinct, thousands of different looks. But in all their faces, as though giving uniformity to this immense and heterogeneous multitude, happiness without reservation and the enthusiasm that entones patriotic anthems." A transclass chorus harmonizes itself lovingly with Liberal Costa Rica.

Fernández Ferraz might well have approved. Though a foreigner, he had penned the words to the patriotic anthem in question. The lyrics, however, filled to the brim with cumbersome republican allusions to the classical age, would soon fall victim to the populist trend in Costa Rican official nationalism: by century's end, they were considered overly intellectual, and in 1903 were replaced by new lyrics after a state-sponsored competition. The winning entry (which is still sung today) was written by a young Costa Rican poet, José María Zeledón, and it used local imagery of humble farmers working the soil, more in tune with the myth of the laborer from Alajuela who served as drummer boy and gave his life in the people's army that preserved the fatherland in 1856. We might conclude by pointing out that the choruses described by Darío and Fernández Ferraz were not composed of sheep. Nationalist discourses that lack genuine popular resonance might still fail to mobilize the people behind the overarching objectives of the powerful. Costa Rican liberals were rather daring in their choice of a hero from the very lowest ranks of society before whom all Costa Ricans were asked to worship. This meant that even the elites had to acknowledge that the people were protagonists in the country's history. This message was not lost on the beholding masses, who would henceforth see themselves transfigured in the new secular passion called National History, staged with ever greater frequency in the classrooms and plazas of Costa Rica.

The Burning of the Mesón

Enrique Echandi

Enrique Echandi, oil on canvas, 1896 (Museo Histórico Cultural Juan Santamaría)

Enrique Echandi (1866–1959) was one of Costa Rica's few innovative visual artists in the late nineteenth and early twentieth centuries. He struggled against the academicians of the day, and so found himself excluded from the benefits of official cultural adulation. His dramatic canvas of Santamaría burning the mesón (inn) during the battle of Rivas, painted in the ghoulish style of Goya's Disasters of War, *caused a scandal on submission to an art competition in 1897. It depicts the hero as a mulatto in peasant dress whose act seems to bring death without apotheosis, and so mocks the trim soldier in uniform portrayed in the official, French-made statue erected in Alajuela in 1891. Echandi anticipated a larger group of iconoclastic young intellectuals, most notable among them Roberto Brenes Mesén, Carmen Lyra, and Joaquín García Monge, who began to subvert the liberal myths and other establishment pieties beginning at around the turn of the twentieth century.*

III

Popular Culture and Social Policy

In 1935, the young dissident intellectual Mario Sancho published an acid critique of the state of society in a book whose title, *Costa Rica, Switzerland of Central America*, mocked the national mythology. Sancho reserved his greatest indictment for the moneyed classes of the country: "With rare exceptions, [they] are characterized by a lack of altruism and an absolute incapacity for social cooperation." His diagnosis of Costa Rican social life was that it was "anguished and disenchanted," suffering a "moral crisis." Its middle class was demoralized by poverty, and a widespread atrophy was leading to national despair and perversion. The book appeared at the height of the depression era, when a backdrop of rising class conflict and sporadic bouts of political violence created a chronic sense of unease. What critics such as Sancho failed to grasp was the new tissue of governance bonding society with state, which had grown with a series of social-policy initiatives begun at the turn of the century. They included the successful extension of a primary school system throughout the country and the rise of an ambitious public health service to go along with an effective, if still incomplete, extension of voting rights and some state recognition for workers' rights. Despite Sancho's dire predictions, the country did not descend into militarism and dictatorship during these dark economic times, as happened everywhere else in Central America, not to mention in most places in Latin America and the world.

A better compass for reading the political culture of this era comes in the form of the delightful *Marcos Ramírez: Adventures of a Lad*, a fictionalized memoir of childhood in the lower-class barrios of Alajuela and San José in the early twentieth century. The book has aptly been called Costa Rica's *Tom Sawyer*. Its author, Carlos Luis Fallas, one of the country's strongest literary voices, was a shoemaker and a banana worker who became a communist leader of the 1934 strike against United Fruit. From the ritualized confrontations between the teenage gangs of the capital's popular barrios to his first journey as a thirteen-year-old ragamuffin to find adventure and fortune in the banana enclave, Fallas portrays a lively, rich, and playful popular culture. This was a working people's world that straddled the urban and the rural and possessed creative ways of confronting serious economic hardship, political manipulation, and exclusion from social benefits.

The country's working and middle classes, urban and rural, began to organize into mutualist associations starting in the 1880s. After 1910, the West Indian dockers and banana workers of Limón created a dynamic labor movement, engaging in a series of wildcat strikes and founding the country's first trade unions. The artisans of San José followed suit, knitting a progressive and spirited working-class culture that ranged from football teams and reading clubs to trade unions and political protest. In the 1920s, the first effort to create a cooperative association of small and medium-sized coffee growers sent a warning shot across the bow of the oligarchy. After the onset of the Great Depression, organized resistance galvanized throughout the country, from the Hispanic banana workers, who paralyzed the United Fruit Company in the great strike of 1934, to artisan groups in secondary towns around the country. It was this popular culture, with its trenchant demands for social dignity and inclusion, that served as a base for political parties like the Reformist Party (founded in 1923) and the Communist Party (founded in 1931). And it was this popular culture that Dr. Rafael Ángel Calderón Guardia melded with a socially oriented and activist Catholicism to forge a formidable base for his reformist presidency when he came to power in 1940.

Marcos Ramírez concludes with the beaten-down young protagonist walking the streets all night. As the sun comes up, he finds himself at the station, waiting for the train to Limón. "The day's clarity dissipated all my doubts and vacillation: I would definitely go to Limón. There was the vastness of the sea, and a boat ready to take me to all the ports of the world. And waiting for the train, I started to pace up and down, still freezing to death, but very content, happy, whistling. The great adventure of my life was about to begin!" Costa Rican society was not without bitter class antagonism and biting poverty, but it also provided opportunities to fashion a modern identity in an economic and political structure somewhat flexible and porous, even for the underdogs.

Alleyway of Open Wounds

Claudia María Jiménez

Claudia María Jiménez, oil on canvas, 1937 (Courtesy of Julio Jiménez)

The first generation of women artists emerged in Costa Rica in the 1910s, many of them associated with education and with the growing workers' movement. The female artist best known internationally was Carmen Lyra, who combined fiction with experimental pedagogy and political activism. If the majority of Costa Rican painters during the first half of the twentieth century preferred to represent the country as a rural idyll, Claudia María Jiménez was among the few who broke that mold and portrayed the urban world of the popular classes.

Women of the Barrio

Luisa González

No professional roles were available to women in Costa Rica prior to the end of the nineteenth century. Nevertheless, two types of specialized women's work existed that trespassed the boundaries of the public and private spheres, vocations in which women could accumulate particular power and status — midwifery and prostitution. Both figures, the prostitute and the midwife, fascinated the young Luisa González in the first decade of the twentieth century as she grew up in San José's poorest neighborhood and contemplated the possibility of escaping a desperate fate (she would eventually become a leading educator, communist activist, and writer). Her portrait of the formidable barrio midwife is one of the best extant descriptions from Latin America, as is her depiction of the local wisewoman, while her view of the prostitutes who lived next door reveals the degree to which they were secretly envied by girls and women for their privileged access to leisure time and autonomous consumption.

Round about the year 1912, La Puebla was the poorest, dirtiest, loosest, and most disreputable barrio in the capital. It was a place where vice, misery, and prostitution grew unchecked. There, in that part of town, that "zone of tolerance," lay my "home, sweet home." La Puebla's notoriety was basically due to the fact that it harbored twenty or so prostitutes of the lowest possible type whose business lent the barrio the crudest, most violent and grotesque colors. For children of proletarian families like us, the streets and shacks where these women lived offered a daily spectacle that was inciting, full of mystery, curiosity, naughtiness, and unhealthy and precocious instruction in the raunchiest sexual matters. In some way, all of us kids secretly wove the craziest and strangest fantasies about the life and feats of those who were called "good-time gals," "women of the night," and "whores."

"Good-time gals." Why do they call them that? Good times? What was good about them? What times? My God. No, no, they were hardly having a good time, those women whose strange faces etched themselves so deeply into my child's mind. I could never forget those human specimens, women deformed by poverty and vice. Podgy old women some of them, others just skin and bones, wrinkled and made up garishly like masks whose horrible expressions justified that foul society. Who could ever forget that thick-lipped black woman, whose exuberance perched on a pair of tremulous buttocks that gained her the nickname Black Pudding! And how to forget that corn blond woman who they called Soft-Boiled Egg? And poor Silvia, skinny and pale, surely suffering from tuberculosis? Where are they now? Maybe they're wandering around someplace begging, or are they just a little anonymous mound of earth in the cemetery for the poor, the Calvo?

All the kids of the barrio knew better than the multiplications table the names and legends that circulated from mouth to mouth about the "extraordinary lives of the little whores" of La Puebla. One time, innocently, we even thought of playing "hookers." We dressed up in some of our aunts' long dresses, we painted our cheeks and our lips red, and we burned dry leaves, imitating the incense that those sinners burn, just as virtuous women do, to attract the better sort of male clients. . . .

One day, a difficult moral issue arose that provoked a long and violent discussion in the heart of our family. A philosophical, political, or religious issue? No, it was more complicated than that: a decision had to be made about whether or not we could sell those sinful women the articles produced by our incipient household enterprise, the one that sustained our family economy. The temptation was great and the scruples of conscience wavered before the possibility of getting good clients from among those neighbors who did not haggle over prices, and who, moreover, paid cash on the nail.

The devil had perhaps directed the leader of that band of "rare birds" to the door of our house—a woman they called the Limpet due to the gaudy colors of her provocative outfits that announced from afar the illicit business that earned her fat profits. The aforementioned Limpet arrived, then, to drop off a pair of white pumps for my uncle Daniel to patch up the heels. Flirting and joking around with him, she engaged his services, and naturally my uncle lickety-split offered to deliver them personally to her that very night at her house. Poor Limpet hadn't walked ten paces when the dust started to fly, protests and recriminations flung against the bold woman who had dared to come to provoke the men of this family of hard workers.

"Shameless! Scoundrel! How dare you speak to that indecent wench?!" shouted my aunt Lola, a confirmed spinster, who wore an impeccable habit of the Virgin of Carmen which, according to her, gave her the prerogative and the authority to judge who was good and who was sinful in every which way. With unspeakable fury, as though she was the Archangel Saint Michael expelling Adam and Eve from paradise, she grabbed the pumps—evidence of the crime—and threw them into the middle of the street in an effort to save the honor of our home. I can still see the pair of white pumps swimming in the mire of the street, looking like ducks plucked by the virtuous hands of that intransigent spinster.

In two shakes, my uncle, furious, jumped into the street and recovered the shoes; in cruel revenge he polished and cleaned them using Aunt Lola's Carmelite slip, trying to stain her saintliness with the human sins of poor Limpet.

"Hell's bells!" my uncle shouted. "Let's clear this crap up once and for all. Can we or can't we deal with those women? Is it that their money isn't worth as much as doña Lucrecia's or doña Lupita's?"

"It's not the same. Don't make such disgusting comparisons," said my aunt Carmen. "You know very well that that money is ill-gotten, that it's dirty money, filthy money, that it can bring curses and misfortune on us."

"Do you really think," retorted my uncle, "that the money of those old bags is perfumed and washed in holy water? Give me a damn break! Everyone knows where the pristine bills come from, and the checks signed with scribbles, produced by waiving a magic wand in the most disgraceful and scandalous business dealings. Isn't that money dirty and ill-gotten? You think just because it comes out of a fine leather check book it's holy, blessed money?"

"Child of God!" replied my aunt Chana, taken aback. "Where are you getting those outlandish ideas? According to you, all the monies in the world are dirty and cursed, even those in church collection boxes?"

"Well, yes, ma'am, even those are dirty if they come from the pockets of the villains and gangsters," affirmed my uncle.

Poor Aunt Lola couldn't take any more, and she hurled herself at my uncle Daniel, shaking him by the shoulders and spewing hearty insults: "Blasphemer! Foulmouth! Mason! Atheist!"

That uproar paralyzed family activity because it was a moral problem of the first order, complicated, like all the things of this society, by cursed money which, like air, we need every day in order to live.

All the members of the family threw themselves passionately into the discussion. My grandmother forgot the tortillas, and they burned on the *comal* [skillet], the milk boiled over on the stove, and the iron, burning Dr. Esquivel's shirt, sounded the alarm with clouds of black smoke. The debate was suspended.

Out of that free-for-all came logical and practical conclusions, imposed by the reality of life. "Morality" was left in tatters: every member of the family, except poor Lola, had to bend to the naked, realistic arguments of Uncle Daniel. The "moral" problem, hotly discussed by every one in the family, was defined perfectly in the face of reality: we might just as well sell tortillas to poor Silvia as to doña Elisa, the high school teacher, a resident of a classier neighborhood; we might just as well stitch dresses for doña Lucrecia as for Limpet, or wash clothes for doña Lupita as for Soft-Boiled Egg. Side by side, beneath the shoemaker's workbench, in strange and ridiculous fraternity, the pumps of honorable daughters of Mary waited together with those of the "women of ill repute." What a tangled world! We kids were sent equally to leave finished work in the barrio by the station, in the barrio of La Dolorosa, or in the shacks where the hookers lived. . . .

★ ★ ★

Fairies, gnomes, elves, even the fantasies of the *Thousand and One Nights* played no role in that barrio, La Puebla. Our young imaginations were nourished on stories and tales that we heard told at nighttime with great gusto and detail in the regular informal gatherings of neighbors and family members in the shop of the shoemakers and seamstresses. Those social circles and the gossip sessions every morning among the women in the courtyards hanging clothes on the line, they left us with our mouths open, with our hearts on a string, and twisted our nerves and children's imaginations into an unhealthy tension. The gossip, the most absurd stories and tales, formed an essential part of the happy greetings and the daily agenda of that din of women, children, men, boys, and girls who lived bumping up against one another in order to survive.

The majority of the neighborhood women were expert and erudite in tales, legends, beliefs, and witchcraft effective for resolving the intricate problems of love that in the poor barrios were mixed up with the tragedies of want and ignorance, while in good neighborhoods vices and immorality are covered up by dazzling elegance and refinement. With propriety and authority, the honest women of the barrio exchanged recipes, prayers, beliefs, and concoctions that they always had close at hand to cure whatever deviation their husbands might be suffering.

Doña Dorila, the old woman who played evenly with the just and the sinful, was the most authoritative figure in those gatherings. She had a hoarse voice that emerged from fleshy and mustachioed lips that revealed a few gold-capped teeth, like those of a manager type. She was very accomplished. When she had the floor, she impressed with a picturesque repertoire of tales and legends that she told with wit and conviction. I remember that she even had a notebook with entries, like a reference book, with the recipes for potions, rites, beliefs, explanations of dreams, lists of aphrodisiacs, prayers, and so on. That notebook, covered with gold and blue fabric, held the great catch of her vast experience, which brought her many colones a month. She was no fool:

she had discovered a rich vein for making money, and she quickly freed herself from the iron and the baking tray that sucked so much sweat from the poor women of the popular ranks.

The recipes and counsel of doña Dorila never failed. That's why she had gained the confidence and the affection of the honest women and of the sinful women, whom she attended without discriminating, observing only a slight difference: on Tuesdays she saw the honest women — the married, the widowed, the virtuous spinsters. Fridays she dedicated to the body and soul of the "rare birds." In the purse that she kept in her exuberant bosom the shining coins paid her by one or the other of her groups of clients came together equally. My uncles, vulgar and ill-spoken, gave her the nickname Three in One, because the purse fit nicely between her two breasts. Her generous and believing heart was the source of many of the colones given to the altar of La Dolorosa Church; many children of the barrio took first communion because doña Dorila bought them the outfit and the shoes for the grand occasion. The old woman was no miser, you had to admit; she was splendid and generous with all the families of the barrio that made her enterprise grow and prosper. . . .

★ ★ ★

Mariana, the old barrio midwife, forever awake all night, rings under her eyes, covered head to toe with a black fichu, came in discreetly, smoking a cigar and bringing half a bottle of liquor and a quart of honey in a string bag. She lit a candle in my mother's room and with great urgency started to recite the prayer to San Ramón Nonato.

O San Ramón, the unborn, prodigious: to you I come moved by the great generosity with which you treat your devotees. Patron saint of pregnant women. Here, my saint, is one of them who puts herself humbly beneath your protection and shelter. My saint and advocate, I humbly beg you to secure from my God and Father that this creature who is shut in the dark prison of my core be preserved in life and health. Help me to come out of this trance to offer a new servant at the feet of the Lord: Kyrie eleyson. Christe eleyson. Pater de Coelis Deus, miserere nobis. . . .

The extravagant Latin verses, enveloped by the smoke and bustle of our house, were recited dramatically by the empiric midwife, at that time an eminent and respectable figure who directed the entire process of the birth of this new being with great mastery. My grandmother fanned the firewood to hurry the boiling of the great pots of hot water, while my aunts shooed away all the little kids whose curiosity had led them to try to see what was happening on the other side of the kitchen partition. My aunt Chana handed out cookies, a bag of peanuts, and beans in tortilla wraps so that we'd entertain ourselves eating underneath the anona tree that looked so fresh at the bottom of the garden.

With lowered voice, fearful, and with malicious curiosity, little sisters and cousins together commented anxiously on the great mystery of human procreation, wrapped in absurd myths and legends that tried falsely to protect the youthful innocence of the children of that era. The truth is that already the eldest didn't believe in those wives tales, and like experts we explained to the other, smaller ones the entire natural process of sexual relations among people. We had received so many crude lessons in that barrio, La Puebla, that we no longer displayed any signs of ingenuousness or mystery about those problems that in the lower-class barrios just form part of the air you breathe every day.

After five long hours of waiting, the tension in the air was broken by the strident wailing of a newborn announcing that he had arrived in this vale of tears. All the women recited in chorus the prayer of San Ramón Nonato and gave infinite thanks to the Lord for the arrival of that "little one" who came to augment the interminable gang of children in our family, faithful servant to the biblical mandate "Go forth and multiply."

"You've got another little brother," my father shouted from the porch that rainy afternoon in October, while he helped my grandmother take two buckets and a basin filled with dirty clothes and blood-tinged water from the room.

"Didn't you hear? You've got another brother," my father repeated insistently. I was cornered in the garden shed, trying to flee from reality, because that kid was the fifth brother who'd come to squeeze even further our impoverished family economy. . . .

My aunt Chana hid the dirty clothes underneath the sink and emptied the bloody water on the hollyhock, chamomile, and mint to make them flower in all their splendor, while my father dug a hole in the corner of the courtyard to bury the afterbirth of the newborn.

"Don't bury it," cried my grandmother from the kitchen window. "Put it into this box to take to Puntarenas and throw it into the ocean. That will bring good luck and the boy will never die by drowning."

"Those are nonsense tales," said my uncle Daniel. "How many placentas have you saved now from this idiot story that you're going to throw them in the sea? Have you even got as far as the river down the road? Don't give me those stories."

Legends and beliefs of all types, not to mention unnamed fantasies, grew out of that little strip of guts that leaves such a singular and happy scar on the stomach of all mortals. According to women, it had miraculous powers due

to it being the thread of life that is tied off, assuring the biological independence of the new being. Wrapped in cotton, like a scapular, they made men
take it with them when they left on long voyages; especially for sailors and
fishermen, it was an indispensable amulet to save one's life during the adventures and perils of the sea. Kept in alcohol, it made a magnificent relic of great,
miraculous powers for warding off the curses and misfortunes swarming the
houses of the poor like bats.

"Don't be silly," said my uncle. "Sell it to old Dorila, she knows how to get
the most out of that bit of tripe."

"Are you nuts? How could you ever think such an awful thing?" answered
my aunt Carmen, alarmed by the audacity and cynicism of that unbelieving
and cynical shoemaker.

Mariana, the old midwife, who was wolfing down a delicious lunch in the
kitchen, joined the discussion.

"Those are sacred things, they have their mysterious side that we Christians
don't know about and so should respect until Judgment Day. It would be blas-
phemous to accept money for it; you could be cursed. I suggest that you give
it to doña Dorila as she is the benefactress of the barrio; it couldn't be in better
hands. She has deep knowledge of these mysteries and knows how to apply
them well for each case and occasion. Some day it might even help you people
out; you never know how things will turn out."

All gave their silent consent, obeying the respectable counsel of the midwife, who was no fool and immediately offered to take the little piece of skin
to old Dorila, her pal and colleague in those high-level goings-on in the life of
the popular barrios. . . .

A District Laboratory in Costa Rica

John Elmendorf Jr.

The role of state medicine and public health in fomenting political legitimacy can be grasped in this 1916 report of a Rockefeller Foundation officer after visiting a foundation-sponsored hookworm disease treatment station. Hookworm disease — the "germ of laziness," as it was called in the United States — was caused by a parasite that produced severe anemia and weakened the body, thus making the affliction a problem of individual and national production. In 1914, the Rockefeller Foundation took over funding and direction of an antihookworm program first developed by Costa Rican physicians. Between 1914 and 1921, field laboratories and propaganda campaigns of the kind described here were undertaken in almost every area of the country. The work would metamorphose into a network of rural health clinics and, in 1927, one of Latin America's first national ministries of health.

After having ridden horseback for some three hours from the nearest railroad station over roads which appear to the outsider to be impassable, it is with quite a surprise that we were met in the small pueblo of Miramar with placards [in Spanish]: "Please don't spit on the ground" — "Campaign against hookworm disease" — "Avoid typhoid fever — infant cholera — dysentery" — and other such like inscriptions, but they are the outward evidences that the work of controlling disease and public education along the more common medical lines has been inaugurated. The laboratory is the center of the medical activities of the village and here we may say of most of the other activities as well. The police are an ever present factor seeming to take great interest in the work and the carrying out of regulations.

On the day on which the Assistant Director and his retinue (John Elmendorf) arrived — a reception was held at the school building and the work explained to a gathering of attentive people — its object — methods of addressing the problem and the finances were discussed. The Assistant Director, a native Costa-rican [sic] evidently knew his people, for when it came to dwelling at length on the dire consequences and sequelae of neglecting common ordinary

A public conference on hookworm disease and germ theory, 1915 (Rockefeller Archive Center)

Learning to defecate the modern way at a hygiene exhibit in Puntarenas, 1915 (Rockefeller Archive Center)

sanitation and of overlooking the treatment of diseases in its incipiency, an emotional determination could be seen written on every face to "off with the old and on with the new."

There were no wise-acres there to scoff at the truth of the statements because it was uncomfortable to believe them — the meeting was taken seriously by all.

The laboratory is equipped with microscopes, and such materials necessary to the diagnosis of intestinal parasites and haemoglobin determination, educational placards demonstrating common sanitary measures, the life cycle of hookworm disease, clinical pictures of patients in different stages of the disease and its sequelae and finally with materials for treating common intestinal infections, primarily hookworm. In passing it is well to mention that the technique of laboratory diagnosis was both quick and accurate, the laboratory diagnostician being able to locate the foreign material in the specimens in a shorter time than the visiting M.D. It is to this laboratory that the people with specimens were sent by the inspector and came with as much enthusiasm as was accorded the director on his visit.

Sunday morning, the treatment day, contrary to most established beliefs, the clan assembled about 6 A.M. to receive the treatment. All ages were there from two months to over sixty years, the men all stepping up in the answer to their name much as in answer to a patriotic call to arms. The women merely took the medicine. It was a sad day for the few quavering children who faltered, as all remedies for this condition were immediately applied by many. Whether the remarkable interest shown is a desire for health, an attraction to something new or an answer to the appeal "Free to all" is hard to say, probably a combination of them all; but attribute it to what cause we will, the people long enough for the treatment and when they once grasp the beneficial results, we may feel that preventive medicine has obtained its permanent foothold in Costa Rica.

Autobiography of a Shoemaker

Juan Rafael Morales

By the beginning of the twentieth century, some formal schooling had become the norm for the working men and women of Costa Rica, both urban and rural. A literate working class took shape, and it displayed a good deal of geographical and occupational mobility. Juan Rafael Morales worked in both vectors of rural capitalism in the Central Valley: the medium-sized and large farms around Alajuela, to the west, which contracted salaried field labor but were part of an agrarian structure that had a strong component of peasant production; and the large estates east of Cartago, which were worked by sizeable contingents of laborers uprooted from their homes — a model more akin to that of the banana plantations. He then returned to a life of urban wage labor as a shoemaker. His story offers glimpses of the possibilities for radical instruction within the public education system, the growing secularism of the popular classes, and the marriage of working-class leisure and politics.

My father, José Gabriel Morales Rodríguez, was a man without vices, studious and dynamic, with a lively intelligence and exceptional faculties. He did every kind of work: farmer, tailor, builder, teacher, and finally, trader. In the canton of Poás, he owned a small shop that sold fabric and clothing that he made, and a small plot of land for farming in a spot called El Chilamate. He also owned a kiosk for selling clothes in Grecia, where he worked Saturdays and Sundays. My mother, María Alfaro Ulate, a native of Naranjo, was like my father, a homemaker of noble sentiment and with a great capacity to love her children and her husband. My parents were people full of religious faith and devotion to their Christian principles. This was how they raised us. . . .

In 1923, my father sold the small piece of land that he had in San Pedro de Poás, and we moved to Grecia, where he bought an old adobe house two hundred meters from the southeast corner of the church. . . . I enrolled in second grade at the local school, Eulogia Ruiz. The teacher was señorita Dora Suárez. I got to know other schoolmates there, and I was enthusiastic and happy. I was taught to participate in presentations and sing the national anthem and other tunes that you still hear sung; to write compositions, something that wasn't difficult because I was easily able to describe how a cat was, its size, color, agility, habitat, prey, and so on. Also mathematics; I understood everything well. At home I did the chores, took coffee and meals to my dad and my older brothers at work. I also played in the street with spinning tops and marbles. . . . At school they gave us lessons in the morning and in the afternoon. I was able to work my way to the position of best student in the class; this was what senorita Suárez told my father and confirmed with my grade, as I passed with ease.

In March 1924, I started third grade with doña Isabelina Barahona. . . . We didn't have time to play, not even at home, because as soon as we arrived, we had to do our homework in order to be able to play. With doña Isabelina's teaching method, you had to really study and dedicate yourself to be the best student. Still it wasn't difficult for me to be among the best in the class. . . . In the month of April, doña Isabelina gave a History lesson and, referring to the first of May as the date of the surrender of William Walker, she also told us that the date was celebrated as workers' day. She told us that don Omar Dengo was part of a group interested in the celebration that took place in other countries. She told us that in Russia the workers had power in their hands and that it was being made difficult for them to govern and that they were going through a difficult time; that many people were starving to death and so the group directed by Omar Dengo was collecting money to send aid to them. From what the teacher explained, I was left with the idea that the Russian workers had taken power, since in that year a workers' party [the Reformist Party], led by a priest called Jorge Volio, was campaigning with the emblem of an owl with large, lively red eyes. My studies continued within the economic limitations of my family, which were getting worse by the day. . . . [Morales continued school until 1926, when, at the age of thirteen, he "understood" that he would have to leave school to help his family economically.]

In Grecia, as the oldest child, it fell to me to put my nose to the grindstone and work to maintain the remaining family. I began to work as a day laborer in the sugar hacienda of the German family Niehaus. The hacienda was to the east of the town and had thirty-two *manzanas* [1 manzana = 1.75 acres] planted in cane, all divided into production quadrants separated by roads and laneways. My job was to make furrows with a hoe during planting and harvest of the cane, from 6 A.M. to 12 noon. In each quadrant, the daily tasks were directed by an overseer who was also the *orillero* [the one who worked the edge and was expected to set the pace], and as a result his salary was twenty-five cents more per day than that of a peon. The workday started with lines of ploughing or cutting. As the man who was in with the company, the foreman enjoyed a few

Juan Rafael Morales in 1999 (Courtesy of Juan
Rafael Morales)

other benefits: a house on the estate, firewood, *dulce* [brown sugar loaf], and
sugar; but in return he had to set the pace for the others in his work rhythm.
Generally, the overseer was the strongest man, and so he did the most work,
forcing the peons to toil a long and exhausting day in order to meet the grade.
The name of our overseer was Zeto Arias, and he was a coarse rustic of a man.
He was followed in rank by Chico Otoya, a humble, brave fellow who aspired
to be orillero because if he attained the position, he would rise in prestige and
respect in the eyes of the bosses and the other workers. He said that if he got
the *orilla* and took over from Zeto, he would not mistreat the peons. I considered myself among the best workers, and I was able to get close to Chico and
put myself in third place.

The months went by, and we remained in a precarious situation at home because my salary and the little that my father gained weren't enough to maintain
the family. I woke up every day at four in the morning; my mother prepared
my small lunch: five tiny tortillas made by her own hand, a boiled egg, rice and
beans, a small piece of brown sugar, and a bottle of lemon or orange juice to
go and endure the scorching sun all morning and put up with the harsh treatment of the overseer. In this humiliating situation, my mind would turn to
memories of school, recesses with those games of leap frog, bucking bronco,
and so on, and of my brothers' trade: making shoes.

One morning Zeto started verbally insulting Chico Otoya because he was
gaining on him in his cutting. The incident turned into a physical fight, with the

danger that it could end up involving machetes. The peons stopped working to intervene and avoid serious consequences. The boss, Mr. Barrantes, once he figured out that the peons supported Chico, proceeded to make changes: he made Chico the orillero, transferred Zeto to another sector, and offered me a move to the hacienda Margot in Turrialba. . . .

On the hacienda in Turrialba, I was put in a camp bunkhouse: twelve rooms extending side by side, with a door for each one, all of them tiny and dark. The space allowed only for a cot, a bench, and a table; they had a dirt floor, and there was a corridor running down the front with a common sink at the end. The toilet facilities were somewhat removed from the bunkhouse; they were of the crude outhouse variety and they gave off a foul odor and swarmed with flies and mosquitoes. Every day at five in the morning, the mill's siren went off, our notice to get ready and head for work for the cane fields. This was the same work that I had been doing in Grecia—ploughing with a hoe, cutting grass with a machete, cutting cane, stripping leaves from the cane (a very uncomfortable job because the leaves scratched your hands and face).

We started work at six in the morning, and we quit at noon, afterward returning to the camp, tired and dirty, to clean and sharpen tools and wash our clothes—in some cases it was tough to get rid of the odor of soil and sweat—and later bathe ourselves if we could still move. At night time, I took to practicing drawing: I drew images of animals and sometimes even of a few people, as well as landscapes; my workmates admired the pictures; I gave them as gifts to everyone as a way of making friends. Others played cards or checkers; some of the workers gambled at cards, some winning and others losing parts of their salaries. While we engaged in these activities during our rest time, the workers exchanged impressions and told each other their problems. For example, that they'd injured someone else, and for a reduction of their sentence, they were allowed a certain conditional freedom as long as they worked in Turrialba; others had abandoned their home suspecting their wives of infidelity. One night I found a man sad and suffering in his room, on the verge of tears; I asked him what the matter was and how I might help him. He thanked me but told me that he was thinking of his wife and children because their situation was so critical that with what he was sending them, it was hard for them to get by, and he was desperate to see them. . . .

One night at 6 P.M., a group of us from the hacienda headed for the center of Turrialba. We walked around the town and visited the Quesada Theater where cowboy films were showing every night and where we could drink an unforgettable papaya shake, made with milk, for ten cents. We bought our tickets and went up to the balcony seats to watch a film about Texas. The plot of this film had to do with the US acquisition of Texas at the hands of its armed forces during its classic project of territorial expansion. . . . One of my workmates told me that the movie theater needed a sign painter; he suggested that since I was good at drawing, the job would be easy for me. A few days later, I decided to show up at the theater. I was looked after by the owner, Rafael Quesada, who had his residence and family in Cartago but owned the theater and a bar in Turrialba. As a result, he had an interest in hiring efficient employees and treated them well. I told him with respect that I hoped to work preparing the signs that were used daily to announce which movies were going to play in the theater. I also told him about the time I wanted to take off to see my parents. Don Rafael proposed to test my painting skills. He recommended that I come to the apartment where films and signs for the theater were kept and, together with the employee who had announced he was leaving the job, go through my paces in order to learn the method I would have to employ on returning to the work. A few days later, I showed up at the apartment where the signs were kept. I found a young man of color there, Teófilo Wilson, who greeted me warmly. Later he oriented me in the preparation of the signs, the paints, and in how to figure out the distribution of the films for the following week according to the schedule assigned by the distribution company, Teatro Variedades. The apartment had a bedroom, a toilet, and a bathroom. There was room for large stacks of newspaper, which were used to cover boards so that they could be painted over later. . . .

The day after [returning home for a family visit], I went to the Teatro Quesada, and in conversation with don Rafael Quesada we agreed that I would paint the posters and collect the tickets from the people who came to see the movie. For the work Mr. Quesada agreed to pay me a weekly salary of twelve colones plus meals, and the room in the painter's apartment. A new period began for me, with new friendships. I ate in the same house where my boss ate. The family was the Lauritos; I became good friends with Leonardo, the son of the woman of the house. He was a champion swimmer in the region, and he taught me the sport. Sometimes he would show up at the painter's apartment and together we'd go and poster; he helped me collect tickets at the door of the theater; then we'd settle down to watch the movies.

They were silent movies. . . . On Sundays, Mr. Quesada would hire an orchestra to provide music for the films. On other occasions he put me to operate an *ortofónica* [a kind of gramophone], but it was very difficult to synchronize the music with what was happening in the film. That was when I got to know that musical apparatus, which also had a radio that only got foreign stations. The films lasted for hours, even when the actual movie time was short, because they were projected by the reel, and there was a break between each reel. During the time between reels, my drawings, done on slides, were projected onto the screen; I got a lot of appreciative comments about them, as well as about the images of certain artists that I painted on a large billboard located in the park by the train station. . . . I had to come up with suggestive billboard advertising for the film *Santa Mía*, starring Agustín Lara. The film formed in my mind a concern about social problems because it featured people living in great misery.

[Homesick and ready for a change and greater independence, Morales leaves Turrialba and returns to his family in Grecia.]

Working on one of my father's machines, I learned to sew pants and shirts. In the afternoons, I would go to the Norma shoe shop to learn the trade of shoemaking with my brother, Gilberto. I had a certain notion of how to tailor and cobble, and this allowed me to learn more easily. . . . I learned how to make pants, and with that I earned a salary equal to what I'd earned in Turrialba, and I was able to widen my circle of friends making pants for people. At the end of the year, Gilberto told senor Umaña [the owner of the shoeshop] that I was good at making the Romano shoes, and could do stitching for men's shoes, and asked him to give me work. Umaña asked me for a demonstration, and after I had made a few pairs, he invited me to look over a contract that he had with the United Fruit Company and told me that every worker in his company had to sign it and follow it.

The contract was tricky because it established certain mutual norms. In one of its sections it said, "in case of illness, every worker will have the right to a doctor's attention, the prescription and the first medicines only." If the illness continued, he would be sent to a charity hospital. In case of this eventuality, the company was authorized to deduct from the employee's salary twenty-five cents per week. In case of epidemics, the company would cover the first costs, but the funds that accumulate would be the company's property. Another section set out that during the existence of the contract, the workers had no right to seek a raise. . . .

My fellow shoemakers were happy for my success and told me that I had to be baptized to be a real shoemaker. I was surprised by that. The baptism consisted of being drenched with one or two buckets of water in which soles had been soaking for a few days and decomposing; so much so that it had leeched all the color of the mangrove and one was left with a smell of clay. That same night, they would celebrate a dance in one of their houses. And so it was: they bathed me well so that I had to go to the company bathroom—in the midst of huge laughs, applause, hard slaps on the back, and the invitation to the dance.

That night, although I didn't know how to dance, I couldn't forsake the opportunity, and I arrived at the place. They welcomed me sympathetically. The musical group was made up of three people: a singer, one with a mandolin, and one with a guitar. They played dance tunes, two-steps, mazurkas, and I remember one song, "Júrame." . . . The owner of the house passed around glasses of liquor that livened up the event, and one of the young women tried to teach me how to dance. For me, that moment meant a very distinct page in my life had turned to a greater responsibility in the face of my destiny. I understood that I belonged to a class, the one that works; that the owners of the cane fields, just as the owners of the shoe factory, were the ones who set the price of the work that one did; that it was not the farmworker or the shoemaker who could set the price for his labor. . . .

In the shop, on a few occasions when the boss and his son, Aquiles, would leave, the workers would debate the problem of the economic crisis, the high price of essential products, and the fact that we weren't allowed to ask for a raise; to the contrary, salaries had actually been lowered. We asked ourselves what to do and where to start. Sometimes we'd listen to the radio that the boss had installed, and we'd hear on the news about the workers movements in other countries and their struggles for wage increases. Such news, although sporadic, woke us up and made us want to struggle for the improvement of our working and living conditions.

Within the shop a struggle was gestating, one I had determined to play a role in. Outside the shop things were different. I left work at five or six, went home to bathe, ate, and dressed up to go to some place where I would see the brown-skinned beauty who I fancied. Sometimes I would be successful when she left the house to bring the neighbor a plate of delicious food made by her or her mother. I always tried to show her tenderness and avoid us being surprised in our talks by her parents because she would have been horribly punished. Although she lived on a corner that had street lighting, the place was dark at night and gave us cover. Each encounter lasted only minutes. When I didn't have any chance to see her, I would visit some center, often the Workers' Center that had been set up years earlier as a mutualist society. There they celebrated birthday parties, dances, weddings, and so on. I also participated in sporting activities, and along with other mates, we decided to reactivate the Club F.C. "Football Club" of Grecia, since there was no longer a team. The interest was born out of the fact that the majority of the players were shoemakers who worked in the different workshops of the city. . . .

On the tenth of August of 1934, we heard the news that ten thousand banana workers on the Atlantic Coast were on strike. They were demanding better working and living conditions from the United Fruit Company. We, the shoemakers of La Norma, which was financed by the same company, were also victims of that exploitation because of the contract that they had imposed on us. . . . I thought of the shoemakers of Grecia who, on top of the fact that we were dealing with the sharp economic crisis, had other problems at work. We didn't have any protection for our health or for our rights, and I thought that something might be done, taking advantage of the awakening that we were experiencing. But I knew that to talk about a union could lead to immediate dismissal. I also knew that the political party created in San José with the name Workers and Peasants Bloc [the Communist Party] had elected two deputies, and that one was a shoemaker. A few of my workmates felt sympathetic to the work that the party was doing for the good of the working people. So I thought it necessary to talk to each one, dedicating the time necessary. I undertook these overtures very discreetly, using the football practices that we had in the afternoons. . . .

We studied the conditions, and considering that it was always in December when the demand for shoes was greatest, November would be the month to present our demands to the owners. So it was. We put together our list of demands and tabled them on the first of November. . . . The owners refused to discuss our demands, and the shoemakers declared a strike. The commission became the strike committee, and four shops were affected: La Norma, Cruz, Villegas, and Jano. The strike committee decided to form vigilance committees for each shop with the object of stopping strikebreakers getting in and to rent a location for meetings; from there the orders were issued. We informed the shoemakers union in San José that we were on strike. . . .

Since the majority of the shoemakers had been sugarcane workers, we went to the workers in the cane fields to see if they would help us, and we received economic help from them. We met every day in the local. In one meeting, I proposed the idea that the philharmonic made up of shoemakers could begin the celebration of the open-air band concerts on the Thursdays of the strike in order to raise funds. The idea was taken up and put into practice to good effect. From the Shoemakers Union of San José, from the banana workers, from the Workers and Peasants Bloc, we got help, which was distributed daily to the 135 shoemakers on strike.

The weeks passed and the owners, seeing our firm stance, asked the Governor of the province to repress our movement because it was influenced by the Communists. During the first week of December, we were holding a large assembly in our local when the rural police of Alajuela showed up. They fired off a few rounds in the air and then with sabres in hand tried to remove us from the locale. One shoemaker, Juan José Solano, was injured in this confrontation and so was the policeman Lioncio Miranda, in the heel. In the face of this situation, the district administrator [jefe político] called both sides to discuss the list of demands in an effort to avoid further violence. A 5 percent raise in salaries was achieved, as well as an agreement that workers should administer the benefits fund and that the contract with the United Fruit Company cease to apply in terms of worker obligations. The agreement signed by both sides, the strike was lifted. We worked intensely that month, but with some tension still. . . .

At the end of the year, the electoral campaign got under way in the public plaza. The presidential candidates were León Cortés and Octavio Beeche. The Workers and Peasants Bloc was now competing at the national level. In January 1936, those of us who had been involved in organizing the shoemakers expanded our activities to join the activities of the Bloc. We thought it necessary for the people of Grecia to hear the platform of this Party through the word of its leader, Manuel Mora. We prepared his visit, and I was put in charge of painting signs to receive him and march with Manuel on the Sunday he arrived; we displayed what the people of the town wanted help with. In one, I painted a fat, smiling, and mustachioed landowner, mounted on his good horse, whip in hand, before a skinny peon who had his belt tightened to its final notch. The reception for Manuel was enthusiastic, but I was detained by the authorities for having painted realities.

That February on election day, I acted as a scrutineer for the party at a balloting table located in the school at Tacares de Grecia, defending the interests of my class.

Maternity

Francisco Zúñiga

Francisco Zúñiga, sculpture in stone, 1935 (Museo de Arte Costarricense)

The creation of the Colegio de Señoritas in 1888 and the College of Midwifery in 1899 led to the training of a cadre of titled women professionals — teachers, midwives, school nurses, and home visitors — to staff the rapidly expanding systems of public education and public health. In the context of their new social responsibilities, educators and intellectuals tended to redefine women's attributes, and in particular maternity, as fundamental civic virtues. In 1932, Mother's Day was officially promoted and as-

sociated with the day celebrating the assumption of the Virgin Mary. One of the most powerful traces of this process is a 1935 sculpture by Francisco Zúñiga, the principal Costa Rican sculptor of the twentieth century, who left the country to take up permanent residence in Mexico in the very year that this rendition of maternity provoked a public scandal: it was declared pornographic by some, while Jorge Volio, the founder of the progressive Reformist Party, in declaring the work "absurd," remarked that the mother figure looked like a "reclining cow."

Prospectus

National Association of Coffee Producers

In 1922, a national association of small and medium-sized coffee growers tried to form in order to extract a better price for preprocessed coffee from the large growers and owners of processing facilities. The attempt failed, but the National Association of Coffee Producers was formed in the context of the depression, and its members' struggle contributed to the founding in 1933 of the Institute for the Defense of Coffee, an agency charged with insuring the prosperity of the coffee industry in general. They also helped to force passage of a law that permitted the state to regulate the profit margins of the owners of processing facilities. Ultimately, these small and medium growers were the ones who consolidated the image of Costa Rica as a country of yeoman farmers, the idea that rural smallholding was the basis of democracy, and the promise that the benefits of coffee growing should be shared even with the peons. In our era of "fair trade" coffee, it is interesting to note that this early effort of small coffee producers to get a better deal for themselves even included attempts to secure norms in international wholesale and retail markets against the fraudulent labeling of coffee origins.

The principal objective of the Association is to free the producer from the exporter completely and absolutely. How can this be achieved? In isolation it is utterly impossible. But if, as we hope, producers respond to our call and subscribe among themselves to the actions we here propose in brief, the Association would be able to count on strong social capital that would be put immediately at the service of the collective. With that base, the Association would acquire whatever coffee processing facilities were necessary according to the number of its associates. This would make it possible to formally conclude negotiations for the acquisition of credit (the deals have already been accepted in principle). These monies would provide credit to our associates and so break the current domination of the processors over credit, the difference being that our credit would be made available at a much lower interest rate and with highly advantageous conditions.

If the coffee processing facilities and yards were the exclusive property of the associates, and no one outside their group had influence or participated, the associates would be immediately transformed from simple producers into exporters of their own coffee. By cooperating, each would gain separately the benefits and utilities that currently remain in the hands of the exporter. Aside from this, the producer-member would be converted into a direct importer of all that he needs, like shovels, machetes, hackles, and even his very clothes, and retain for himself the abundant profits that are currently generated by this trade. This would mean, then, that the producer-member would enjoy the following benefits and advantages through the Association:

1. The power to be at the same time a producer and an exporter of his own coffee, garnering at the time of sale the same price that coffee has been fetching in European and American markets—that is, an effective profit of between 20 and 30 percent over what the processors have been paying

2. The ability to acquire the money necessary for his annual work schedule and his subsistence at an interest rate much lower that that currently charged, and under better conditions, without being exposed to the constant danger that his properties might pass into the hands of the moneylender

3. The ability to acquire specialized tools at prices much lower than are actually charged, since the Association would order from abroad all the necessary tools for its members

4. The ability to dispose freely of the fertilizers and chemicals necessary for achieving a greater production by area, and without feeling the cost; and also of the discard of his own coffee, which currently remains for the benefit of the owner of the processing facility

5. Access to an Association office at the service of its members, one made up of competent professors and experts in coffee, who would instruct them appropriately in order to achieve a greater harvest than that currently produced. Through conferences, pamphlets, and publications, these professors and experts would convert the coffee farms of the associates into true founts of wealth and would be always at the beck and call of the members for any consultation and information of use to their crops

6. The unconditional help of the Association in liquidating the mortgages that weigh on the associates' farms, which, little by little, as they are taken on by the Association, would make available the money for this at an interest rate of 8 percent annually and at a minimum of a five-year term

7. And we think it also just, in enumerating the incalculable benefits that the Association would mean for the producer, to think of those advantages that will also be gained by the same peons who assist each of us with their work, since we are not interested in freeing some in detriment of others, but rather in attaining a complete liberation of Costa Rican workers in general. With that end in mind, and with common agreement, a minimum wage will be established, one that must be received by each worker, as well as [restrictions on] the number of hours that he must devote to these tasks. It is important that every member understand the advantages that will be obtained by having peons satisfied with their remuneration and not having to worry constantly about how they will survive the next day, a preoccupation that saps the strongest spirit and destroys all noble ambitions. To gain in order to give: that should be the motto of the Association

Aside from all these benefits, the Association would begin to make the appropriate petitions to get, if not a total suppression of the tax currently levied on the export of coffee of one and a half dollars per quintal, at least a reduction according to the possibilities of the State. This is because a violent suppression of the tax without already being able to count on a substitute of the same or greater amount would be the cause of awful economic unrest that would directly prejudice the country to which we belong and for whose glorious growth we must force ourselves to work. A rich country produces citizens who are of healthy body and soul by means of the common welfare, while the economic ruin of the state, whatever the reasons that might cause it, will only produce sickly spirits and a damaging collective scepticism. Let us labor, then, so that the country might always move forward, and let us be the ones who take it always toward a greater prosperity and wealth.

It will also be necessary to undertake an active, systematic, and duly organized propaganda campaign in order to ensure that the excellent qualities of our coffee are given credit in the markets of those countries where other types are sold under our name, even though its origins and quality are quite different. Trade promotion is in this sense totally necessary, and there is no sum ill-spent if it achieves our objective, since through such efforts sales of our coffee will improve, and we will obtain better prices than the current ones. . . .

The social capital of the Association will be established by common consent in the first general meeting of shareholders, with the value of each share set at fifty dollars, which will be paid in coffee from the next harvest or in currency if preferred. Each member will immediately begin to enjoy the benefits and advantages that we have listed. Having already tabled discussions with an important foreign bank to get the sums necessary for advances to the members at an interest rate of 6 percent annually, the only thing left to be done is to see that the shares are subscribed to by the majority of producers as we believe and hope they will be.

The Red Door

Teodorico Quirós

Teodorico Quirós, oil on canvas, 1945 (Museo de Arte Costarricense)

The ideology of the rural middle classes found a complement in the nationalist paint-ing style that emerged in the country toward the end of the 1920s. Teodorico Quirós's Red Door, though from a later date, is a classic example of this genre: it depicts the wall and door of an adobe house in the country, with blue shadows in the white wall, red door, and red tiled roof (the colors of the national flag). In reality, during this era, the majority of adobe houses were not painted, and those that were, generally featured other colors, especially pink and green.

Banana Strike Confidential

Diplomatic Service of the United States of America

The 1934 strike of banana workers against the United Fruit Company's operations in Limón is one of the most famous labor actions in Latin American history. The pioneering agribusiness giant was notorious for wielding immense influence over local governments and for having a stranglehold over local economies. The following report of Leo R. Sack, the chief US diplomat in Costa Rica at the time, reveals how the strike was viewed by the company, US observers, and Costa Rican political elites. The report also underlines just how important Franklin Delano Roosevelt's Good Neighbor Policy might have been for some Latin American countries. Had the United States heeded the call of the United Fruit Company director in 1934 and intervened to end the strike, it is not an exaggeration to say that the entire subsequent democratic history of Costa Rica might have been fatally undermined. This is the first time the document has been published.

Legation of the United States of America
San José, Costa Rica
August 25, 1934

No. 407
Subject: Communist Activities

Strictly Confidential

The Honorable
The Secretary of State
Washington

Sir: —

For the strictly confidential information of the Department I have the honor to report suggestions which were made to me yesterday afternoon in this Lega-

tion by Mr. G. P. Chittenden, chief representative of the United Fruit Company
in Costa Rica.

With the passage of the strike of banana laborers into the third week and
following the decision of the United Fruit Company not to attempt to cut any
fruit whatsoever this weekend on its own plantations, Mr. Chittenden's nervousness over the strike situation has greatly increased. Up to now he has proceeded calmly and coolly and in my opinion with discretion and judgment. As
heretofore reported he has at no time asked this Legation to request American intervention as has been suggested in conversations between other banana
growers; neither has Mr. Chittenden requested this Legation to be more aggressive in what I believe has been the tactful manner in which I have discussed
the strike situation with officials of the Government. As reported to the Department my objective has been to obtain maximum protection, within the
Government's means, of the American lives and property. At the same time
I have refrained from doing anything or offering suggestions or making criticisms which in any way might add to the Government's nervousness.

But yesterday afternoon Mr. Chittenden's calmness seemed to have disappeared and he came to me with suggestions along these lines:

After discussing the Communist background of the strike and the apparent
fact that the movement is under the direction of politically minded agitators
who in the last analysis are hopeful of taking charge of the Government — an
opinion in which I concur — Mr. Chittenden then inquired if the United States
Government would not look with disfavor upon a Communist form of the
Government in Central America?

"The form of Government decided upon by other nations is no business of
the United States Government as I interpret the policy of my Government,"
I replied to Mr. Chittenden. "The United States Government recognizes the
responsibility of other peoples and their rights to have a form of government
of their own choosing. This policy, I am quite sure, has been made exceedingly
clear under President Roosevelt."

Then Mr. Chittenden asked me if I were not concerned as to whether or not
the strike movement might not result in the establishment of a Communist
Government in this country.

I replied that the form of Government chosen by the Costa Rican people
was, in so far as I was concerned, a matter wholly within their own province
and not one for interference in and from me in any way. I added that personally
and officially my views were in strict accordance with the views of the State
Department and of President Roosevelt.

Then Mr. Chittenden put out this feeler:

"Don't you think that if a Communist Government would be established in Costa Rica that it would be very dangerous for President Ubico in Guatemala, who has succeeded heretofore in stamping out Communism in that country before it could get a start; for President Martínez in El Salvador who stopped Communism at a loss of three thousand lives; for President Carías in Honduras and for old man Sacasa in Nicaragua? Do you think it is possible to get word to them through your American Ministers in those countries and from you to their representatives (of other Central American countries) in San José to point out to them the grave danger which exists here and which would affect them if carried to its present conclusion in order that they might bring pressure upon President Jiménez to let him know that the Governments in these countries are watching the situation in Costa Rica with much concern."

"Are you making the suggestion to me that I do that?" I asked Mr. Chittenden.

"Yes," he replied.

"Well, if you have that in mind suppose you communicate with your attorney in Boston, Mr. Jackson, and let him make the suggestions to the State Department on your behalf because I can not do anything for you," I answered.

"Oh, no, I don't want to do that," Mr. Chittenden replied.

"Well I can not do anything for you because I am not in sympathy with your suggestions. It will only make a bad matter worse and to my mind it is interference in a Costa Rican internal affair."

"I'm sorry," Chittenden continued, "but I may make it formal before I get through."

"Then, if you do, put it on your official stationery in writing above your signature and as a courtesy and as a duty I will transmit your suggestions to the State Department," I told him.

Mr. Chittenden seemed much annoyed because I did not show any enthusiasm over his suggestion but because of the possibility that the United Fruit Company, which has widespread ramifications in Central America, may yet attempt to bring outside pressure on the Government of President Jiménez, I am reporting the above conversation for the information of the Department. The Department, perhaps, may feel that I am attributing too much importance to Chittenden's "feelers" which arise from his unquestioned nervousness nevertheless I prefer to report the conversation fully.

In this connection, I should like to report that Mr. Chittenden informed me that he had personally suggested to Foreign Minister Guardián on last Thursday the need for martial law in the strike area. Apparently his view appealed to Mr. Guardián because on Thursday afternoon when visited by Secretary Trueblood and myself he told us that he was going to recommend to President

Jiménez the establishment of martial law in the fruit zone. In his conversation with the President, however, that afternoon the seventy-five-year-old Executive apparently persuaded his Foreign Minister that the need for martial law was not apparent at this time. Likewise the President apparently persuaded Mr. Guardián that this was no time for him to submit his resignation (my telegram No. 42, August 23).

Respectfully yours,

Leo R. Sack

Notice to West Indian Farmers!

West Indian Strike Committee

The United Fruit Company promoted a policy of divide and rule whenever necessary to weaken potential labor solidarity. In the multiethnic and multilingual world of banana production on the Limón coast, one obvious strategy was to foment racial enmity and rub salt into old racial wounds. This is an example of a flier that circulated during the strike, probably emerging with the company's blessing.

NOTICE

—— TO ——

West Indian Farmers!

Fellow Country Men;

        Greeting:—

We beg to call your attention to the movement now on foot, that if you allow yourselves to be intimidated by self-seeking people, who are against the coloured people and refuse to cut the fruit from your farms, we are the ones who will suffer, our wives and children will starve.

Remember for years we have been working in harmony with the Co. and they have always treated us right, now is the time for us to prove that we are no cowards, your fruit is your own property. Allow no one to prevent you from cutting same for delivery to the Co. Awake to your own interest. This is not a strike, but a dangerous movement to destroy the Banana industry of Costa Rica.

Remember brothers, if there is no fruit there will be no jobs for any of us, The Co. can send their ships to other countries to obtain fruit, whilst yours will rot on the farm and everybody will suffer.

If we have no Bananas, there will be no ships, no machine shop, no trains, no commissaries and everything will be at a stand-still.

The Government has offered you protection. This movement is only to scare you. Don't be afraid cut your fruit.

        THE WEST INDIAN COMMITTEE

Express Printery

(Archivo Nacional de Costa Rica)

Woman in Window

Max Jiménez

Max Jiménez, oil and sand on canvas, c. 1939 (Museo de Arte Costarricense)

After the banana strike of 1934, the Caribbean began to acquire a certain presence in Costa Rican literature and plastic arts, as evidenced by Carlos Luis Fallas's world-famous novel, Mamita Yunai, *a Spanish nickname for United Fruit (1941), and by paintings such as this powerful portrait of a* mulatta *woman by avant-gardist Max Jiménez. Jiménez was Costa Rica's most internationally celebrated artist of the period.*

A Governor and a Man Faces

the Social Problem

Rafael Ángel Calderón Guardia

In 1940, the charismatic San José physician Rafael Ángel Calderón Guardia was elected to the Costa Rican presidency with over 80 percent of the vote. Rather unexpectedly, his government undertook an ambitious social reform that involved the introduction of social security (including medical and maternity benefits), the passage of a labor code, the inclusion of social guarantees in the constitution, and the founding of the University of Costa Rica. In this 1942 pamphlet, Calderón Guardia offers a highly personal explanation of the sources of the reform, magnifying his own importance in typically populist fashion and remaining silent about the degree to which the struggles of the workers had forced reform onto the agenda of political elites.

No one can deny their convictions without denying themselves. That is why I have constantly striven to be faithful to my religion as I lived it in my parental home: without exclusionary fanaticism or sectarian limitations, in an atmosphere of tolerance and charity, constantly inspired by the ideas and feelings of a true, integral Christianity. As the son of a Doctor [Rafael Calderón Muñoz, one of the leaders of a circle of Catholic politicians with social concerns], I became aware from a very young age of the pain and suffering that surround us. My father knew how to inspire the apostolic sense of his profession in me. As soon as I became a medical student, I knew that by devoting myself to the profession, I could not hope for fame or fortune: I was not unaware how arduous and lacking in laurels is the profession of those who struggle against death in a country where the population often lacks the bare necessities. From the time I left for Belgium — a center of civilization, an emporium of culture — I could not get out of my mind the idea that the pain and suffering of my people needed a remedy. Not a remedy drawn from class hatred or from violence — products of a state of injustice that only engenders a thousand more injustices and never achieves peace among social classes. What was needed was a remedy of harmony that emerged as the fruit of an attempt at perfecting our democratic institutions. . . .

Could a student in a European University be indifferent to the social question? Was he not obliged to study it in all its manifestations? In order to end the catastrophe [of the First World War], the great military powers tried to reconstruct the world politically. But they did nothing to restore the Christian morality that was threatened by parties extolling the exploitation of man by man, and by Marxist revolution based on the dictatorship of the proletariat. The frenzy produced by the war threatened to sink the human race into a greater moral misery than during the very days of killing themselves. For those believers at heart there was only one road: that of the Church. . . . Everything I could have hoped for as a response to my concerns was foreseen and addressed in the Social Code, the sketch of a Social Catholic synthesis, a document that emerged from the National Union of Social Studies founded in Malines in 1920 under the presidency of Cardinal [Desiré Joseph] Mercier [a Belgian Catholic sociologist whose writings proposed a third way between materialism, both communist and positivist, and the hyperindividualism of a classical liberalism discredited by the Great Depression]. There . . . the most admirable analysis of human life is achieved, not from the point of view of a negative individualism or a negative materialism, but rather starting from the Christian conception of man, Society, and the State. This is done without deifying man as individualism does; without deifying the State, as Socialism does; and without deifying Society, as positivist sociology does. . . .

The university years passed by. The student became a Physician and returned to his homeland with youthful fire and optimism. And what did he find? Waiting for him was a painful and awful experience. His people, living in a rich and fertile land, were dying of pain and suffering. How many nights did that hopeful man have to hang his head and feel in his heart a good measure of responsibility for the agony and vulnerability of the dispossessed! He was in the presence of profound social injustice. In those sad houses, without air, without light, prostrate before illness and indigence, many men surrendered their souls to the Creator without leaving their children a crust to raise to their orphaned mouths. Was that reward for a life of work and sacrifice? And how many times did a poorly nourished mother die giving birth because the child sucked the last vital reserves from her debilitated organism?

No less painful and pathetic is the case of the sick father who cannot earn his pitiful salary, who cannot provide food for his family or acquire medicines to combat his illness. Those workers awash in misery without the least protection against the contingencies of age, injury, illness, or death moved me to profound piety and at the same time to a natural feeling of rebellion. Where was the justice in such economic treatment of those whose families are the backbone and the great mass of our nationality? It is easy to see where the problem lies. Those men have been denied all that their work entitles them to receive. Charity and occasional acts of kindness shown to them are improper because they are humiliating. Society owes them the retribution that they have the right to demand and so for which they should not have to beg. They are most definitely not a load borne by those elements of society who have used the working people's strength and taken advantage of their economic activities; they are victims of an injustice. . . .

Social Christianity, unlike Marxism or the parties that deify the State, does not arbitrarily seek justice through violence. Hatred is not a proper goal, nor is it logical or just to use it as a weapon. One can and one must fight injustice, but not by substituting the existing economic dictatorship for the dictatorship of the proletariat, or of any other social class. We must feel the need to struggle against the evils done to the disadvantaged, but not seek or wish for bad ends for other sectors of society. To believe that justice is done or must be done as vengeance, by repressing ruling groups or those who possess wealth, is an error that has cost much innocent blood. The violence of those above and the violence of those below are equally wrong. Faced with those antagonisms that emerge inevitably out of the ideas and tendencies of multiple ideologies, one feels the need to appeal to a power superior to that of man, one that for that very reason conciliates all coexistence among human groups and finds a possibility for a life in common based on justice; one that eliminates class struggle; one founded on the understanding and the spirit of true Christianity, leading to a solution to the crises and divisions that dominate modern societies. . . .

But as I am one of those who create wealth with which they can subsist if need be, I did not forget nor could I forget that those who have no other weapon to defend themselves than their debilitated arms need government help. I have tried to make sure that my sympathy for our peasants and workers is not pure rhetoric. Rather, I have tried to identify myself with their needs and limitations, to try to get closer to understanding these humble brothers with a heart free of prejudices. And listening to their voices and their complaints, I have felt that we cannot be indifferent to their pain and their suffering because discontent, poverty, lack of personal esteem, economic inequalities cannot subsist in a well-organized democracy. . . .

I understand that the social project has barely begun; that for those who try to achieve it as I have, there will be neither glory nor benefit, but only an abundant harvest of bitterness and displeasure. I understand, equally, that what I have been able to achieve is worth very little. In the years to come, other governors will have to confront—as I have confronted in an era of universal upheaval and emergency—the grave problems originating in the misery of the great mass of the population that belongs to our working classes. I know that those governors shall fulfill other stages in the difficult battle and complete the great edifice that must be built by the Costa Rican nation to secure its future progress and culture and to guarantee, it must be said, not only the dispossessed their legitimate rights but also the propertied classes the enjoyment of their goods and the social peace they so badly need for the maintenance of current riches and well-being.

IV

Democratic Enigma

Latin America has had notorious difficulty establishing, maintaining, and strengthening democratic institutions, and this is what makes the success story of Costa Rican democracy so important. Many of the historical forces used to explain the failure of democracy were powerfully present in Costa Rica. Like most Central American countries, Costa Rica was predominantly rural and had an economy dependent on coffee and bananas, and during the nineteenth century, the country was not immune to periods of instability, coups, and authoritarian rule. Curiously, Costa Rica's great democratic opening in the period after the elections of 1902 coincided with a prolonged slump in the export economy, one that deepened with the outbreak of the European War in 1914. After a temporary rebound in the 1920s, the country was hammered as hard as any other by the Great Depression and the closing of European markets during World War II. Costa Rica also had its share of labor militancy and political radicalism. After its creation in 1931, the Costa Rican Communist Party played a directive role over that movement — at the peak of the depression leading unemployed workers in a march on congress that ended in a bloody confrontation with police, and organizing banana workers in a famous strike against United Fruit. Yet the country suffered only one, brief spell of military dictatorship during this trying period, that of the Tinoco brothers (1917–19), which was overthrown by a coalition that quickly restored civilian government. Costa Rica, alone among Central American countries, survived the 1930s without electoral politics falling to dictatorship.

The democratic miracle was tarnished by a terrible civil war that ripped the country apart following the elections of 1948. Until very recently, the civil war remained the symbolic reference point of modern Costa Rican politics. The regime of popular Catholic physician Dr. Rafael Ángel Calderón Guardia was overthrown, and his welfare and labor reforms put in jeopardy. It was the bloodiest political event in the country's history, with a death toll of at least four thousand in only five weeks of fighting. In the war's aftermath, the country's jails were filled with political prisoners (some of whom were executed summarily), and thousands of supporters of the defeated coalition were forced into exile. But the victors of that war, José Figueres and his followers, rejuvenated electoral institutions and renewed a state commitment to social democracy, while famously abolishing the military as an institution and strengthening electoral laws and the agencies charged with overseeing them.

How did Costa Rican democracy survive the turbulence that left virtually all Latin American countries mired in authoritarianism, violent social and political conflict, and brutally repressive military rule? An earlier generation of Costa Rican scholars argued that a "rural democracy" had taken shape among freeholding peasant farmers in the eighteenth century and that this constituted the democratic backbone of society to the present. A more theoretical and academic school, influenced by the debate over the transition from feudalism to capitalism and the arguments of the famous sociologist Barrington Moore, has proposed that during the expansion of coffee in the nineteenth century, the large coffee barons were unable to forcibly expropriate the peasantry to make them work on their haciendas. As a result, these small farmers maintained enough economic autonomy to give them a political voice. Other observers insist that the main explanation for the success of democracy is to be found in the way institutions were built to promote effective conflict resolution among politicians.

We think it is best to consider social and institutional factors together. By the end of the colonial period, a pattern of legal and institutional mediation of individual and collective conflicts had already been set, and the Costa Rican state reinforced this tendency after independence. Despite the authoritarian nature of presidential succession in certain periods, electoral practices were rarely interrupted during the nineteenth century. According to the electoral census of 1885, 67 percent of adult Costa Rican males of twenty years of age or older were inscribed in the electoral register (in Great Britain in 1884, only 59 percent of men of twenty-one or more were). Registration of voters reached 100 percent of adult males in the first decade of the twentieth century, with voter turnout surpassing 70 percent of those registered.[1] The decisive turn toward electoral democracy took place between 1889 and 1909. A first wave of political parties emerged and electoral participation broadened, as did the political space available to the opposition. The electoral campaign of 1889 for the first time saw two parties competing openly for the presidency without the process being interrupted by the withdrawal of one of them or by a coup d'état as had always occurred in the past. Also, the opposition party won the first round of voting with more than 80 percent of the vote, a figure that reveals the government's limited ability to manipulate the electoral result. According to mythology, the Liberal faction's decision to concede defeat in the face of the popular uprising of November 7 marked the beginning of electoral democracy in Costa Rica. We find this interpretation questionable since José Joaquín Rodríguez, the victorious candidate in 1889, governed in an authoritarian fashion and five years later installed his son-in-law, Rafael Iglesias, in the presidency, thereby ensuring his own reelection in 1897 by dubious means. But in spite of the authoritarian character of the regimes of Rodríguez and Iglesias, from 1889 onward, presidential succession depended on more or less competitive and regular elections. In 1901, a pact between the moderates in the opposition and Iglesias eased the removal of the strongman figure from the executive.

This was the backdrop to the transition to the direct vote in 1913 (up to this point elections had taken place in two stages, with voters going to the poll in the first round to choose an electoral college). And these were also the years when the proportion of the budget spent on the military and police began to decrease, while that dedicated to public health, education, and public works began to increase. Pressured by the demands of urban and rural popular communities, politicians and parties progressively modified the distribution of spending. They did so in an effort to consolidate electoral clientele, and this contributed decisively to the social development of Costa Rican democracy. Somewhat later, as a result of an electoral reform between 1925 and 1927, the secret ballot was instituted—a modification that increased the voters' power at the expense of the control formerly wielded over them by parties. Little by little, elections were converted into a way of channeling popular demands. Because the basic connection between society and politics was of an electoral nature, politicians and parties became key actors, strategically positioned to direct the demands of urban and rural communities and transform them into public policy. The electoral nexus was important in another sense: to the degree that political competition intensified, parties made an effort to enlist and mobilize the greatest possible number of citizens. In the process, the electoral dynamic developed its potential as an agent of integration, operating against discrimination based on ethnicity or class (but not sex, since women did not win the vote until 1949).

Many students of Costa Rican politics take 1948/49 as a moment of clear rupture, since they suppose that the civil war and the writing of a new constitution marked the beginning of a fundamentally distinct phase in the political life of the country—one that continues to the present. Given that right through to the 1990s many of the principal actors in Costa Rican politics had formed their identities and their power bases during these intense months of violent confrontation, it is not surprising that they saw it as an act of creation that had established an entirely new political universe. Now that over half a century has passed, it is easier to see the civil war era as merely one crucial moment in a longer period when Costa Rican political institutions, identities, and practices were reformulated but not fundamentally transformed. This turbulent time, lasting almost three decades, began in the 1930s when the National Republican Party achieved a virtual monopoly over the vote and then split into two factions in 1941 (Calderonistas and Cortesistas). It came to an end in 1958, when the Party for National Liberation (PLN), the political party built by José Figueres and the other military victors of the civil war a decade earlier, determined to respect the election results of that year even though they had lost. The long view also helps to explain the curious outcome of the civil war — the return to the welfare state program of the defeated regime and the handover of power on two occasions by the faction who had led the military victory. The invention of Costa Rican national identity in the late nineteenth century had occurred in tandem with the expansion of electoral participation. The two processes reinforced one another to create the Costa Rican citizen not simply as an ideal aspiration but as a key actor in practical politics. The political identity of the losers of the 1948 civil war (anti-Figueristas or anti-Liberacionistas) shared a founding principle with the political identity of the winners (Figueristas or Liberacionistas): social justice and the exercise of the right to vote as the sources and objectives of legitimate political power.

Note

1. A three-tiered system of citizen voters was established in Costa Rica in the constitution of 1825. In 1847, a two-tiered system was introduced, and it endured until 1913. Aside from the major restriction of sex (the vote for women was not approved until 1949), restrictions on voters really only applied to electors of the second tier, who had to fulfill certain economic requirements. In order to vote in the first-round elections, the only thing required other than being Costa Rican and an adult male was to work in a useful occupation or have known means of subsistence. That changed in the constitution of 1848, which stipulated that to be a citizen and to vote required a degree of economic wealth. This clear restriction on citizenship disappeared with the constitution of 1859, where citizens were defined as all men of twenty years or over, or of eighteen and over if they were married or "professors of some science," owners of property, or engaged in an honest occupation that permitted them to maintain themselves in a condition proportional to their station. The widening of citizenship was ratified in the constitution of 1871, which, except for two brief interruptions, remained in force through 1948.

Petition for Recognition of Voting Rights from a Humble Citizen, 1859

Santiago Córdova

Except for the decade of Juan Rafael Mora's presidency in the 1850s, constitutional development tended more toward political inclusion than exclusion. The following petition from an ordinary citizen allows us to glimpse the political culture of a Costa Rican farmer who had been denied the right to vote toward the end of the era of Mora, when property restrictions were introduced. The subtext of the son who had died in the war against William Walker suggests that it might be worth considering the degree to which the Mora government's restriction of citizenship contributed to discontent with the regime, which was overthrown in 1859.

Your Excellency Mr. Captain General President of the Republic,

I, Santiago Córdova of Heredia, farmer of majority age, come before Your Excellency to humbly declare that the Eligibility Committee of my town has dealt me the notorious injury of not registering me on the list of eligible citizens, as Your Excellency will deign to see from the certificate duly attached. The Committee has listened to neither the voice of justice nor the echo of reason, and so I find myself with no choice but to rise up against that fate. The only reason that the honorable Commission has given for refusing me the enjoyment of citizenship is its insistence that I do not own real property worth at least three hundred pesos, as required by the Newest Constitution. And given that this is the sole justification for their resolution, I promise to undo it by appealing to Your Excellency's illustrious intelligence. Please dignify me with your worthy attention.

The attached certificate demonstrates that the Trustee don Joaquín Orosco, with full knowledge that I possess a house within one block of the plaza in my community, one worth three times the property required by the law, and knowing that I am constantly engaged in work that provides me an income of more that 250 pesos [a year], asked the Eligibility Commission to register me in the list of citizens. I insisted that that petition be respected, due to the truth of his declaration, and because this was the only criterion used against me in this matter, but no, sir, this did not happen, because the Commission resolved the opposite and so took away my civil being.

The honorable Commission knows that I worked hard here during my youth in order to acquire goods that would allow me to survive in my old age, and that I was able to make my efforts prosper, but a series of misfortunes and the desire to provide useful sons to the fatherland made me lose everything I had. The Commission knows that I dedicated my life to educating my late son, Father Bruno Córdova, and that after spending everything I possessed, Divine Providence in the guise of war and cholera snatched him from me while he was serving the fatherland. And they know that when I lost him I also lost all my solace, all my hope, leaving me now decrepit in my old age and unable to earn like I used to. So, despite such powerful reasons, the Commission buries me with a single stroke, condemning me to live alone outside society and without that sweet name of citizen of the fatherland.

Naturally, I am taking these steps because the law has stripped me of the rights of citizenship, and no matter what I read or think, I find no reason for this stain on my honor and for the fact that today I have had taken from me that which yesterday I possessed. I speak in this way precisely because in the previous electoral period I did have the letters, and as such I carried out public duties the good of which nobody can deny.

It is true, sir, that as a result of a debt, a coffee plot that I had with some seven thousand bushes was auctioned along with my residence, bought by don Paulino Ortiz, and this man donated the house to my younger children. But it is also true that at that time it was worth six hundred pesos, and today it is worth more than nine hundred or a thousand pesos, meaning that the difference, by virtue of the improvements that I have made to it, constitutes the wealth required by the law, together with the two hundred pesos I possess in belongings. But even if this were not the case, does not the house belong to my children, and since I am of them, can I not use it as the basis for the faculties that the law concedes me? Of course the answer is yes, and Your Excellency knows it well, and all I need is an indication from you along these lines to produce a correct result.

For all the aforementioned,

Without anywhere else to turn, I ask Your Excellency and implore you to show me the dignity, due to the merits of the sworn affidavits attached and the arguments I have made, of recognizing my eligibility and ordering the honorable Commission to register me on the list of Citizens, since to do so would give me mercy and justice which is what I beseech, swearing, etc. . . .

Heredia, 25 February 1859

The Night of San Florencio

La Prensa Libre

In 1989, the government of Oscar Arias Sánchez celebrated "one hundred years of Costa Rican democracy" by organizing a summit of American presidents in San José, one that even drew US president George Bush the elder. The historical basis for this claim was the popular rising of 7 November 1889 which ensured the triumph of the opposition Constitutionalist Party in the presidential election of that year. Overlooked in the centennial festivities was the uncomfortable fact that the opposition triumph deteriorated after two years into a decade of authoritarian government. Still, the 1889 election proved significant in that it was the first time two parties competed openly for the presidency. The uprising can also be seen in a wider light than strict electoral democracy, since the popular explosion in large measure expressed the discontent of urban and rural communities, supported by the church, with the liberal reforms undertaken during the 1880s. Here was how one opposition newspaper of the day reported the uprising.

Spirits were relatively tranquil on the night of the sixth after the official visit to the Señor Presidente of the Republic, don Bernardo Soto, by a group of respectable citizens who are members of the Constitutional Party clubs. Our Magistrate president acknowledged the electoral victory of the Constitutional Party. All that was left was to wait for the electoral commissions to start reporting the respective results of balloting and resolve the petitions to annul election results in a variety of locales after hearing the arguments of the two competing groups. This was how things stood when at about 5 P.M. on the seventh of this month, a platoon from the police force started going around the main streets of the capital acclaiming the candidate of the Liberal Party, don Ascensión Esquivel, and shouting death to don José Joaquín Rodríguez of the Constitutional Democratic Party.

On a number of occasions, members of the Liberal Party had put out the word that they could count on the support of the Army, and that Esquivel . . . would be proclaimed the Supreme Ruler. We understand that the people thought that the carrying-on of the police was the first sign that such a move was afoot. And so they started to move themselves as if with a single will to look for weapons, which they had totally lacked up to that point in time. Withdrawing to the outskirts of town, they began to surround the capital, organizing themselves militarily and preparing to defend themselves.

The cry of alarm was sent by word of mouth at an astonishing speed to the surrounding towns, and the towns started responding according to the number of their inhabitants with columns, battalions, companies, and squadrons of men who flew rather than ran to the capital. They streamed in over a three-hour period . . . until San José was surrounded by somewhere around seven thousand men, without including those of Cartago who, numbering almost three thousand, concentrated themselves around that city, nor those of Santo Domingo and Heredia, who gathered around the second of these towns with nearly two thousand men. . . .

It would have been nine at night when a group of notable men, led by Dr. Carlos Durán, the third designate to the presidency [these were men designated by congress at the beginning of each administration who could be called on if necessary to exercise the presidency], and Licenciado don Ricardo Jiménez went to the Palace with the objective of holding talks with President Soto so that they might explain the situation to him and determine the road that had to be taken in such a critical emergency. We are not informed of all the details of that conference, but the tangible result was Soto's call at approximately ten at night for the designate, Durán, to occupy the office [for the remainder of the outgoing president's term]. The outgoing president dictated his final decrees, and the incoming president dictated his first decrees (the most outstanding being the recognition of the new President by the Army High Command and the naming of the distinguished don Ricardo Jiménez as Cabinet Secretary). While all this was going on, some small skirmishes were taking place outside between groups on either side. One occurred on the corner where the Liquor Factory meets General Fernández Street: Román Zumbado and Joaquín Quirós were killed and [various men] wounded. Hard on the heels of that, in the small plaza in front of the Palace, bullets put a tragic end to the life of don Teodorico Quirós — we are told fired from the Palace itself. The unlucky and innocent victim had been passing in front for who knows what reason.

By this point, the human circle besieging the city had been supplied with miscellaneous arms and a more unshakeable resolve than ever. They watched over the dawning of the new day, without knowledge of the agreements reached in the Palace, in order to assure with arms the victory at the polls that they believed was being stolen from them. Still, before the break of dawn on the eighth, the improvised besieging army got word that their blood would be spared so that they might struggle in work instead, and that the new [interim] ruler would put into effect on behalf of the people of Costa Rica that huge majority vote deposited in the coffer of suffrage.

To conclude, it is enough to point out that those who would have to relieve the forces of the barracks and the gendarmes were quickly chosen from among those citizens in arms. Within the space of a few hours the chosen changed the coat of the worker for the blouse of the armed soldier who defends rights and the law. Nevertheless, it was only when they were sure that the barracks troops in the other provinces had also surrendered their weapons to the Nation, that the people united in this capital put down their arms, after putting down their anger, in order to return in short order to their farm, work instruments clenched in hand, to extract from the breast of mother earth the juice that gives nourishment to the individuals of the State. It is worth noting that the only Costa Rican blood shed during this brief but riveting democratic drama was the generous blood of the Constitutional faction. Despite this, the winners wish only to see the losers as brothers.

An Outsider's View of

Political Society in 1914

Dana G. Munro

Dana Gardner Munro was an astute young student from the United States who spent time in Costa Rica in 1914. He witnessed the democratic opening of the new century. To read Munro's description today is jarring in that Costa Rican democracy as it existed in the early twentieth century looks surprisingly contemporary: essentially conservative, personalistic, lacking in clear or meaningful ideological choices, encompassing popular participation without the leadership necessarily responding to public opinion, but at the same time socially oriented in terms of public expenditures and with opportunities for social and political advancement.

The inhabitants of Costa Rica now enjoy more stable and more nearly democratic political institutions than any of their Central American neighbors. Constitutional government works in practice, and the letter of the law is generally respected, even though its spirit is often ingeniously circumvented. The president walks through the streets much like a private citizen, without fear of assassination or of being captured by his enemies, and the leaders of the opposition carry on their propaganda in San José without hindrance or persecution, and at times are even called in to consult with the president on matters of great importance. The press criticises the administration fearlessly and at times scurrilously, and animated political discussions may be heard every day on the principal corner of the main street of the capital. The elections are participated in by about as large a proportion of the entire population as in the United States. If one candidate receives a majority of the votes cast, he becomes president, and if no absolute choice is made by the people the question goes to the Congress, where it is decided by intrigues and deals between the political leaders. The administration is able to exert a decided influence in the selection of its successor through its control of the patronage and the army; but the final decision rests with the people or the popularly elected deputies, and it is not probable that any president would resort now to the forceful methods by which official candidates were placed in office a few decades ago. . . .

Government by the people, however, has not really advanced so far as the number of votes cast at the elections would seem to indicate, for the great majority of the Republic's inhabitants still take little interest in political affairs. So long as order is maintained and their property rights are secure, they do not care particularly which group of politicians is in control and they are guided in voting more by the inducements held out by the rival candidates than by their judgments. Personalities rather than questions of national policy are the issue, for it is rare that any candidate makes his campaign upon a definite political or economic platform. Between the elections, public opinion, although far more influential than in any of the other Central American countries, exercises little real control over the policy of the government. The newspapers are very widely read, and the people as a whole are remarkably well informed about current events, but the press nevertheless has comparatively little power, because no one believes in its impartiality or its incorruptibility.

The choice of candidates for public office and the conduct of the government are left almost entirely to a small number of landed proprietors, lawyers, physicians, and professional politicians residing in San José. These owe their influence partly to social position and wealth, but more especially to education; for although the members of the old principal families are still prominent, there are also many influential leaders who have risen from the lower classes by availing themselves of the educational advantages which the Republic offers to all its citizens. The ruling class is divided into a number of small political cliques, each of which professes allegiance to a party chief. As might be expected in an aristocracy composed chiefly of the leading people of a town of thirty thousand inhabitants, ties of blood and personal feeling play a very large part in the formation of these groups, especially as the prominent families are very large, and each is closely related with the others by intermarriage. A leader is often able to derive the major portion of his strength from his relatives alone, for the aid of ten or fifteen active and popular sons-in-law, together with that of several scores of brothers and cousins and nephews, is not to be despised in a country where there are at most only a few hundred active politicians. Besides his relatives and his intimate friends, however, each party chief has also a number of followers who are attached to him by the hope of obtaining employment in one of the government offices, for a very large number of persons among the upper class have little occupation aside from politics, and little income beyond that derived from official positions when their friends are in power.

The various leaders may have different political ideals and economic theories, which to some extent influence their relations to one another, but it can hardly be said that any of the present parties have definite principles or programs. Each desires primarily to win the elections in order to put its followers in office; and the platforms and the utterances of the leaders are shaped with this end in view, with the result that they receive little attention and less credence. When it is necessary in order to obtain control of the government, leaders of widely different points of view will join forces without any suspicion of inconsistency, and it is not a very uncommon occurrence for a prominent member of one party to join another and very different group, because of a quarrel with his former associates or simply because the change improves his chances of advancement. Sectional jealousy is no longer a force in politics, since the capital has so far outstripped the other towns in population and wealth, and religious questions are rarely injected into the campaign. Attempts have been made to organize a popular party among the laborers and peasants, and this party has achieved some notable successes at the polls, but its policy when in power is very similar to that of the other factions. There is in reality little ground for political rivalry between the different classes of the population.

The so-called parties have so little permanent organization that they can hardly be said to be in existence during the greater part of the presidential term. About a year before an election, the heads of the stronger groups, who are often perennial candidates, begin to organize their own followers, and to bargain for the support of the less powerful leaders, with a view to inaugurating their campaigns. Committees and clubs are organized in each town and village, and desperate efforts are made to secure the support of influential citizens who are not permanently affiliated with any party, and to arouse the interest of the voters in general. Processions and serenades are organized to show the popularity of each candidate, and orators are sent to every town and village on Sunday afternoons to entertain the voters with abuse and denunciation of the rival aspirants. Party newspapers are established, but they confine themselves to printing long lists of local committees and adherents and to describing meetings and ovations. One may search their columns in vain for serious discussion of the issues of the campaign. Several of the regular newspapers take sides more or less openly, while others maintain an ostensible neutrality, but the press as a whole seems to have little influence over the voters. As the contest progresses, feeling runs higher and higher among the politicians, and the voters become first interested and then excited. The meetings and ovations, the continual political arguments on the streets, resulting in an occasional riot, and the wholesale treating by the party workers in the drink-shops, distract the attention of the people from their ordinary occupations, and temporarily disorganize the entire community. Elections are therefore looked forward to with a certain amount of dread by the more respectable classes.

Since the adoption of the law of 1913, the President, the members of Congress, and the municipal *regidores* [councilmen] have been chosen by popular vote instead of by electoral colleges. The balloting takes place on the same day in all parts of the country. Each citizen must inscribe his choice in a book where all may read it, and every party has representatives at the polls to secure fair play. This system prevents fraudulent counting, but it also encourages corruption and the exercise of improper influence on the individual elector. Bribery is practiced openly and on a large scale by all parties, and the voter is often prevented from exercising his own discretion in casting his ballot by the fear of offending the local authorities or other powerful personages in his village. The amount of intimidation and coercion, however, is insignificant as compared with that in the other republics, and attempts to influence voters by such means are generally condemned by public opinion. The president is prevented by the constitution from seeking his own re-election, but one of his associates is usually frankly supported by the administration as the official candidate, and thus has an immense advantage over his opponents, even though recent presidents have refrained from using the army and the police to interfere with their enemies' campaigns or to keep the adherents of the opposition party away from the polls on election day.

The large supplies of money which are perhaps the most important factor in the campaign are obtained by contributions from members of the party, who hope to obtain offices for themselves or their friends in the event of a victory, and from native and foreign business men who desire special concessions. The banks of San José usually assist one candidate actively though secretly, and considerable amounts are also obtained from certain rich speculators, in return for favors contingent on the election of the candidate whom they support. Consequently a new administration comes into office bound by numerous more or less improper pledges, and burdened by a considerable party debt. After the election of 1913–14, the victorious group liquidated a portion of its financial obligations by a levy on all office-holders, who were presumably the chief beneficiaries of the party triumph.

The choice of the voters does not always inspire the respect which it would in a democracy more conscious of its power and more jealous of its rights. The people of Costa Rica have more than once shown that they were ready to compel respect for their will when their interests were at stake, but as a rule they are disposed to recognize any administration which controls the capital, regarding civil war, with its attendant destruction of crops and livestock, as a greater evil than submission to an illegal government. It is not strange, therefore, that a defeated faction should occasionally attempt to seize the barracks in San José by force or by strategy, or that the president should exact conditions from an opponent victorious in an election before turning over to him the command of the military forces. No candidate opposed by the government has ever obtained the presidency without either making a compromise with his predecessor or else overcoming the latter's resistance by force, for even the freely elected presidents of the last decade have in every case had the approval, if not the active support, of the previous administration. The strength of the government, however, in reality rests far less upon the army than upon the disapproval of the people as a whole of any attempt to displace the constituted authorities in a disorderly manner, for the army itself is almost insignificant as a military force. There are a few troops in the barracks of the capital, but elsewhere order is maintained entirely by the civil police. It is a proud boast of the Costa Ricans that their government employs more school teachers than soldiers.

The President of the Republic has an almost absolute control over the machinery of the government. He not only appoints all administrative officers, but also in practice exercises a dominant influence over the deliberations of the Congress, where his ministers initiate the most important legation. Even when his personal followers do not have a majority in the Chamber, he can usually command one by the use of patronage or of money from the treasury, which is often paid to the Deputies in the form of fees for professional services to the government. As party lines break down soon after an election, the minor political leaders who make up the legislative body are apt to be influenced less by hostility to the administration than by a desire to maintain their following in their own districts by securing public works for their towns and employment for their constituents. In times of emergency, moreover, the Congress itself frequently invests the President with practically absolute power, as it did when the country was passing through the economic crisis which followed the outbreak of the European war.

The Judicial Department, however, is far more nearly independent of the Executive. The Supreme Court, which is elected by the Congress every four years during the political slack season in the middle of the presidential term, appoints and removes all subordinate magistrates throughout the Republic. Politics enters very little into the composition of this body, partly because of the strong sentiment in favor of a non-partisan judiciary, and partly because party lines are almost non-existent at the time when the judges are chosen. The subordinate positions are also saved from the spoils system which rules in other departments of the government, although it is inevitable that purely personal considerations should enter to some extent into the appointments.

The administration of justice is on the whole prompt and efficient, although the magistrates are not always distinguished for erudition or ability and those on the supreme bench sometimes show a human desire to make sure of their re-election as the time for this draws near, by keeping on good terms with the President and with the members of Congress. They are generally honest and impartial in their decisions, however, and their incorruptibility, with hardly any exceptions, is undoubted. That not only the people themselves but also foreigners in the country have confidence in the courts is shown by the fact that there has been a conspicuous lack of the complaints of denial of justice which have complicated the relations of some other Latin American republics.

The local administration is highly centralized, but the people of each district enjoy a certain amount of local self-government through their municipalities. The representatives of the central government are the executive officers of these bodies, and the Department of *Gobernación* [the Interior] has a final veto over all their acts, but the regidores are freely elected by the people of each town and village, and have very wide powers in matters of purely local interest. The lack of funds, however, arising from the fact that the municipalities have no source of revenue except certain license fees and fees for public services, forces them to leave to the central government many of the functions which are assigned to them by the constitution, and especially the support and direction of almost all the more costly public works, and at the same time makes them politically subservient to the President and the Congress, which can provide or with-hold appropriations for local purposes. President Alfredo González attempted to make the local units truly autonomous, by authorizing them, in the fiscal legislation passed just before his fall, to levy direct taxes upon their inhabitants by adding a percentage to the national direct taxes. . . .

An examination of the work of the government shows that the men who control the destinies of the Republic, however regrettable their political methods sometimes are, do not seek power solely for their own profit. If there is a large amount of favoritism and graft in official circles, there is also much progressive spirit and true patriotism. Most of the government employees are appointed for political reasons, but they ordinarily perform their duties with as much energy and zeal as can be expected in tropical America. Public money is often misused and improper considerations sometimes govern the letting of contracts, but public works are nevertheless well executed. Wholesale theft from the treasury, which is too often regarded with cynical indifference in other parts of the Isthmus, would not be tolerated by public opinion in Costa Rica.

Democrats and Feminists

Steven Palmer and Gladys Rojas Chaves

In 1917, the government of Alfredo González Flores was overthrown by the military, in part because it had introduced progressive banking and taxation measures to alleviate a severe economic crisis. The ensuing dictatorship of the Tinoco brothers, important members of the Costa Rican coffee oligarchy, resorted to increasingly repressive measures to maintain itself in power. But in June 1919, a popular mobilization led by women educators and normal school students in the capital city succeeded in breaking the back of the Tinoco dictatorship. The Colegio de Señoritas had been founded in 1889 to train schoolteachers for the new public education system; its staff, students, and alumni played a central role in the protests of June 1919 and in the subsequent founding of the Costa Rican Feminist League.

The international context was one of popular rebellion. A university reform movement was sweeping through Latin America, sparked in 1918 by students in Córdoba, Argentina. The Russian Revolution and the widespread socialist rebellion and labor militancy of the postwar period were also making their mark in Latin America. It was fitting, then, that the popular rebellion against the Tinoco dictatorship ignited during a conference for schoolteachers featuring the Argentine educator and labor leader Julio Barcos, when a woman teacher stood up to denounce the political persecution she had suffered for being a member of the same family as some of the rebels. The floodgates of criticism were opened, and that night plans were made to create a national association of educators to protect the rights of teachers and to lobby for more education funding. The Tinoco regime responded by summoning the directors of all the country's secondary schools and demanding that they circulate a form that educators could sign in order to voluntarily donate a portion of their salary to the war effort. The threat was clear.

The forms went up on the walls of educational institutions, one for those who wished to collaborate, one for those who wished to dissent. After some hesitation, the first two to sign what came to be declarations against the military regime were school inspectors José Guerrero and Esther de Mezzerville, the first a former teacher of the Colegio de Señoritas, and the second a distinguished graduate of the institution. The majority of the country's leading educators in San José and at the normal school in Heredia followed suit. The dictatorship retaliated by ordering schools and colleges closed in order to facilitate a "reorganization of personnel." Students from the Liceo de Costa Rica, the elite male secondary school, marched to the Colegio de Señoritas in support of the teachers, but police dispersed the protest. That night, the regime sent military police to prevent a meeting where the national teacher's association was to be formed.

The following day it was announced that the school year was suspended and that there were plans to eliminate school inspectors, dismiss personnel, and raise the salaries of the remainder (in other words, to reward those who supported the regime). This time it was the students of the Colegio de Señoritas who initiated the march to San José's Morazán Park, joined by teachers, students from other schools, and workers. The core of the marchers—the students of the Colegio—was a fairly representative expression of San José society. Enrollment records from the time tell us that virtually all students came from the capital and that one quarter of them were of working-class extraction, while about a third were of professional or white-collar families. The strong contingent of girls from artisan families sheds new light on the adhesion to the march by the city's popular classes, since the revolt is often represented as one led heroically by a middle-class intelligentsia, backed by a faceless mob. The presence of this female working-class contingent among the protagonists also suggests that these anti-Tinoco street protests formed part of the same wave of working-class militancy that peaked less than a year later in the successful strikes in favor of the eight-hour day.

Some of the more audacious of the students addressed the crowd from the kiosk in Morazán Park. The police used physical force to stop them from speaking, but women teachers defended the girls, and the fight was on. Fire hoses were used to disperse the crowd, which reformed and continued the protest by marching to the US Legation, only to be broken up again, this time by machine-gun fire. The next day, the students of the Liceo marched to their sister school once more, quickly generating a popular throng that would finish their protest by burning the installations of the pro-regime newspaper, *La Información*, and skirmishing with police and soldiers at the cost of numerous dead and wounded.

The normal school in Heredia was the symbol and center of a masculine democratic radicalism because of the numerous young male intellectuals who taught there. But it was the women students, teachers, and graduates of the Co-

Colegio de Señoritas students march c. 1927 in solidarity with Nicaragua, then occupied by the US Marines. (Archivo Colegio Superior de Señoritas)

legio de Señoritas who played the leading role in organizing the resistance that finally broke the back of the dictatorship, which collapsed less than two months later in August of 1919. Indeed, their heroic leadership of the urban protest movement was so widely recognized that it almost won women the right to vote. Julio Acosta had led an armed resistance to the regime based in Nicaragua. During his successful campaign for the presidency in 1920, women's suffrage was part of the former rebel leader's platform. The leading role of educated and educator women in the ouster of the Tinocos was underlined by students of the Colegio in June 1923, when they presented a petition in favor of female suffrage to the national congress, arguing that "through the instruction of many women, a large number of significant projects has been realized in our country; it was the virile activity of these women that made it possible on one occasion to overthrow a tyranny." The audacity and novelty of this act should be underlined: these *normalistas* [normal school students] were declaring on the country's main political stage that it was legitimate—and even necessary for the democratic life of the republic—for women to assume a virile public stance.

Partially out of resentment for the public emasculation of the patriarchal order in 1919, the petition was only the first of many in favor of female suffrage to be ignored by the male congress, despite a great deal of lip service from leading political figures in favor of granting the vote to women. Nevertheless, on 12 October 1923 (the anniversary of Colón's "discovery" of the New World), the Liga Feminista Costarricense (Costa Rican Feminist League) was officially formed at a ceremony in the hall of the Colegio de Señoritas, attended by President Acosta and the first lady, Elenita Gallegos. Its first board was made up of the director of the Colegio, Esther de Mezzerville, the institution's most academically distinguished graduate, Ángela Acuña (though, interestingly, a Tinoco regime sympathizer), and its physical education teacher, Ana Rosa de Chacón. Among the rank and file was a contingent of schoolteachers, many of them graduates of the institution.

The league was formed during a particularly active period in Latin American suffragism. Although, as we have seen, women's suffrage had been placed high atop the national agenda due to dramatic local political circumstances, the Costa Rican movement did emerge out of the Western network of suffragism. Ángela Acuña had spent some years in France and England following her graduation from the Colegio in 1907, and she had been inspired by the activities of the English suffragettes in particular. On returning to Costa Rica in 1912, she became the first woman to enroll in the Liceo, with an eye to gaining access to the College of Law, which she did in 1916. She became the leading proponent of women's emancipation, her essays were published in the press, and though from an elite background, she spoke frequently on the plight of the woman worker. In 1922, both Acuña and the conservative Catholic suffragist Sara Casal de Quirós attended the Conference of the League of Voting Women in Baltimore, prior to going on to the Panamerican Women's Conference in New York City. In both meetings, they met with Latin American and US feminists, including the Uruguayan Paulina Luisi and the head of the League of Voting Women, Carrie Chapman Catt (who would later tour South America to help promote women's suffrage organizations). The immediate organizational link, however, was Iberoamerican rather than Pan-American: the Liga Feminista Costarricense was founded as a local chapter of the International League of Iberian and Hispanoamerican Women.

The founding of the Liga Feminista in the hall of the Colegio de Señoritas gave dramatic expression to the real and symbolic link between the institution and women's emancipation. The presence of the president of the republic at that act underlines the extraordinary degree of political legitimacy that women had achieved in Costa Rica by the 1920s, although the battle for women's suffrage would not be won despite such a promising conjuncture. Though the Liga Feminista was unsuccessful in its primary goal of winning the franchise for women, the organization—and the Colegio de Señoritas more broadly—had forever transformed women's public roles. In 1928, from his Paris exile,

Federico Tinoco would poetically express the sense of betrayal felt by the patriarchs who had created this institution without realizing its radical potential. He wrote that in June 1919 teachers and students had transformed the streets of the capital into a garden, "but like roses in an unusual outburst of anger, they stuck their thorns into the heart of the governor, leaving the beauty of their petals and their fragrant aroma and carrying in their flower tomorrow's innocent seed to be spilled in the odious terrain of the imagination."

Women's Vote — the Day

That They Get It

Paco Hernández

"Women's Vote —
the Day That They
Get It," cartoon by
Paco Hernández
(*Diario de Costa Rica*,
15 July 1923)

In 1925, there was another discussion of a possible electoral reform to enshrine the secret ballot and the vote for women. The introduction of the secret ballot modified the institutional framework in which the political parties had competed up to that point and increased the margins of uncertainty in the presidential elections of 1928. Given these circumstances, passing women's suffrage into law as well would have practically doubled the size of the electorate and increased even further the uncertainty in the midterm elections of 1925 and the presidential race of 1928. So, even though sexist prejudices weighed in the failure to approve the vote for women (as the caricature reveals only too well), the basic reasons had more to do with electoral calculations. The propitious political moment passed, women's suffrage organizations waned, and Costa Rican women did not get the vote until 1949.

Hail to the Jefe

Alejandro Alvares Duartes Mora

Even though the United States did not intervene militarily in Costa Rica as it did in so many other countries in Central America and the Caribbean during the first half of the twentieth century, US influence was palpable: to the north was US-occupied Nicaragua (1912–34), to the south was the Panama Canal Zone, and inside Costa Rica, the United Fruit Company clearly expressed the economic interests of the United States. The omnipresence of US imperial power is the reference point for this letter, mailed to the US diplomatic mission in San José and duly forwarded to Washington for the consideration of higher officials in the State Department.

16 June 1937

Dear Mr. President of the United States, Eye rite to you, Mr. President, hoping that you will be good enuff to back me in my campaign to win the government of Costa Rica. helped by the American and put In the Presidency of Costa Rica by the American Government to suppress the Red flagg of [the Communist leader] Manuel Mora.... Eye hope that the President of the United States will immediately send a plane to Liberia [capital of the province of Guanacaste] to bring me now In these days of June to Go and discus national affairs with the government of the United States.

Your close friend

Alejandro Alvares Duartes Mora
Liberia

Unlikely Threesome

Reformist Summit, 1943

(Archivo Nacional de Costa Rica)

With the growing division of the National Republican Party into two personalist factions, one around the figure of Dr. Rafael Ángel Calderón Guardia, the other around ex-president León Cortés, the former skillfully played the social reform card to gain electoral advantage, allying with Archbishop Sanabria and with the Communists (against whom the reform had originally been directed). The photograph shows the unlikely reform troika, (from left to right) Communist Party leader Manuel Mora, Sanabria, and Calderón, at an Independence Day celebration in 1943.

The Polarization of Politics, 1932–1948

Iván Molina

It is difficult to provide a comprehensive yet brief explanation of the causes of the 1948 civil war. The breach was sudden, uncharacteristic, and relatively short-lived, yet the forces at work were sprawling, contradictory, and a very long time coming. Many explanations concentrate on the dictatorial tendencies of Calderón Guardia and his insistence on social reform and an alliance with Communists even as the cold war set in. Others magnify the role of the Figueres camp prior to 1948 to make its victory seem much more preordained than it was. Explanations from the Left propose that 1948 was a social conflict: a growing working class committed to a Communist Party allied with a reformist fraction of the bourgeoisie caused a backlash from the reactionary oligarchy. The following explanation takes the long view of a series of mutations that polarized Costa Rican political society and gave legitimacy to the violent political challenge of José Figueres and his followers.

In 1931, seeking an unprecedented third term in the presidency, Ricardo Jiménez organized the National Republican Party (PRN). Voters welcomed Jiménez's charisma and integrity at the peak of the depression: the party received almost 50 percent of the votes in 1932 and would become increasingly dominant for the remainder of the decade, augmenting its share of the vote in each subsequent midterm and presidential election all the way through to Calderón's victory in 1940. The architect of this political success was León Cortés, a lawyer with anticommunist and profascist leanings, who served in the Jiménez cabinet as secretary of public works. After he became president in 1936, Cortés, between 1936 and 1939, invested 36 percent of the national budget in building roads, bridges, and a health and education infrastructure, allowing him to consolidate support in the rural areas, especially those of the Central Valley.

The PRN presidential candidate for the 1939 campaign was Dr. Rafael Ángel Calderón Guardia, who had a strong link with the Catholic sector of his party. Cortés backed Calderón's candidacy with one condition: Calderón had to help Cortés get reelected in 1944. Calderón was elected with a whopping 82.5 percent of the vote and assumed the presidency in 1940. Confrontation with the Cortés camp began when Calderón showed his intention to consolidate his own hold on power, and it reached the point of open breach in May 1941 when Calderonistas voted their man, Teodoro Picado, into the key post of president of the congress instead of supporting the Cortesista candidate. After this challenge, Cortés decided to leave the PRN and initiate a campaign to discredit the government, taking advantage of the economic difficulties associated with World War II.

From 1932 to 1942, then, Costa Rican political elites had displayed an overwhelming tendency toward unity in the PRN, and the voters had backed this to the point of making the country a one-party system. The minor exception to this rule came in the form of the Communist Bloque de Obreros y Campesinos (BOC), or Workers' and Peasants' Bloc, which had provided the only serious opposition to the PRN in the midterm elections of 1938 and 1942 and in the presidential election of 1940. Though the BOC could not rival the PRN, it had gradually increased its share of the popular vote until it reached 16.3 percent in 1942. Now came an unexpected turn: the Communists began to negotiate an alliance with Calderón's PRN, both with an eye on the 1944 presidential elections. The Communist interest in this alliance had a decisive electoral background. Calderón had introduced his social reform: the creation of social security, establishment of the Labor Code, and a chapter in the constitution on social guarantees. The social reforms, part of a strategy to secure support from workers and to attract urban voters away from the Communists, challenged the electoral fortunes of a Communist Party that had committed itself to a democratic route to power. An alliance with a government committed to social reform would allow the Communists to promote social policies as part of the government. On their end, Calderonistas secured the patronage of a minor party that had disciplined and organized support from the banana workers, as well as from urban artisans and wage laborers, as they prepared for their 1944 showdown with Cortés and his new party.

The BOC dissolved and reorganized in 1943 as a (formally noncommunist) party called Vanguardia Popular (Popular Vanguard). The pro-reform archbishop Víctor Manuel Sanabria could then endorse this alliance and even encourage Catholics to support it and get involved. This endorsement also reflected the relations between the Catholic establishment and the PRN hierarchy since the PRN had built its agenda on the social doctrine of the Catholic Church and promoted the repeal of nineteenth-century liberal anticlerical legislation. Therefore, in a context in which the United States and the USSR were allies in the fight against Nazism, in Costa Rica Communists and Calderonistas participated in the 1944 presidential elections as a coalition. Calderón himself could not be reelected, but he was now the dominant player in the PRN. He supported Teodoro Picado as the PRN candidate in 1944, but continued to exercise influence behind the scenes and prepare for his return to the presidency in 1948.

The PRN-Communist coalition handily beat Cortés's Democratic Party in the 1944 elections, but the opposition denounced their triumph as a result of fraud, insisting that the elections "constituted a coup d'état perpetrated by President Rafael Ángel Calderón Guardia and a group of politicians and falsifiers of votes that on this occasion annihilated the right of the people to choose a ruler for itself." The charge was based more on faith and sour grapes than on evidence. Formal mechanisms existed for challenging tallies believed to be fraudulent, but the opposition appealed the results in only 30 of the 324 districts. Even had all those votes proved tainted, the electoral fraud could not have explained Picado's impressive victory: 66 percent of the votes, against 34 percent for Cortés. Former president Ricardo Jiménez thought the difference "impossible to explain through barter and coercion on a big scale," instead suggesting that "the popular sectors supported Picado's political group because it promised not only to continue policies that could be beneficial for them but also to broaden them." It was in the same 1944 interview that he famously commented: "How many surprises elections offer when it comes to a single man, alone with his conscience or with his convenience, voting the way he wants. That is why the ballot box always holds the unexpected."

A similar story was played out after the 1946 midterm elections, with the PRN-Communist alliance winning 56 percent of the vote for congressional deputies and the opposition crying fraud but failing to present credible evidence that fraud had been decisive in changing the electoral result. And yet Costa Rican society increasingly believed that fraud played a significant role in its electoral life—something that would prove crucial in giving legitimacy to Figueres's armed rebellion after the presidential elections of 1948. There are a number of reasons for this widespread belief, beginning with the fact that the opposition systematically accused the Calderón and Picado administrations of corruption and disorder, of engaging in dictatorial methods, and of being dominated by the Communists. The PRN-Communist alliance resulted in political differences being portrayed in terms of increasingly sharp ideological distinctions, especially as the cold war dawned.

As far as the actual practice of fraud is concerned, the 1940s did see a marked change in patterns. Prior to 1940, the majority of accusations of fraud, and the most serious (coercion of voters, votes emitted by foreigners, votes by underage citizens, and ballots cast by the dead), came from Guanacaste, Puntarenas and Limón—peripheries populated by ethnically distinct minorities located on the margins of national political life. But in the 1944 and 1946 elections, the majority of denunciations came from San José, Cartago, Alajuela, and Heredia—areas that concentrated over 70 percent of the electorate. The residents of these provinces considered themselves respectable, well-educated, white citizens who were small and medium property owners or independent workers. They witnessed the proliferation of a phenomenon that up to then had only been frequent in marginal areas populated by poor peasants and agricultural workers, with high levels of illiteracy and visible indigenous or African heritage. This shift in the geographic patterns of fraud, so damaging to the dominant political culture's sense of legitimacy, explains why growing confrontation between political parties after 1942 resulted in deteriorating electoral practices magnified by the press and the opposition.

In this atmosphere of political decadence, the opposition itself split into two factions. One faction was led by León Cortés, who sought a return to the presidency by means of elections or a political transaction. The second faction was led by José Figueres Ferrer, who insisted on a civil war as the only way to emancipate Costa Rica. Figueres had spoken out strongly against Calderón's style of government in a radio speech in 1942 (while wartime censorship restrictions were in force), something which earned him a period of exile. A year after his 1944 return, he founded a political party called the Social Democratic Party and incorporated into its ranks a group of reformist social democratic intellectuals who had begun a think tank called the Center for the Study of National Problems. Although they wanted political and economic modernization for Costa Rica, and were committed to certain aspects of European-style socialism (especially a large technical and economic role for the state), they were deeply anticommunist and very much against Calderón's style of personalist and patronage-steeped government. While in exile, moreover, Figueres had forged links with antidictatorial groups from other Latin American countries, and he shared with them a willingness to take up arms to destabilize dictatorial regimes and create political space for reform. Starting in 1945, the Figueres faction carried out a series of terrorist acts that intensified in 1947. Its emphasis on the military option is explained by the fact that this faction had very little electoral support and that they could only achieve power by means of disrupting the constitutional order.

During the four years of his administration from 1944 to 1948, Picado tried to resist the increasing polarization through a conciliatory policy, and in 1946 he promoted the approval of the so-called Electoral Code, which separated the organization and supervision of the electoral process from the executive branch and put the power to resolve disputes concerning elections in the hands of an independent National Electoral Tribunal. Then, in March 1946, the great opposition leader León Cortés died quite unexpectedly, and along with him died an ongoing process in which governing party moderates and the opposition tried to achieve an understanding. Within a few months Figueres was condemning negotiations, and by February 1947, the opposition had designated as their candidate Otilio Ulate, an archconservative and anticommunist businessman who had contributed to the conflict's polarization from the pages of his newspaper, *Diario de Costa Rica*. The tension between the groups that favored Picado's administration and those backing the opposition led to the *Huelga de Brazos Caídos* (sit-down strike), a stoppage promoted by employers between 23 July and 3 August 1947. The strike basically asked the government for electoral guarantees. This movement ended when the major political groups compromised and accepted that the new National Electoral Tribunal's decision concerning the upcoming February 1948 presidential elections would be definite and not subject to appeal.

There were no important incidents in the elections held on 8 February 1948, and official results suggested a convincing victory for Ulate and the opposition. Nevertheless, the next day Calderón Guardia, who had run as planned as the PRN candidate, refused to recognize the results and claimed that his opponents had practiced systematic fraud. On 28 February, the National Electoral Tribunal provisionally declared Otilio Ulate president. Meanwhile, Calderón presented a demand to have congress annul the elections. On 1 March, the congress, overwhelmingly Calderonista and Communist in composition, accepted the demand and started an intense lobby to try to find a negotiated end to the conflict. But on 12 March, Figueres began his armed uprising in the southern part of the province of San José. This was supposedly in defense of the February electoral results, even though Figueres had signed the so-called Pact of the Caribbean with rebel exile groups from other countries on 16 December 1947, committing signatories to support efforts to overthrow the dictators in the region. The civil war was on.

Costa Rica's armed forces were already weakened by almost thirty years of underfunding and neglect, and they soon fell apart in the face of Figueres's rebel army (which had been reinforced and supplied by foreign supporters, exile groups, and professional soldiers of fortune). The Communists stepped into the breach and organized a disciplined force of working-class militias made up of urban workers and agricultural laborers (the so-called mariachis). Calderonista supporters also answered the call to irregular arms, while supporters of the opposition joined the ranks of those fighting under the command of Figueres. After five weeks of nasty fighting, especially in Cartago, a final battle for San José (still held by Calderón and the Communist militias) was averted through mediation by members of the international diplomatic community.

The outbreak of conflict had not stopped negotiations among the main electoral contenders, proving that the political elites did not pay full attention to it at the outset. In late March, when Calderón Guardia and Ulate agreed that Dr. Julio César Ovares could serve as compromise candidate and assume the presidency for two years, Figueres rejected the deal and intensified the conflict. Figueres only achieved the capacity to negotiate when his Army of National Liberation captured the cities of Cartago and Limón on 11 and 12 April, and after the bloody *Batalla del Tejar* (Battle of Tejar, Cartago), fought on 13 April. These battles were the prelude to a new set of negotiations in which Figueres's presence proved decisive. The Pact of the Mexican Embassy (Pacto de la Embajada de México) was signed on 19 April, and on 1 May, Figueres and Ulate agreed that an executive council, or interim junta, would govern for eighteen months, but without congress and with Figueres at its head. In return for control over a provisional government, Figueres had agreed to respect the social reforms, maintain the legality of the Communist Party, and respect the lives and positions of Calderón and his backers. But once the Executive Council assumed power on 8 May 1948, it broke the last two promises and systematically persecuted Calderonistas and Communists, driving Calderón and thousands of his supporters into exile.

On the surface, Figueres had been fighting to defend Ulate's electoral victory. In this sense he represented the forces of reaction against those of social reform. However, his own ideological position remained quite distinct, and he now had the upper hand. Instead of handing power over to Ulate, he called a national convention to write a new constitution for what he grandly called the "Second Republic." In the meantime, he would be president of the provisional junta that would oversee a transitional period during which order would be restored to the country. Only then, with a new constitution, would Ulate become president. Figueres was able to push through a number of important reforms prior to restoring the presidency to Ulate in 1949. Indeed, his Executive Council implemented a vast institutional transformation which laid the foundations of contemporary Costa Rica. Among them were the nationalization of the banks and the abolition of the army. Significantly, neither Figueres nor the constituent assembly tried to roll back Calderón's social reforms. Social security and labor guarantees had become surprisingly entrenched in the fibers of Costa Rican political culture in a very short time (though they had not been very enthusiastically received at the time of their implementation), and electoral interests stopped even conservatives from proposing their elimination.

Many people had feared that Figueres would himself become a dictator, but even if he had entertained such ideas, the balance of forces was not in his favor. Ulate's supporters won an enormous majority in the constituent assembly. After leaving power in 1949, Figueres and his closest associates concentrated their attention on founding a social democratic political party that could serve as a successful electoral vehicle. The resulting Party of National Liberation would become the country's dominant political force from Figueres's first electoral victory in 1953 until the party's decline in fortunes in the 1990s. In the process, they built up one of Latin America's most comprehensive welfare states. So, although the civil war emerged out of a bitter conservative backlash against a Communist-backed reformer, and though the latter was decisively defeated, the reform process Calderón had initiated remained intact and was extended in many directions by the political faction most responsible for his defeat. The 1948 elections and the civil war remain polemical issues. Recent research on the 1948 election strongly suggests that Calderón Guardia was deprived of the presidency through electoral fraud committed by oppositionists who managed to deny thousands of Calderón supporters their right to vote.

Memories of Girlhood in '48

María E. Robles Solano

The civil war of 1948 was a bloody affair that aroused deep hatreds and left many people displaced and grieving. Surprisingly, almost all the literature on the conflict has concentrated on its political and ideological dimensions. The following testimonial, written in 1998 on the occasion of the war's fiftieth anniversary, provides one moving description of how the conflict was lived by ordinary civilians.

In March 1948 I was ready to start sixth grade at Jesús Jiménez School, but because of the events that took place the school year did not start until May.

I still live on the same site in Cartago where I lived in '48—just south of the Courthouse, once known as the Plaza de la Soledad—but in a new house. My old family house was spacious, with walls of wood and wattle, and a door made of colored glass that all of us kids really liked. I remember a large dining room that was undergoing repairs, where there were a lot of bricks piled up. During the days of the civil war, they served as a place where I and my sisters took refuge during the tremendous gunfights that broke out and that struck such fear in us.

We were a family of six children, three older than I, and two younger. My father was a telegraphist, my mother a schoolteacher, and an uncle on my father's side who was also a teacher. Politics were always a topic of discussion around the house, and ever since I was little, I was used to hearing the older ones comment on all the political goings-on in the country. And so I knew of things like the deaths in Llano Grande and La Ceiba [places in Cartago and Alajuela where people were killed after the election of 1944], the voting irregularities, and the disturbances that took place here in Cartago during the Sit-Down Strike, which also form part of my childhood memories. Around the house they were saying that as a result of all these things the people were going to react with nonpeaceful means, and that meant a civil struggle in the not-too-distant future.

Because of my age, I was not able to see clearly the way that the impact of these events was dividing families, some loyal to the government of the day and others suffering persecution by that government, but in the conversations that were going on around the house and with people who dropped by for a visit, I picked up on these resentments.

During the months of March and April of '48 there were a lot of rumors about the approaching civil war. I remember that handwritten pamphlets circulated from person to person. They said that in the mountains to the south of Cartago an army was being formed to overthrow the government. I heard my parents talk about boys, sons of relatives and friends, who left surreptitiously in the middle of the night to join the movement, and I heard them say that the commander of this army was José Figueres.

I also recall that dad was on a committee in charge of stockpiling basic food-stuffs, which were stored in different houses in preparation for the shortages that would occur when the Revolution broke out.

Of the anecdotes that I have deeply etched in my mind about the final weeks of March and the first ones of April, I remember the house contiguous to ours, where some old women lived along with a granddaughter of one of them who was my age, and with whom I had enjoyed a friendship of many years. A little olive grove divided the two houses and marked the limit of the two properties, and through it we could go from one house to the other without going out onto the street. That house became a meeting place for the neighbors since the women had a small radio, and on its shortwave band they tuned into the clandestine frequency that transmitted messages and made announcements about the arrival of the troops, obviously without giving names. One funny message heard on the radio circulated around the neighborhood: "Hello, Tamarind Seed has arrived all right; greetings to Red Pepper." Tamarind Seed was the code name for a neighbor of ours, and Red Pepper was the name of other neighbors who were followers of the government.

I remember another funny thing that took place in the middle of all the distress. It happened one afternoon when the neighbors were gathered around the radio and the kids were playing in the hallway. One of the older ladies, who we fondly called "Auntie," had stayed in bed because of her age. Suddenly someone said "Police!" This was enough for everyone to be seized with fear, and they put us kids inside the house and told us not to make a sound. In the nervous state that they were in, one of them had the idea to tell the old woman, "Auntie, play dead." Their idea was that the police would think we were waking her and that this was the reason for the gathering. They arranged the bed and the old lady obediently closed her eyes and started breathing very lightly and without making a sound. The next few minutes were very tense as we waited for the police to arrive. There was great surprise, and later laughs, when one single policeman appeared, mounted on a skinny horse and laboring under a strong afternoon sun, and passed by the house without even throwing it a glance. Of course, Auntie revived instantly.

Everyone was jumpy those days. You couldn't go out at night for fear of police patrols, and on top of that, there was a curfew after 6 P.M.

I remember very well that dawn on the twelfth of April 1948, when before first light we were awoken by a plane engine and later a distant noise that gradually became more perceptible. They were gunshots, and a little later we were startled by the boom of cannon fire.

We didn't know what was happening; we were very afraid; Dad came to the bedroom and told us to put the mattresses on the floor. Mom and the littlest ones, we cried with fright. A little later we heard voices and shouts of "Viva José Figueres, long live the Second Republic," and the shots seemed very close. When the older ones in the family confirmed that the troops were those of Figueres, they became happy despite the fear that still gripped all of us; Dad and my uncle, forgetting the gunfight that was raging, went out onto the street to greet the first troops to arrive, inviting them into the house for coffee. I remember them as very tired, with blue bandanas, a lot of beard, dust covering their clothes and shoes.

When the early hours of the morning had passed, a sad piece of news arrived at the house. A neighbor, a man who belonged to a family that had always been near and dear to ours, had been hit by the bullets. It was a huge blow for everyone. He was a farmer, and he customarily woke at the crack of dawn each day to make his way to the finca north of Cartago; the gunfire was very heavy, and he had died caught in the crossfire on a corner two blocks from his house.

After this news that so affected the family, we spent a worried day, since the shots did not cease. During the afternoon, we heard that the Colegio San Luis Gonzaga had been taken by Don Pepe and that it was now the headquarters for the Army of Liberation. The night was more worrisome; I think they had cut the electricity off because I remember we illuminated the place with candlelight, we slept on the mattresses that were still on the floor, huddled tightly and praying a lot together with my mom.

The next day, Tuesday, is etched in my memory as one of the events that most terrified me of all the things I remember from my childhood. That was the afternoon of the famous Battle of El Tejar, an all-out confrontation of the government and the Liberation troops.

The gun battle, although somewhat distant, was terrible. We all stayed in the house, hardly moving. At the same time as the battle was being waged, a huge fire broke out here in the center of Cartago, in the block exactly to the south of the barracks. I remember that from the yard of my house, I saw the plumes of smoke, they seemed like cauliflowers as they billowed up and gave off large flames; it was a block with a lot of businesses, and it burned easily. While we were enduring that bit of anxious business, one of my dad's cousins showed up at the house with his son because the fire had broken out in the block next to their house, and they'd had to abandon it. They arrived in tears, terribly upset, since the night of the eleventh of April my dad's cousin's brother and another son had been detained after finishing work in their bakery, and they had been locked up in the prison. I remember they had a white napkin in their hands, which they waved as a symbol of peace. They stayed with us while the civil war lasted.

Someone had given Mom a basket filled with peas in the pod, and since food was scarce we had to make use of them, and I and my little sister were given the job of shelling them. I remember that we set ourselves up behind the bricks in the dining room, frightened to death, since we could sense more than once bullets ricocheting off the roof of the house, as guns were being fired crossways over the house, with Figueres's troops to the south of the city and the government soldiers situated in the barracks and the ministry offices, which in those days were on the corner across from the Bárcena store (today the Rayo Azul supermarket).

The days of anguish and uncertainty continued until the civil war ended. In our house it was said that there were many dead on both sides. I remember my father, my older brother, and the daughter of my cousin who was in the house went to help with office work in the Colegio San Luis Gonzaga, where Figueres's headquarters were. We were still worried, especially mom, since in order to get to the Colegio you had to cross the mouth of the road that led directly to the barracks, and from where they were constantly firing. When they returned to the house, they would tell us that they crossed from one street corner to the other practically on their hands and knees for fear of the gunfire. I recall that in the house we had a puppy called Moro, who was their loyal friend every time they went to the Colegio—he went out happily to accompany them, and there was no way to keep him in the house.

About the last days of the civil war I don't remember what happened very clearly, except for a vague impression of the celebrations that broke out in Cartago. What I really wanted was for everything to end so that I could go back to normal, everyday life; I think all the kids felt the same way. We wanted to go outside, sleep in our beds, eat the things we liked, go back to school and talk with our schoolmates and our friends, and play. Finally, we just wanted to do all the things that were part of the life of a child.

Fifty years have passed since the events took place. I feel very sentimental about those memories. A lot of the people who lived them with me, family, friends, and neighbors alike, are no longer alive. It was an extraordinarily difficult time that forced maturity on my childhood, marked a very definite stage in my life, and I think in the life of all those who lived it.

Democracy on the Brink:

The First Figueres Presidency

Kirk Bowman

How did the pieces of the democratic puzzle get put back together after '48? Scholars have largely avoided the question, with an unspoken assumption that because the opposition to Calderón was fighting for democracy and against electoral fraud, naturally they resumed and perfected the democratic path after winning the war. Recently, political scientist Kirk Bowman has explored with fresh eyes the explosive newspaper wars of the post–civil war period and interviewed many of the surviving key political players of the era. The results of his investigations underscore the tremendous political instability of the 1950s, and the real threat that the United States might intervene to thwart Figueres's social democratic agenda. Though the importance of Figueres's famous abolition of the army in 1949 has often been dismissed as more symbolic than real, Bowman sees the absence of generals as key to the bootstrapping of democracy after the civil war.

The Costa Rican national myth of a democratic, egalitarian, consensual, pacific, and homogeneous culture both contributed to and was enhanced by the account of a quick return to stable democracy in the post-1948 era. Many political scientists have argued that the 1948 civil war constituted a minor blip on the Costa Rican democratic path and that the willingness of José Figueres and Otilio Ulate to alternate power after that violent engagement ushered in the foundation of consolidated political democracy. Yet the evidence is unambiguous: elites were willing to employ force throughout the 1950s to overthrow elected politicians.

During the four years of the Ulate administration, Figueres and his supporters were busy trying to regroup from their two electoral disasters in 1948 and 1949. The Party for National Liberation (PLN, or Liberación), founded in 1951, was soon organized throughout the country. It was a programmatic party, with a very specific platform supporting strong state intervention to spread economic benefits and to curtail the power of foreign capital. Figueres knew that he had to develop support within the United States, and he spent a great deal of time traveling and giving speeches. Don Pepe (as he was popularly known) had spent some years in Boston in his youth, read the *New York Times* daily, had an American wife, and could quote Thomas Jefferson and John Locke. He charmed many US officials, but his blunt talk made others bristle. Figueres developed allies in the U.S. Senate, in the American Federation of Labor (AFL), within the important liberal group Americans for Democratic Action (ADA), and in some members of the State Department.

The CIA and elements of the State Department, however, were highly dubious of Figueres. During a 1952 trip to the United States, Figueres announced that "we do not want foreign investment." He equated foreign investment in important sectors of the economy with economic occupation: "This is not a fantasy. I know of what I am speaking. I am a citizen of a banana republic." Figueres also raised a few eyebrows when he criticized US foreign policy: "Militarism and graft are perfectly acceptable to the US in our relationships with you as long as your men in power pay lip service to our side in the world struggle and we see to it that foreign investments are properly respected." The United Fruit Company (UFCO) expressed concerns over Figueres after he stated in a 1952 public interview that long-term contracts could be broken if breaking them served the interests of the country.

Despite the meager showing of Figueristas at the polls in 1948–49 and the ascendancy of Ulate to the presidency, many of the country's elites viewed Figueres as a continual threat. Indeed, don Pepe looked so bad that former president Rafael Ángel Calderón Guardia no longer looked like an enemy but a potential ally. As early as January 1950, a movement began "to unite Ulatistas and Calderonistas against Pepe Figueres." By February, representatives of Ulate were meeting with ex-president Teodoro Picado in Nicaragua, though the rivalry between Ulate and Picado and Calderón was still heated, and a true united front would not be forged until after Figueres regained the presidency in 1953.

The elections of 1953 became a two-man race. Don Pepe with the PLN and Fernando Castro Cervantes of the Partido Demócrata (PD, or Democratic Party). Castro, a wealthy landowner and businessman who based his entire campaign on smears and attacks on Figueres, was closely linked to reactionary elements and did not oppose violence to take power (he had financed and planned the failed uprising against the government in 1946). It is hard to imagine an election so divided along class lines. The economic elites, fearing that Figueres planned to finance his development program by taxing the rich, and worried that he was a socialist, gave Castro solid backing. In contrast, the PLN laid out a specific program of improved education and living standards for the poor, government programs to improve housing and health care, rising wages, control of foreign investment, and support of democracy throughout the Caribbean Basin.

Castro had communism as his trump card, and he tried furiously to make the charge stick to Figueres. Today, Castro's attacks seem juvenile and ridiculous. Yet at the height of the cold war and McCarthyism in the United States, such attacks often proved very effective. In the six months leading up to the election, the conservative paper *La Nación* called Figueres a liar, a thief, an assassin, an enemy of the Catholic Church and Costa Rican women, a Marxist-Leninist colleague and supporter of Stalin, and uninformed about soccer. It is interesting that for all his charges against Figueres's communist leanings, it was Castro Cervantes who attempted a pact with the still underground Communists in order to get their votes. Despite the fact that Castro Cervantes was reactionary and Communist leader Manuel Mora had publicly supported Figueres's policies of bank nationalization and the 10-percent tax, the Communists agreed to vote for the Partido Demócrata. Enthusiasm for Castro among ordinary communists remained modest, however, and many of them simply refused to vote.

Turnout for the 1953 election was low considering the fact that women were enfranchised for the first time. Figueres won 121,509 votes, compared to 66,874 for Castro. To nobody's surprise, the Castro camp immediately cried foul. The first evidence pointing to fraud, and one to be mentioned for years to come, is the so-called jeep incident. A jeep wrecked on the road to Puntarenas a few days before the elections, and the crash site revealed an already sealed ballot box containing five thousand ballots, almost all for Figueres. Clearly, the election involved some questionable practices. The PD analyzed 59,944 ballots and found 14,000 fraudulent. Lightly veiled threats were made by anti-Figueristas such as congressman Venegas Mora: "I believe that we are again approaching cloudy days for the tranquility of Costa Rica." While the amount of fraud or irregularities was probably not enough to have changed the outcome, the opposition believed that Figueres wanted power and would resort to fraud and irregularities if that was needed to maintain power. *La Nación* also published the "Manifesto of the National Independent Republican Party," the party vehicle of still exiled Calderón Guardia, which blasted the recent elections as a fraud and a coup d'état.

José Figueres Ferrer, a political unknown just a decade earlier, now came to power in a special four-and-a-half-year term, with an overwhelming electoral mandate, a well organized party, and two-thirds of the deputies in the

Legislative Assembly. Figueres already had serious enemies, both domestic and international. Thousands of Calderonistas and Communists detested Figueres both for the war and for the atrocities, exiles, and seizure of property after the civil war. The business elite considered Figueres a socialist and feared creeping statism and new measures that would reduce their share of the economic pie. Marcos Pérez Jiménez in Venezuela, Anastasio Somoza in Nicaragua, and Rafael Trujillo in the Dominican Republic all vowed to destroy him, and all were much better armed. And powerful elements within the United States, particularly within the CIA, viewed Don Pepe as a deceitful and dangerous leftist. By 1954, all of the leading voices in Costa Rican politics — Calderón, Picado, Ulate, Echandi, and Castro Cervantes — reached the conclusion that force must be used to oust Figueres. There was no elite pact for democracy. Costa Rican culture did not inhibit a violent uprising. Institutions did not channel preferences toward support of ballots over bullets. Figueres survived for one reason only: without a military, the opposition did not have the means to overthrow him.

If anyone thought that Figueres would be a more moderate and cautious president than leader of the junta, they were quickly disappointed. One month after taking office, Figueres sent a letter to US ambassador Robert Hill, calling for a new contract with the United Fruit Company and denouncing existing contracts as "a vestige of colonialism employed by other countries in past epochs." United Fruit sought assistance from the State Department, but Figueres was masterful at promoting his nationalism as better than what Jacobo Arbenz was offering in Guatemala, and he still had allies in the State Department, the Senate, labor, and academia. In the end, Figueres was able to sign a new contract that gave Costa Rica nearly 30 percent of the powerful multinational's profits.

Of all his audacious political actions, Figueres's decision to boycott the Caracas Conference of the Organization of American States (OAS) was probably the most ill advised. Secretary of state John Foster Dulles had called the meeting to condemn communism in general, and Arbenz in particular. Figueres immediately refused to attend because the Pérez Jiménez regime in Venezuela was dictatorial and a number of political prisoners were in jail. American diplomatic pressure was intense, but Figueres remained firm even when members of his own cabinet pleaded with him to reconsider as this would give ammunition to those who already charged don Pepe with being soft on communism. Costa Rica was the only no-show at the Caracas conference, and Dulles was furious. On 1 March 1954, the *Miami Herald* reported from Caracas that Figueres had provided a victory to the communists and that senior observers of the region suspected that the regime of President Figueres was pro-red, pro-Russian, and opposed to cooperation in the hemisphere. The enmity between the Dulles brothers and Figueres was now cemented. As one former intimate of Figueres put it, "We knew that we had a permanent enemy in John Foster Dulles. And we knew that Foster Dulles was a friend of Pérez Jiménez, a friend of Somoza, a friend of Batista, and a friend of Trujillo. . . . Everyone associated with the Dulles brothers and with the CIA were hostile to Figueres. And they believed that they could liquidate Figueres."

Figueres also sent a clear message to wealthy Costa Ricans that they would be expected to share their wealth with those numerous less fortunate who voted for the PLN. By March of 1954, the PLN economic plan was clear—high tariffs, higher wages, and state-directed industrial expansion. In May 1954, agricultural employers sent a letter to the labor ministry decrying minimum wages in the agricultural sector as "an excess of socialism." The opposition deputies in the Legislative Assembly, led by Mario Echandi, and the commercial elite strongly opposed such measures.

Meanwhile, the heated rivalry between Ulate and Figueres turned into open confrontation. The 1949 constitution stated that a president must wait eight years to run for an additional term. During his tenure as president, Ulate had held a successful plebiscite to change the wait to four years, which would mean that Ulate could run again in 1958. However, in May 1954, the PLN-controlled Legislative Assembly voted against the measure, and the constitutional change was rejected. The opposition saw the PLN action as a blatant attempt to eliminate the most popular opposition candidate in the next election and as more evidence that the PLN would use whatever tactic possible to maintain power. Ulate supporters rioted in the streets, and violence erupted in the Legislative Assembly. After the riots, Figueres proclaimed in a speech that "I am tired of saving Ulate." Ulate countered with a bold front-page story claiming that Figueres "wanted the communists to collaborate in his government." From this moment on, Ulate worked tirelessly via his two newspapers and in trips to the United States to meet with Dulles and US newspaper editors to enlist domestic and international support to oust Figueres.

The hatred for Figueres and the desire of the major players to overthrow him helped to unite the once factionalized opposition. Castro Cervantes had been meeting with the exiled Calderón Guardia, and a headline in *La Nación* announced what was once thought impossible: "ULATE ALLIES WITH CALDÉRON GUARDIA." Ulate made this new alliance public in Washington, D.C., announcing that he had no other choice to combat the tyranny that ruled in Costa Rica. It is clear that Picado, Calderón, Echandi, Castro Cervantes, and Ulate were in agreement that nondemocratic means should be employed to get rid of Figueres. Some three to five hundred Costa Rican rebels were training in

Nicaragua. The United States' role in the training and preparation of the rebel forces is not fully known. The US Ambassador to Nicaragua, Tom Whelan, toured the rebel training area in Coyutepe and reviewed the troops preparing to invade Costa Rica. Whelan was a close friend of Somoza and Sumner Welles. Some reports claim that the CIA was actively involved in planning the invasion and termed the invasion against Guatemala "Plan G" and that against Figueres "Plan C."

On 11 January 1955, opponents of the regime started the war by capturing the small Costa Rican city of Ciudad Quesada. The next day, the other rebels invaded from Nicaragua. The key for Figueres was getting the support of other American states by invoking the nonaggression pact of the 1947 Rio Treaty. Figueres and his lobbyists tried fiercely to portray the war as a Nicaraguan invasion of Costa Rica. With the seizure of Ciudad Quesada, the opposition attempted to demonstrate that this was an internal affair. Costa Rica immediately asked for intervention from the OAS and combat airplanes for self-defense. The OAS sided with Costa Rica, invoked the Rio Treaty, and requested that the United States provide four P-51s for Costa Rica, which the United States sold for one dollar each to the beleaguered country, which helped to turn the tide of conflict. It may be that had it not been for the success of the CIA-supported Carlos Castillo Armas invasion of Guatemala to oust Arbenz a year previous, the United States would not have saved Figueres. After the fall of Arbenz, and when the US denial of involvement was discovered to be false, the Eisenhower government faced heavy criticism at home, in Europe, and throughout Latin America. The United States could not watch a second elected president fall with CIA complicity.

Had an autonomous and powerful military existed in Costa Rica, the opposition would not have needed to ally with Somoza for the force. Figueres would not have been able to seek help from the OAS. The CIA might even have used allies in the military to topple Figueres. As Figueres's lieutenant Gonzalo Facio put it, "If there were a military here, the events would have played out differently. There would have been a force to unite the opposition. With a military, the calculus is completely different." As a leader of the opposition insurgents, Miguel Ruiz Herrera, put it, "If we had our own military caste and did not need to get weapons from Somoza, it would have been simple to unify the opposition and overthrow Figuerismo in 1955."

From March of 1955 until the elections of 1958, a number of major political controversies swirled. First and foremost was an amnesty for all participants in the civil violence from 1948 through 1955. The nonconfrontational and conciliatory political culture often invoked when people talk of Costa Rica was not evident in the mid-1950s. Not only had the Figueristas exiled and jailed thou-

sands, they had seized properties with the Tribunals of Immediate Sanctions—
"a kind of Nuremberg" as Oscar Bákit, one of the defendants, described it years
later. By 1955, no amnesty and no healing had occurred. As leading PLN figure
Luis Alberto Monge recalled it,

> There were many pressures from people who had suffered under the other
> governments, people who had been jailed and mistreated and people who
> had been killed for defending the polling stations. And these people put on
> lots of pressure to form a hard line [against an amnesty]. . . . The amnesty
> was also postponed because of the two invasions. We were talking of an
> amnesty when the invasion of 1948 occurred. Then when we were consid-
> ering an amnesty again there was an invasion. . . . The hard-liners around
> Figueres were saying: "How can we pronounce an amnesty if they are in-
> vading the country. They are not willing to contend with us in the electoral
> arena, only with force; they want to take power with force.

The absence of a military also proved crucial to a further critical test of Costa
Rican democracy: the decision of Figueres and the PLN to accept the party's
defeat in the presidential elections of 1958. The PLN had suffered a split into
two factions, with lifelong Figueres friend and public works minister Francisco
Orlich running as the PLN candidate and finance minister Jorge Rossi breaking
off and running as the candidate of the Partido Independiente (PI, Independent Party). Meanwhile most of the opposition united behind Figueres's arch-
enemy, Mario Echandi. Rumors of impending revolts and widespread electoral
fraud were constant. In Costa Rican elections, votes were cast at tables, and
all registered parties had officials at each table—this group of officials would
determine if a person could vote or not. The opposition registered "phantom"
parties to stack the voting tables, and the PLN responded with a full-page ad
in *La Nación* titled "The Invasion of the Polling Stations." The ruling party
charged that these new parties were phantoms invented by the opposition to
commit massive fraud against the PLN. "Look carefully, Costa Ricans. Look at
what is happening. Be alert. Remember that concessions such as these were
what fortified Caldero-Communism in Costa Rica. We must cut out the infection now, or within a few short years, we will have to resort to the means that
we employed in 1948." The three major candidates were shamed into signing
a pledge to accept the verdict of the Supreme Elections Tribunal as final and
to use legal norms to appeal claims of fraud.

In the peaceful and orderly February 1958 elections, Echandi received
102,528 votes, Orlich received 94,788, and Rossi 23,920. Echandi did not get
over half the votes, but he received slightly more than the 40 percent needed
to avoid a runoff and so was declared president. The PLN did not immediately

recognize the results. Orlich complained that the electoral registry was deficient and estimated that "at least 40,000 supporters were unable to vote." The party asked that the votes from three hundred voting tables be annulled, and a major battle erupted within the PLN over the course of action to take. Mario Echandi, who had plotted to overthrow the regime and who had been beaten, nearly lynched, suspended from the congress, and whose office was burned by Figueristas, would now be president. As Luis Alberto Monge recalls it, "There were people within [the PLN], fanatics who said how are we going to hand the government over to Echandi if we are the majority, our two blocks received many more votes than they did." Indeed, one of those most opposed to handing the presidency to Echandi was José Figueres Ferrer. Gonzalo Facio remembers that "when Orlich lost the election, Figueres said 'whoa, I am not going to recognize this election.' Many within [the PLN] did not want to give up power. Figueres did not want to surrender power. This would have been fatal for Costa Rican democracy."

Fortunately, the losing candidate and longtime Figueres confidant Francisco Orlich was able to convince Figueres that this was madness. Another PLN insider, Alberto Cañas, remembers that "Orlich was the one person who could put the brakes on Figueres. He was the one person who could bang on the table and make Figueres listen." A childhood friend of don Pepe's, Orlich saw no reason to gain the presidency through illegal means. The PLN still controlled the Legislative Assembly. He could easily win the 1962 elections with a unified party (which he did). And without a military hierarchy, there was no force in the country powerful enough to keep the opposition in power and cheat the PLN out of winning in the electoral arena. In the words of Facio, "With a military, the calculus is completely different." Monge echoes the sentiment: "If there would have been a military here (in the 1950s), the opposition would have allied with it, as they did with the security minister Cardona in 1949."

Echandi ultimately took office, and the PLN and Independent Party deputies in the Legislative Assembly reunified under the PLN banner. Hope for true democratic consolidation and a commitment to wage political battles in the electoral arena had now become possible. The Supreme Elections Tribunal gained stature as an institution and as a guarantor of free and fair elections. In 1958, a general amnesty was finally pronounced, and Calderón Guardia returned to the country after a ten-year exile. Thousands lined the Paseo Colón to greet him. He ran unsuccessfully for the presidency against Orlich in 1962.

V

The Costa Rican Dream

For thirty years following the civil war of 1948, Costa Rica lived a dream of electoral democracy, middle-class prosperity, and social services that expanded in tandem with a buoyant economy and an exuberant public sector. The period was dominated by the Party of National Liberation (PLN), the political vehicle built by José Figueres and his followers after their victory in the war. The PLN guaranteed cheap credit to a new entrepreneurial sector and committed itself to social justice and social mobility while remaining stridently anticommunist. The PLN trinity that sustained the Costa Rican dream is expressed perfectly in a photograph from 1956 showing President Figueres and a new archbishop, the conservative Monsignor Odio, throwing the switch to inaugurate a hydroelectric plant: progressive technocracy, conservative morality, and state investment in infrastructure.

The social improvement rested on a spectacular wave of growth, itself the product of the awesome expansion of the global economy after World War II. The traditional export sector generated extraordinary profits that were channeled through the state banking system to provide financing for technological improvements and agricultural and industrial diversification. Coffee plantations tripled their productivity between 1950 and 1970 thanks to the use of agrochemicals, something also employed by the banana industry to further enhance their cultivation of disease-resistant varieties of the fruit. Meanwhile, the income distribution policies of the PLN increased people's spending power. Greater numbers of consumers provided a basis for the capitalization of other activities, particularly rice and dairy farming. For a decade after Costa Rica joined the Central American Common Market in 1963, industry grew enormously: over one hundred companies were formed in Costa Rica between 1963 and 1975, the majority of them foreign-owned. In the process, the workshops of days gone by gave way to the impetuous advance of the factory.

A new public sector that grew and diversified at an incredible rate nurtured and guided this economic growth. The number of state employees tripled to

Dream Ignition (Archivo Nacional de Costa Rica)

51,000 between 1950 and 1970, when they made up 10 percent of the workforce. Over fifty new state agencies were created during the same period. Public investment manifested itself in schools, colleges, roads, highways, hydroelectric plants, health clinics, hospitals, and other infrastructure projects. Neither was the formation of "human capital" (that is, people) forgotten. An expanding group of technicians and professionals, graduates of the University of Costa Rica and foreign centers of higher learning, took over the direction of public administration. The PLN utopia was a world of cheap credit, endless salary increases, support for cooperatives (the most successful of which were those of coffee growers, who founded twenty-three between 1963 and 1972), stable public employment, opportunities for social mobility through education, and promotion of the internal market. The main beneficiaries of the Costa Rican dream were the urban and rural middle classes, who prospered with the growth of the export economy, the expansion of public-sector employment, the increase in the size of cities, and the expansion of industry. The rise of strong unions of public employees, which occurred during the 1960s, gave ballast to middle-class prosperity.

Economic expansion combined with social justice not only provided legitimacy to democratic politics but consolidated the ideological and political leadership of the PLN. Ironically, the putting into practice of the party's so-called social engineering credo, which was supposed to depoliticize the exercise of power, converted public employees into faithful followers of the PLN.

The party used this technocratic thrust to disguise traditional forms of electoral patronage and to propagate a statist ideology. Meanwhile, the deep conservatism of the opposition became more exaggerated in the context of the cold war. This made it easier for the PLN to assume the role of a progressive party. Aside from promoting modernization, PLN governments practiced a more active international diplomacy in defense of the prices of export products and critical of US support for the dictatorships of the region. This did not stop Costa Rica from backing the blockade of Cuba and generally acting as a US ally.

Striking improvements in the standard of living were achieved despite a demographic explosion that had increased the population from some 800,000 to almost 2 million between 1950 and 1973. Of course, a variety of social conflicts during the long boom years also shook Costa Rica. Between 1948 and 1954, the protests of urban artisans and workers, and those of banana laborers, emerged as the most significant, as these men and women bravely stood against the persecution of the post–civil war period. Small and medium-sized coffee farmers mobilized in 1961 seeking to regulate better their relationship with the coffee merchant establishment. During the same period, the discontent of poor peasants began to assume a public form, sometimes through the organization of leagues and committees with a leftward orientation. The total number of rural squatter families (*precaristas*) grew, and more than two thousand struggles over land flared up between 1963 and 1970, most of them in the Pacific north, the Pacific south, and Limón Province (areas in which ranches and banana plantations were expanding). The state met this and similar challenges by creating specialized agencies that devoted their attention to specific social problems. The desire to deal with popular discontent through legal and peaceful means, which had predominated in the Central Valley since the eighteenth century, culminated almost two hundred years later in a complex and diverse array of institutions.

The unequal distribution of prosperity had a very visible geographical dimension. The urban world (with San José by far the most prominent center) concentrated 42 percent of the populace in 1973. It boasted the best services, infrastructure, and income, but these advantages came at the expense of the rural areas. The Central Valley, given its political and electoral weight, benefited in proportionally greater terms from state investment than did Limón, Puntarenas, and Guanacaste. San José experienced consistent growth. Aside from those who lived in the city proper, five hundred thousand people visited San José every day in 1976. The majority came from nearby communities, whose civic life dissipated as they became commuter suburbs. The growth of slums was still extremely limited as late as 1973, but lack of planning meant that urban expansion would become chaotic. San José lost the European charm that had impressed the great modernist poet Rubén Darío in the late nineteenth century and became an ugly place, lacking in parks and facilities for pedestrians and cyclists, and with an increasingly polluted atmosphere.

As the 1970s wound down, Costa Rica could boast social indicators far better than those of most Third World countries. The average Costa Rican could expect to live to the age of seventy, infant mortality was a healthy twenty per thousand live births, and 90 percent of the people were literate. Three-quarters of the labor force were covered by social security, and unemployment hovered at a mere 5 percent. Then, in 1978, the severe shortcomings and risks of the postwar development model became evident with cruel suddenness: growth came to a screeching halt, and then Costa Rica seemed to move backward in time as the creditors came knocking all at once and Nicaragua, El Salvador, and Guatemala exploded in revolution.

Means and Ends for a Better Costa Rica

Rodrigo Facio

The program proposed by Figueres and followed by the Party of National Liberation from the 1950s to the 1970s had been developed by the Center for the Study of National Problems in the 1940s and was based to a great extent on the thinking of Rodrigo Facio, an overlooked figure in Latin American political economy. As this 1943 diagnostic study reveals, Facio was ahead of his time, proposing (six years before the Argentine economist Raúl Prebisch's famous report for the United Nation's Economic Commission on Latin America) the expansion and transformation of the state in a technocratic direction, the nationalization of key public services, support for cooperatives, and defense of small agriculture and industry. A clear blueprint for the PLN program, the study can also be seen as a legitimate precursor to the theory of dependency and to the idea of long-term state economic planning as a way of confronting that dependency.

Corporations like the United Fruit Company, the Electrical Company, the Standard Oil Company, and others of lesser importance distribute good dividends from profits made in Costa Rica among their shareholders. Meanwhile the country is not receiving its just share for contributing men, lands, forests, and waters. The country becomes poorer, it sees its lands exhausted, its forests cut down without thought, its waters consumed, without any current advantage or future gain. . . . Costa Rican capital is timid and cowardly, in large part as a result of the uncontrolled penetration of foreign capital, whose competition naturally cannot be resisted; and in part due to a national psychic modality. As the Center said in a recent editorial, "Costa Rican capital does not risk itself in difficult enterprises, regardless of how great the rewards of success might be; it refuses investments that are not covered by outright monopolies; and it is especially afraid to assume the role of pioneer, the valuable creator of new sources of national wealth."

As a semicolonial country, with an economy based almost completely on agriculture and a nascent industrial sector, the numerically predominant social class is the middle class, made up of small agriculturalists, artisans, professionals, teachers, small merchants, business workers, and so on. As for the capitalist class identifiable as bourgeois, it is made up by certain tiny agroindustrial sectors and financiers of big business. Particular sectors of the incipient urban industrial scene account for a definably proletarian class of wage laborers. In the consciousness and the feelings of the majority of the population individualism rules, an individualism determined by the smallholding backgrounds of most people, by a white and homogeneous ethnic composition, and by the peaceful and liberal political traditions of the country. . . .

As a result of the social makeup of the country, economic interests have not defined or established themselves in such a way as to set some classes openly against others. Because of its eminently agricultural nature and the great reserves of uncultivated land, the country offers a wide margin of new productive activities, which is an escape valve for any possible social friction. . . . In general, socioeconomic struggles that have emerged and extended themselves throughout the country over the last two decades—in the city and the countryside—do not assume a class expression, nor do they have their origin there. Rather, they manifest themselves as struggles of professional groups (importers against exporters, industrialists or landowners protected by monopolies against merchants, etc.), or as demands by certain general popular interests against an oligarchic or exclusivist situation (consumers against abusive commerce, for example). . . .

Due to this economic reality, the state is essentially an instrument of the interests of imperialist and large national capital, which it has scarcely ever dared to touch. . . . Also a product in part, though at the same time a cause—of economic disorganization, and in part of the great-man and individualist tradition of the liberalism of 1889—our struggles for power do not take place in a permanent form around defined ideological groups and their corresponding programs of government, but rather in exclusively electoral form and around people in whom one finds some kind of individual merit. This system has naturally made it impossible for certain healthy ideological tendencies—economic nationalism, tax reform, and so on . . .—maintained by civic groups, to extend themselves and realize a concrete political expression. . . .

An element of extreme importance in our international panorama is without doubt the "good neighbor" policy toward Latin America propagated and sustained by President Roosevelt. Unfortunately, up to now, the country has not known how to use it beyond pure protocol and minor meetings, and it has continued its policy of passivity in the face of the penetration of private yankee capital, without realizing that it could find its best ally and the greatest guarantor for its rational control in the very democratic government of the United

States. The meaning of the present war, the proposed arrangements for the construction of peace, the ever greater understanding of social problems by the large democratic powers, the great influence of Russia, are other facts that tell us that the evolution of the world in the next few years will be toward socialism. This tendency, which cannot help but be reflected in culture, politics, and the economy, will be a factor of maximum importance in our immediate future.

Given this reality, it falls to us, the new generations, to fix on goals and paths: the necessary goals, those which the country needs; and the possible roads, those which the country can take to realize such goals. In the economic sphere, the country must as an issue of fundamental and vital importance control and make equitable for the Republic the investment of foreign capital; and control and make productive for the Republic the investment of national capital. It must impede the first from exercising its current role of unrestricted exporter of national wealth; it must eliminate the exercise by the second of its current role of monopolist and speculator in national wealth.

Now, in one sense, the country enjoys adequate social forces, and ones that can be mobilized: the great rural and urban middle classes and, by their side, the small proletarian class. They are sufficient because they form the majority of the popular sector; they can be mobilized because they are quite aware of the immediate origin of their social inferiority and economic misery and will be willing to fight to remove the evil. Naturally this struggle could and would have to take place in an evolutionary form and through legal means, not through revolutionary or direct action, and so it could and would have to take on a Political expression in a party made up of those social forces and directed toward those economic goals: that is, a permanent and ideologically based party, as much for its organic composition as for its concrete objectives of reform. At the same time, it seems clear that such a party would be the adequate instrument for the realistic and nonviolent adaptation of the country to the International socialist evolution that is beginning at the present time. That would be for us centrists . . . the most fully and naturally popular, nationalist, and progressive Costa Rican movement. . . .

In terms of monopoly economic activities in the area of national services: exploitation of hydro-electric energy, aerial navigation, the railroad to the Atlantic, and so on . . . ; and in terms of export agriculture in bananas, abaca, rubber, and so on. . . . As can be seen, in this area of the economy the subject is foreign capital. As for national services, it would be sufficient to nationalize them, if through indemnified expropriation, in favor of an autonomous technical institution . . . by the inclusion in the respective contracts of a special clause that would leave the companies, at the end of the contracts, in the hands of the

State, without detriment to the owners of the investment capital. In treating export agriculture, nationalization or state takeover of companies seems logically impossible. . . . Until such time as there is a total change in the economy of the great powers, the road to take will be public contracting that controls foreign investments and guarantees that they have stimulating effects on the national economy.

As for semimonopolized activities in the realm of the industrial processing of coffee and sugar cane; the grain trade; certain branches of import trade (an exemplary case would be gasoline), and so forth, here the need is for direct public control by means of autonomous State institutions in the style of the Costa Rican National Bank. In certain cases this could even turn into nationalization or indirect control by means of cooperative organization of the sectors that suffer a semimonopoly, as well as the immediate creation of special social legislation adequate to the level of economic power of different companies. . . . In terms of activities subject to the free market like agricultural production based on small properties and industrial production based on small capital, what is required is self-defense through the organization of cooperatives directed by the State. They would be stimulated and promoted by autonomous State institutions providing credit, technical advice, equipment rental, product storage, transportation, colonization, immigration, land redistribution, and other activities judged convenient for the strengthening of the sector. This strengthening, on the other hand, would begin to indicate the need for the gradual establishing of special social legislation.

What would we get by the realization of this program for Costa Rican economic rectification? We would greatly democratize the distribution of national wealth via the control of private and foreign capitalist enterprise or — in certain cases — by way of substituting them for autonomous State institutions and cooperatives; by organizing national production; by making intervention in the economy an institution of public law oriented not by profit but by social necessity; by augmenting the volume of production; by organizing it and eliminating anarchy and insecurity from the market. . . . ; [and] by obtaining the growing adhesion of the popular majority to a regime that they see modifying itself in order to benefit them. . . .

We will, then, have abandoned economic liberalism. But we will not have destroyed it with a totalitarian statism. Rather, we will have overcome it with a mixed regime of autonomous cooperative organization of the democratic economic forces and with the intervention of the State, through its "services" in the oligarchic or monopolistic economic forces. . . . We will have also put an end to the divisive agitation of communism by integrating the middle and proletarian classes into the national economy through constructive collaboration and the effective improvement of their standard of living that will evolve with collective benefits. We will have fortified our democracy by providing it with stronger and more independent social bases, without overthrowing the liberal political regime whose maintenance is indispensable if our People are to have the government they desire—in terms of its composition and its politics—through the free operation of parties and elections.

In Defense of the Corner Store

Constantino Láscaris

Constantino Láscaris was a philosopher, originally from Spain, who played an important part in the intellectual life of Costa Rica during the 1950s and 1960s. At a time when Costa Rican society remained relatively provincial and its unique qualities difficult to grasp, he analyzed the corner store (pulpería) not only as a center of supply and consumption but also as a hub of popular sociability in both urban and rural areas that revealed national peculiarities.

According to the dictionary of the Royal Academy of the Spanish Language, the term *pulpería* derives from *pulpo* [octopus]. But though this may be the finding of illustrious academics, I don't believe it. There is no question that the pulpería is a store, and that in it everything is sold. Its classic name in Spain was "store with goods from overseas." . . . But I have never seen, read, or heard tell of a pulpería that sells pulpo. Due to a simple semblance, I relate *pulperías* with *pulpa*, which is definitely not the feminine of *pulpo*, but rather a word meaning all classes of flesh, from the flesh of animals to that of fruits. So, a word with a variety of meanings, all of them under the same general heading of fleshly being. . . . You might say, then, that a pulpería is a store where everything is sold. The difference between this and a market is that the latter has many sellers or merchants, while the pulpería has only one. Nevertheless, a market is not the juxtaposition or the spatial union of various pulperías. In a market, no matter how small, the merchants specialize, while a pulpería approximates the entire offerings of a market. During the 1960s, so-called supermarkets have begun to appear in all the cities of Costa Rica. This name already suggests a loss of stature for the word *pulpería*. Supermarkets should have been called super-pulperías, since each offers the totality of products on the market, with only one merchant (though it tends to be a company), which distinguishes them radically from the concept of a market. Also, no matter how large they are, they tend to be spatially smaller than markets, but we'll come back to this.

Pulperías have received bad press of late. I will cite here only the judgments of Luis Barahona, in his book, *El gran incógnito* [The Great Unknown], who gives pulperías an awful image as a place of time wasting and alcoholism. Clearly, I think these judgments suffer from a lack of perspective. The entire history of Costa Rica, its authentic history, the history of the everyday life of concrete men and women, has centered on the pulpería. The pulpería has been the only tie binding Costa Ricans dwelling deep in the highland valleys, the only place of provisioning and social relations.

This point demands that we make a prior distinction between two types of pulpería. The original one, and that which still today makes up the circulatory system of the country, is the peasant pulpería. With urban development, the pulperías of the small locales that have been encroached on by the development of the cities have been gradually transformed into pulperías servicing neighborhoods or marginal sectors of the population. And from this there has developed a marked association since the 1960s of the urban pulpería as a "poor store." Let's look first at the rural pulpería.

Costa Rica is the result of the unplanned, organic penetration of the frontier by Costa Ricans. A man throws an axe over his shoulder and with machete in hand burns a piece of forest, plants it, and builds his shack. The norm is that he has to make a two- or three-day trek to provision himself. Little by little others arrive, burn forest and build cabins. They rarely meet one another, although they know of one another. Slowly the footsteps of the folk forge tracks and paths that intersect in a point, whether in the center of the valley or a small clearing or in a canyon. One day, a farsighted man installs himself at that point. He doesn't burn the bush and he doesn't build his shack. He builds a slightly bigger shack and uses it as a storehouse. He spends his entire day waiting for someone to come and buy from him. In order to achieve this he has to:

1. Offer for sale everything that the frontiersmen need (from salt and sugar to fat, from cheap pants and shirts for working to fabric for the women, from rope and machetes to needle and thread)
2. Give credit, since the frontiersmen live from the coming harvest and not from the one past
3. Accept with some frequency payment in kind instead of in money

Wandering about the plains of San Carlos one time, I came on the greatest commercial enigma I had ever been faced with. The horizon was thick with forest. There was a junction of roads over which, even in dry season, a four-wheel drive would find it hard to negotiate. And right at that spot there was a pulpería. Not a single house was visible anywhere in the surrounding area, not a single sign of human life—just the roads. The pulpería was without paint, its wooden body was eaten by termites. It was big and long, with a counter that could accommodate simultaneous service for more than thirty or forty clients. It had an overhanging roof outside that could protect more than a hundred people from the rain. Inside the pulpería there was only the *pulpero* [proprietor of the pulpería]; it was a weekday morning. The merchandise hanging from the walls and ceiling was worth many tens of thousands of colones. In medicines, tonics, and toiletries alone there was as much as you would find in many small-town drugstores. It was not, then, a town pulpería, because there were no townspeople. It was a pulpería that served the frontier dwellers who, once a week, "came down" to the pulpería to "buy" a wide variety of things and to bump into other folk.

With the growth in population, the most frequent outcome is that the pulpería becomes the nerve center of a group of houses. It might be ten or it might be fifty, but they are still without pseudo-urban structure because they still lack a plaza. In settlements that have already grown relatively large, it's rare to find that the pulpería, or usually now the pulperías, are on the plaza. If the town is small, the plaza is principally a soccer pitch. To one side, the church; to the other, the building housing the public offices. On the third side, the best house. The fourth side of the plaza is occupied by a large number of tiny houses all close together. If there is a pulpería in the plaza, it will not have the typical characteristics; it will have evolved into a general store, and these days it is quite probable that it will have a bar or a food counter. One or two blocks off the plaza, one or more pulperías will be found, and the "campesinos" — that is to say, those who live far away — will go there to make their purchases.

On top of everything else mentioned, pulperías sell alcohol, though using that word wouldn't help me because if I asked for "alcohol," I would be served fuel alcohol or rubbing alcohol. What they sell is *guaro*. Officially guaro is spirits made from sugarcane. In Costa Rica, I suspect, guaro means spirits made from sugarcane, from maize, or from whatever. And this poses a serious problem. The production of spirits and alcoholic beverages is a State monopoly based in San José in the Fábrica Nacional de Licores (National Liquor Factory), a large establishment where they sell liquor wholesale. In the countryside, everyone makes it themselves, though underground, of course, and always in grave danger that the rural policeman might want to settle an old score and sniff them out. This is bad, because it ends in the penitentiary. In the pulpería, there are a few bottles that come from the National Liquor Factory. There are also a few more of unknown origin (of course this is a secret which I must not reveal). The campesino, the frontiersman, who has come to truck, has made his purchases and has a few free hours in front of him, so he stays in the pulpería, chats, and throws back a few shots of guaro. The norm is that he gets "buzzed." Sometimes he goes a bit overboard and ends up snoring on a bench or on the ground.

I remember in some places on the banks of the Sarapiquí, a Saturday, there were neither paths nor tracks. The only road was the river. A few launches arrived, loaded with bananas and people. By mid-afternoon, the bananas had been unloaded and a large number of bags and packets had been piled up in the center of each launch. At five, three women began to herd the men from the pulpería toward the boats. They were the grandmother, the wife, and the sister-in-law. Using the most varied methods (one young, trembling lad by the hair, three strong, robust men with punching pushes, and a pleasant old fellow carried between two), they were able to round up all the men of the clan in the space of a half hour and deposit them in the launch. They cast off and headed back up the river. That Saturday there was no dancing.

I confess that the spectacle awoke a real sympathy in me. I saw it with tenderness. It is easy to criticize drunkenness. It is not easy to live a frontier life without once in a while warming the spirit with the *agua-de-vida* [water of life] of the best Alchemy. On the frontier, there are no alcoholics. Alcoholism is an urban problem. On the frontier it doesn't exist as a problem because the alcoholic would die quickly. To get happy once in a while is a tonic for the body and the spirit. Moreover, in this difficult life, it is the secret of the explosive birthrate, since those stout, strong women, after depositing the "happy" husband in the cot, still had work to do. . . .

One takes a few drinks in the pulpería in order to liven up the conversation. Different from the classic Andalusian pulpería, drinking is not for livening up sales or haggling. The Costa Rican makes his purchases stone sober, with total attention, with the brow knit and the hands vigilant. And a few coins are put aside for later. There is total honesty, and he knows that they will not rob him. That only happens in the cities. And so, to converse, to break the silence in which the frontier has kept him for many days, he downs a few drinks and loosens up the tongue.

I remember a place near the Aguas Zarcas River, a pulpería that sold "witch's milk." I wasn't able to get them to divulge the secret of its making. It wasn't very strong. It wasn't very sweet. It placated the stomach. Even the termites on the walls looked good.

And if there is a dance, things change. I remember a settlement of thirty-two houses. The pulpería had a "dance hall," which might be better called a "party room." Open on two sides, half closed on one, and bordered on the fourth by the store, on whose wall was the door and the counter. In other words, little more than a floor and a roof. Little advertisement flags hung from the ceiling.

Almost a hundred people arrived by river. Pants and shirts very clean, and all with shoes. The women were decked out and done up nicely, many of them in pants and semi–see-through shirts. The music came from the jukebox. And there was a six-hour dance, all merengue and boleros. Huge volumes of guaro and beer were drunk. There were very few drunks and no scuffles. There was a dance once a month, and it was the great fiesta of life. The "frontier folk" came down to partake of the liveliness and cheer of the "burg." Hungry for human contact, for the sight of pretty women, or for the sense of being looked at by like men, to be able to tell how the corn patch was coming along or to ask after the distant neighbor who had married recently, to show off the pretty and brightly colored "rags" and look good in the garb while moving to the beat.

At that point it becomes a social center, a place where the community comprehends itself, among all the machinations of the mutual acquaintances. In that center, before anything else, they dance. They also talk politics, they engage once every four years in electoral campaiging, they discuss the problems of the community, they write up petitions for a road or a bridge, they collect funds. . . . The history of Costa Rica's demographic expansion in such territories can only be written as a history of the development of the pulperías. Of course, when it has become a social center, it is no longer a pulpería. It has become something else, painted with lively pictures and selling beer.

The urban pulpería has had worse luck. Cities are stratified according to economic class. The barrios are not always separated along those lines. For example, it's common that a small town has been surrounded by suburbs, or that the city (and this always happens) segregates marginal zones of settlement. Then we have a market and large stores, sometimes a supermarket or "Más por Menos," and the whole gamut of semicommercial and semi-industrial establishments. In each case, there will also be pulperías.

Now it's an urban pulpería. It only sells cheap things and in small quantities. Often the sales are measured in fractions of cents, and they rarely reach five colones. Vegetables, squashes, chayotes are usually a fundamental part, and there is, of course, no meat. In a few strategic places, between populous but poor barrios, there are large pulperías in which sales run into a few thousand colones a day, but they remain pulperías in their look and also because they sell in tiny amounts.

Of course the profit margins are, in relative terms, very high—how can one charge a mere 10 percent on an item that sells for a fraction of a cent? But to take the most typical cases, the urban pulpería will have a notebook or a list as its commercial axis. The pulpero opens a line of credit that he tallies in the book, with no more guarantees than the client's word . . . and the necessity he or she has to maintain the credit by paying up from time to time. In the pulpería, the notebook functions just as the checkbook does in the supermarket.

In the cities that have been invaded by automobiles, the difference has become starker still. So-called *auto-servicio* [autoservice] has been introduced, and even *automercados* [automarket]. Of course, the term *auto* means, etymologically, "for oneself," but in fact, crucially, it has come to mean "with a parking lot for your automobile." You go to the automercado in an automobile; you go to the pulpería on foot.

And if it is a pulpería, they sell drinks. If they don't sell drinks, it's called a *verdulería*, or vegetable stand, even though they also sell threads and toys. And the urban drinks are not always as nice as the rural variety. Although they might dress the same, it is a different thing to be a farmer on the frontier than to be a suburban peon. In the second case, one is living side by side with the thresholds of poverty. And the larger the city, the more it seems like poverty, the poorer the pulpería, and the worse the digestion of the "bad guaro" [*mal guaro*]. In one concrete region, and it is one that the study mentioned at the outset might refer to, it is a common thing on Saturdays to find cases of mal guaro that devour the entire salary of a family.

But the suburban pulperías also fulfill a vital role of public relations. They opened the country to televisions, acting as a transitional phase of familiarization. They sold millions of transistor radios, which mute men have stuck to their ears for hours at a time. They are the place where the news of the day is discussed, newspapers being rather dear for half the population, and they are also the place where the news of the neighborhood can be gotten (which is not published in the papers). And in order to justify another purchase on credit, a good woman's hardships are listened to, which, after all, gives comfort.

To see this evolution, this urbanization of the pulpería, leaves a certain sadness in the spirit. It's another aspect of the conversion of country life into city living, and not one of the better ones. The man with drive prefers to head for the frontier again rather than become marginal. Demographic expansion continues to disperse the population, which follows the course of rivers to the sea, and in those rivers new peasant pulperías are still appearing.

A Costa Rican Godfather

J. L. Vargas

Costa Rica was not a country transformed by mass immigration from Europe in the late nineteenth century, as occurred in the Southern Cone countries and North America. Still, immigrants had an important qualitative impact on the society's evo-lution. Among the elite, one can find many families tracing their recent ancestry back to Germany, Lebanon, and Spain. Often they created space for themselves by opening new roads in commerce and manufacturing. In the modern era, many found success by taking questionable risks and betting on José Figueres, the political underdog, in the process forging a whole new network of influential contacts outside the traditional ruling class. This is the tale of one such immigrant family.

José F. and Julia P. arrived in Costa Rica at the beginning of the twentieth cen-tury. They had left the Canary Islands for Cuba along with their five children, friends, and neighbors from Tenerife with the conviction that they would have a better standard of living in America. Some of the group stayed in Cuba, while others moved on to Venezuela and the United States. Julia and José decided on Costa Rica, attracted by the contracts and land concessions that the govern-ment was offering to European immigrants. Once in Costa Rica, they went with their children to work in the coffee plantations of Turrialba. Government promises weren't kept, so they left for San José, where Julia set up a conve-nience store while José, who had always farmed, worked in the countryside. Finally, José secured a job as caretaker of the parks in the misty city of Cartago, and there his children grew up.

One of them, Teobaldo, fell in love with the beautiful María Prota. As was expected of the young couple, they reproduced bountifully, until six children graced the household. Teobaldo owned a bakery in El Molino barrio, and María opened a famous beauty parlor in one of the rooms fronting on the street in their spacious home in the center of Cartago. Their hard work and commit-ment rewarded, by the 1930s the young couple had amassed a modest capital.

Of the six children, three became industrialists, two graduated as professionals, and one became, as he himself defined it, "an entrepreneur."

The "entrepreneur," Rodrigo, was better known around Cartago in the 1940s as "Pajizo" for his straw blond hair. With his six-foot frame, his light skin, and his enterprising manner, he was the very picture of a middle-class son. Yet he lived his life on the edge. From a very young age, people saw him as a leader of his generation, a notable figure. He was innovative, aggressive, adventurous, and without fear, and he loved to keep the adrenaline pumping by pushing for change and challenging the way things worked. The rebel personality got him kicked out of the Colegio San Luis Gonzaga by a distinguished intellectual who was the director of the high school, and provoked Hugo V. and his wife to try to put an end to the romance he was carrying on with their daughter, Claudia María. Despite their opposition, the courtship continued and became one of the legendary ones of the day, inspiring other would-be transgressors of social mores. Without even finishing high school, Claudia María married Rodrigo and, though declared sterile on her first medical exam, later brought seven children into the world—five of them in less than six years.

Rodrigo was one of the youngest of Teobaldo and María's children, but it fell on him to help them out. Between gambling, drinking, women, and escapades, Rodrigo assisted his father in the bakery, making it possible for the other children to get ahead. During the politically turbulent 1940s, the family opposed Calderón Guardia and bet on change, helping out a group led by José Figueres. While his father confronted the government in the city, Rodrigo—scarcely sixteen years old—trained with the rebel troops in the mountains of San Isidro de El General. The military experience forged important friendships and contacts, especially the political and commercial alliance that Rodrigo formed with F. M., one of the principal military leaders of the Figueristas in the civil war of 1948. From flirtations with new political parties, to the importing of peaches, apples, grapes, and liquor, Rodrigo's association with F. M. endured.

With the beginning of the Central American Common Market in the 1960s, Rodrigo set up a transport company, initially based in Costa Rica. After the success he enjoyed with this, he consolidated an import-export company with F. M., and together they opened a commercial office in Colón, Panama. The transport of foodstuffs throughout the isthmus became the front for the biggest and most successful illegal liquor-trafficking operation in Central America. While the booze smuggling grew and left juicy profits, Rodrigo began to diversify his investments, buying a jam factory from its Cuban owner, getting into the black bean business, and backing local television production (including one of the country's leading children's programs).

Even though the smuggling operation allowed him to diversify, Rodrigo also built a network of businesses associated with the consumption of alcohol. He organized a national liquor distribution network, and he owned hundreds of liquor licenses and a large number of cantinas. He started up a huge ice factory and opened various dance halls. Presidents, ministers, bureaucrats, police officials, and "socialites" partied with him despite being quite aware of his illegal business dealings. Claudia María and her children spent New Year's Eve with presidents, politicians, public officials, and the select of Costa Rican society in an exclusive social club in downtown San José.

Rodrigo's motto was "you can only profit from the poor" — which for him meant the working and the middle classes. And he was faithful to this creed in his investments. The cantinas never lacked clients and the dance halls filled up every weekend. Rodrigo even brought popular foreign pop stars to sing in his larger venues, and he contributed to the growth of a national music scene by contracting local groups to play in his so-called *bailongos* — dance fests that he held at different venues around the country.

Of course, gambling and other activities connected to it were also among his interests. Filling a niche, Rodrigo opened a casino in San José, the Típico Camacho, which operated twenty-four hours a day, seven days a week. The patrons, of course, were men, and so the casino was attached to a "nightclub." The gambling venture allowed Rodrigo to become owner of one of the most important collections of antique cars in the country: a member of the Costa Rican elite lost them one after the other in the course of a night at the tables. The cars were beauties and — proof of Rodrigo's extravagance — as a measure of his support for a certain political party, he painted the most valuable "machine" in the collection in the green and white party colors for a parade that kicked off the 1978 presidential campaign.

The name of my father elicited fear and respect. He was known as the Godfather. By that point, in his mid-forties, he had long since left the business in the hands of administrators. He decided to combat the absence of challenges by returning to the highways. He bought a car and drove it to Acapulco, where he lived for a while. Later, he bought another vehicle and drove it to Miami, where he settled for a while on the beachfront. Finally, when his children started to marry in the early 1980s, he decided to return to a small property he had in Tárcoles. Rodrigo loved the sea — it gave him strength.

The end of the 1970s brought changes for Rodrigo. The smuggling business was systematically persecuted, the unconditional support of certain politicians began to wane, and the daily bribes became more expensive. Rodrigo's lists were populated by the highest public functionaries on down to the humblest civil guards. Daily harassment by the police began to form a constant part of our lives. Our phone was tapped, our house watched, and sometimes we suddenly had bodyguards and chauffeurs. We knew little about Rodrigo's activities; clues were provided by snippets heard on the street, stories in the papers, or the especially careful way we were treated. A number of times we actually went to collect him from police stations, where he'd been brutally interrogated. On top of everything came the calls from his many women and the cries of his illegitimate children.

As were the houses of a lot of men of his generation, Rodrigo's home was the site of domestic violence. Claudia María could not go out alone because Rodrigo thought that no good woman had any reason to leave her house. The blows were part of everyday life. During my last year of high school, somehow Claudia María managed to kick him out. At last she was able to ask for a divorce. After many years and multiple occasions on which we'd gone with her to the authorities so that they could take her statement and get photographs of her injuries, finally, one day, an officer processed that last, decisive charge. Rodrigo never forgave Claudia, so he never helped us economically: estranged, he continued with his prosperous dealings and his multiple women. At age forty, Claudia María for the first time had to look for a job.

I was the first of my brothers and sisters to marry, and I did so on Rodrigo's birthday, giving him what he called "the worst birthday present" and marrying in the same church where he and my mother had married twenty-five years earlier. The ceremony began at five in the afternoon on a Friday in May, and, to my surprise, when we came out of church, we found that out of deference to Rodrigo, the Civil Guard had sent a small honor guard, at attention waiting to accompany the newlyweds to the limousine. Concerned for my safety because I was going to live on a finca, an uncle presented me with the gift of a gun; my dad made me the special present of a permit to carry it. I say "special" because with his one call to the Ministry of Security, the office in charge of permits extended one that allowed me to carry any weapon, from an AK-47 to a .22. When I went to renew the permit in the 1990s, after Rodrigo had died, the person who looked after me asked if I would have a problem with a permit limited to the gun I owned.

Married and with children, I sometimes went to visit him, until one day, as he would have put it, he "exploded." His disordered life presented him with the bill. He was fifty-four when he died. The wake and the funeral were an apotheosis: four thousand people signed the registry at the funeral home. Hundreds shared stories of my father: "don Rodrigo bought me the little car and the taxi license"; "don Rodrigo believed in me and gave me a job"; "don Rodrigo gave me the money to buy my house"; "don Rodrigo financed my little business"; "don Rodrigo paid for my education or the education of my children";

and so many others. We were astonished. Ex-presidents, ministers, high functionaries, leading business people, the Civil Guard, the Red Cross, the police, transport officials, municipal workers, and members of the clergy sent hundreds of funeral wreaths and telegrams and representatives to walk in procession with the body. Rodrigo had an honor guard of police on motorcycle, in cars, and on foot, all in military formation. A caravan of taxis formed part of the procession. His funeral was more a spectacle than a ceremony: people of different walks of life mixed together—the humble, the bureaucrats, the politicians, and those of "high society."

His death was like his life, his final wish perfectly and precisely reflecting his philosophy. He asked to be cremated because he felt that he could not be buried in one single place. In his own words, "I always lived shared out, and shared out I must remain." His ashes were divided in four parts: one for my mother (his "number one"), one for his favorite lover, one to be thrown into the sea, and the final one scattered by one of my sisters in another of don Rodrigo's favorite places: on the stage of "It's a Small World" in Disney World, Florida.

Growing Up in the Dream

Manrique Mata-Montero

What was it like to grow up in Costa Rica's golden years? Experiences varied a great deal, of course, but the following recollection might be taken as representative of that of a middle-class child from a large town on the rural periphery whose family moved to the capital city in the 1960s, along with so many others. Mata-Montero is now a professor of computer science at a large North American university, and he maintains strong ties with Costa Rica and other countries in Latin America.

Oh, we are so civilized in Costa Rica! We are so different from the surrounding countries. We are so democratic. We are so . . . so French. We learn the national anthem in school, but side by side with the Marseillaise. The primary, secondary, and postsecondary education systems are based on the French model. We have lycées, we have *licenciaturas* [a degree between a B.A. and an M.A.]. . . . A technical school degree?

Those were my thoughts as I walked with our maid en route to the corner store where they packed rice, sugar, and beans in brown paper bags, wrapped meat in plant leaves, and sold milk in glass bottles. Little Richard was on the radio — heralding the coming of a new age — intertwined with Mexican tunes and classical pieces. No Costa Rican music, though. There was hardly any. When we felt the need for cultural and artistic and popular traditions, we looked north to the province of Guanacaste, whose people we'd otherwise abandoned, and learned to call their folklore our own.

The last years of Costa Rica's relative isolation and patriarchal political regimes. The beginning of the end of my childhood. The early '60s. San Isidro de El General, Perez Zeledón. Commercial center of the Zona Sur. Ugly and dry, without the ocean, but economically buoyant: tobacco, tomatoes, vegetables, bars, and whores.

A sociopolitical phase transition was on the way, fueled by don Pepe Figueres and his Party of National Liberation. Modernization was making me realize that I lived in an underdeveloped country; that our economy was based on a few exports—coffee, bananas, cocoa, and beef; and that we were not that different from our brothers in the rest of Central America to whom we had always shown the greatest contempt, particularly when their national soccer teams played ours. More shocking was the realization that the means of production were controlled by a handful of oligarchic families in cahoots with a few transnational companies. These facts had long been known to a small percentage of the population—mostly manual laborers who worked for the international fruit companies, and don Manuel Mora Valverde, leader of the occasionally banned Communist Party. The world was collapsing—indeed, it had collapsed. The corner store no longer bagged its goods in brown paper. The age of plastic bags and television had arrived.

The national and international news did not pacify my prepubescent anxieties. Newspapers and television warned us of atomic annihilation. Realizing that Costa Rica was no longer the center of the universe—my universe—but a small banana republic in the middle of nowhere, I believed an atomic war would not be of much consequence to us. Who would want to drop an atomic bomb on Costa Rica? What for? We didn't even have an army.

Fidel Castro was another issue. The Catholic school I attended warned us of the dangers of communism, and particularly of the atheist Fidel Castro, dictator of Cuba. He was spreading his oppressive atheist ideology all through Latin America.

"Why doesn't anyone kill Fidel Castro?" I asked one of my older sisters. I do not recall her answer, but I do remember that it was quite unsatisfactory, similar to the one she had given me when I asked her what infinity was.

I felt, nevertheless, a kind of perverse curiosity that frequently led me to tune in to Radio Havana Cuba on the shortwave radio in the TV room of our home. The issue was always the "Norteamericanos" [North Americans]. Of course, those in Cuba must have had it wrong. The *Norteamericanos* were not imperialist warmongers, they were the ones who brought us the Alliance for Progress, JFK's economic relief package aimed at promoting "US-style democracy for Latin America," which was just now being challenged by "exotic ideologies," and. . . . What else did they bring us? Oh yes, the Ford Thunderbird station wagon that my parents owned, canned fruit, and movies with subtitles. How angry Radio Havana Cuba made me feel! I could not wait for the day that someone would shut them up.

Nevertheless, I continued tuning in, mostly at night. I deeply disliked Fidel, and even more the enigmatic Che Guevara. They scared me.

I recall vividly the first time I saw a photograph of Che Guevara. It was at the home of don Danilo, a dentist and high school chemistry and biology teacher in our small town. He was my friend's father. One day I saw a photograph on the night table in the parents' bedroom: a bearded guy dressed in fatigues. I asked my friend who it was. My friend said in an offhanded way that it was "el Che Guevara." I did not say anything and neither did my friend.

Don Danilo was a peculiar man, pretty eccentric. I admired him a lot. (Many years later, during my university years, away from the little town where I had been born, I would find out at a consciousness-expanding get-together that he was among the handful of "old people," besides my grandfathers, who had had a lasting impact on my life.) I did not know what to think. Don Danilo a Che Guevara sympathizer? Something was wrong. I justified the presence of Che Guevara—the communist—in don Danilo's home by the fact that don Danilo's sister was married to don Manuel Mora, leader of the Communist Party. The photograph was due to family pressure from don Manuel. That had to be the reason. I did not want to think more about it.

The police, reorganized with each new government, were becoming professional. In my town, movie theaters showed Hollywood films. There were some that still showed Mexican and Latin American movies, but eventually American films took over. The Americans were winning the cultural war. I became a fan of cowboy movies and Tarzan. Roy Rogers and the Lone Ranger were my—our—new heroes.

One inconsequential day in the comfortable life of an upper middle-class teenager, the front page of the conservative newspaper *La Nación* had a photograph of the dead body of Che Guevara in a glass sarcophagus. He had been assassinated by the Bolivian armed forces for spreading communism—or was it fighting for the natives and the unprivileged? He had been killed in a small-town schoolhouse in Bolivia where he'd been held captive. His death should have made me feel happy, but no, I felt shivers running down my spine as if a bucket of ice water was slowly being poured over me. I felt an irresistible urge to cry, and I still do.

Was I reminded of the body of Christ in a glass sarcophagus in the cathedral across the street from my home? I was not religious even as a child . . . my contradictions mortified me, for weeks ghosts haunted my sleep. I knew that I would not find solace until I could see what El Che represented. No one understood what I was going through. Had my family known, it would have explained my new ideas about social justice and politics and, of course, my bitter fights with them. Particularly with my father.

Central America again found itself in another cycle. Hundreds of years before, it had been the Aztecs from the north and the Incas from the south. This time, the turmoil was coming from further north—the United States—and from further south—Chile, Argentina, Brazil, and Uruguay. Navigating through ordinary life was like maneuvering a sailboat in a pot of boiling water. From the south and neighboring countries came political refugees, many of them very well educated and with Marxist or socialist ideas. The artist Rubén Pagura came from Argentina, Luis Enrique Mejía from Nicaragua, Santiago Quevedo from Chile and many, many more. The north contributed Bob Dylan, Rosemary's Baby, The Doors, Jimi Hendrix, Janis Joplin, Abby Hoffman, Timothy Leary, The Beatles, Coca-Cola, and Katty. Yes, beautiful Katty.

She was the only daughter of an American preacher—from somewhere in the midwestern United States—who had settled in my hometown. I fell madly in love with her as soon as I saw her. But the first time we talked she lost all interest in me when I told her that I was twelve years old. She was thirteen. Months later, after she showed me the pleasures of carnal love, she revealed that she hadn't expected me to know about sex, so she'd lost interest in me. Katty was amazing. She fucked everyone I knew—everyone. I wasn't jealous. My consolation was that it was me who loved her the most. I proved it to myself the night she broke the news in our coffee shop hangout that she was pregnant. No one wanted to have anything to do with her, even talk to her. I gave her a ride back to her place on my motorcycle.

Katty said good-bye, gave me a peck, and said, "You are nice. I love you."

Her expression hinted that I would never see her again. And I never did. Her father, unable to reconcile his profession with his daughter's behavior, sent her back to the United States to live with his mother. She wrote a letter to one of her lovers and told him she had run away to become a hippy. After that no one ever heard from her again.

In 1969, fearing that the environment of a small town was not favorable for raising her children, that the capital would offer far more educational and social opportunities to her children, my mother decided to move the family to San José. I was enrolled in the Colegio Calasanz, a Catholic school run by the Escolapio Order of Spain. It was interesting to see how the class struggle had permeated the order. On the one hand, there was Father Llombard, who ingratiated himself with the aristocratic parents of some students; on the other, Father Juan, who had been kicked out of Nicaragua for reasons unknown— though we knew it was because he was a communist. I realized with amazement that even the Catholic Church was not immune to the winds blowing through. The Theology of Liberation, prominent in Brazil, was ravaging the clergy like a wildfire on the grasslands. Young priests were "going back to their roots" and denouncing the social, political, and economic inequities that were somehow overlooked by the Catholic establishment. Misery loves company. Seeing these priests as confused as I was made me feel better.

Father Juan persuaded some of the more advanced students and daytime professors to teach night high school classes to underprivileged students. The exclusive Colegio Calasanz by day became a free educational institution by night. Although I was ideologically closer to Father Juan than to any member of the school community, we disliked each other a great deal.

The economy of the country was changing. International organizations had created an economic development plan for Central America, and Costa Rica had subscribed to it. The plan benefited a small sector of the population, but it was never clear whether the well-being of the country as a whole had improved. For the first time, Costa Ricans witnessed the emergence of urban areas that taxi drivers refused to enter after sundown. The most appalling sight of all in San José: street children. The image of the first handful of street children I saw in San José is imprinted on my brain. There were six or seven of them. They used to hang out in the grassy areas around the Central Bank of Costa Rica, across the street from the first McDonald's. Photographs of the kids were published in the newspapers.

In the early '70s, I started university. Two groups were fighting for power, one influenced by the north, the other by the south. The Left was represented by Vladimir de la Cruz and the charismatic Alberto Salom. The hedonistic extroverts—for lack of a better term—were led by Cotico, son of a supreme court judge. The communists promoted social justice and Latin American culture. Cotico only believed in the justice of the *carapacho*—a big seashell—the object that he blew while dancing nude around the university campus.

I had reached a fork in the road: communist or hippy, each with their conditions. All my friends had chosen. For several years I would waiver between the two paths until I found out that for some people there is no path.

The university students and its faculty rapidly polarized.

An ordinary Monday:

My literature professor, conservative in appearance, prompted by the noise of a demonstration in front of the library, asks us what Karl Marx would respond to what she had just said. Before we can react to her question, she continues: "Probably nothing because he would be out there," pointing with her right hand in the direction of the incoming noise. Then she looks coldly at us. At lunchtime I go to the washroom and walk in on a young economics student holding the dick of a well-known philosophy professor—a man who had a column in a conservative newspaper. At 2 P.M. I write a philosophy exam while my European-educated professor entertains himself at the front of the classroom with a *Playboy*. I am wearing white bell-bottoms, leather sandals, and a tie-dye T-shirt. I scratch my long beard.

Everyday reality is surprising, alive, continually changing. Every road is open to travel.

Cotico was viciously attacking the status quo. He scorned traditional ideologies, regardless of whether they were from the left or the right. It took him a couple of attempts to win the election for president of the student union. This was a student union that routinely organized and participated in demonstrations joined by thousands of students and other sectors of the population. For example, when the Left had run the show, they had demonstrated against the exploitation of bauxite from southern Costa Rica by the transnational Alcoa. The country had never seen tens of thousands marching through the streets of San José united in an effort to prevent the government from allowing a foreign company to exploit precious mineral resources. The conservative president of the country, ex–university math professor José Joaquín Trejos Fernández, seemed to favor the project, as did most of the members of congress. The episode concluded dramatically with an individual spitting in the president's face.

So a student union that had been controlled by the Communist or Socialist parties was facing a takeover by Cotico. The Left never understood him or what he represented—possibly no one ever did. They attempted to destroy him in every possible way. The most pathetic attempt came during one of his pre-speech dance performances. The left wing had arranged for a sexy professional stripper, masked and dressed in black tights, to confront him. It was like witnessing a tête-à-tête between the Clash and the English Chamber Orchestra playing the Brandenburg Concertos. What an embarrassment for that beautiful woman! . . .

When Cotico finally won the presidency, his performance was anticlimactic. Once so articulate and quick-witted, he became unintelligible, unable to express what he had so successfully expressed before the election. There were allegations of corruption, that the offices of the student union had become storage space for marijuana and booze (the same space had sheltered illegal political refugees many times). Some blamed an LSD trip from which the man had never returned, others attributed his demise to existential burnout, while still others saw it as the result of a sudden realization of the magnitude of his influence. Whatever it was, speculation that he was going to run for the presidency of the country died.

In the early '60s, almost by decree, we had become an underdeveloped country. In the mid-'70s, a well-known luminary who was a professor at the University of Costa Rica (and one of the ugliest men I had ever seen, but who somehow had stunningly beautiful daughters—a fact that earned him the nickname *pinga de oro*—gold dick), decreed during the 6 o'clock TV newscast that Costa Rica was a developed country. I kind of recall that his argument had to do with the quality of life, that it was comparable with that of the developed countries. I do not recall if the fact that eating disorders were becoming more and more common also helped to upgrade our classification. Most people did not believe him; so we compromised and accepted the classification of "developing country."

The '70s were coming to an end. I had finished my undergraduate degree at the University of Costa Rica and was preparing to leave the country. I learned of the triumph of the Sandinista revolution in 1979 while in graduate school in California.

Alcoa No!

Student Protests, 1970

(*Semanario Universidad*)

Costa Rica's "May '68" came in April 1970, when high school and university students mobilized against government concessions to the transnational mining giant, Alcoa. Approval of the contract on 24 April resulted in the stoning of the legislature and a violent confrontation between students and riot police. Beyond the motive that provoked it, the movement that identified with the cry of "Alcoa No" expressed the cultural dissatisfaction of youth with the provincial and conservative Costa Rica of the 1950s and 1960s. Youth radicalization made a decisive contribution to democratizing access to higher education and led to a new flowering of the Costa Rican Left.

(*Semanario Universidad*)

The Crisis: 1980–1982

Jorge Rovira Mas

The social democratic system began to come apart at the seams with the economic crisis of 1980, inaugurating Costa Rica's "lost decade" with a resounding crash. The eminent sociologist Jorge Rovira Mas painted a frightening portrait of the causes and consequences of the economic collapse that brought an end to the Costa Rican dream and that served as midwife to the new economic model based on the application of orthodox free-market policies (known in Latin America as neoliberalismo*).*

The Crisis: Some Indicators

In September 1980, Costa Rica had enjoyed more than three decades of accelerated dependent capitalist economic growth characterized by social evolution and a political picture that strongly reinforced democratic life and gave great legitimacy to the country's institutions. The devaluation of the colon decreed that month marked a now clear and unequivocal point of rupture with the entire dynamic followed by Costa Rica to that point. The economic deterioration that followed this devaluation, and that made 1981 and 1982 the most difficult years in the nation's economic history since the Great Depression, clearly showed that the country's *style of development* had entered a profound crisis now irreversible. The decline resulted from three factors, but in overall terms it must be understood as essentially the product of a socioeconomic model of dependent capitalism.

The primary expression of this was the stagnation of production in 1980 and the abrupt collapse in 1981 and especially 1982. In contrast to the historic rate of economic growth in the postwar period, which averaged 6.2 percent between 1950 and 1980, between the latter year and 1982, the annual rate of growth was minus 3 percent. This was made worse by the fact that the decline in GDP per capita, which was actually greater than the fall in GDP, combined with a dramatic drop in the investment of fixed capital, which plunged by 25 percent in 1981 and by 28 percent in 1982. The average salary fell more than 40 percent in terms of real purchasing power in the same period, and if it is measured in terms of the number of essential foodstuffs that can be purchased with a salary, it dropped by more than half. The official unemployment rate went up from its postwar average of about 6 percent to 9.4 percent in July 1982.

Inflation in Costa Rica, traditionally very low and in no way comparable with that prevailing in many South American countries, went from 17.8 percent in 1980 to 81.8 percent in 1982, a figure unseen in the country's prior economic history. And the exchange rate, a fundamental variable in the case of such an open society as that of Costa Rica, went from the 8.6 colones to the US dollar, which prevailed prior to the beginning of the successive devaluations in September 1980, to an amount greater than 60 colones to the dollar in July 1982, something that badly affected the returns to exporters as well as to consumers. The public foreign debt more than tripled by 1982 if compared to the average annual indebtedness of this sector between 1976 and 1979. Finally, another persistent disequilibrium in the Costa Rican economy — the public sector deficit. This had been quite high throughout the second half of the 1970s when compared with the GNP, but the deficit grew even more in 1980–81 and would have reached the order of 17 percent of the GNP had the fiscal policies of the Carazo administration continued after the change of government in May 1982, when Luis Alberto Monge became president. Also, if we look quickly for other indicators that can sketch the depth of the crisis experienced by the country between 1980 and 1982, we might note that the number of strikes during the three-year period reached eighty-one, much greater than the sixty-five that took place in the six-year stretch from 1974 to 1979. Take into account that the number of strikes in the 1970s was already extraordinarily high, a response to the international crisis of the oil shocks and the general downturn. . . .

In terms of the strictly political dimension of the crisis, it is clear that the manner in which President Carazo came to power in 1978 had many consequences. Supported by a coalition of political and social forces whose alliance was based on so-called *antiliberacionismo* — dislike of the PLN — they lacked a firmly shared common project to govern the country. The government of Carazo in general, but particularly his economic policies, was in large part held prisoner by the contradictions extant among the political and ideological groups that had carried his presidential aspirations. Already during the first year of his mandate an absence of precise political direction became evident, and this left him unable to face the delicate situation that Costa Rica was passing through with any degree of coherence. And a trait of the final year and a half of this government was the ruling group's definite loss of credibility, which left the president guiding the country in a mistaken direction with an extremely reduced number of supporters. His social base was so meager we might say that he was almost completely alone, and he showed all the signs of being a ruler who had lost his senses, railing against a society that waited hopefully for a change in the executive. The government reached such levels of weakness and discredit that if one thing draws attention from these years, it is precisely the solidity of political institutions that had emerged following the civil war of 1948 and the subsequent development of Costa Rican society — a solidity that essentially allowed the country to avoid the possible overthrow of the president of the republic by the force of events.

At the end of 1980, on 15 December, there also began what would become a wave of terrorist acts that would persist until the middle of 1983, though the large share of them took place in 1981–82. It is true that many of them were intimately connected with the worsening regional political tensions in Central America and the presence in San José of a variety of political groups and organizations of different ideological stripe. Such was the case, for example, of the capture in October 1981 of a SANSA airplane by a commando group called International Saviors of Nicaragua against Communism, or the kidnapping of the young Iranian Kavek Yazdani on 8 January 1982, or the failed attempt to capture the Salvadoran businessman Roberto Palomo three weeks later. This also accounted for the bomb that exploded in a parking garage in the center of the capital in June 1983, presumably intended to kill leaders of the Democratic Revolutionary Alliance of Edén Pastora, an anti-Sandinista who nonetheless refused to ally himself with the CIA-backed Contras. This resulted in one death and material damages.

But it is also true that some other terrorist acts had their origin in the way some Costa Rican youths understood the internal situation, perhaps believing the crisis had opened the possibility of novel political action whose road had to be prepared through a series of armed operations. This was evident, above all, in the attack on a group of US Marines traveling in a minibus in March 1981; in the shoot-out in Barrio La Granja in San José in April 1981 which ended in the capture of four people; and particularly in the armed confrontations between a group of young people and a Civil Guard patrol on the night of 12 June and the morning of 13 June 1981 — fighting in which three guards were killed and one of the captured young attackers, Viviana Gallardo, was assassinated in her cell soon after, on 1 July. These last cases involved a series of unprecedented events concentrated in a short period of time and which clearly suggested a questioning of the sociopolitical order prevailing in the country.

The Causes of the Crisis

There were a number of causes that led to Costa Rica's postwar development style entering into a pronounced crisis at the end of the 1970s. First of all was the socioeconomic structure implanted into the country after World War II, largely as a result of the dominant political project from 1948 onward, a typical model of dependent capitalist production. This featured an agricultural sector in which agroexport production played the front-line role (representing half of the production of the sector). It was the base, major premise, axis, and motor of national economic growth. This is what generated the foreign exchange that Costa Rican society required in order to operate as it wished, as well as a large share of the profits that various mechanisms have increasingly transferred to the industrial and the public sectors.

Throughout the period 1948–80, a significant increase in the principal export products could be seen, along with a certain diversification of exports. The following facts tell the story: between 1957 and 1980, the rate of growth in the GDP of the farming sector averaged 5 percent annually, a little lower than the economy as a whole; between 1957 and 1969, however, the best period was registered, with the GDP of the farming sector growing at 6 percent annually, declining to 3.5 percent between 1970 and 1975, and then worsening considerably to an annual rate of growth of 2 percent between 1976 and 1980; from that point on stagnation set in. It should be noted that not all products have performed homogeneously. In the 1950s, the growth of coffee production was notable, an increase achieved not only by expanding the area under production but also through a development of productivity that made it among the highest in the world. This was also a period that saw an important increase in farming for the internal market. In the 1960s, it was bananas and sugar that showed the greatest dynamism. Finally, in the 1970s, rice production saw an annual growth rate higher than 10 percent.

Meanwhile, the industrial sector that emerged was one that benefited enormously from a large number of incentives starting in 1959, when the Law of Industrial Protection and Development was passed. These incentives have included tax, credit, and finance policies designed to privilege the growth of this sector, whose production rose by an annual rate of 9 percent between 1960 and 1974. The principal characteristics of industrial development, broadly speaking, are the following.

By and large, this has been industrialization oriented toward the production of consumer goods using a large proportion of imported materials, which does not lead to a greater articulation of industry in other parts of the economy. No serious steps have been taken at the national or regional level to move toward the production of capital goods or processed primary goods that might dovetail with the kind of industrialization promoted. The consequences are clear. One is a strong dependency on the import of these materials for an important portion of the productive structure, bringing with it a growing rigidity in the patterns of imports. Another is a redoubled technological dependency, since there exists no stimulus for internal scientific and technical research linked with material production. Finally, this type of dependency constitutes a structural companion to the reproduction of the industrial sector in terms of the dynamic followed by the agroexport sector and its capacity to generate a growing amount of foreign exchange earnings required by the industrial sector for its expansion.

From the point of view of the market, limits have existed on this class of industrial development. Even if at the beginning, with the creation of the Central American Common Market, the demand for industrial products widened, the great restrictions on a sustained increment of this type of industrializing process in a region like Central America became patently obvious three decades later: a social structure that ensures that the benefits of economic growth reach only certain small parts of the social body. It should be noted, however, that in the case of Costa Rica, this affirmation needs adjusting in the sense that the country's social composition and continued actions (not always successful in terms of the formal objectives pursued) directed toward improving the distribution of income have been an appreciable factor in industrial growth.

In terms of the property of capital invested in industry, an important presence of foreign capital is patent, and particularly US capital, in the industrial concerns established in the country after the approval of the Law on Industrial Protection and Development of 1959 and Costa Rica's joining of the Central American Common Market. This was notable especially in the period 1963–75, and in the newer branches of industry (chemical, metal products, etc.), and also in the most dynamic of them. Among the implications worth mentioning with respect to this situation are the effects that an industrial sector composed in no small measure of affiliates of multinational corporations have on the balance of payments, particularly on the entries corresponding to the payment of technical services, royalties, profits, and interest that the multinational houses extract from the country by way of these affiliates or of mixed-ownership companies charged for production licensing agreements and a variety of other services.

A third element that forms a substantial part of this model of dependent capitalist socioeconomic reproduction is the creation of a new form of state, with an interventionist character, that has had so much impact on the economy and on social formation. In terms of that social structure and the tendencies in distribution and redistribution of income, one must reiterate that the most significant aspect of this in Costa Rica has been the expansion of middle-class groups in the postwar period. Those groups best situated in the social structure, whether due to property or just income, and the middle-class groups have acquired imported habits of consumption, reflections in many ways of habits of the central and dynamic capitalist societies of the international economy. These habits have spread widely in national society, and because they promote the use of foreign products or of products with an elevated imported component, they contribute to the sharpening of certain imbalances in the economic structure, especially the current accounts deficit in the balance of payments.

This completes our sketch of the most important elements that make up the socioeconomic model of dependent capitalist reproduction. The place where they are most clearly manifest is precisely in the balance of payments current account. The best expression of the vulnerability of this pattern of reproduction is its tendency to *chronic and growing deficit*. All the Central American countries exhibited serious deficits in current accounts and balance of trade starting in the 1960s, but Costa Rica experienced the sharpest imbalances in both areas from 1965 onwards. It is also interesting, however, that in terms of the structure of income distribution and income level per capita in each of the Central American countries in the late 1970s, Costa Rica had the best situation in terms of the portion of total income going to the middling sectors (the 60 percent who are below the richest 20 percent), as well as in terms of the distribution of average income across that 60 percent range. All this allows us to propose the hypothesis that, given the similarities between the economic structures of the Central American countries—ones that undoubtedly signal a persistent deficit in the areas mentioned—the difference in the magnitudes of those deficits in the case of Costa Rica is likely to be associated with its social structure and distribution of income.

It is also clear that given this propensity of the socioeconomic model to generate a growing deficit in the current account of its balance of payments—including during the best moments of the agroexport sector during the postwar period—this situation has only been able to be vented via the constant input of a growing amount of capital, whether as direct investment or as loans. Direct investment and the foreign debts accumulated by private capitalists occupied a key place in the meeting of external sector balance throughout the 1960s. In the '70s, especially after the world crisis in the middle of the decade, there was no alternative but to be dragged along in the international current of public and private loans from the central capitalist countries in an already well known and thoroughly explained process which Costa Rica was in no way able to escape.

The second cause of the Costa Rican crisis was the international crisis of 1974–75 and, a little later, the renewed effects of the subsequent rise in the price of fuel and in the international interest rates at the end of the 1970s. During these years the country was severely hit by a deterioration in the terms of trade, due to the unleashing of international inflation and the resulting deficitary rise in the commercial balance and in the balance of payments current account. And starting in 1978, on top of the prevailing situation (one that was mitigated only by a rise in the price of coffee in the world market in 1976–77) the Central American political crisis was added to the country's woes, due to the serious effects this had on weakening intraregional trade.

But if the Costa Rican crisis has something specific about it in comparison with those of the other Central American countries, it is that when the international economic crisis erupted in 1974–75, Costa Rica was going through an internal process of accentuating some characteristics of national development. This was a product of new social interests congealing around President Daniel Oduber Quirós, and of the political will of those at the head of the dominant political project. They were oriented toward deepening certain distributive tendencies in the postwar model: the state of that time not only chose to unveil a new moment in its economic intervention through CODESA, a consortium of state industries, and by getting involved in ambitious infrastructural projects, but also by undertaking a highly vigorous welfare policy. And to achieve these objectives, they engaged in a systematic and accelerated expansion of public expenditures, with fiscal deficit constantly rising and the state's indebtedness to both internal and foreign sources growing.

The third cause of the crisis had much more to do with the deepening of the most significant manifestations of the national crisis than it did with the actual reasons for its appearance. This was the economic policy put into practice during the government of President Carazo. Its severe contradictions were the result of the complex and equally contradictory amalgam of political forces that led to Carazo becoming president of the republic, as well as of the resistance that its application met in the heart of distinct social and political forces.

And so, by September 1981, the government of President Carazo, overwhelmed by the weight of circumstances and given its inability to conclude a final agreement attempt with the International Monetary Fund two months earlier, made known that the country was incapable of meeting its international financial obligations, including the payment of interest on foreign debt. These were the final conditions that led the economy to drift, and it would not reach a new and definite direction until the second term of 1982.

The Family

Anonymous

In the early 1980s, popular revolutionary movements were apparently on the verge of victory in Guatemala and El Salvador, Sandinista revolutionaries held power in Nicaragua, there was a pronounced increase in US military presence in the region, the national economy was in free fall, and the government found itself in chaos. Many young Costa Ricans felt compelled to act. Some took halting steps down the road to revolution. This is how one of them remembers the way this period dramatically and tragically transformed his life.

Saturday, 13 June 1981, I woke up to eat breakfast and heard on the news that the night before there had been a shoot-out near the El Gallito factory in Guadalupe [a suburb of San José]. It was stated that in the process, three police had died, along with an unidentified person. Later, I went to my son's kindergarten, where we as parents were lending ourselves to a series of tasks so that we could later celebrate Father's Day with our children. We commented on how strange the events of the night before were. At midday I went home for lunch, and I was at the table with my wife, my five-year-old son, and my one-year-old daughter. Then, through the window, I saw a vehicle stop in front of the house; two people got out—one was a cousin of mine and the other had been a classmate in university. They greeted me and told me please to come with them to clear up a few things about my brother Carlos having to do with the events of the night before. I said good-bye to my wife and told her to relax.

The car took us to the offices of the Dirección de Inteligencia y Seguridad [DIS—the state secret service]. There they took me to a room and left me sitting alone. Later, my cousin appeared and said that unfortunately it seemed that the person killed in the confrontation the night before was my brother and that they had to take me over to the Organismo de Investigación Judicial [OIJ—the state judicial police] to identify the body. I felt crushed, stunned. When we arrived at the basement of the OIJ headquarters, I was quite surprised because they immediately took away my belongings, filled in a file on me, handcuffed me, and threw me in a cell. Everything seemed like a nightmare, and in minutes, I felt more suffering come on, thinking of my parents, of my wife, of my children, of my brother. Later they took me to an office where a number of officers asked me a pile of questions about my brother, his friends, and they told me that I was involved with him and hurled all sorts of insults at me. They said that in order to convince me, they were going to take me to where they had his body so that I could identify it. They took me to the morgue where they were doing the autopsy, and it was shocking because the head was open. I could no longer contain myself, and I let loose sobbing, and in that state they took me back to the cell where I continued crying for a long time.

Later, they took me to another office where there were other officers. I didn't know what time it was because I had lost all sense of time. They began to interrogate me again, but this time in a friendly and familiar tone. I told them the same thing, that I didn't know anything. One of them told me that he had been my brother's high school companion and that he had been with him in a leftist group, as a result knowing all of the people involved with my brother. They told me that they were going to free me and take me to my parents' house so that I could make arrangements for my brother's funeral.

Sunday the fourteenth, we went ahead with the funeral, which was attended by some family members and neighbors. While I carried the coffin with my brother's remains, even with the pain, I observed how, among the tombs, there were police everywhere, including the officers who had interrogated me the night before. Later I realized that as we left the cemetery, they interrogated and photographed everyone who had participated in the burial.

On 1 July, at 6:30 in the morning, my wife woke me up, distraught, with the newscast: Viviana Gallardo had been assassinated in prison. She had been identified by the police as my brother's accomplice, and since her arrest on the night of 12 June, the media had converted her into a monster. In reality, Viviana had been my brother's romantic partner. We cried again at the news.

Meanwhile, on 19 June, they had arrested two people in a house and seized a large amount of documentation. This led them to believe that there existed a leftwing political organization in which the police claimed a number of people were involved. They began to make a large number of arrests and house searches. A witch hunt ensued.

Classes at the University of Costa Rica were over. I was overwhelmed by events and with a great uncertainty. I knew that they were watching me and waiting for any reason to arrest me. That moment arrived on 6 July: I left the university for my parents' house. My wife and children were waiting for me there. Around six at night, we left for our house, and after about one hundred meters, I passed a parked car. I looked instinctively and saw that there were a number of occupants inside looking at me. In the rearview mirror I saw that the car's lights turned on, and it began to follow me. When we arrived at my house, I got out of the car to open the garage door, and as I was driving the car into the garage, the other car drove up and parked itself right in front of the garage door. Two men got out, identified themselves as members of the OIJ, and told me that I had to go with them. Again, I told my wife to stay calm and to call my lawyer so that he could show up at the OIJ building. As I got into the vehicle, I saw that there was another officer in the back with a large-caliber gun.

Again they processed me and took me, handcuffed, to a cell. They took me to be interrogated, and this time it was done with insults and great belligerence. They told me that this time they had me and that I was going to rot in jail, since they said that this time they had the evidence against me and that I was the intellectual leader of this group that they called "The Family."

Many things went through my mind, and I tried to think what had happened.

I thought back to September of 1973, when I left classes and heard the news that a military coup had put an end to the government of Salvador Allende in Chile. That day marked me, since I had not been a political activist, but I reacted immediately and joined a march that left the university and went through the streets of San José until very late at night. By the time of the electoral campaign of 1974, I was a member of the Socialist Party, and in 1975, I was part of the student leadership of the Left, which challenged the Communist Party's approach to the struggle over university budgets, during which time we promoted a strike. In 1976, starting a career as a university professor, I was elected representative of the teachers in the union of university workers. At that time the war against Somoza was heating up, and in El Salvador the popular movement had developed a great deal. In that context, I began to collaborate, first with a group in solidarity with the Sandinista Front, and later I came in contact with Salvadoreans from the Popular Revolutionary Bloc (BPR). In the elections of 1978, I voted for Pueblo Unido [the new name for the Communist Party], but the personalist wars among the factions and the lack of a clear and organized project left me rather disenchanted, as a result of which I left the Socialist Party. My goals were very clear: I was going to keep working for the Central American revolution. In that vein, I kept collaborating with the Sandinistas and with the Salvadoreans of the Bloc. At that time my brother, who had just returned from El Salvador where he had participated as a combatant in the Popular Forces of the Farabundo Martí Liberation Front, proposed that I collaborate with an organization that they were creating as a new revolutionary alternative in Costa Rica and that would also keep helping the Central

American revolutionary organizations in the war of counterinsurgency that the United States was carrying out in the region.

Because of its nature, the group was clandestine. It came out of the Central Americanization of the war and, as a result, it was committed to a strategy of prolonged popular war. According to this perspective, Costa Rica could not remain on the margins of what was happening in the isthmus, since within the regional counterinsurgency, the country was playing a particular role — namely selling the image that liberal democracy was viable and serving as an example for other countries of the area where the popular movement was seeking to establish socialist governments. At the same time, to avoid any fissures in the model offered by Costa Rica, the US government increased its training and preparation of the Costa Rican security apparatus and upgraded their equipment. Meanwhile the government of Carazo began to face a series of economic problems that made it ever more unpopular. All these things, according to the political view of the organization, tended to create propitious conditions for Costa Ricans, especially for the popular sectors, to consider an alternative way of organizing and struggling.

Due to the frustration with the traditional Left among certain sectors, especially in the university, and also due to the influence that Central American events had on our world, the ideas of the organization began to percolate in some parts of the population. My participation was limited to the political domain, and to that end I prepared reading and study materials, as well as conjunctural analyses. The organization did not have a fixed name because it was in the early stages, and the issue of a name was left aside until a time when it had developed more. And so, for internal use, in code, the name "the family" was adopted. The police later used that name to denigrate the organization's political objectives. The embryonic work of the group took place as work with the masses, with peasant and worker groups, and in the military realm. Around 1980, I had had a few disagreements with members of the leadership, and I was rather disenchanted with the project, as a result of which, by common aggreement with them, I shifted: I would continue to collaborate, but only on the periphery, where my participation was occasional. It was at that moment that the events of 12 June 1981 took place, which later led to the organization's dismantling and my detention for a period of almost three years.

Imperial Eagle versus Peace Dove

Hugo Díaz

The US war on revolutionaries in Nicaragua, El Salvador, and Guatemala (1980–89) almost swept Costa Rica up in the general militarization of Central America. The Party of National Liberation (PLN) was just barely able to keep the country out of the vortex by astutely playing a peace card that proved very popular with the citizenry. This maneuver culminated in 1987, when president Oscar Arias blindsided the United States diplomatically with his Central American peace plan. Despite efforts by the Reagan administration to undermine the initiative, the plan proved irresistible to Central American leaders (Arias was awarded the Nobel Peace Prize). Hugo Díaz, the most important Costa Rican caricaturist of the second half of the twentieth century, captured the moment.

Arias: "Alright, in keeping with the agenda it's time to feed this dov . . . ," cartoon by Hugo Díaz (*Semanario Universidad*, 7 August 1987)

Arias holds a document entitled "Peace Plan." (*Semanario Universidad*, 14 August 1987)

A Dictionary of Costa Rican Patriotism

Álvaro Quesada

During the 1980s, while some sectors of the government cooperated with the United States' dirty war against Sandinista Nicaragua and key elements of Costa Rica's security services were under the control of the US embassy, programs under the direction of the United States Agency for International Development were undertaken for the economic transformation of Costa Rica. The country's business elites began a campaign in favor of the free market economy that included slogans like "Private enterprise produces freedom." One of Costa Rica's leading literary critics, the late Álvaro Quesada, regularly wrote scathing columns on the semiotic absurdity of the intense propaganda that accompanied the measures. Many of these appeared in the University of Costa Rica's newspaper, including this piece from 1987.

The ineffable economic, political, and military transformations promoted in our country by patriotic organizations like the ANFE [National Association for Economic Development], CINDE [Costa Rican Investment and Trade Development Board], United States Agency for International Development (USAID), the CIA, the American Chamber of Commerce, and so on require, as far as we can see, a parallel effort at ideological redefinition. We must prevent campaigns directed by exotic ideologies separating our people from their sacred mission: that of converting themselves into a cheap labor force so that international trade, private enterprise, and the free market—bastions of Western civilization—can flourish in the world. This dictionary is a humble contribution to this urgent effort. Since for their fullest understanding words always refer to one another, we have stressed in the definitions those words that find definition in other parts of this dictionary.

> **Capitalism.** See *democracy*. A regime constructed according to the laws of the market.
> **Christianity.** An ambiguous doctrine. When it preaches the submission of the poor to their fate, and of the workers to the *entrepreneur*, it is *demo-*

cratic and forms part of *Western civilization*; when it preaches love and equality among men, it contradicts the *laws of the market*, acquires subversive overtones, and forms part of *communism*.

Communism. Intrinsically perverse doctrines or regimes opposed to the teachings of the *liberal economists* and the *laws of the market*.

Democracy. 1. Government of the *entrepreneurs*, by the entrepreneurs, for the entrepreneurs. 2. *Capitalism*: A regime in which the value of men, their qualities, their words, or their acts, are determined according to the quantity of money that they produce or possess. In a democratic regime, the *government* and the *people* are at the service of the *entrepreneurs*.

Dinero. In *democratic* American regimes, a measurement of the politicians, the countries, and the people.

Dollar. In *democratic* American regimes, a measurement of the politicians, the countries, and the people.

Entrepreneur. *Democratic* archetype of Man. Said of all those capable of selling their soul, their country, or their people, with the noble goal of protecting or incrementing their properties or their business.

Facism. A nationalist, *militarist*, or racist doctrine that defends Western civilization from communism.

Freedom. Exercise of obedience to the *laws of the market* and to its spokespeople, the *liberal economists* and the *international financial organizations*.

Freedom of the Press. Application of the *laws of the market* to information. In general terms it guarantees, in *democratic* regimes, the *freedom* of *entrepreneurs* to publish what they wish and to hide that which they find inconvenient; and freedom for the *people* to find out what has been ordered published by the *entrepreneurs*.

Government. The ensemble of functionaries and institutions whose duty it is to protect the business and the property of *entrepreneurs* and ensure that Costa Ricans adopt the dispositions of the policies of the *international financial organizations*.

International Financial Organizations. Organisms that govern the *government*, in collaboration with national *entrepreneurs*.

International Relations. In *Western civilization*, a system of relations among countries that reproduces the *laws of the market*. The relations between *entrepreneurs*, *government*, and *people* that are established in a democracy are equivalent to the relations between the rich countries, the government, and the people, in which the entrepreneurs act as intermediaries in the buying and selling of peoples and poor governments by the rich countries.

Liberal Economist. A type of modern oracle, whose voice interprets the laws of liberty and of the market.

Market. Nature. God. Omnipotent and superhuman mechanism whose laws of supply and demand, and of the survival of the fittest at making money, determine in *democratic* regimes the value of men and of human relations.

Mercenary. Foreign *military entrepreneur* who collaborates with national *patriots*.

Patriot. 1. Someone who generates profits. *Entrepreneur.* 2. Said of those who defend the *government, freedom,* and *democracy.*

People (the). Inexpensive and submissive labor force that works for the firms of the *entrepreneurs.* In a *democratic* regime, the *government* must ensure that the wages of the people go down, so that the incentives and profits of the entrepreneurs go up.

Soldier. Guardian of order, *freedom,* and *democracy.*

Western Civilization. See *democracy; capitalism.*

VI

Other Cultures and Outer Reaches

A walk down any downtown San José street or a trip to any of Costa Rica's out-lying regions will immediately reveal that Costa Rica's "ethnic homogeneity" is more mythical than real—and not just because of the recent internal migra-tion of Afro-Limonenses to the Central Valley or the influx of tens of thousands of Nicaraguans. At the time of independence in 1821, not even one-tenth of the population was of direct Spanish descent, while over half were mestizos, blacks, and mulattoes. The indigenous population, having experienced a re-bound from the postconquest demographic calamity, accounted for about 10 percent of the inhabitants of the Central Valley. In the ranching area of Gua-nacaste, with its free-range herds, a vibrant culture of semisedentary peasant cowboys predominated and combined elements of mulatto and indigenous culture. In the inhospitable areas of the north and south, an indeterminate number of indomitable *indios bravos* (wild Indians) still lived free of Spanish rule. In the late nineteenth century, Costa Rica's ruling groups attracted very little of the European immigration they hoped would overcome their chronic shortage of labor. However, starting with the building of the railroad to the Caribbean coast in the 1870s, hundreds of Chinese and thousands of Afro-Antillean laborers entered the country.

The notion of a homogeneous Costa Rican race has underpinned nation-alist ideology since the mid-nineteenth century, and the racism of this myth constantly resurfaces in panics about the contamination of a supposedly pure national phenotype. In practice, however, Costa Rican society has been able to absorb and homogenize racial Others with great success. Of course, consider-able violence and physical displacement often accompanied the assimilation process. Many of the country's surviving indigenous societies bore the brunt of this when the first export booms of the mid-nineteenth century expanded the frontiers of agricultural colonization, breaking through their defenses, and claiming their lands and, in many instances, their lives. The period from 1950 to 1990 saw the gradual assimilation of Limón's once distinctive anglophone

West Indian culture into the dominant Hispanic mode, a process favored by the settlement of the zone by people from the highlands, by racism, and by the state's refusal to offer English instruction in public schools. More recently, the tourism boom, the new highway from the Central Valley to Limón, and the increasing concentration of opportunities in greater San José have quickened the pace of integration.

The most extraordinary challenge to the homogenizing powers of Costa Rican culture has been the steady arrival of Nicaraguans since the Sandinista revolution began to collapse in the mid-1980s. Long held in suspicion and contempt by Costa Rican public opinion due to their alleged culture of criminality and political violence, Nicaraguans in desperate straits have faced an uphill battle. They have developed an array of institutions, social networks, and cultural expressions to help them deal with exclusion and hardship in a potentially hostile land. Because they have arrived in such large numbers and in such a short period of time, this latest and greatest wave of immigration will be the acid test for the absorptive capabilities of a national culture that, in practice, has proven quite flexible and inclusive despite its absolutist and racially exclusive rhetoric.

For a good part of the country's history, discrimination against those considered racially or ethnically distinct had a geographical basis, since the bulk of the population of African or indigenous origin were located outside the Central Valley. This differentiation, in turn, had a decisive demographic and political background, given that the majority of the population of Costa Rica — and so of the electorate — lived in the Central Valley. Demographic and political imbalance, accentuated by ethnic difference, meant that during the twentieth century, the Central Valley also received a disproportionate share of public spending. Nevertheless, just as prior to 1950 education and electoral participation played important roles in integrating people despite ethnic and geographical discrimination, since then the social policies pursued by the state (and particularly by the PLN governments) have helped to compensate for the differences between the Central Valley and the rest of the country.

Since at least the end of the nineteenth century, discrimination has been counterbalanced by socially and culturally integrating forces, generally promoted by the political sphere. Currently, an official culture now promoting the idea of Costa Rica as a multicultural society is in the process of abandoning the view of Costa Rica as a country of white people. The ministry of culture is currently institutionalizing the celebration of "regional" ethnicities and customs. The embrace of multiculturalism marks an extraordinary rupture with the past. It seems to be related to the fact that areas that were once peripheries exhibiting distinct cultures—like the Caribbean, Guanacaste, and the areas around Puntarenas—are currently epicenters of the tourism industry. The following pages present unofficial expressions of the cultural and geographical differences becoming more visible and more acceptable in Costa Rica today.

Indigenous Figure

Juan Manuel Sánchez

Juan Manuel
Sánchez, stone
carving, c. 1932
(Museo de Arte
Costarricense)

Although the country's indigenous people have rarely served as subjects in the work of Costa Rican painters, sculptors have sometimes recuperated their past, as evidenced in the work of Juan Manuel Sánchez, one of the country's leading twentieth-century sculptors.

Dispossessed

The Indigenous Community of Orosi

The final thirty years of the nineteenth century proved disastrous for Costa Rica's remaining indigenous peoples, both those who lived in communities that had recreated some cultural and economic autonomy within the confines of Hispanic domination and those whose communities had survived in the dense forest and jungles to the north and south of the Central Valley. The international rubber boom motivated rubber tappers to penetrate the northern area between the Central Valley and the San Juan River, and the trade led to the rape, murder, and enslavement of hundreds of Guatuso-Maleku people. To the southeast, the rapid expansion of United Fruit Company banana plantations led to devastating incursions on the lands of the indigenous groups of the Talamanca region. Sedentary communities of Indians in the highlands, who maintained traditions of common land ownership by the village (ejidos), were overrun and had their access to resources cut off in the context of the boom in coffee production. That story can be read from the following petition rediscovered by the historian José Antonio Salas — one rejected by the authorities on the grounds that the Indians no longer had the right to request particular treatment on the basis of their ethnicity since the laws of the republic did not recognize race or caste distinctions.

The undersigned, Toribio Serrano, as Mayordomo of San José de Orosi and the other indigenous people of the same pueblo of Orosi, before your exalted person respectfully declare: that in accordance with the title issued in the year 1777 in the name of the King of Spain, the pueblo of Orosi was bestowed with fifty-three *caballerías* [1 caballería = 112 acres] around the Indian settlement for its *ejidos*, farmlands, and sowing. No right of property was conceded to any individual, not even an indigenous person, except that of possessing the lots that would be used for their houses and their crops. Since remote time and especially in the more recent era there has been no lack of attempts by ladinos (that is, white people) to purchase portions of this land from the Indians, even by reprehensible means such as by depriving them of the use of their reason by plying them with alcohol. But beyond that, when they have been refused such acquisitions, they have become hostile to the indigenous people and have used any and all means to make them flee into the mountains, forcing them to cede the small portions of land that they occupy, either with their houses or their plots. By these means a primitive people that was owner of these lands, not only by nature but also by grace of the Conquerors, today finds itself reduced to a barbarous state, withdrawn into the mountains, thanks to the greed of invader landowners who have dispossessed them even of their last patch of land that had been conceded to them by the Spanish Crown by the same right of conquest.

In the past, the indigenous people have claimed their exemptions and their rights over the lands in question, and they sought to exclude the intruders who possess portions of the community's land. We have always received justice. We refer you to the resolution of the Governor of Cartago [of 20 April 1881], which ordered: "Above all, the indigenous residents of the community in question, the Pueblo de Orosi, must have their rights protected and their ability to use the land in conformity with the established laws." Despite these dispositions protecting the indigenous people of Orosi, the Municipality of Paraíso, in whose jurisdiction the pueblo of Orosi is located, proposes to ignore all of these precedents in order to make available to ladinos certain portions of the lands belonging to the pueblo. Moreover, the very inhabitants of the pueblo have been refused unfettered transit to places adjacent to the pueblo where we water our animals and gather our fuel for domestic use. All of this has arisen because the ladinos have taken possession of the lands, as well as roads or paths that previously served our most urgent needs.

We must also declare at this time that the savanna where the pueblo of Orosi is situated has always been considered by the indigenous people to be a pasture for the cattle belonging to [the religious brotherhood of] Señor San José. Now, with the invasions of the ladinos who chase away this cattle, we have nowhere to pasture our animals with security. In addition to this, we note that since certain ladinos among those who have devoured our lands insist that the indigenous people are indolent and even inclined to take what is not theirs, especially animals, we offer to prove the extreme opposite: that we are hard workers and that we work and possess rich planted fields. If there are some [Indians] who have tried to take what is not theirs, this does not happen only here but everywhere. Perhaps, if these illegal acts really exist, they are rather caused by the excesses of those who usurp our lands and take advantage of the simplicity of the indigenous people and not by the malice of Indians.

For all the reasons stated to Your Excellency, we implore you to help us as destitute subjects worthy of your compassion, and to declare: (1) that no one, other than the indigenous people, can acquire the right of possession and even less of property in the area of land belonging to the indigenous community; (2) that only the indigenous people and the brotherhood of Senor San José can use the savanna of the pueblo to pasture their animals; (3) that indigenous people cannot be stopped from using the watering sources that they have hitherto used for their cattle and those of Senor San José, and likewise from using the woods to supply themselves with firewood and especially from having access to the banks of the Rio Grande.

San José de Orosi, August 9, 1884

Signed by 214 indigenous people of both sexes

West Indian Limón

Paula Palmer

Paula Palmer has worked with the people of Limón to generate a valuable body of material describing the extraordinary history of the area. Costa Rica's Caribbean shores were the destination for thousands of West Indian migrants between 1880 and the 1920s, most of them from Jamaica. Afro-Antilleans provided the labor that built the railway, they taught US banana companies how to grow the fruit, and they did most of the clearing and planting of the first large banana estates. A highly literate Anglophone community took shape in Limón Province, with a thriving press and a lively culture connected to all points of the Caribbean world (including New York). The United Fruit Company enclave became one of the principal stops on the Caribbean migratory circuit of small farmers, banana workers, stevedores, teachers, prostitutes, Protestant ministers, and activists like Marcus Garvey.

An organization that was especially effective in promoting English education, as well as cultural and social programs, was the UNIA—the Universal Negro Improvement Association. Mr. Marcus Garvey founded the organization in his homeland, Jamaica, in 1919. Two years later, he arrived in Limón on the organization's Black Star Line ship, the *Frederick Douglass*, to establish a branch in Costa Rica. Garvey was no stranger in Limón, having worked as a timekeeper for the United Fruit Company on the Old Lines in 1916 and 1917. When he returned, he registered the UNIA with the government, published the constitution, and gave a well-remembered speech at the ball ground in Limón. Marcus Garvey established a worldwide reputation as a leader of black people and a champion of human rights. The UNIA branches organized in Old Harbour, Cahuita, and Penshurst played a vital role in the life of these communities from the 1920s through the 1940s.

Mr. John Burke, of Cahuita, first joined the UNIA during his years in Cuba, later participating in activities of the Limón branch. He gives this explanation of the purposes and programs of the UNIA:

In Cuba I joined an association called the Universal Negro Improvement Association. I was secretary there for quite a few months. That was in Garvey's days; he was an organizer. The idea was to organize the Negro people to have one substantial idea of who they are, where they are from. Because the facts had been hidden by the other people.

Garvey gave us a lot of lessons, let us understand the position that we were in. Because we were told in the early days that the colored people were very much inferior. So Garvey go and get the history from Africa. And then we find out that the Negroes were ruling the world before, but through their waywardness, God turned them down. Sin came in, and they were taken away like Israel as slaves. That was how a certain amount of people came to Jamaica, Barbados, Trinidad, all around the West Indies. So Garveyism came in to let us understand more about ourselves, our people. And it really did help. It's a big history.

The UNIA only want to bring the people together to understand about their history and to expect a better future. They had plans for better education, Liberia was a substantial country in Africa where all the most intelligent Negroes went to get a certain amount of training. And they were building Liberia as the first independent republic. And it is the first independent republic in Africa. But in Barbados and Jamaica they had teachers trained in Liberia to give a better education to the colored children than what was being given by the other teachers before.

When I came here I attended several meetings in Limón. Mr. Mitchell was the president. They had instruction of the past history of the Negro people and plans for the future. Today, a good amount of the people, this new generation, didn't seem to take much of that teaching. They got some of it, but they never had it as how we had it in the older days. Because, you see, we suffered more with the white people in the older days, so then we were determined to have a way out, that we could have our own administration.

So under that strain, the UNIA worked a lot. They had a school, and they teach the same English and the history. Take like the history of the West Indies under the British control. The history that we got from England, you see, they give it their way. We got to make with a different one altogether for the colored people.

You know, from the early days some of the colored people never believed there was any equality with the whites. And Garveyism bring that matter in. They had a way of saying everything got to be "yes, sir; yes, sir," but, you see, Garvey let us know it wasn't necessary under that compulsory way. So to me and to the whole world, Garveyism meant that the rest of the African nations, after Liberia, were so organized that today we have thirty-two independent nations in the continent of Africa. That's the fruit of Garveyism. . . .

When I came to Costa Rica, you could scarcely find a colored man in any kind of important position. Now and then you may find one. But the work of the UNIA in Limón with the assistance of the Costa Rican government make plenty changes. I never get the opportunity to have a talk with the last governor they have in Limón. I have it in mind, but never get the chance. I was going to give him a word of encouragement that I live to see in the Province of Limón we had a Negro governor. It was something wonderful. And when I went into the post office in Limón, and I saw the young man there in charge of the post office, I said, "Very good!" I could see the improvement of Garveyism along with the assistance of the Costa Rican government. And in other departments. I'm pleased to see it.

Mr. Selven Bryant remembers the establishment of the Old Harbour branch of the UNIA: "You have men come in from Limón, and afterward they form a branch with president from right here, and secretary, treasurer, and all. Practically all the families around was in it. They was trying to unite the people, get all the Negroes together, say they was fighting to go to Africa, to go home back, for they claim that Africa was the home of the Negroes. But they didn't succeed in that part of it. But you had about two men come from Africa here visit all the UNIA branch."

The large UNIA hall in Old Harbour is still standing, although the branch is no longer active. Mr. Mason recounts building the UNIA Liberty Hall in 1922:

That was the first board building in Puerto Viejo. All the lumber they cut with a handsaw and drag by men, women, and children by night and day, from the woodland to build that building. For about fifteen years the UNIA was strong in Old Harbour. It was through the UNIA we get English teachers here and they form a school board. We always wear the UNIA uniform. The colors of the flag was red, black, and green, so we make tie, shirt, dress out of those same colors. We were always marching, have Scouts, give concert. Now we realize it was something great.

Old Harbour people say Miss Daisy Lewis was one of the greatest singers and actresses to perform on the Liberty Hall stage. "What a voice that woman had! How I used to love to sit and listen to her sing!" says her neighbor Clinton Bennett. Today, at the age of sixty, Miss Daisy nostalgically remembers the concerts and plays that she enjoyed in her youth:

Anytime a program coming out, we put a notice at the shop here and send some to Cahuita and Manzanillo, inviting the people them. In those days, they had to walk or come in boat if the sea was good. But it always be crowded. When the people hear a program, they is coming!

Sometimes we win prizes for the best singer, the best musician. Once I played the organ, and I won the prize; I won two books. Mr. Roper had an organ at his home, and I went there every evening at 4 o'clock to practice. I had to work in the farm in the day, and sometimes I come out late, and then I had to run and practice. But I love music, and I was interested. And the little that I get, I grasp it. The piece I played came out of religious books: Children Hosanna and Choral Praise.

In those days, when we are going to have a dance, a group of boys here always be the musician, such as Vibert Myrie play the trumpet, Dudley Waite play the guitar, Clarence Patterson play the drum, and we had this great man, Mr. Lewellyn from Hone Creek, and sometimes he comes to accompany on the clarinet. We had sacred concert and we had rag concert. Rag concert is a joke, just to make people laugh.

One of the best piece we always have was the parson. The Baptist minister, his church was full, and the minister preaching and telling the people them not to do wrong things. But meanwhile he's preaching, some people come in on the other side of the stage away from the church, and they start to dance with a sweet music. And one of the church members gone over to them. And so on and so on, and when the parson look, only one member leave in the church. Everybody take off and gone to the dance. Total, the music get sweeter and sweeter, and when the parson look, the one member gone. And after, him put down the Bible and him take off him gown and him start to dance. The people always like that joke.

One time we made Noah's Ark. We had to get a lot of cardboard to make this big boat. And then we had some very strange animal, ugly animal, all kinds, and everything by pair. So they all going in the ark, and as they go, they all make sounds: the horse going "neeeeigh," the pig going "ugh, ugh," the cow going "muuu, muuu." Oh, the people love that. And everyone have on this costume, mask, tail and all, and we walk on we knee. A lot of children have to act in that for the small animals.

And when everybody get inside now, the door close. And the rain start to fall. Somebody outside pouring water! And the rain can't stop. And then the people come around, some of them with their babies, begging, "Lord, have mercy on us. Master Noah, open up the door and take us in." It was a little solemn, too, you know. You see all the people all outside begging. Some of we try to tear down the ark. We try to perform it just how we read

Miss Daisy Lewis (Courtesy of Paula Palmer)

of it in the Bible. And after, we just throw down ourselves around the ark. We were dead people. And then they draw the curtain.

In addition to its cultural and educational programs, the UNIA wanted to demonstrate that it could make real the dream of black people returning to Africa. The organization's ships of the Black Star Line docked in ports throughout the Caribbean and welcomed the people on board. Mr. Mason remembers a time when the *Frederick Douglass* made a stop in Port Limón and people were invited to go on board to take a look. He says he met the captain of the ship, "a black man named Cockburn. He was the first black captain sailed over the ocean."

Mr. Humphries, who was working on the docks in Limón at the time, also remembers the ship's stay in the port: "They did have a big place for the UNIA in Limón. They sell the ticket there for the people to go look on the ship. People come all in from the country. Train make special excursions to bring them in. All the day you see people on the docks there looking at the ship. I think it stay there for one day and then it went down to Bocas. I hear when it get to Almirante they just throw a rope off the boat, they didn't even use winch, the people alone them haul in the ship to the dock. They was so glad to see that ship. They claim the ship was to go to Africa."

In Cahuita, the UNIA hall was located on the lot where John Burke now lives. It was the site of many concerts and meetings, sometimes serving as a classroom for the English schools. The UNIA also operated a grocery store in Cahuita for a number of years. The popularity of the organization declined in the 1930s, when Marcus Garvey experienced legal difficulties in the United States. Although the Limón branch remains active, the organization no longer functions along the Talamanca coast.

Our Blood Is Blackening

Clodomiro Picado

The rise of an English-speaking, Afro-Caribbean province under the sway of a US multinational made Costa Rican nationalists extremely uneasy. As eugenics seized hold of a new generation of progressive and nationalist intellectuals in the highlands, and the results of the 1927 census revealed that West Indians were far and away the largest immigrant group in Costa Rica, there was an ugly upsurge in racist hostility directed at the West Indians of Limón. Dr. Clodomiro Picado was one of Costa Rica's most important scientists, a microbiologist and serologist who was an alumnus of the Pasteur Institute and director of the national laboratories of the Hospital San Juan de Dios during the first half of the twentieth century. His classic 1939 expression of the racism of the elites, contained in a letter to the historian Ricardo Fernández Guardia (who was then director of the National Archive), tries to give a scientific underpinning to the white legend of Costa Rica's racial origins. It is worth underlining that Picado's "blood science" is specious.

Dear and Esteemed Friend,

Authorized representative, because of your lineage and your noble and notable efforts to become one of the experts on the history of our origins, I believe I must respectfully make you aware of what I have realized concerning the blood of our ancestors of a century ago and the differences apparent in the current situation.

The object of these lines is to signal something akin to the latitude and longitude that in the ocean mark the site of a ship in motion. The modus operandi is, for those whose interests are most involved, rather unfamiliar, so I am going to explain to you what instruments have been used, what calculations have been made, and what possible routes may still be available to us.

The case is this: the diverse blood types of men can be classified into four principal groupings: I, II, III, and IV. These four groups are immutable and hereditary, so that the different percentages of one and the other present in each region mark the hematologic characteristics of the country. The Europeans living by the Mediterranean have more or less equal quantity of blood from group II and group IV. Asians, by contrast, have a high percentage of blood from group III, and the American aborigines are almost 100 percent from group IV.

For years I have been studying the distribution of our sanguineous groups, and the many thousands of exams done permit me to know what our current "blood" situation is. Moreover, by means of sampling, I have been able to determine the constitution of our ancestors a hundred years ago. This is easy, since we simply examine individuals of seventy or more years of age who by definition must have inherited the hematologic constitution of their fathers. By these means we established the typical formula, while we also do the same with young people of today and we see, strikingly, the changes suffered in our sanguineous formula.

A century ago, our formula had all the characteristics of the European race with more or less 25 percent of the Indoamerican, as is the case currently in the principal cities of Argentina, Brazil, and Chile. Later, little by little, through the immigration of diverse races, the formula has undergone change. Our immigration waves have been made up of Europeans, Asians, and Africans, while our aboriginal people disappeared before our eyes. Now, in the space of a century, our current sanguineous formula has taken a turn: that portion which is group IV, and due to conditions which remain to be explained, has had an addition of 10 percent African blood. There can be no other satisfactory mathematical calculation.

When [Vicente] Lombardo Toledano, the renowned Mexican humanist leader, came to a Costa Rican congress held by students from throughout the Caribbean area, he said in a moment of fervent fraternity for which we must thank him, "Costa Rica might very well be the crucible where the archetype of the future vigorous race of America is forged." Let's hope that this is the case, but the truth is a different one: OUR BLOOD IS BLACKENING! And if we continue like this, it will not be a nugget of gold that comes out of the crucible, but rather a piece of charcoal.

Perhaps there is still time to rescue our European sanguineous patrimony, which is possibly that which has saved us up to now from falling into systems of African type, whether in the political or in pastimes that imitate art or distinction in sad and ridiculous styles. Perhaps you, whose prestigious voice is heard by humanists of substance who are still to be found in these parts, might manage to point out the precipice toward which we are currently walking.

Yours truly, C. Picado T.

Everyday Racism, 1932

Anonymous

The racism of common folk was often motivated by the job-seeking anxieties of average Hispanic Costa Ricans, newcomers to the Limón labor market, who felt that blacks were shown preferential treatment in hiring by the United Fruit Company. Historian Ronny Viales discovered this petition to congress while researching the history of Limón.

Deputies Urbina, Ulate, and Ortiz,

As a worker and a Costa Rican, I believe it is my duty to bring to your attention in order that you might assist me with your investigation that the United Fruit Company is getting around the law that requires them to have a certain number of Costa Rican employees by instructing its negro employees in the methods of naturalizing themselves and giving them all possible means so that they might achieve this in the fastest possible term, so that when this requirement is finally applied to the company, they will be able to present the whole bunch of darkies [*toda la negrada*] they have as Costa Ricans and so get out of paying the benefits that are being demanded of them, since if the company wanted to help the country in confronting the problem of the unemployed, this would not exist in the Atlantic coast region if they only gave preference to our own; but they only give preference to the blacks, maybe because they speak the English language that the company has imposed in this area so that anyone who doesn't speak it is screwed, and it seems a contradiction that, to get work in our country one must speak another language as though our own was an Indian dialect which they were coming to civilize. I believe it is a principle of true nationalism that the companies that come to extract the juice from our land should be imposed on to respect and even adopt our language. The congress should begin to pay attention to this Jamaican race that is not only the owners of the Atlantic region but is also invading the interior of the country without anyone concerning themselves with the fact, and when they do begin to pay attention to it, it will be too late. Blacks, Chinese, Polacks

[Eastern European Jews], Coolies [South Asians], and all manner of undesirable scum who get thrown out of other countries or are kept out enter and exit our borders like it's nothing without the authorities showing any interest, and this has worsened the agonizing situation of workers like us. I will leave this letter unsigned for fear of worsening my situation since even in telling the truth and complaining of our troubles we have to hide our names.

My Mother and the Seawall

Eulalia Bernard

When the United Fruit Company shifted its operations to vast new tracts of virgin land on the Pacific coast in the early 1930s, the Costa Rican government prohibited the corporation from relocating their black labor force. Those who remained in Limón faced a double depression through the 1930s and 1940s: world economic collapse and regional economic devastation. Following the civil war of 1948, the new policy of José Figueres was to "incorporate" Limón into Costa Rican life—a policy that has meant a steady Hispanization of the area through state education policy, encouragement for new settlement by Hispanics, and a gradual increase in the flow of Afro-Limonenses to educational and employment opportunities in the Central Valley. The contemporary search for the historical identity of the Afro–Costa Rican minority is eloquently expressed by Eulalia Bernard, the best known of the community's contemporary poets. The poem was originally written in Spanish.

MY MOTHER AND THE SEAWALL

I never got tired
of seeing the sea
when I was a child
with my mother.

Like lovers
we loved it my mother and I:
she would take me by the hand
and lead me to the highest pedestal
of the seawall.
She and I would laugh
like swallows,
in the joy of finding
the treasure of life,
in the breeze of the sea,

in the scent of the sea,
in the sound of the sea,
in the distance of the sea.

I never got tired
of seeing the sea
when I was a child
with my mother.

From there, from the seawall,
I learned from her lips
the solemn truth
about my ancestors
(abandoned in this land).
From there, from the seawall,
I learned that I would be a soldier
with the unshielded word
in my hand.

She would show me
imaginary spots
that I turned into stars.
"There they are," she'd say,
"Your Koromantine grandparents,
your Fante grandparents,
who know nothing
of identity cards, nor of
crucified Christs
on the rails, nor of
deaf saints, nor of
black virgins."

The sea rumbled
(with her words)
while she told of all this
with breathless speech
and a look of far-off pride.

(Whilst the waves . . .)
the waves bowed their heads
in awe.

The Devil and Don Chico

Marc Edelman

*People from the Central Valley often jokingly refer to Guanacastecans as Nicas rega-
lados — Nicaraguans who were given to us — referring to the fact that the Nicoya
Peninsula was a separate district under Nicaraguan jurisdiction during the colonial
period (residents decided to annex themselves to Costa Rica in 1824). These peasants
and small herders have strong Mesoamerican cultural characteristics (most tellingly,
a diet based on maize) that separate them from the people of the Central Valley. An
idealized image of their cultural tradition is plundered freely by state intellectuals and
the tourist industry in order to fill with dances, dress, and marimba music what would
otherwise be a rather empty basket of national folklore. The people of Guanacaste register their difference from the people of the Central Valley in a rich oral tradition whose
distinctiveness and humor can be glimpsed in tales about the exploits of Francisco Cubillo, a legendary hacendado (large rancher) of the early to mid-twentieth century.
Anthropologist Marc Edelman collected Cubillo stories from people all over central
Guanacaste and reinscribed them in a groundbreaking article on devil pact narratives
as a cultural matrix of peasant community.*

Filadelfia, seat of Carrillo Canton, was a town of little more than one thousand inhabitants in the late 1920s, and only slightly over five thousand in
1984. Wedged between the Tempisque River and a road (now paved but once
a branch of the colonial-era royal road, or *camino real*), the settlement was
known until the late nineteenth century as Sietecueros, a term for a variety of
tree which literally means seven hides or skins. Older Filadelfinos recall that,
before the construction of levees in the 1950s, rising waters in the rainy season
frequently inundated the entire town. Residents would string ropes and cables
between tree trunks in the central plaza so that children and nonswimmers
could traverse it without drowning or being swept away. Schools of fish would
splash through the unpaved streets, sometimes remaining stranded when flood
waters receded. In the dry season, the town, only a few meters above sea level,

is dusty and hot. Filadelfia was (and is) a poor municipality, smaller and visibly less prosperous than the nearby towns of Liberia and Santa Cruz.

Shortly after the turn of the century, a destitute Nicaraguan immigrant, Francisco Cubillo Incer, appeared in Filadelfia. According to one account, echoed by many others, he came looking for work as a peon, "with his little suitcase, his rope, his [canteen made from a] gourd, his knife and sharpening stone, his machete, and his sandals." His nickname was Chico. This sobriquet was completely unrelated to his size which—judging from the formal portrait that hangs today in the municipal offices—was not especially diminutive. Within a few years, don Chico became the wealthiest and most powerful man in the canton, called by some "the owner of Filadelfia." In many respects he resembled the classical flamboyant *gamonal* (rural boss) familiar to devotees of Latin American magical realist fiction.

Between the mid-1920s and his death in 1948, Cubillo was one of the top half dozen suppliers of steers to Alajuela, the main livestock market in central Costa Rica. He ran Filadelfia, in the words of one agriculturalist from a nearby village,

> like a paternalist state. He was the one who sponsored the fiesta. He treated everyone. He gave horses to everybody so they could come. Everyone would take a horse, show it to him and go to the fiesta. He provided the bulls [for riding competitions], the bullring. He paid for the whole fiesta because he was the man with the money. He put at the service [of the people] the stores and bars, [so that] the people would go to buy the clothes they would wear and the cane liquor they would consume, the refreshments and all that. And at the culmination of the fiesta, he used to go around paying, like a birthday party, to demonstrate the power he had.

Despite his clear economic importance and his ostentatious personal style, Cubillo left little of the paper trail that members of the elites typically generate. Yet if Cubillo left few documentary traces, he did leave a more vivid imprint on the popular memory of central Guanacaste than any other twentieth-century landlord. In a region still dominated by huge underutilized estates, the family names of wealthy hacienda owners are universally recognized, and the reputations of individual hacendados past and present are widely known and discussed. Some are respected for being (or for having been) "democratic" and generous; others are reviled as imperious autocrats. None, however, evokes the same kind of richly elaborated narratives as Cubillo, or the same degree of passion in the narrators. Thus the gamonal who died over four decades ago and who is nearly invisible in the conventional documentary sources emerges as the most visible of all in the oral tradition.

Virtually all narratives coincide in citing Cubillo's sudden economic ascent. Jerónimo "Chombo" Ortega, for example, born in 1909, told how his father worked together with Cubillo and other peons on the farm of José María Obando. According to don Chombo, Cubillo "was like any other worker, like us." Then Obando lent him some land to grow maize, tobacco, and beans, and

> he began to work. And when finally he felt he could do something more, he began to buy mares, cows. . . . And in a little while he bought his first small piece of land. The man went along working, working, working, and buying little pieces of land next to the first lot he bought. El Coyol was where he bought . . . [and] from there he headed inland, buying, buying, buying, buying everything, all the farms, part by part. He bought two hectares in La Jirona and continued buying there [until] it became 1,600 hectares. He went little by little to La Penca, right up to Santa Cruz.

Zoila Medina was born in 1903 and turned eighty-eight on 11 July 1991, the day of a total solar eclipse. A few days later, I spoke with her in the dilapidated wooden house she inherited from Francisco Cubillo, the father of her nine children. Referring to one of Cubillo's earlier wives and hinting about the dark rumors that still swirled around the figure of her late husband, doña Zoila recalled that "when he had the first woman who helped him work, they lived through really hard times. He didn't even have enough to give baby clothes to the woman when she had his child. He was a poor little fellow. And here he went raising himself up, working until he became a big rich guy. Working, nothing more. Not because he had those bad things."

The stories of "those bad things"—Cubillo's pact with the devil—employ a rich imagery that bears detailed examination. Some maintained that the devil had left his mark on Cubillo's back or shoulder, a claim doña Zoila dismissed as "lies" and a "calumny," pointing out that when she went with her husband to bathe in the river, she saw that "his back was clean."

Other versions of Cubillo's pact with the forces of evil emphasize quasi-magical objects given to Cubillo by the devil or by his sons or helpers, variously referred to as "the dwarves" (*los enanos*), the "seven little devils" (*los siete diablitos*), or "the seven little blacks" (*los siete negritos*). The most prominent of these objects is Cubillo's *alforja*, a term that in English and in the different narratives refers to a "shoulder bag" or "saddlebags." The "seven little devils" figure either as a tireless workforce that toils ceaselessly for the signatory of the devil pact and helps him accumulate wealth or as the devil's watchmen and timekeepers, accompanying the signatory for the duration of the contract.

The motif of the alforja as a literal representation of wealth occurs repeatedly in stories about Cubillo, whether or not it is viewed as a gift from the forces of evil and whether or not the particular narrative touches on the theme of the devil pact. Doña Zoila recounted one confrontation that also highlighted Cubillo's ironic sense of humor and his impulsive, violent temper (an oft-cited personality characteristic that, calculated or not, likely bolstered widespread beliefs about his malevolence).

> They said that at night don Chico would go to a pasture, and that he would bring bags full of money, because he had a contract with the devil. One time a man from Belén came on a horse, with little saddlebags.
>
> "Don Chico," [he says]. "I want to talk with you."
>
> "Fine. Wait a minute" [says Cubillo].
>
> "Look, don Chico, is it there by the Tempisque River that you go to the pastures and come back with saddlebags full of money and that you have a contract with the devil and that you have the little devils here?" he says.
>
> "Do you want to see them?" [don Chico asks].
>
> "Yes," says the man.
>
> "Hey! You, you, and you!" [he calls to his children]. "These are the only little devils I have, a pile of them." [Loud laughter.] "Wait, wait, don't go," [he says to the man]. "Senora," [he told me]. "Bring my pistol, the silver one. I'm going to give 'silver' to this man and enough of this damned story!" [Loud, prolonged laughter.]
>
> The man left running. He didn't wait.

In some accounts, the pact is envisioned as a compromising piece of paper whose signatory or possessor becomes fabulously wealthy. Francisco Cortés, an agriculturalist from near Filadelfia, gave the following narrative:

People thought that [Cubillo] signed a pact, a document, with the devil, because of the fact that from night to morning, well, in the night he didn't have anything and in the morning he did. Because there's a tree, a wild fig tree, where he had his house, that's where he had the contract buried. That's where Chico Cubillo used to go to meet that man [the devil]. His peons tell that at night first there would be a strong wind, and then he would get up to go and converse [with the devil]. . . . The new generations have been digging around that tree, tearing it to pieces, looking for the treasure that people think is there. So the tree's tiny now and really it has been lost, because wherever [a piece] flies it takes root, so nobody knows where it was [originally].

The idea that don Chico had a contract with the devil was by no means universally believed. Many narratives, in explaining his rise to riches, emphasize instead his hard work and his business acumen. Jerónimo Ortega and Eliécer Zúñiga, elderly Filadelfinos who own small farms in the nearby countryside, marveled excitedly on what they remembered as Cubillo's extraordinary intelligence.

JO: He was the biggest millionaire in Guanacaste. . . . And he didn't know how to read. A son of his taught him to read and to add and subtract when he was already mature. And he did sums like this [points to his head], mentally, nothing more. And he didn't make mistakes.

EZ: He didn't make mistakes. That man was a computer! [Much laughter.]

JO: After that he bought cattle in lots of two hundred or three hundred steers.

EZ: With different prices. I admired that man, because he had the corral there full, and he would arrive one day and [tell me]: "From here on down the cattle are worth so much, and from here on up they're worth so much." Ta, ta, ta! Like that! There was a division in the corral according to the weight. Some fatter, some leaner. That's how that man was! Of those that are in high school here, there isn't a single one with the head of that man!

JO: No, no way!

EZ: You know what it is to have one hundred steers with different prices? And to say, "And this one is so much and this one so much?"

JO: Not even with a pencil, with just his head. "And this one is so much."

EZ: It's that some were fatter than others and of a better breed, some thinner.

JO: He handled all those accounts in his head.

EZ: Yes, just in his head. Of course, in his head. "If you deceive me, it's because I want you to," he would say. [Laughter.]

Another individual—who, like many, affirmed a belief in the teachings of the Catholic Church that led him to dismiss stories of Cubillo's devil pact as "legends" or "drivel"—nonetheless explained them in terms similar to those of foreign anthropologists:

He made a lot of money fast because, I'll tell you, his sagacity, the intelligence that he had for business, made him get big. . . . But what's the first thing [people] say? It's as if you, being poor, find yourself a diamond mine and soon they see you with a Mercedes Benz, that you bought a big mansion, that you bought a yacht. [in a dramatic whisper] "But how the devil did he do it, if the man didn't have money?" "Well, for sure he made a contract with the devil." [Laughs.] Because there's no other explanation. Of course, if later they find out that you found yourself petroleum or diamonds or a gold mine, and you turned it into money, well. . . . [Laughs.] He came from Nicaragua with that mentality. And when he arrived here he found the mine.

The image of the destitute Nicaraguan migrant finding a "mine" under the equally impoverished but less astute or less fortunate Filadelfinos provides a poignant indication of two other themes that infuse narratives about Cubillo and help to explain their persistence over time. One is the narrators' profound identification with Cubillo, marked by conflicting mixes of envy and esteem. The other, clearly tied to the first, is the image of vast wealth tantalizingly close yet hopelessly unobtainable. In contrast to other large landowners, who were usually from elite families and remained aloof, Cubillo's humble origins and his willingness to hobnob with the populace fed Filadelfia residents' pervasive sense that "there but for fortune go I." Many remember that when he was out drinking, he would invite any and all to imbibe with him and that he always paid the bill. Although he sometimes wore a special belt set with gold coins, most of the time he looked and acted like everyone else. "He used to walk around like a beggar," one contemporary recalled. "[With] a homespun shirt, his hat all broken, with unkempt hair, and a very old alforja."

Even the belt with the gold coins, an ostentatious marker of big-man status and wealth, serves in the narratives as a redistributive mechanism that illustrates Cubillo's generosity. "In his drinking sprees, when there was a fiesta, he would walk around with a belt with big gold medals on it. And when he was drunk, the people would come and tear them off [laughs] and take them, and he didn't even notice. 'Ah,' [he would later remark], 'They stole one of my gold coins.' And he would order that another one be put in its place."

This proximity to vast, unattainable wealth, tempting and frustrating at the same time, is also evident in the story of the lost alforja, one of the most commonly related anecdotes about Cubillo.

> In one drinking spree he had, he had a leather alforja, one of those that they used to use, full of money. And in the spree, he ended up asleep underneath a tree. And a guy came along, and he sees don Chico lying there, and he opened the alforja.
>
> "Son of a bitch!" [he said] "Full of money! A ton of money!" [Lots of laughter.]
>
> And then you know what the guy did? Honest, eh. Honest. [Laughs.] When the drunk had worn off the next day, he said, "Look, don Chico, here I bring you your alforja with all your money."
>
> Then [don Chico] said to him, "I'm going to give you fifty centavos, for you to buy an oiled rope to hang yourself," he said. "Because I didn't even know that I had lost it."

In some versions of "The Lost Alforja," the virtuous but hapless finder not only could have kept all the money but is also so honest that he does not even look in the bag before returning it to its owner. Then Cubillo gleefully taunts him by opening it, exhibiting the cash, offering a pittance of a reward, and urging him to use it for a rope to hang himself, presumably the only way he can escape the torment of knowing that he had millions in his grasp and needlessly gave them away.

"The Hotel Costa Rica" is told even more frequently than "The Lost Alforja." In this tale, narrators are strongly identified with Cubillo as stigmatized, second-class citizens of impoverished northwest Costa Rica who—in contrast to the "European" residents of Costa Rica's central plateau—look, speak, and act like mestizo "Nicaraguans" or *cholos*. When don Chico's new-found class position is briefly inverted, the association with the narrators is reinforced even more. Then, both narrators and listeners vicariously exult in how the protagonist turns the tables on oppressors with pretensions of ethnic and class superiority:

Cubillo arrived in San José, and logically he was walking humbly, he dressed humbly, and he arrived in San José with the two big saddlebags, and he went into the Hotel Costa Rica, the famous Hotel Costa Rica of that time. It was the best hotel in Costa Rica. And he arrived there, he sat down, and he waaiiiiiited and waaiiiiiited for them to attend to him, and nobody looked twice at him, like when a millionaire sees some poor bastard, like a cockroach; that's how they saw him. [Laughs.] Look, then he arrived with the alforja, and he sits down and waits for them to serve him, and an hour or so later he calls the supervisor, "Look, sir, please, why don't they wait on me?"

"No, no, no," [said the supervisor]. "Here only people with tuxedos, with fine ties and jackets and the whole business." [Much laughter.]

But a poor humble person, how were they going to wait on him? Then [don Chico said], "Call the owner for me; I want to speak with the owner, eh."

They called the owner, and he came. And he said, "Sir, what's the problem? What do you want?"

"Why don't they wait on me here?"

And he took the two saddlebags and lifted them up like this [raises his arms], and he let go a torrent of paper money. And he said, "I'll buy the hotel from you with all the employees in it!" Because he spoke like that [angrily, using the familiar form of address]. "I'll buy the hotel from you with all the employees in it!"

And then the owner said, "Yes, yes, don Francisco." And from then on it was pure pats on the back, eh. Because then they saw the man and the money he was carrying.

One account affirms that the hotel altercation brought Cubillo—and by extension the poor Filadelfinos with whom he is implicitly identified in the story—to national attention: "It was like a bomb blast in San José, in the entire country, because at that time radio stations were beginning to appear, and it was big news." One of the most striking aspects of "The Hotel Costa Rica" is the bond that narrators, typically Filadelfia residents of modest means, establish with Cubillo, the regionalist hero who triumphs over the discrimination of "white" Costa Rica (with money, as in much of Latin America, compensating for membership in a subordinate ethnic group). Importantly, this identification appears more salient than the class antagonism central to the devil contract narratives, which stress the evil behind rapid accumulation of wealth. Indeed, the most commonly told stories about Cubillo do not even mention the devil pact and are frequently related by individuals who reject it as mythical or superstitious.

Despite repeated references to Cubillo's bargain with the forces of evil and frequent allusions to his apparently irascible and impulsive personality, Cubillo does not emerge in the devil-pact or alforja stories as especially diabolical or greedy. Even accounts of his fifty centavos to the man who returns his lost alforja place greater stress on Cubillo's caustic sense of humor and on the luckless finder's lost opportunity than on the niggardly size of the reward. Indeed, generosity rather than stinginess is a constant theme in reminiscences about Cubillo. In this, he is viewed nostalgically, much like the hacendados of earlier decades, as epitomizing the more humane style of class relations, which predated the aggressive agrarian capitalism of the 1950s and 1960s.

Passing: Nicaraguans in Costa Rica

Patricia Alvarenga

The withering of the Sandinista revolution, which started with the US embargo and the Contra war of the 1980s, resulted in a growing number of Nicaraguan refugees coming to Costa Rica. The failure of the post-Sandinista Nicaraguan economy in the 1990s brought an even greater wave south as illegal aliens. This most recent migration of "Others"—totaling an estimated half million in a country of four million—has created a xenophobic panic. The presence of "los Nicas" (a diminutive for Nicaraguans, the equivalent of "Ticos" for Costa Ricans) in Costa Rica is impressive, especially in the urban heart of the country where most have settled and where large, marginal barrios of Nicaraguans have appeared. Social scientist Patricia Alvarenga interviewed Nicaraguan immigrants to establish how the clandestine immigration is organized, what types of solidarity networks exist among Nicaraguans in Costa Rica, and how they deal with assimilation and discrimination.

The stories of Mexican migrants to the United States cause deep concern among Costa Ricans. The same people are almost totally unaware of the conditions faced by hundreds of thousands of Nicaraguans who have crossed the border into Costa Rica, or of the perils that they have had to undertake to evade the border patrols. It is difficult to believe that a journey of some one hundred kilometers can require a physical exertion that, on top of the hunger of the poorly provisioned migrants, often brings them to the point of starvation. For Marlene, who came to Costa Rica in 1992, the journey began in her hometown, Pueblo Nuevo de Estelí. She left there with thirty men and one other woman. The group, which, according to Marlene, was led by a "coyote," headed toward Granada, and from there to Papaturro on the border. From Papaturro to the last immigration post in Upala took them eight days. According to Marlene, "that's how we got here, putting up with hunger, and when we were finally in Costa Rican territory eating ripe cacao that we picked where we were hidden on the side of the road so that they couldn't see us. . . . We couldn't even take a bus because they'd get us further down the road."

On top of these obstacles, they had to face an unforeseen circumstance: in Naranjo the young man who was leading them got sick and, without any possibility of going to the hospital, they decided to ask for help from the guard of one of the farms in the area. Marlene narrates: "Instead he kicked us off the farm, gun in hand, and went and called the police, and us there, with the guy really sick, we had to hole up in the middle of a field planted in coffee, and then we walked and walked and that day a great rain fell, and we didn't have anything to put on because, well, the clothes we had were all wet." Gender made the difficult migrant adventure even more of an uphill battle for Marlene. Even though, according to her testimony, the majority of the thirty men who were traveling with her were good, some "who wanted to take advantage began to bother me. I didn't pay any attention because I was thinking, 'right, tell me when?' "

The conditions under which they traveled were really adverse, but thanks to the solidarity of the group, they all managed to avoid the surveillance of the border posts. One of the traveling companions hawked his watch and used the money to buy everyone a bus ticket to Orotina. Marlene remembers that she sold her gold necklace "for a thousand colones [a few dollars] to help all of us out." Still, the amounts from these transactions were not enough to buy food; they barely paid the costs of transportation once the distribution of immigration control posts allowed them to move about in local buses. Hunger stalked them until they got to Higuito, an encampment of sugarcane cutters.

Mayerli, a seventeen-year-old domestic servant who arrived in Costa Rica in late 1996, came together with a girlfriend. Both, like Marlene, paid a coyote to get them secretly into Costa Rica. But in this case, the coyote basically left them at the border. They had to use their wits to get past the border posts in the Zona Norte. Mayerli and her friend stayed for five days and nights in the hallway of the house of a woman from whom they bought, at exorbitant rates, a bun, a few cookies, and a Coke. With this meager nourishment they survived until they were able to phone a fellow countryman, Gustavo, a Nicaraguan who was resident in Costa Rica. He organized a rescue for the young women by convincing two truck-driver friends of his to hide the women in their cabs. Although the border posts inspected the trailers, according to Mayerli "they hardly looked at anything, just kind of glanced at the canvas, but we were hiding underneath it. In San José at last, Gustavo accompanied the two disoriented, filthy, and hungry travelers to the Parque de la Merced [a historic park in downtown San José that, during the 1990s, was an important meeting point for Nicaraguans], from where they were able to call a girlfriend resident in Costa Rica who could come and get them.

The journey is not always so troubled. Marvin came with two young men who had already entered the country illegally on a number of occasions. They had good experience with how to hide in the woods and hills to avoid detection by the immigration police. Also, Marvin, a man of about thirty years of age, made good use of his experience in the Nicaraguan jungle as a soldier with the Sandinista army to overcome the obstacles on the trip. Marvin didn't suffer hunger like Marlene did thanks to his knowledge of wild plants. According to what he told us, "in the wilds you can find anything—if you're smart and you've lived a bit in the wild, you know what you can and can't eat." He and his friends expertly avoided the immigration posts. On arrival in San José, Marvin bid his friends farewell, asked where he could find a place that was cool, was told that San Antonio fit the bill, and so he took the road there.

Doña María Eugenia, an engineer with the ministry of public security who is in charge of building a command post in Los Chiles on the border, tells of her experience in the Zona Norte. During her trip to the border areas at La Cruz, Peñas Blancas, Upala, and Los Chiles, she was surprised to see "many Nicaraguans hidden among the coffee fields and some plantations that are around there." When the illegal immigrants that she happened to run into on the road saw an official ministry vehicle, they ran to hide, fearing that it was the border police. She tells us that they will soon build modern installations for the border police, a corps created during the Figueres administration (1994–98) due to the massive Nicaraguan migrations. According to this ministry employee, the project is intended to improve the "infrahuman conditions" in which the border police work.

Those migrants who are detained are shut in a basement where they have access to only one toilet facility "in very poor state," three benches, and dreadful ventilation. This barracks, however, located in an installation belonging to customs and immigration, does not figure in the plans of the projected new works. Detained migrants remain in this basement until enough illegals have been rounded up to fill a bus—that is, for only a few hours. After that, they are sent to the other side of the border with Nicaragua. Generally the number detained in Los Chiles alone is more than fifty a day, and our informant tells us that the immigration authorities always try to effect the deportations as quickly as possible to avoid having to feed the detained since "if a lot of time goes by, they have to give them something to eat . . . for example, if they arrive in the morning, at lunchtime they have to get something to eat." Nevertheless, according to members of the Central American Human Rights Commission, on their visit to the basement at 4:30 P.M., many of the Nicaraguans waiting for expulsion had been there since nine in the morning and had still not received a meal. The drama of these migrants is summed up by doña María when she comments that those who have traveled such a long journey without success "look worn out, hungry, sometimes with their clothes filthy, torn, without suitcases."

In the 1980s, due to the existence of the migratory status of "refugee," the trip into Costa Rica was not nearly as painful as it tends to be now. The great difficulties of the journey were met on the Nicaraguan side. While the war was going on in Nicaragua, the Costa Rican government openly favored the Contras and, as part of its anti-Sandinista policies, promoted the migration into Costa Rica of Nicaraguans who also opposed the Sandinistas, creating refugee camps in the north. As a result, even though the guerrilla war taking place on the Nicaraguan frontier made the trip difficult for those who were fleeing the war, once they had entered Costa Rica, far from avoiding the authorities, they sought them out and surrendered in order to be transferred to the refugee camps where, although deprived of their freedom, they could count on a roof over their heads, food, and clothing. . . .

The thousands of Nicaraguans who came as refugees from the countryside during the 1980s, taking advantage of the opportunities offered by the Costa Rican state, looked for ways to make links with the outside world. The camps became centers of reproduction for a new labor force, achieved through a complex system of controls whereby the authorities distributed refugees as workers to rich coffee and sugar growers. This system of labor recruitment was explained in clear terms by don Arnulfo: "Owners would arrive from San José and from Alajuela, and they would say, 'I need ten people.' They'd talk with the director, with the administrator of the camp, and he would give them a permit. In the permit it would say that he had to provide food, a place to live, a bed, even if it was only a cot, and give them money for their return fare too. There were some bosses who fulfilled the promise and others who didn't, but I myself have had luck with the bosses."

Basically, the situation in the camps was tough because of the strict supervision which the refugees were subject to, and because they had to live in very close quarters with dozens of strangers. But despite these drawbacks, the basic necessities of the refugees were guaranteed, and they could count on valuable possibilities of integrating into the labor market on good conditions. The story is different for the hundreds of thousands of Nicaraguans who have crossed the border since the Costa Rican government decided there was no longer any reason to apply the category of "refugee" to them. . . .

Don Arnulfo tells us that when his current employer asks him where he's from, he says that he's from Guanacaste because, as he puts it, "I tell all people who ask me that question that I'm from Guanacaste, not because I want to deny my homeland, but because you can't just tell anyone that [you're from Nicaragua]." He goes on to reflect that according to him, Nicaraguans have acquired a reputation as liars. As a result, he insists that he does not like to lie much. Obviously, when he says this, he means that he does tell lies, but as little as possible. In fact it would be very difficult for Nicaraguans, especially those who are illegal, to avoid lying. Lies are weapons they use to defend themselves.

One of the strategies used by Nicaraguans to evade identification by immigration agents and to avoid discrimination by Costa Rican society is to identify themselves as Guanacastecans. This is what Marlene did when, while taking a taxi ride with two Nicaraguan women, the woman taxi driver asked her what country she was from. She replied that she was from Guanacaste. They happened to be passing by the Parque de la Merced, and so the taxi driver who, according to Marlene, had believed her lie, "began to talk about 'the Nicas'! [saying] 'This bunch of *muertos de hambre* [literally, "starving people," the common derogative term used by Costa Ricans to refer to Nicaraguans], they've taken over the whole park. Now we Ticos can't even use the place to relax.' " Marlene is probably exaggerating her capacity to "pass for" a Guanacastecan since her accent pegs her as a native of the north of Nicaragua. What Marlene didn't realize is that the taxi driver, realizing that she was trying to fool her, was being aggressive.

Henri, on the other hand, insists that he never denies his nationality. He himself, however, tells us of his experiences trying to pass as a Tico. When he escaped from a refugee camp, he found work in a pharmacy owned by an Israeli woman who had employed a number of illegal Nicaraguans. Henri learned how to change his accent to talk like a Costa Rican in case the immigration police came into the pharmacy. Mayerli didn't like to pass herself off as a "Tica" either. Nevertheless, she laments, when she spent a month looking unsuccessfully for work, she felt that she had to accept that she was a Nicaraguan. For Mayerli it was impossible to lie because "they immediately said to me, 'You're a Nicaraguan,' without waiting for me to tell them." . . . After six months in Costa Rica, it's impossible for Mayerli to talk like a Tica, especially because it's difficult for her to pronounce the letter *s*. By contrast, her friend Olga is "an expert." After dedicated practice at pronouncing Spanish like a Tica from the Central Valley, Mayerli claims her friend is able to fool even the immigration police.

The capacity to use these defensive strategies in the face of ethnic discrimination depends on two factors: experience and physical appearance. The more time the migrants have been in Costa Rica, the greater their ability to put on a Central Valley or Guanacastecan accent. The choice here depends on the talent acquired to "fake" a Central Valley accent, which is harder for Nicaraguans than the Guanacastecan accent. As we saw in Marlene's case, those who have recently arrived might think that they can pass for Guanacastecans without trying, but this is not true, especially in the case of migrants who come from the north, a region whose accent is easily distinguishable from that of Guanacaste. But to pass for someone from the Central Valley, the ability to imitate the accent does not suffice. Physical appearance is very important. The more light-skinned Nicaraguans, and those who have been in the country for a number of years, are those who can more easily fool Costa Rican nationals into taking them for Vallecentralinos. If they are not found out, this permits them to adapt better to the environment when they feel it necessary to put their transformative capacity to the test than would passing themselves off as Guanacastecans who, though Costa Rican, are second-class citizens.

These processes of mutation are very nuanced. Sometimes, as in the cases of don Arnulfo, Henri, and Marlene, they are used only occasionally when, in a given moment, the migrants consider it inconvenient to reveal their origins. In other cases, however, the mutation expresses a high degree of assimilation to the dominant culture. This change is no longer just done purposefully; it becomes a form of everyday behavior that the subject reproduces without intention. In other words, in such cases the migrants have "interiorized" the dominant culture.

Doña María and her daughters were brought to Costa Rica by don Arnulfo six years ago. The family lives in the Carpio shantytown where don Arnulfo visits regularly, especially recently, having bought a house in the neighborhood for one of his daughters. But her relation with don Arnulfo is the only friendship with a Nicaraguan that doña María will accept. Although she lives in a part of the barrio where Nicaraguans predominate, doña María plainly avoids contact with them. She and her daughters are fair, and so they easily pass for Ticas. Although her Costa Rican neighbors in the barrio know that they are Nicas, they accept them as "different from their countrymen" as much because of their behavior as because of their physical appearance. In this way, the same forms expressing discrimination promote alienating behaviors on the part of Nicaraguans who are trying to integrate into the Costa Rican community.

Doña María spoke ill of her Nicaraguan neighbors, because "they go on drinking binges and fire off guns. How they go at it! And they come to do the same thing here. They're all Nicaraguans, but there are some who are not bad." So, for doña María, good people are an exception among her compatriots. She explains that she uses the following strategy to avoid them: "Although we might all be from the same place, I keep my distance to avoid problems with anyone. I don't have any ties. The only one is don Arnulfo." ... Doña María also "protects" her daughters from the unhealthy Nicaraguans, "locking the front door so that they can't go out and they stay here watching TV." According to Marlene and her cousin Idalia, who accompanied us on our visit, doña María got furious when she found out that her oldest daughter had a Nicaraguan boyfriend.

In part, doña María's behavior is a response to the difficulties she faces trying to raise her daughters in Carpio, a marginal barrio of the capital that is frequently the scene of violence. On the other hand, she is also a classic representative of that group of Nicaraguans whose response to discrimination is to reject, openly or subtly, their fellow Nicaraguans, which manifests itself in conjunction with an eagerness to show the dominant society that they, too, can behave like Costa Ricans.

Taking Care of Sibö's Gifts

Gloria Mayorga, Juanita Sánchez,

and Paula Palmer

Costa Rica's indigenous people are holding onto cultural survival by a thread. Accord-
ing to the census of 2000, 63,876 indigenous people live in Costa Rica, 1.7 percent of
the total populace. Many of them make their homes on reserves in lands once consid-
ered marginal but that have sometimes become desirable again for tourism develop-
ment, logging, hydroelectric projects, or mineral exploration, a dynamic that inevitably
ends with enormous pressure on indigenous groups to accept displacement and ques-
tionable compensation yet again. Fewer than two hundred Cabécar and Bribri people
live on the KéköLdi Indigenous Reserve in the Caribbean lowlands near the border
with Panama. Here, some of their leaders outline the environmental projects of the
KéköLdi Reserve Development Association, part of their bold and innovative attempt
to rejuvenate indigenous culture and society in Costa Rica. Sibö is their creator and
inspiration.

Define and Defend the Boundaries of the Reserve

The people of the KéköLdi Reserve are petitioning CONAI [National Commission for Indian Affairs] to demarcate the boundaries of the Reserve so that all
our nonindigenous neighbors know exactly where they stand in relation to the
Reserve. We also hope that CONAI will buy the farms of nonindigenous people
within the Reserve as soon as possible. In the meantime, it is our responsibility
to keep the paths which currently mark our boundaries clean, and to enforce
the Indigenous Law within the Reserve.

The responsibility of the KéköLdi Reserve Development Association is to
keep the boundary paths clean so that nonindigenous people will not trespass
to hunt or clear land. The nonindigenous people whose properties are within
the Reserve have the right to keep farming the parts that are already in cultivation, but they do not have the right to clear forest without our permission. . . .

Right now there are squatters occupying parts of our Reserve. They say, "Why do you Indians want so much land? You don't even cultivate it!" We have explained to them that we are taking care of the forests and the animals, but they only want to destroy everything. . . . We are poor. We don't have money to buy zinc, so we need to protect the plants whose leaves we use to make thatch roofs. The forest gives us lianas that we use to make baskets and fences and houses. The forest gives us medicinal plants. And we like to have the forest around us. To us, a big pasture, say ten or twenty hectares, is not beautiful. The forest is beautiful because Sibö created it. Yes, we clear small parts to plant, to live, but we would never cut down the whole forest because it is valuable to us just as it is. We need it to live, too.

An indigenous person without the forest is a sad person. We know that without the forest, we wouldn't have water. We only have a few sources of water in our Reserve, and already some squatters have destroyed several of them. One squatter family took some land high on a hill at the source of a river. They cut all the trees along the riverside to make a big pasture, and the river is almost dry now. What water it carries is contaminated from their cows, so the people below can't drink it. It's hard to move these people off the land. Sometimes we feel sorry for them, and we tell them they can stay, but they can't cut any more trees. But really they are endangering all of us.

Actually, the people who live in the lowlands surrounding the Reserve should be grateful to us for trying to protect the sources of their water, for trying to prevent droughts and soil erosion. Even if they don't know it, they are benefiting from our conservation efforts.

—Gloria Mayorga

Stop Illegal Hunting in the Reserve to Protect the Wildlife

Not long ago, the KéköLdi region was rich in wildlife. Now the animals are so scarce that we rejoice when we see signs of them. To give the animal populations a chance to reproduce and repopulate the Reserve, we are voluntarily restricting hunting among ourselves, the residents of the KéköLdi Reserve. The Indigenous Law prohibits hunting by nonindigenous people, but this law has been very difficult for us to enforce. When we talked to the poachers, they ignored us. Even when we denounced them to the authorities, they kept coming back. Since 1987, the Wildlife Department of the Ministry of Natural Resources, Energy, and Mines has authorized four indigenous Wildlife Inspectors to enforce the antipoaching law in the Reserve. The poachers pay high fines, and most of them have finally stopped hunting in the Reserve. But we always have to be vigilant.

We have already seen some results from our efforts to restrict hunting: our animals are returning to the forests. We rejoice when we see the tracks of wild pigs, pacas, peccaries, and wild turkeys, and we are seeing many more of them now than we did just five years ago. White-faced monkeys have returned, and parrots and toucans. We have hopes of some day seeing again the tapirs and deer and jaguars. For all the animals to return, we have to stop killing them, and we have to protect the forests where they find food and shelter. That is why we are asking our neighbors to cooperate with our No Hunting policy.

Thirty years ago, the animals were abundant here. You saw wild pigs, red monkeys, howler monkeys, and white-faced monkeys. There were macaws and wild turkeys, deer and wild goats, tapirs, jaguars, peccaries, pacas, hawks, iguanas, sloths, mountain hens. You saw them all the time, anywhere you walked. When I was a young man, I went out hunting with the older men. . . . In those days, the wild pigs traveled in bands, up to two hundred of them all traveling together. They trampled down the bush and left wide trails where they passed, so the men would follow those paths until they found the wild pigs. We would kill one or two and return to the house. Indigenous hunters carry the whole carcass of the animal to the house. We don't leave anything in the bush. We always share the meat with all our family and our neighbors so that they are happy and Sibö is happy with us. Sibö doesn't permit us to waste the meat of wild animals or to sell it.

In about 1956 or 1957, the government made a law that said that everyone has to respect private property. That means that you can't hunt on private property without getting the permission of the owner. But we didn't enforce that law on our farms here. White people started coming in to hunt, and we didn't do anything, we didn't say anything to them. They would walk right through our yards, by our houses, with their rifles and their dogs. And we never said anything to them. Why? Because we were so timid, we were afraid to say anything to them. At that time, this was not an Indigenous Reserve. And we didn't know our rights.

One time I remember they came to this creek here to hunt deer. From six in the morning till five at night they were chasing a deer, and they finally killed it right here in front of my eyes. I didn't say anything to them. But now it's different. Now we have the courage to defend the animals. Now if I see a hunter come in with his dogs, I tell him he can't hunt on my property, and if he doesn't leave, I report him to the police. For years you could say we were asleep; now we're waking up. It's the Reserve that has given us this courage. Now the police have to fine the poachers that we report. But before, people were coming in all the way from Cartago to hunt. They would kill three or four peccaries, three or four pacas, and they would sell the meat in Cartago. They came here every other week. That's why the animals were becoming extinct. . . .

—Rodolfo Mayorga

The worst problem we have with poachers is on the Margarita side of the Reserve. The squatters that live over there keep coming into the Reserve to hunt. They sell the meat in Panama and get paid in dollars, so it's a good business for them. I don't know what more we can do. We denounce them, and they keep coming back. Our Wildlife Inspectors are working hard, but they can't guard all the Reserve's boundaries every night. When will these squatters and poachers ever begin to respect our Reserve?

—Tranquilino Morales

The white people don't respect the borders of the Reserve. They come right through my yard to hunt. One day I went out to report them to the authorities, and they got furious with me. They said this place doesn't belong to the indigenous people, they said they would beat me, they said they would kill me, and I don't know what else. They keep coming in to hunt. They live from that. I hear their dogs about three times a week.

When I came here to live, just four years ago, there were pacas here, but the poachers killed them, they killed two of them right here in my yard, next to my house. I haven't seen any more pacas. A few weeks ago, they killed a tapir up in the mountains there. The monkeys used to come here close to the house, but no more. They hide way back in the mountains. A howler monkey used to wake us up every morning with his roaring, but those people shot him. And a wild turkey used to come here, she was practically tame. She came right up to the house. And they shot her.

—Carmen Leiva

The /awapa/ [shaman] always used certain animal hides in our healing ceremonies. When the people hunted, they always kept the hides for the /awapa/ to use. Now, since there are no animals, some people make wooden figures of animals, and we have to use those in our ceremonies.

—Aníbal Morales, /awá/

For the animals to live, we have to preserve the forests. And that is what we want. We want the animals to return and reproduce. We have the faith and the hope that the animals will come back again.

—Rodolfo Mayorga

Semidomestication of the Green Iguana

The green iguana is an endangered species. It has many natural predators, but its greatest enemy is man. When female iguanas are ready to lay their eggs, they are particularly vulnerable to hunters because they come down from the trees to lay their eggs on the beaches and riverbanks, where they are easily spotted. Deforestation along riverbanks also deprives them of protective vegetation. Their meat and their eggs are delicious and nutritious. Their numbers are rapidly declining throughout Central America.

The KéköLdi Association is now managing an experiment in the semidomestication of the green iguana. Our goals are to repopulate this species in our Reserve, train people in other communities in the semidomestication techniques, and eventually, when iguanas are abundant, rely on them for protein in order to protect other wild animals in the forest. This project is funded by the Norwegian government through the International Union for Conservation of Nature and Natural Resources (IUCN) and Asociación ANAI [a national indigenous organization]. The Costa Rican Ministry of Natural Resouces, Mines, and Energy is also contributing to it.

When the ANAI people learned that we are restricting hunting in the KéköLdi Reserve because we are so concerned about the disappearance of the wild animals, they offered us the opportunity to start a green iguana semidomestication experiment. First, they sent a Costa Rican biologist, Julio Barquero, to study in Panama with a German iguana specialist, Dagmar Werner. When Julio came back to Costa Rica, we had several meetings. The ANAI said they could finance the project. They would buy materials to build the iguana nursery and pay Julio to supervise the work and to train KéköLdi volunteers in all the techniques of raising iguanas. The KéköLdi participants would eventually be able to take iguanas to their own homes and start nurseries in their yards. It seemed like a good way to begin to repopulate endangered species in our Reserve, so we accepted the project and started to work.

We chose Juanita's farm as the site for the nursery because it is close to the road; it would be easier to bring all the materials there. We cleaned the site and started building the cages and a storehouse for supplies and tools.

Since the iguanas lay eggs in March, we started the construction in January. When the storehouse and the cages were finished, we started building the artificial nests where the iguanas would lay their eggs.

In the wild, iguanas live in trees, but the females go down to the beach or the riverbanks to lay their eggs in sandy soils. They make a hole in the sand or under a rock or a trunk, and they cover the eggs with sand after they've laid them. So we built artificial nests, making hollow tubes out of the *jira* tree, and we filled them with sand. When the iguanas were ready to lay their eggs, they dug out the sand inside the jira tubes. A few of the females didn't use the artificial nests, but most of them did. Then we carefully took the eggs out of the nests, trying to keep them in the same position without disturbing them too much. We counted the eggs to keep records of how many eggs each iguana laid, and then we placed the eggs in baskets, marked with the identification number of the mother, and put them in the incubator. . . .

We're learning a lot about what the iguanas like to eat. The people are planting these plants in their yards, so they won't have to keep the iguanas in cages. They'll let them loose near their houses and provide them with the plants they like best, to keep them close. They like yam leaves, hibiscus flowers, ripe bananas, and lots of other plants. Dagmar sends us dry food that the iguanas like, too. All the people who are working have set up feeding stations in their yards, with dry food and water. We've seen some wild iguanas come and eat the dry food.

A female iguana starts laying eggs when she's two or three years old. In Nature, very few iguanas grow to maturity. If a female lays sixty eggs, maybe only two or three survive to be able to reproduce. Raccoons eat the eggs, and snakes, hawks, basilisks, dogs, cats, and other animals prey on the baby iguanas. In our nurseries, their chances of survival are much higher, but still many babies die. So Dagmar says we have to produce lots of iguanas before we can start thinking about using them for meat, or marketing them. We have to let them grow to maturity and begin to reproduce naturally and repopulate the whole region. And we want to extend the project to other communities throughout the country, so we will always be giving iguanas away and training people to start their own nurseries. . . .

A lot of people from all over the world have come to see the nursery. They write their names in our Visitors' Book, and you can see all the different countries where they come from. So we realize this work is important because if we're successful, people in other countries will be encouraged to try to repopulate iguanas and other species that are endangered. So we're trying to keep good records of everything we're learning about taking care of the iguanas.

— Demetrio Mayorga

Protect the Forests and the Plants We Depend On

In addition to providing water and a home for the wild animals, the forest gives us a great variety of plants that are very useful to us. Our medicines come from the forest, and so do the lianas, trees, and plants that we use to make our houses, baskets, bags, and blankets. Luckily, we still have some virgin forest within our Reserve. It is a natural nursery for the plants we depend on. We have to protect the forest and be sure not to overuse the plants we need. We are also starting to experiment with cultivating some of these plants on our farms. . . .

The KéköLdi people have resolved to prohibit cutting trees in the forest. There are valuable woods for construction in our forest, but we have no right to cut them and sell them because we didn't plant them. Sibö made them, and it is our responsibility to care for them. We have no right to exploit them for personal gain. We have talked about this in many meetings in the Reserve, and we have all agreed on this policy.

If someone wants to cut trees on his farm to build a house, he has to go to a meeting of the Association and explain what he wants to do. If he wants to cut trees to make a house, we usually give permission. But if he wants to sell the wood, first he has to convince the Association to give him permission, and then he still has to get permission from the Forest Department of the Ministry of Agriculture. If he gets the permissions and cuts the trees, he has to pay a fee to the Association treasury. He has to share his profits with the community, because the properties in the Reserve belong to all of us collectively.

—Gloria Mayorga

The plants that are most useful to us are becoming very scarce in the KéköLdi Reserve. This is partly the fault of the squatters who have cleared the forest in the Reserve. Maybe they don't know, or maybe they don't care, but they cut the jira and *chonta* trees, they cut the plants that give us leaves to make our thatch roofs, they cut the pita that gives us thread, they cut the *guarumo* and *mastate* trees that we use to make *chácaras* [string bags] and blankets, they cut the trees that support the lianas from which we make baskets. We also have part of the fault ourselves, because we have used up most of the plants in the lower regions of the Reserve, on our farms, and now we have to walk far into the mountains to find them.

Now we think we should be very careful not to destroy the last of these plants. That is why we have started an experimental nursery to see if we can cultivate them and transplant them on our farms. A Peace Corps volunteer, Marco Lowenstein, helped us make the first nursery in Rodolfo Mayorga's farm. The jira seeds didn't germinate, but the chonta did. The /uko/ leaves didn't grow, but the /sekamo/ leaves did. We have also been successful with pita cultivation, and we have a nursery of *cachá* and cedar for wood.

Now we are working with Rafael Ocampo to try planting these same species and many others directly on our farms. This is a project sponsored by CATIE

(Centro Agrónomico Tropical de Investigación y Enseñanza, an agricultural college) and ANAI. We are planting the same plants we tried in the first nursery, plus *cabuya* [agave] and guarumo for thread, and lianas for basket-making and binding materials. We're also planting medicinal plants like Chinese root (*Cuculmeca smilax*) and sarsaparilla (*Smilax officinalis*), and ornamental plants. These are all plants that grow naturally in our forests, but the idea is to cultivate them for our own use and also for sale. If we're successful, this project will demonstrate how valuable the forest is, how it gives us plants that can bring us economic benefits, if we take care of them.

—Juanita Sánchez

Medicinal Plants

All indigenous people know certain plants that we use as medicines. This knowledge is passed from one generation to the next. We use leaves, roots, flowers, bark, lianas, seeds — all different kinds of plants. Some of them we can cultivate. We plant those in our yards. Some of them grow along paths and on farms, where they get a lot of sun. But most of them grow only in deep forests.

We use more than twenty different lianas to cure snakebites, rheumatism, dizziness, headaches, kidney infections, itching, diarrhea, cough, and fevers. These lianas are only found in the forests. The /awapa/ use these and other lianas in their ceremonies to cure sicknesses that result when we don't obey Sibö's laws.

For us the forest is a pharmacy, full of medicines. Our /awá/, Aníbal Morales, collected more than fifty medicinal plants for botanists at the National Museum to identify and study. We are happy to assist scientists who want to analyze the medicinal properties of the plants in our forests. We only ask them to assist us, too, in our efforts to protect our forests. We don't want these valuable plants to only exist in scientific laboratories and Museum basements. We want them to exist in Nature, in the forests where Sibö left them for us to use as we need them. This is another reason why it is so important to us to protect our forests.

Reforestation

The KéköLdi Association is seeking grant funds to reforest some parts of the Reserve. One site we want to reforest is a four-hectare pasture abandoned by a nonindigenous resident six years ago. The site is in the hills of the Reserve above Olivia, at the headwaters of the KéköLdi River. Our plan is to plant trees whose fruits the wild animals eat. We want to plant *javillo* along the riverbanks for the iguanas; ojoche for the pacas, agoutis, and mountain hens; *almendros* [almond trees] for the pacas and parrots; *molinillo* for the monkeys, toucans, and parrots; *níspero* [medlar], *zapote, sonzapote,* and *caimito,* which are loved by all the animals. We would also plant native hardwood trees like laurel and *kativo.*

Nearer to the residences of KéköLdi people along the UkabLi trail, we are already planting fruit trees and trees whose leaves we use for thatch. A grant of one thousand dollars from a Dutch church enabled us to start a nursery of native fruit trees: mangoes, star apples, monkey head, water apples, avocados, and peach palms. The fourteen people (adults and children) who are working in this project will transplant the small trees near the Community House, where their fruits will be available for everybody. We also planted some fruits that have been brought to Costa Rica from other tropical areas by ANAI. And we are planting medicinal plants *(hombre grande, sarsaparilla),* native hardwoods (níspero, *cedro macho,* ojoche) and /uko/ to make thatch.

To accomplish these reforestation projects, KéköLdi people will have to dedicate many months of work to the tasks of collecting seeds and seedlings, preparing, planting, and maintaining nurseries, and transplanting and maintaining the young trees. We will need funds to pay KéköLdi people to work full-time in these reforestation projects and to buy tools and materials. The KéköLdi Association is seeking these funds from national and international organizations.

Indigenous Education

The children who live in the KéköLdi Reserve attend public schools in the nonindigenous communities surrounding the Reserve. In these schools, they study the national curriculum, but they learn nothing of their own language, culture, and history. Since April 1990, KéköLdi children have been attending an indigenous education program offered on Sundays at the Community House. Marian Caplan, a student volunteer with the Institute for Central American Development Studies (ICADS) helped to organize the program, through which KeköLdi adults pass their traditional knowledge on to the next generation. Artisans teach their skills and techniques; /awapa/ teach the /sorbón/ dance and the uses of medicinal plants. Elders narrate the history of the Bribri people and the lessons Sibö gave to the first generation of the indigenous men and women.

One of the program's main projects is the making of storybooks based on these narrations and illustrated by the KéköLdi children themselves. The first storybooks retell in Spanish and Bribri the histories of ShuLakma and MuLurtmi; income from the sale of *Taking Care of Sibö's Gifts* will be used to make more of these storybooks and to support the indigenous education program.

Land Purchase within the Reserve

The KéköLdi Development Association is actively raising funds to help CONAI purchase farms within the KéköLdi Reserve. Once purchased, these properties will be included in the single title to Reserve land, held collectively by the KéköLdi people. Resource management policies of the KéköLdi Association will be applied on these properties. Forest, wildlife, and watershed will be protected, reforestation will be encouraged, and technical assistance for sustainable agriculture will be available through collaboration with CATIE and ANAI. The farmland will provide subsistence for young KéköLdi families who will pass on Sibö's teachings to another generation.

Many people wonder what they can do to help preserve the tropical rain forests which are so important for sustaining life on our planet. Doesn't it make sense to lend support to the indigenous people who have lived within the rain forests for thousands of years without destroying them? With increased political autonomy, secure claim to land, and the support of environmentalist organizations, indigenous people can continue to play a crucial role in saving the rain forests.

To effectively take care of Sibö's gifts in the area defined as the KéköLdi Reserve, the KéköLdi people need to be able to purchase hundreds of hectares of land within the Reserve boundaries. To everyone who wants to do something to help preserve the forests, we invite you to consider donating funds to bring these lands under the management of the KéköLdi people.

★ ★ ★

To contact KéköLdi leaders,
send an e-mail to
   Sebastian Hernández Balma, deyedi@costarricense.cr
or send letters to:
   Juana Sánchez
   Asociación KéköLdi wakkakoneke
   KéköLdi/Cocles
   Puerto Viejo de Talamanca
   Limón
   Costa Rica

VII

Working Paradise

Costa Rica has become a popular destination for ecotourism, and its public authorities have made some praiseworthy efforts to create national parks and pass environmental protection legislation to shelter wetlands, beaches, and rain forests from unbridled development. Still, although the last few years have seen the rate of loss of forests drop from twelve thousand hectares per year in 1987 to only three thousand per year in 1997, it is estimated that a quarter of Costa Rica's remaining forests may disappear by 2016.[1] Environmental protection requires the investment of public funds and the creation of state monitoring agencies, but the past two decades have also focused on cuts to public spending and reductions in the size of the state. Meanwhile, the enforcement of environmental legislation reduces the easy profits of some powerful corporate interests and, arguably, the chance to earn a livelihood for many people who are in desperate need of one. With influential foreign governments and world trade bodies pushing hard for deregulation and nonintervention in the "natural" operation of the market, the hidden hand is drastically rearranging the state of nature. For all its good press, much of it deserved, Costa Rica is no exception to the devastating dynamic that is leading humanity to ecological catastrophe. Institutional mechanisms and legal channels for addressing criminal affronts to the environment have been created in Costa Rica, and they are enforced. Yet critics point out that this enforcement often comes too late, that environmental devastation takes only the blink of a developer's eye, while the wheels of justice do not move quickly enough to block the bulldozers and the chemical contaminants, especially given the sparse fleet of overburdened emergency response vehicles operated by the government.

Focusing on the problem this way, however, perhaps falls into a romantic fallacy of imagining that there exists something like a pristine natural environment that needs "saving." In one sense, the entire history of Costa Rica since the conquest has been the exploitation of the rich ecology in which the people found themselves—from the extraction of exotic herbals by the crate for trade with Europe in the seventeenth century, to the hunting of bird, animal, and plant specimens for natural scientists from the Smithsonian Institution and the Berlin Herbarium in the nineteenth century, to the exchange of rain forest for export agriculture over the past 150 years. In good measure the Costa Rican approach to the environment has been conditioned by the demographic "emptiness" of a country that, though small in size, crested 1 million inhabitants only in the early 1960s, the vast majority of whom lived in a geographically restricted area in the Central Valley. The people have tended to see the environment as an obstacle that needs to be overcome in order to extend the agricultural frontier and as something that can be consumed without checks given the apparent abundance of natural resources.

This has changed dramatically in the past two decades. Even as they were granting questionable concessions to local and foreign investors to transform mangrove swamps into five-star resorts, recent governments have begun to promote public awareness of the value of the country's uniquely rich ecology. Despite many contradictions, the overall policy of promoting ecotourism is, on balance, a success story. And the Costa Rican government has been a world leader in signing bioprospecting agreements with giant foreign companies like Merck, which exchange access to the potential pharmaceutical wonders of the rain forest for guarantees of conservation, employment for local scientists, and a share of any future profits. In a short period of time, Costa Rica has had to confront urgent questions of resource management and sustainability — issues of extreme urgency in a country of such small landmass explored and exploited annually now by a million pairs of tourist feet, dozens of multinational hotel chains and small national and foreign hospitality entrepreneurs, cruise ship lines, cosmetics companies, logging and mining multinationals, and a growing number of Costa Ricans with an interest in touring their own country. It is also worth mentioning the growing presence of conservationists, many of them foreign and of an educational ecotourism bent, whose "research" and "protection" stations often bear an uncanny resemblance to the intrusive agencies they seek to protect the area and its wildlife from.

Finally, and in many ways most worrisome of all, is the ecological catastrophe known as the Greater Metropolitan Area. San José and its environs have become a largely unplanned urban sprawl of almost 2 million people — 51 percent of the national populace living in little more than 2 percent of the national territory and concentrating the great majority of the country's roughly 700,000 vehicles. Behold a conurbation with few green spaces, a chaotic traffic picture, a lack of effective vehicle pollution controls, grossly inadequate sewage facilities, and utterly inappropriate development governed by quick returns and paved by corruption and overmatched public institutions. No program of ecological protection or conservation alone can solve this extreme and dreadfully ironic coexistence of dense natural diversity with postmodern humanity's limitless capacity to despoil its environment. The indicators point to political struggle and some very tough sacrifices for all contenders if Costa Rica is to remain an ecological jewel in an increasingly degraded and depleted global treasure chest.

Note

1. Proyecto Estado de la Nación, *Estado de la nación en desarrollo humano sostenible*, vol. 8 (San José: Proyecto Estado de la Nación, 2001), 212.

A Community Takes Care of Its Environs

Owners of Montaña de la Candelaria

In the 1840s, Costa Rican communities still had extensive jurisdiction over their own natural resources, and they regulated them carefully. The following disposition shows the way that each town generated its own laws on the use of property shared in common. The basis of this community self-regulation was the extensive common land vital to a community's reproduction, something that disappeared with the privatization of lands for coffee agriculture over the course of the nineteenth century.

In the city of San José at ten in the morning of 5 June 1845 I, José L. Valverde, serve as witness that the men who are owners of the mountain of Candelaria and who are founders of that community came before me to say that they were suffering grave damages from those who are not owners and who are extracting materials in such a way that they are senselessly destroying woodlands. They want to formalize the method by which they will conduct themselves in the future, they desire that their families might enjoy the fruits of their own work, and they wish to insure that they will not be misappropriated. As a result, they have agreed that they will regulate their property by judicial accord, making everyone's interests even under the following terms:

All those interested parties of the community of owners of the mountain of Candelaria, wanting to regularize their property under the auspices of the authorities, are in broad agreement that a commission shall be named from among themselves, made up of a president and two members, and if necessary of a secretary without voting rights, which will hold sessions to emit dispositions for the good of the community and of society, and for which we are obliged to fulfil the following Statute.

> Article 1. All those of the community wish to be part of and held to that which the commission in session agrees is in the best interests of the community. . . .
>
> Article 5. There shall be a warden who cares for and keeps watch over the

extraction of firewood and other materials from the forests, and he shall be paid with the wood, firewood, and other things that he confiscates, and his obligations are also to assure that no person causes unnecessary damages or upsets.

Article 6. Only members of the community can use wood for their own purposes.

Article 7. Any person who is not in agreement with this Statute and who wishes to settle up and divide their share from the community must do so at their own expense.

Article 8. No member shall cut down or extract wood in quantities that exceed four trees, without getting the permission of the commission, which will assure that the warden enforces the fulfilment of this disposition. . . .

Article 11. Each member recognizes as sacred the right of each member to the land that was apportioned them.

Article 12. Each individual among those who work on the edge of the mountain and toward the area of the border dividing our lands from those of Aserrí shall plant a living tree at precisely every four by four yards. . . .

And finally they say that they are obliged to fulfil all the prior clauses, and to reinforce that obligation they agree that all their wealth shall be left unprotected for the payment of legal damages.

And so in my presence it was said, authorized, and signed by those who knew how, being instrumental senors Martín Mora, Jesús Vega, Pablo Alpízar, and Pablo Benavides, of this locale, married, farmers, and of age, except the first who is single, before whom this document was read and all those present said that they were in agreement with what was expressed in it, which I certify to be true.

Caffeinated Miasmas

Residents of Santo Domingo de Heredia

The booming coffee economy created Costa Rica's first large-scale struggle over environmental contamination. In 1878, residents of Santo Tomás de Santo Domingo de Heredia, one of the hubs of coffee agriculture, lodged a protest against the contamination of water sources by the rotting husks discharged by coffee processing facilities. The petition, discovered by historical geographer Gladys Rojas Chaves, demonstrates that community action against agro-industrial contaminants in the environment predates the 1960s and was not something invented by the Western middle classes. It is interesting to compare the political context of this petition with the preceding one, because by 1878 the law had been alienated from the community and jurisdiction over resource issues lay in the hands of the national state, which would henceforth become the key mediator of environmental conflict and politics in Costa Rica.

District Administrator of this Canton, Sir:

We, the undersigned, of various estates, farmers and residents of the barrio of Santo Tomás of this jurisdiction and before You with all due respect, do come to declare:

For some time now the residents of this barrio have been suffering damages that public hygiene and the police should not permit for this can lead to grave illness or plague in all the inhabitants of the neighborhood, and even extend itself to the entire population. The damage we are suffering is from the fetid matter and the miasmas of the fermented coffee water that pours into the street that leads from this town to "Turres," "El Raicero," and so on, issuing from the courtyards of the processing facilities of senors don Manuel Bonilla, Pedro Bolaños, Mercedes Castro, Ramón Villalobos, Pedro Diego Sáenz, Rafael González, and Martín Rojas.

According to articles 40, 197, 198, and in accord with article 42 of the Police Code of 20 July 1849, the Police Chiefs must take care that no filth or mess sullies the towns, and drain the swamps and clean them of all objects that produce unhealthy miasmas, or anything that threatens the public health. . . . Up to now, despite the repeated complaints that we have made with the goal of prohibiting these men from spreading their water in the town with notable prejudice and danger to our health, this abuse of the cited laws has been tolerated. We can no longer consent to such tolerance, because even if it is true that the authorities must protect agriculture, it is also true that individual interests must be subordinated to the general interest. Beyond the fact that this tolerance is illegal it favors seven people, namely the owners of the processing facilities. . . .

Senor Jefe Político [roughly, Your Worship], taking into consideration all the arguments presented . . . [we request that you] prohibit the named Gentlemen from draining their coffee processing basins in the place they are accustomed to and order that they deposit the waste within their haciendas or remove their processing facilities to sites that will not damage the townspeople. This is justice.

Santo Domingo. 1 October 1877.

[Signed by thirty people, including two women. Neither of the women knew how to sign their name; of the men, sixteen knew how to sign.]

National Palace. San José. 8 January 1878

In view of the resolution of the Governor of the Province of Heredia which conciliates the interests of agriculture with those of Public Hygiene for the population of the town of Santo Domingo, we resolve:

1. That Messrs. Manuel Antonio Bonilla Jr., Mercedes Castro, Pedro Bolaños, Ramón Villalobos, Pedro D. Sáenz, Rafael González, and Martín Rojas provide a regular channel for the waters in which they wash their coffee, without allowing even the smallest deposit to build up. Also, they are obliged, at their own cost, in a formal manner, under their responsibility and with sufficient capacity, to cover the channel from where the flow begins and up to the street that borders on the west with the pasture of Mr. Joaquín Rosa Ocampo. The object of this is to avoid exhalations of the putrefaction from the waters that endangers the residents where it passes by them

2. Taking into consideration that there is already coffee prepared to be processed in the courtyards of the facilities and that the work of covering the channel is quite costly and cannot be done quickly, for the summer underway, the drainage will be permitted to continue as it is. Prior to November of this year the owners of the processing facilities are obliged

to carry out that which has been ordered to the satisfaction of the Police, ensuring a perfectly clean channel with substantial capacity, covered as ordered, and with a considerable current of water to carry off the corrupt residuals of the coffee

In agreement that the resolution of the Governor is appropriate for the interests of agriculture just as for the health of the population of Santo Domingo, His Excellency the General President has determined to give it his supreme approval.

Migration and the Costa Rican Environment since 1900

Uli Locher

Since the eighteenth century, colonization by peasant farmers has been one of the central dynamics of Costa Rican history. Initially its negative environmental impact was limited by the relatively small size of the society and the regulations of the communities themselves. That changed with the expansion of coffee and the development of agrarian capitalism, which coincided with a growth in peasant numbers and a progressive elimination of fertile state lands. Uli Locher offers an iconoclastic analysis of the environmental cost of the migration promoted by changes in Costa Rica's agricultural sector and state land policies in the twentieth century.

Costa Rica's open economy and integration into international markets have made it easy for migration to play the adaptive role it so often does. As long as the population was predominantly rural and much uninhabited land was available, the mechanism could function as smoothly as anywhere else. It is not by accident that Costa Rica has long held the world record in forest clearing—7 percent of total forested area was cleared every year since the 1960s, according to the World Resources Institute. (Although the quality of this information is somewhat uncertain, the magnitude of the deforestation cannot be doubted.) A combination of pro-frontier legislation and nonenforcement of environmental protection laws have made the government into the principal accomplice in the environmental destruction we are currently witnessing.

The state has been active in the clearing and settlement of frontier land. It passed laws in 1909, 1924, and 1934 allowing all citizens to claim public lands. Even better, in 1942, it passed the Ley de Poseedores en Precario (Squatters Law) which de facto legalized all squatting, giving squatters title to even privately owned land and allowing landowners compensation out of land held in the public domain. All three parties involved loved these arrangements. The

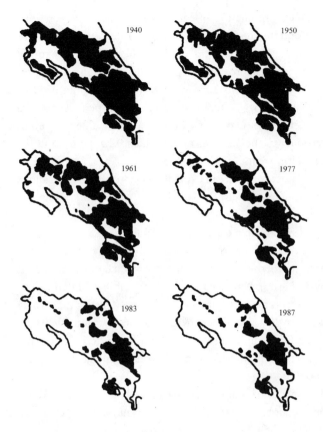

Costa Rican forests
(in black), 1940–1987

state viewed them as expedient and politically less controversial than land reform measures. The large landowners saw them as a means to avert effective
land reforms and an opportunity to expand and round off their holdings. Peasants and landless squatters were offered safe and peaceful access to land. Later,
an institution was founded to regulate frontier settlement, the Instituto de
Tierras y Colonizacion (ITCO, Institution of Land and Colonization), which
became the Instituto de Desarrollo Agrario (IDA, Institute of Agrarian Development).

Whatever the political merits of these generous policies, their effects proved
disastrous for the environment. Great expanses of public land were lost, and
since proof of occupation always came in the removal of trees, large parts of the
country's forest cover were destroyed. Much of the land opened up this way
was not put into crop production, but was either abandoned or used for cattle
grazing. The resulting soil erosion, especially in the hillsides, is now visible
everywhere, especially in parts of San Carlos and Guanacaste.

A much more positive picture emerges in those frontier lands converted to coffee cultivation. The combination of coffee, a labor-intensive perennial crop, with shade trees, and the frequent use of sugarcane to cover the hilltops at least in some areas of the Meseta Central, had the effect of simultaneously protecting the soil from physical erosion and providing work for many times more people than did the cattle farms. However, conventional coffee production does cause significant damage because chemical inputs poison soils and rivers. Consequently, deforestation can have quite drastically different demographic impacts according to the auspices under which it happened and the land use eventually resulting from it.

Bananas will grow almost anywhere in Costa Rica, but the great plantations producing for export need good soils, flat land, much water, good drainage, and hot temperatures. While the demographic effects of banana cultivation were more sudden and spectacular, the environmental effects appear to have been less marked than those of the frontier. The frontier is by definition not sustainable; it has left much of the country denuded of forest cover and exposed to highly visible physical erosion. Banana cultivation is, at least theoretically, sustainable. But such appearances are hard to substantiate. The fact that visible scars of soil erosion are largely absent in banana regions is attributable to the topography alone. In addition, indirect environmental effects derived from the rapid increase in population and hillside farming around the plantations also should not be overlooked.

All Central American countries have urbanized rapidly since 1950 and have reached levels between roughly 40 percent and 60 percent in 1990. Costa Rica ranks third, with a population that is 47 percent urban. The role of migration in such urban development is well known but sometimes exaggerated. Rural-urban migration directly explains only 17 percent of the increase in Costa Rican urbanization between 1965 and 1990. Nevertheless, the absolute numbers are impressive, especially when combined with the evidence on interregional migration. A very significant shift in the distribution of population is taking place, favoring the urban center of the country and constantly increasing its dominance. Urban pull factors have certainly played a major role in stimulating migration since the 1960s. Import-substitution industries, free trade zones, the rapidly expanding state apparatus and public payroll, the urban concentration of governmental, economic, and educational institutions, and other factors have created a disproportionate number of urban jobs. However, rural push factors have also proven significant, even dominant, according to some authors. These rural push factors are a lack of nonagricultural employment, the low labor demand of cattle farms, soil depletion and erosion, and the drastic fluctuation in labor demand according to the boom-and-bust cycles of coffee and bananas, which create periodic misery among large numbers of landless rural workers.

One could be tempted to exclude urban bias from the list of causes of rural misery and cityward migration in Costa Rica. This is, after all, a country that can pride itself on having more rural services, distributive justice, and transfer payments than any of its neighbors, as well as on frontier policies and plantation employment stimulating rural-directed migration. All of these points may be true, but they are hardly convincing on closer inspection. The banana enclaves have produced good incomes for the major companies, but they have not caused much rural development. Even the agricultural modernization they represent remains quite irrelevant outside the enclaves. The frontier has self-destruction built in, and the coverage of rural areas by government services and institutions is far from what cities have received. The classic urban bias argument still applies: the accumulation of urban advantages leaves the hinterland ever farther behind. Rapid urban growth has severe environmental consequences in the city itself, its immediate surroundings, and the downstream parts of its watershed. However, its principle environmental effects remain indirect. To some extent, urban dominance feeds on rural poverty, and rural poverty causes indiscriminate deforestation, farming on steep slopes, and other survival strategies buying short-term individual gain at a long-term cost to the collectivity. This link between rural disadvantage, poverty, unsustainable resource use, soil erosion, and migration is all too obvious even in the Costa Rican case; it provides the basis of much recent thinking on sustainable development.

The major migration streams of this century can be summarized in the following way. For many decades there has been a significant amount of frontier migration, which has gradually pushed back the forests in virtually all cantons. This migration has been steady and appears to finally have reached a plateau. Second, there have been great spurts of migration to the plantations. This form of labor migration has been so sudden that it has led to spectacular immigration rates in the three regions affected (Guanacaste, Limón, and Puntarenas). The fateful event happened at the turn of the century with the merger of the two rival banana producers into the United Fruit Company. Many major migration streams over the next six decades were related to the production of bananas in what may have been the first country referred to, in derogatory terms, as "banana republic." Only the recent diversification of agricultural production has reduced the importance of the country's banana-driven demography. Finally, there has been an accelerating rural-urban migration that has increased the dominance of the Meseta Central and its metropolitan agglomeration. Generally speaking, the significant migrations of the past have been to peripheral regions, while those of the present are directed toward the country's center, but the following section will show just how hazardous such generalizations can be.

After two decades of strong growth since 1960, the Costa Rican economy went into a deep recession in 1981 and 1982. The crisis brought about a dramatic change in migration patterns. As buying power and employment in the cities declined, urban destinations became much less attractive to migrants. As rural poverty spread rapidly, the frontier again became a place where the landless could eke out a living as long as there was forest to be harvested. Invadable lands became prime targets once again. Aggregate analysis does not provide sufficient detail, but even at the cantonal level, we observe a connection between rapid loss of tree cover and strong immigration. Virtually all of the squatters who received land settlements between 1979 and 1984 had moved into areas that in 1966 still had more than 50 percent tree cover. Even among the IDA-sponsored settlements, we find that over three quarters of the settlers moved into those formerly forested areas. As far as the environment is concerned, this represents a great deterioration compared with the situation at the time of the previous census.

During the years of crisis, the forest increased its role as the target of frontier settlement. Over the 1968–73 period, only 3,113 settlers (33.7 percent) ended up in districts with more than 50 percent forest cover, but eleven years later, the numbers increased to over 25,000 (58.7 percent). All this excludes the thousands of squatters whose position has not been regularized by an IDA settlement. Forest cover deteriorated rapidly between 1968 and 1984: the number of settlers in the highest category of forest cover was cut in half—not because they moved but because, with their help, so much of the forest was cleared. The great increase in IDA settlements—to the point that in 1979–84 they amounted to over 40 percent of all rural-destined migration—comes as no surprise in Costa Rican political history. It fits well with the various colonization and squatting laws that have proven so effective during this century. What seems particular, however, is that all these laws, as well as the recent IDA-sponsored settlements, have put the emphasis on clearing trees, rather than on true settlement and conversion to agriculture. Squatters can be legally recognized after occupying land for as little as six months and having cut only a part of the trees. They are then free to sell not so much the land as the so-called *mejora*, that is, the improvement they have made on it by cutting trees. The buyer of this mejora can then receive legal title. There have been professional squatters who have treated parcel after parcel in this way, providing ever more land for land-hungry—and subsidized—cattle farmers.

If we generalize the situation around the crisis years of 1981–82, we can state that the central region was shifting the weight of its population from the Greater Metropolitan Area to more rural districts; that Guanacaste Province was showing some recovery but still losing migrants; that the banana cantons were still acting as magnets; and that there were a number of rural cantons, mainly those close to the Nicaraguan border, which show evidence of increasing frontier settlement. Much of the crisis-driven settlement was directed at forested land. The country paid a heavy price in land and forest resources for the ill-advised policies preceding the crisis and those supposed to alleviate it. Since the renewal of frontier settlement was so obviously crisis-driven, it is safe to assume that it has somewhat abated now. Such episodes may well occur again. Continued population increase, illegal immigration, and nonapplication of laws protecting the environment make it unlikely that the assault on the frontier will come to a halt soon.

Public land has not been available for homesteading since 1968; the pattern of squatters' taking over good virgin land and becoming owners simply by staking it out is no longer a problem. Both the IDA-sponsored land reform and the movements of squatters are now almost exclusively directed at poor land. This is, however, precisely how most of the damage is done: poor land is by definition located on steep, easily erodable slopes. In environmental terms, the official land reform policy, even after the changes made in 1968, remains counterproductive. Population density in rural Costa Rica is still low, which means that much forest land is waiting to be conquered. The technique of this conquest has not changed. The professional squatters continue to advance one or two steps a year, selling their "land improvement" to finance their meager survival.

There is every indication that urbanization continues to advance rapidly, despite the official underestimates published twice per year. The example of the district of Pavas proves illustrative. In 1984, this district had 18,068 inhabitants, which the census bureau extrapolated to 43,341 in 1993. According to a census carried out by the local clinic, the population stands at over 79,000 in 1995. Similar increases have been documented in many parts of the Greater Metropolitan Area, exacerbating the numbers of people struggling to achieve urban subsistence, swelling the ranks of the informal sector, putting extreme pressure on efforts to provide social housing, and deepening class segregation.

One of the effects of the increasing urban dominance is that the national capital now increasingly feels the fragility of economic development typical of export-specialized rural regions. Economic downturns are translated into urban unemployment since the free trade zones react almost instantly to international fluctuations, for example, in the volatile textile and electronics sectors.

It would be premature to claim that the country derided as a banana republic has now matured into a maquiladora republic, but it is no doubt engaged in this direction. Whether this will result in higher levels of unemployment, increased stratification, and rapid growth of *tugurios* (shanty towns) is anyone's guess.

As the urban proportion of the population exceeds the benchmark of 50 percent, we can expect urban push and pull factors to increasingly dominate among the determinants of internal migration. The environmental consequences of this development remain unclear. Should the urban political elites succeed in furthering globalization strategies, agricultural producers may end up as losers, and this could accelerate migration both to the expanding frontier and to the city. However, all regimes here since 1947 have been populist, and it is quite likely that farmers will continue to benefit from governmental largesse. "Sin finqueros no hay comida" (without farmers there's no food) is a powerful slogan, especially at election time.

Few studies have demonstrated more than intuitively the relationship between rural poverty, migration, and the loss of natural resources. In Costa Rica, a clear relationship between poverty level and forest cover can be shown to exist by combining census population data with data on deforestation. The poorest cantons in 1984 were those that in 1960 had the most complete forest cover (73 percent), while the cantons with the lowest level of poverty are those with the lowest level of forest cover (28 percent). What is really surprising is the link between this result and the net migration rates: precisely the most forested and poorest cantons proved most attractive to migrants. This seems to contradict prevailing migration theory, which can be stated simply as predicting migration streams from poorer to more prosperous areas. My findings suggest the need to reformulate such theory. What functions as a magnet for migrants is not so much prosperity as such but economic opportunity. The frontier of tropical forest offers opportunities that can be compared to those found in the cities of the Meseta Central or on the banana plantations of the coastal plains. However, the character of the opportunities changes over time; once a population of recent migrants has established itself, it will face a rapidly changing opportunity structure. Urban industry and the agro-industry of plantations continue to produce added value and can maintain viable regional economies. The frontier is different: it resembles a short-lived mining operation in that its resources (wood and topsoil) will inevitably become exhausted over time.

The Costa Rican state has emerged as a strong promoter of foreign penetration in agriculture and its demographic side effect, migration. From the concessions made to the United Fruit Company in the late nineteenth century to the negotiations of the most recent banana accords with the European Union, there has been an uninterrupted stream of measures taken to assure continued banana exports. Since 1947, the state's actions have been two-pronged. On the one hand, foreign companies can act with near-complete freedom. On the other hand, a number of populist policies have assured the military and social peace essential to the continued presence of the multinationals. One of these is embodied in a series of squatters' laws and agrarian reform measures designed to conquer the forests and push ahead the agricultural frontier. These laws have proven fateful for the country as development tools and as sociopolitical safety valves. Numerically speaking, frontier migration may well have been the dominant form of migration in this century, and the state's role and complicity in its promotion remains beyond doubt. All of the available evidence points to the probability that banana plantations will continue as one of the key determinants of migration in Costa Rica. Much of that particular migration appears to consist of immigrants from Nicaragua, a neighboring country with much lower standards of living. Inequality does not explain everything, but it is truly the mother of migration.

Poverty and population growth are linked in a cycle of cumulative causation. The evidence presented here strongly suggests that the cycle should be enlarged to comprise the environmental degradation we are witnessing in many countries today. However, other elements should be included as conditions, such as income inequality, land concentration, and central government policies. Peasant squatters will not usually destroy their own land, but only land which is not and most likely will never be theirs. Secure tenure is the best protection of agricultural land, but it must be established in a context allowing smallholders to keep their land.

The association of migratory cycles and cycles of foreign penetration is an intuitive one at best. With the exception of some instances of expansion and relocation in the banana sector, it is impossible to prove a close correlation of foreign investment and internal migration because the necessary data does not exist. The one instance where we can do more than just speculate is the adaptation to the crisis of 1981–82, but even there the renewed migration to the internal frontier is related to poverty and conditional on a particular policy, rather than directly resulting from falling foreign investment. What is certain is that in either of the two examples—bananas and the frontier—it would be quite inappropriate to speak simply of neocolonial exploitation of national human resources. The problems are largely homegrown. Costa Rica has become a model of the process deplored by world systems analysts: the combination of foreign investment, soft state regulation, and free migration results in short-term advantages for all. The longer-term cost, presently borne by the environment, is now starting to become apparent in productivity declines of hillside agriculture. Migration again is bound to be the mechanism by which the country will adjust to an increasing scarcity of good land. In the end, the net transfer will be one of rural resources to the city, with large long-term costs borne by rural areas and large profits being made by cities, directly or as extensions of foreign interests.

From Rain Forest to Banana Plantation:

A Workers' Eye View

Ana Luisa Cerdas

What was it like to enter the pristine rain forest as the advance guard of the trans-national banana industry? How did workers understand their charge? Testimonies of the working-class men who were specialists in "making" the plantations have been collected by Ana Luisa Cerdas as part of her project to reconstruct from the workers' perspective a history of the "new" banana zone built in the late 1930s by the United Fruit Company in Quepos and Golfito on the Pacific coast.

To start banana production, it was necessary to prepare the future plantations in lands almost entirely covered by virgin jungle and in many cases by swamps. The time required for the preparation of each finca—to "make it" and leave it producing—could vary considerably from one to the next. Topographical conditions had an influence on this, as did the nature of the vegetation and the size of the finca. Generally the work lasted between eight months and a year, though some of the bigger fincas, like Finca 18 in Palmar Sur, took about a year and a half. The company's objective was to start exporting bananas and receiving profits as soon as possible. As a result, they wanted to see the work that had to precede production finished in as little time as possible. They re-cruited large contingents, gangs specializing in this type of work, who prepared a number of fincas at a time.

The Costa Rican Banana Company ("La Bananera" for short) used contrac-tors to carry out the prep work, and each contractor was in charge of finding workers, paying them, lodging them, and so on (this allowed the Bananera to avoid taking on the obligations of an employer, a point of conflict between the union and the company that was finally resolved in favor of the workers after being aired in the courts). The work began with the clearing of a site for the camp where the peons would live, and it finished with the sowing of the banana "seed." In between came a variety of overlapping and carefully coordinated tasks, each one undertaken by separate gangs with particular specialties.

Prolog: Mapping and Siting

The work of making the finca required elaborate preparations even prior to the arrival of the gangs of banana peons in the zone. This was work undertaken directly by the technical and professional staff of the banana company. Elaborate planning in the United States was coordinated with exploratory fieldwork in the zone to plan the layout of operations in the Golfito Division.

> First they brought a corps of topographical engineers, the ones that measure. They brought maps with them, already made up in Boston, well-studied to know where they were going to put the banana plantation in Palmar Sur. . . . The company made its geographical maps, [and] put the teams of engineers to work measuring the drainage in the jungle. . . . It also marked the divisions where the roads for taking out bananas would go . . . and then other smaller roads within each section of eight or ten hectares.
> —Cruz Obando Silva

Once this technical work of delineating and marking off the grid of the future finca was accomplished, the different work teams came in to carry out the work necessary for preparing the site.

Trenching

Due to the wetness of the land, virtually all of the fincas in the Golfito and the Quepos divisions had to be drained by cutting trenches and canals. This work was the first done in what was essentially pristine rain forest, although a narrow band had already been made by cutting just those trees that had stood in the path of the future drainage system. From the beginning to just prior to the end of the classic period of banana production in the Pacific south, this work was done without the help of mechanical dredgers by men known as *paleros* (shovelmen).

> At the end all those ditches, canals were done with dredgers, but at the beginning, no, it was all paleros. They were men, the ones who went to make those trenches with shovels, that was hard work. There were a lot of guys from Guanacaste, a lot of Nicaraguans who earned good money trenching, making trenches with shovels. But the people from here, from the high-

lands, they never made it; they weren't used to it, and so the work seemed too much for them. They said it was for animals . . . that they were being exploited . . . and no, I never considered that they were being exploited, because it was a job that had to be done, but it was work for a man, and it paid well.

—Carlos Vásquez Umaña, trenching foreman

The trenches were measured and calculated in sections of ten meters, depending on the depth they might have. The speed, skill, and output of the worker had to do with the assignment of the sections or lengths to be tackled. For example, when it came to making the trenches, those in the vanguard, where the cut was deepest, had to be the most skillful, quick, and resistant. In this work there existed a tendency toward specialization.

> The trenches were done without clearing because once the trees were chopped down, you wouldn't be able to trench, you had to have the drainage channels cut first. . . . Your chest was really ready to explode from throwing up earth. . . . Some trenches were up to four meters high, and afterward, that little bit of earth tossed up! It was tough, . . . they didn't pay what they should have. For digging out earth from the ground they paid ninety-five cents the cubic meter.
>
> —Cruz Obando Silva

Scrubbing

Doing the scrub involved clearing away the underbrush. Only the large trees were left, without bushes, plants, or grasses; the workers labored using only machetes and axes.

> [We worked] cutting the small brush, everything that was low-lying, and leaving the ground clear. This was dangerous because there were a lot of snakes in the woods.
>
> —Beto Rojas Chavarría

Staking

Once the trenching was done to drain the area and the small vegetation cleared away, stakes were placed to indicate where the banana trees were going to be planted. This constituted lighter work in terms of the physical force required, but it demanded great precision.

> The stakes that the stake-driver had situated so carefully divided the lots into a grid four by four square meters that we workers called "the box."
> —Manuel Aguilar Vargas

The terrain had been marked by the engineers, and the stake-driver had to make further calculations according to these marks. The workers doing this had to have prior knowledge of the work involved in order to make very precise measurements, and a lot of them were people with carpentry knowledge or who had experience doing the job on the plantations in Limón.

> They did the setup, setting the stakes from point X to point Y. These were the famous courses—two furrows for stakes here, two furrows for stakes there—to make the section, and that set up the frame that had to be filled. They'd mark it exactly with a chain and a stick where the stake had to go, because that was where the banana plant got placed.
> —Cruz Obando Silva

Sowing Seed

The seed was brought by ship to the dock that the Bananera had established, was transferred to trains that traveled along the railway lines built to each finca, and from there was distributed throughout the plantations in mule-drawn carts or handcarts that took it right to the stakes where it was sown and watered in by different gangs.

Cutting the Forest

Now the axmen arrived. Their task was to clear the forest. This was the last labor task in the preparation of the finca.

> And the axmen that they had there were such expert folk! Well, because they came from the Atlantic zone, tough people, to teach the other axmen how to fell a tree while leaving the lanes open. Because the contractor paid an axman better if he could avoid the tree falling along the path of the lanes. If it fell like that, it would cost a pretty penny, but if it dropped crosswise, it didn't cost anything. They made a few cuts and with cranes and brute force we'd take those great chunks of wood out of the alleys to leave a clear path. Of course they fell on top of the plantings, and sometimes you'd see a seedling coming out from underneath a fallen tree. . . . A really good axman—one of those axmen who came over from the Atlantic—they'd earn up to nine colones by two in the afternoon. How the wood went in those years . . .

it would rot. . . . Sometimes it would take four axmen working on a tree for an entire day to chop the thing down. Can you imagine how big a tree that was? And there it stayed. You'd climb over it . . . and still when the fruit was being taken in during the first harvest, those trees would still be there in the way. And underneath were the snakes, the viper and the *bocaracá*, and all those other ones, attacking the workers.
—Cruz Obando Silva

Moving On

The contractor and his gang would now move on to other lands to begin preparing a new finca, while in the one just finished, the work of maintenance would begin, the responsibility of other workers, including women and children, contracted to tend the plantations and harvest the banana.

> When we finished cutting down the forest, the land was left littered with so many trunks that you could barely walk through them, and the bananas growing up from under them and in between.
> —Beto Rojas Chavarría

The cut trees decayed with the humid environment and the passage of time.

> Beneath the scattered trunks and branches of those fallen giants, which fertilized the soil as they rotted, a new vegetation sprouted and grew rapidly with the rains. . . . Now I get sad thinking of those forests that rotted away. It was a true crime against future generations. I myself cut *espaveles* [skeels—a tree native to the rain forest] as big as three meters in diameter.
> —Manuel Aguilar Vargas

Pesticides and Parakeets in the Banana Industry

Steve Marquardt

Eco-historian Steve Marquardt has written groundbreaking work on the relationship between the environment as a living and changing system, corporate capitalism trying to create "factories in the field," and laborers and their organizations. In this multiple-award-winning piece, he explores the Faustian dimensions of an early United Fruit Company program of agrochemical use in an effort to spare its new Costa Rican division from the ravages of plant disease.

In 1942, a correspondent for the Costa Rican Communist Party newspaper described for his readers the plight of a new, unsettling group of workers in the plantations of the United Fruit Company's Pacific banana zone: the crews "whose job is to spray poison on the bananas to combat [the banana disease] 'sigatoka.'" The reporter noted that "these poor men with their hats, clothing, and hides impregnated with a repugnant blue-green color" were now a familiar sight in the zone. "The poison stains everything—and penetrating the respiratory passages, it slowly destroys the organism. In a few weeks, the worker is hoarse, emaciated. There are already many tuberculosis cases that have come from the 'poison' crews." The job of pesticide application was still a novelty in Central American agriculture in 1942: United Fruit's "poison"-spraying program had begun only four years earlier as an emergency response to a fast-moving epidemic of the fungal banana disease *sigatoka*. This probably pioneered the use of biocidal chemicals on crops in Central America. By the end of World War II, spraying for sigatoka control had become routine throughout the banana industry of the isthmus.

United's regionwide, fixed-pipe, fungicide application program ultimately lasted twenty-five years; long after its replacement by newer technologies it remained, in the words of a leading tropical phytopathologist, "the biggest job of plant spraying ever done anywhere in the world." And, as the reporter made clear, the program was starkly and dangerously labor-intensive. Wage-workers are, in a sense, the shock troops of industrial agriculture's "war on insects" and plant disease. They suffer as much exposure to toxic chemicals as the organisms they seek to control, and far more than urban consumers. Yet most nonmedical analyses of agrochemical use follow the lead of Rachel Carson's environmentalist classic *Silent Spring* (1963) in focusing on issues of food contamination and environmental degradation, while giving little attention to wageworkers themselves as social or historical actors, instead seeing them as inevitable, largely passive victims—not unlike the robins and brook trout in Carson's jeremiad—of an agricultural order controlled by farmers, agronomists, agribusinesses, and global markets.

The United Fruit Company's confrontation with sigatoka began in August 1935, on the north coast of Honduras. Managers on Farm 15, on the upper end of the company's rich Ulua Valley cultivations, noticed an area of banana plants with damaged leaves. By June of 1936, what tropical agronomists would call "the Great Caribbean Leaf Spot Epidemic," or sigatoka, was underway, with over twelve thousand affected hectares in the Ulua. Infection spread to Belize, Mexico, Jamaica, and the Lesser Antilles in that same year, and by 1937, the epidemic had engulfed most of the Caribbean and Central America. This explosive pace threatened United's empire with what one contemporary observer termed "the greatest crisis of its history." That assessment was all the more remarkable for its context. In the mid-1930s, when the epidemic struck, United Fruit was midway in its epochal, fifty-year battle with a different, soil-borne fungal malady known as "Panama disease."

United remained a multinational banana empire, in control of over 1,400,000 hectares in four Central American countries and held a near-absolute monopoly in the North American banana trade. Nonetheless, Panama disease had seriously undermined its production and resources, devastating (albeit slowly) tens of thousands of hectares of bananas, prompting the closure of whole zones of operation and migration to new regions. Unlike Panama disease, which moved slowly through banana root systems, *Mycosphaerella musicola* leach, the fungal pathogen of sigatoka disease, swiftly attacked the leaves of the banana plant, broke down the entire leaf structure as it gained strength, and first limited the size and weight of banana bunches, then halted their appearance altogether as the infection progressed. Most insidiously, from the company's point of view, lightly, even imperceptibly infected plants often bore normal-looking fruit, which would ripen prematurely during shipment or acquire a noxious taste and odor by the time it reached the consumer.

Both Panama disease and sigatoka have a common—though unacknowledged—basis in the vulnerability of industrial-scale tropical monoculture to epidemic disease. When the fungus appeared in United Fruit's domain, it found a habitat both well chosen and well prepared for its rapid and widespread dispersion. The warm, lowland rain forest ecologies that the company had replaced with banana monoculture offered ideal environments for—indeed, dependent on—a multitude of airborne and soil-dwelling fungi. As the Panama disease epidemic had already shown, plantation zones were no less hospitable to fungal growth after they were stripped of their trees, and the enclave's vast expanses of a single plant species proved far more susceptible to damage by host-specific fungal disease than the incredibly diverse mix of species in moist tropical forests. In the mid-1930s, United's isthmian banana cultivations offered the pathogen 48,982 hectares of susceptible plants, growing in massive, uniform blocks of three hundred to six hundred hectares. Like Panama disease, then, sigatoka was less a "natural" disaster than an artifact of industrial-scale, global agriculture.

The company had responded slowly, haltingly, and without much coordination to Panama disease twenty-five years earlier. With sigatoka, company plant pathologist Vining C. Dunlap's research team began systematic chemical control experiments in November of 1935, two months after symptoms first appeared on Farm 15. Though there were mixed and uncertain reports on the effectiveness of fungicides in the earlier outbreaks in Fiji and Australia, the Lancetilla researchers conducted thorough trials with a series of liquid and powdered fungicides and a host of ground and aerial application technologies. As early as December 1936, "bordeaux mixture," a heavy, blue-green solution of ten pounds of copper sulfate granules and ten pounds of lime in one hundred gallons of water—far too bulky to be sprayed from the air—had emerged as a fungicide that consistently controlled the disease, but only when sprayed lavishly every two to three weeks, year-round, in order to coat each new leaf as it emerged from the main stalk. Ground-based bordeaux spray was thus an expensive, unwieldy, and labor-intensive proposition. But with mounting evidence of the failure of aerial spraying, Dunlap's team developed and refined a system that could put massive quantities of the mixture—250 gallons per acre, twenty to thirty times per year—onto banana leaves. Once the decision was made (by UFCO president Zemurray personally, according to company lore) to proceed with ground application, workers installed these systems with stunning speed. By 1941, the company claimed coverage of over forty thousand hectares.

The spray apparatus represented a major investment for a crop that had just begun to be cultivated in a technologically intensive way. Workers laid

a thirty-meter grid of galvanized iron pipe over the ground of each plantation, contending, on newly cleared land, with the tangled limbs and trunks of
the felled, still undecayed forest. A typical farm's system included over forty
miles of pipe, with 1.5-inch lateral and three-quarter-inch sublateral lines ar-
rayed symmetrically on either side of the two-inch main line, which bisected
the farm. Each pipeline system was supplied by its own central pumping and
mixing plant, where workers would mix the bordeaux solution in a complex
and massive set of tanks, then send it into the lines with diesel-powered pumps
at a pressure of seven to eight hundred pounds per square inch. Finally, each
farm maintained a pair of vats in which workers dipped harvested fruit, first
in dilute acid, then in water, to remove the blue-green spray residue before
shipping.

Installation was not, of course, the end of sigatoka-control costs. Actual
spraying was carried out manually, by the spray crews, with 140-foot hoses
carried from one to another of the more than 2,500 hose couplings (*boquillas*) in
each plantation. In order to maintain a spray schedule that thoroughly doused
each banana plant at intervals of two to three weeks through years of con-
tinuous production, more than a quarter of United's farm labor force in the
bordeaux spray era worked in sigatoka control. Mid-1950s studies of the company claimed that spray crew wages, along with the costs of massive quantities
of copper sulfate and those of pipeline maintenance, accounted for over 40
percent of UFCO's plantation operating costs.

The bordeaux spray program brought the sigatoka epidemic under control
and may well have deserved British banana scientist Claude Wardlaw's praise as
"one of the greatest achievements in phytopathological history." What is certain is that the expense and the perceived technological requirements of sigatoka control would shape the landscape and organization of the Central American banana industry for decades. New divisions, like Golfito, Costa Rica—the
first to open after the adoption of the fixed-pipe method—were laid out around
the needs of sigatoka control systems, while older divisions were impelled to
adjust plantation boundaries and operations. The pump capacity, symmetri-
cal bias, and angular construction of spray systems imposed a new uniformity
of size and shape on plantations: the optimum area of banana farms would
henceforth be eight hundred acres, and rectangular boundaries would dominate farm layouts that had once followed natural contours. For workers on
the sigatoka control crews, the bordeaux spray program represented a major
step toward the implantation of industrial, factory-like work regimes into the
process of agricultural labor. It gave rise to a new managerial hierarchy: spray
workers (unlike their machete-using comrades in "Agriculture") worked in the

"Spray" department and reported to a "Spraymaster" whose orders came from a separate office in the division headquarters, where treatment schedules were planned on a centralized basis.

United's corporate newsletter, for example, wrote glowingly of the transformation of thousands of "machete swingers" into "spray men." Wardlaw, the British observer, claimed that spray workers proudly referred to themselves as "chemists," an assertion echoed a few years later by a company publicist (though the ability of either writer to speak to the men in their own language is doubtful). In fact, however, the quotidian nickname for spray workers in the *zona bananera* was not *quimico* (chemist) but *perico* (parakeet), a term that referred not only to the blue-green bordeaux salts that caked clothing and stained bodies but also suggested the way central pumps drove the spray crews (the *periquera*) through the plantations like flocks of brightly colored birds. The humbler, mocking, job title suggests that plantation workers themselves saw spray work not as a step up into the brave new world of industry and technology, but rather as a humiliating task for those at the bottom of the plantation work hierarchy.

Sigatoka control was, in some respects, more redolent of factory work than agriculture. The distribution of spray crews and the pace of labor were both determined by a machine, the diesel Hardie pump in the central plant. From fourteen to twenty-two spray teams worked simultaneously on a typical farm; once the pump began to run, it was as inexorable as an assembly line, and it was not shut down until the end of the working day. For this reason, lunch stops or breaks of any kind were forbidden until the mid-1950s, when worker resistance seems to have forced at least some plantations to allow staggered rests by one team on each side of the main line. The effort to duplicate the precision and regularity of an industrial plant meshed poorly with the disorder of a growing, changing banana plantation, and it was largely workers who paid the price. On recently planted land, workers had to drag the long, hundred-pound, pressurized hoses over the still undecayed, jackstrawed trunks of the original forest and across drainage ditches not yet bridged. In older cultivations, the banana plants themselves created difficulties, as irregular growths of new stalks succeeded the precise, measured rows in which the original rhizomes were planted—making it easy for sprayers to lose the grid they needed to follow for complete coverage. Most workers knotted ropes at precise distances along their hoses in order to serve as guides in the re-creation of an order that natural regeneration had erased. Workers often complained that the difficulties imposed by these plantation variables (which could occur within a single farm) did not figure into the daily acreage expected of them. Sigatoka control, unlike most other plantation jobs, was mainly paid by the day, rather than the task, probably to encourage careful, thorough work in the crucial labor of controlling the disease. Both rapid pace and perfect coverage were enforced by a high ratio of supervisors to line workers. Surveillance was intense: according to labor newspapers and some judicial records, supervisors often hid behind clumps of bananas in order to catch pericos resting. Sprayers complained that bosses continually, and often without notice, changed their criteria for judging effective spray technique.

But it was the bordeaux spray itself that made sigatoka control work "ugly." Pericos spent all of each working day virtually immersed in copper fungicide. Until the last years of the bordeaux spray period, pericos worked in teams of two; one man (the *manguerero*) carried, connected, and kept the heavy hose from tangling, while the other (the *regador*) sprayed the banana plants with a meter-long wand and nozzle, which workers dubbed the shotgun (*escopeta*). Both workers labored in a fog of blue-green droplets, but the regador was most affected. The Gros Michel banana variety that United cultivated during the bordeaux spray era grew to a height of ten to thirteen meters, and the regador's responsibility was to coat thoroughly both sides of each leaf, especially the uppermost, since research in 1940 showed that coverage of the unfurling top leaf was crucial to disease control. In practice, this meant that in order to direct his spray, the regador, shielded only by the canvas hat worn by most banana workers, kept his face turned upward into the falling spray, constantly inhaling the acrid copper vapor and blinking it out of his eyes. The manguerero suffered some spray drift, but was saturated more directly when coupling and uncoupling the high-pressure hoses. Throughout the day, copper sulfate built up on both workers' clothing and exposed body parts, until it formed a virulent blue-green crust; wash water would remove the bulk of this, but both skin and fabric (often the workers' only clothes) remained stained. These "filthy conditions" (in the words of one union organizer) contributed to the repugnance with which *bananeros* (banana workers) viewed spray work, quite apart from the fungicide's long-term health effects.

The physiological cost of their work was, however, very much on the minds of pericos and their families. A delegation of women who toured the Costa Rican banana zone in 1954 reported to the ministry of public health on what they had learned from workers' wives: "even several months after leaving [the periquera], the men expel green-colored sweat, their teeth are the same color, and likewise the membranes of nose and mouth. Many families are worried, and think that this work could have grave consequences for [the workers'] health." Over the preceding decade and a half, pericos had, in fact, acquired very specific ideas about the effects of bordeaux spray on their bodies. A 1942 spray workers' petition to the Costa Rican president appealed to him as a former physician, presumably alert to the "poisonous" nature of copper sulfate, to intervene with United to alleviate their unhealthy working conditions: "We, spray workers, based on the bitter experience of our work, tell you that headaches, night coughs, and bad eyes are all common among us, that is, we suffer in our vision, our brains, and our lungs; we are very prone to tuberculosis." Ex-pericos interviewed in 1996 clearly recalled the sting of bordeaux vapor in their eyes, and anecdotal evidence from United's Puerto Armuelles Division points to high rates of blindness among longtime spray workers.

But it is the last complaint in the 1942 petition—decrying the vulnerability to tuberculosis among pericos—that had the greatest resonance. Respiratory diseases, especially tuberculosis and pneumonia, were the great endemic killers of the banana zone. Tuberculosis was the most feared, because of its slow, debilitating, inexorable progress. Central American reportage on United's spray program rarely omitted reference to the presumed link between spray work and tuberculosis. Although the UFCO medical department records for the bordeaux era remain closed to researchers, there is no evidence in any available source that the company itself took spray workers' fears of tuberculosis seriously. Indeed, it would have been easy to attribute their association of the disease with bordeaux spray to rumor, superstition, or the malicious imaginations of leftist labor agitators; before the late 1960s, no medical research linked inhalation of copper to respiratory disease.

In 1969, however, doctors in Portugal's wine country—one of the last agricultural regions in the world to use bordeaux mixture rather than newer systemic fungicides—began to notice a set of common symptoms among vineyard sprayers. The Portuguese patients exhibited the precise range of tuberculosis-like symptoms described in the earlier protests from the banana zone: malaise, weakness, loss of appetite, weight loss, dry cough, and headaches. After respiratory failure and death—inevitable in chronic cases—autopsies revealed lung tissues stained blue-green by copper and cavernous regions of cellular breakdown, much like those produced by coal miner's black lung disease. Portuguese vineyard sprayers worked with relatively low-pressure backpack pumps and were employed for three months or less per year, applying bordeaux from two to twelve times during those months. The far greater exposure of sigatoka control crews, whose spray cycle was year-round, involving twenty to thirty applications at high pressure in each plantation, suggests that their likelihood of developing "sprayer's lung" was proportionately increased. In any given year, ten to fifteen thousand men found employment in sigatoka control throughout Central America. Of those, just under half were regadores, whose exposure to copper sulfate vapor was much greater than that of hose carriers or plant operators. Without data on the length of time individual workers remained in the periquera, it is impossible to estimate the numbers of those who may have contracted the disease, but, even allowing for very high turnover rates, the afflicted probably numbered in the many thousands. Technical distinctions between the symptomatically identical maladies of tuberculosis and "sprayer's lung" would have mattered very little to these men.

The respiratory effects of bordeaux spray inhalation were sufficiently pervasive to foster an enduring trope in Central America's body of anti–United Fruit literature and journalism: the skeletal, tubercular, "totally disfigured" ex-perico, dying alone in an urban slum or on the fringes of the plantation zone after the company had no more use for him. In many of these vignettes, the writer is hailed by a frightening, unfamiliar figure, only to realize, with horror and embarrassment, that it is the same man he had once known as a robust youth. The trope of the spectral worker is part of a larger awareness — not new to the bordeaux era, but certainly sharpened by it — of agricultural capitalism's macabre exchange of the lives of men for the productivity of plants. The irony of men becoming sicker as plantations were restored to health was not lost on residents of the banana zone.

The dark comparison of the inversely linked fortunes of "men and bananas" (to recall the phrase of the great Costa Rican writer Carmen Lyra) achieves its most powerful expression in *Prisión verde* (Green Prison, 1950) a novel written by the Honduran writer and ex-perico Ramón Amaya Amador. In one of the novel's most moving scenes, don Braulio, an old regador, "with the face of a tuberculosis victim, sunken chest, and distended abdomen," gives his new hose man, Martín, an "orientation":

All of these farms are plagued with sigatoka, but they still produce well. Look at that fruit! What stalks! . . . If we don't resolve ourselves to live like worms, the Company doesn't prosper. And you see how life is, the more it fattens, the less men we are. . . . When I see sick farms, I think of us, [the bananeros]; it seems to me that there's our full-body portrait, because here my friend, we're all sick, some of sigatoka and others of *mata muerta* [Panama disease], malaria, and tuberculosis. Some will be cured, if they get away in time, others — just a hole in the ground!

Amaya's vision of an eerie symmetry between the robustness of the crop and the emaciation of the men whose labor allowed it to grow was, to a greater or lesser extent, widely shared. Workers' use of the same language of sickness and cure to describe the state of both plantations and their own bodies, along with the underlying sense that what heals one makes the other ill, reveals a conception of industrial agriculture as a zero-sum game, in which both nature and technology were on the side of industry. Against these forces, unfortunately, the plantation union movement seemed an uncertain ally.

One might suppose that sheer misery would lead spray workers to embrace the great upwelling of labor struggle and unionism in the United Fruit plantations during the two decades after World War II. But in reality, the miserable and humiliating nature of spray work, far from inspiring militancy, ensured that the men (or boys) who took the job would not share the backgrounds, ethnic and regional solidarities, or the pugnacious masculine pride that underlay successful labor organizing among "agricultural workers" on the plantations. Costa Rican spray crews seem to have been recruited, far more than other plantation laborers, from a thin stream of youthful jobseekers from the highland Central Valley, whose population prided itself on its European origins. The darker-skinned majority of plantation workers, most of them migrants from the impoverished lowland border province of Guanacaste, Nicaraguans, and some Hondurans, referred derisively to such highland Costa Ricans as *cartagos*, after the colonial capital city. But the nature of the work itself was the most serious barrier to manly self-assertion by pericos. Soaked and stained by bordeaux mixture, working without the machete that was the bananero's emblem of combative manhood and militancy, the pericos received scornful treatment from other banana workers. One union organizer recalled, "Because the poor pericos appeared completely soaked and blue, the workers in agriculture always made fun of them." Another was blunter: "It was work for dumbshits [*pendejos*]."

Though pericos rarely figured among the militants who sustained the labor movement on a daily basis (or even paid dues), labor leaders nonetheless strove, often successfully, to mobilize them for the great banana strikes that shook Costa Rica in postwar decades. One union leader recalled, "We always had to put something in the demands for them, to attract them, treat them well, and unite them with us, to give us strength." Spray workers unmoved by appeals to their interests were convinced instead by the remonstrations of flying squads of activists who sought out sigatoka-control crews in the earliest hours of each strike. The strength that union leaders hoped to gain from spray workers had to do less with the virtues of solidarity than with the economic pain that any significant pause in fungicide application inflicted on United Fruit. Regular application of bordeaux suppressed sigatoka infection but did not eliminate it from banana cultivations. Any deviation from the maximum three-week spray cycle, such as a strike, would allow the disease to reestablish itself. Resumption of control then became a lengthy process "as the entire crop becomes a locus of infection." Harvests could suffer drastic reductions for many months thereafter. In effect, the potential participation of the periquera in strikes changed the balance of industrial power by making agricultural disease a weapon of the workers' movement.

Unfortunately, however, this weapon was double-edged. Potential damage to one of the republic's principal export sectors became an increasingly successful pretext for securing state assistance in suppressing strikes and jailing union organizers. For a decade following the four-week strike of 1959–60, Costa Rican authorities gave United free reign to conduct a systematic policy of union suppression, repeatedly justifying its efforts by referring to "the total loss of plantations in a short period after suspension of bordeaux spraying" during strikes. If the power of striking pericos to damage fruit production was unacceptable to management, the price of employing them during periods of labor peace was no less distressing. Only a substantial wage, comparable with the earnings of the fastest pieceworkers in machete work, could make a spray job attractive to new recruits. Despite the relatively high pay, spray crews had very high turnover rates, often addressing their workplace grievances by voting with their feet. By the mid-1950s, managers complained that spray workers were becoming increasingly difficult to recruit or keep.

Dependence on unreliable, expensive, and strike-prone workers for the crucial work of disease control had always been a sore point for United Fruit's management and scientific corps. The company's famed research department repeatedly strove to eliminate the human element from its sigatoka program, first trying to spray bordeaux mix from airplanes and then from a series of stationary tower apparatuses. After initial high hopes, each of these initiatives failed to check the disease, and the company was forced again and again to return to reliance on the periquera. Finally, in 1962, after a failed attempt in 1959, United succeeded in capitalizing on the French discovery of a new oil-based spray that could be applied by aircraft, and the era of the pericos ended. It is worth emphasizing that the discovery of a new technology for fighting the disease was made outside United's own corps of scientists, whose agenda single-mindedly ascribed crop disease problems to an undisciplined workforce and sought, unsuccessfully, a solution in automation. Once discovered, the new aerial method of combating sigatoka would almost certainly have been adopted eventually, but it is equally certain that the company's problematic relationship with its spray crews fueled the urgency with which it sought to replace them. The postwar evolution of United's sigatoka-control strategy was driven by biological contingency and labor-management struggle in nearly equal measure.

Environmental change has no fixed pace. It may be gradual and cumulative, but it can also be sudden and spectacular, as with the spread of the Caribbean basin sigatoka epidemic in 1935. Yet even explosive change may have hidden origins in earlier, apparently innocuous human interventions. The outbreak of a new, more virulent strain of the *mycosphaerella* fungus in 1973 was almost as rapid as the original epidemic and has had nearly as dramatic an impact on the banana industry. From the outset, this "black" sigatoka (*Mycosphaerella fijienses*, var. *difformis*) has been strongly resistant to oil sprays alone, and it developed resistance to systemic fungicides far more rapidly than the previous strain (now redubbed yellow sigatoka). This has led to the employment of a rotating assortment of "fungicide cocktails" and ever more frequent spraying schedules — over forty applications per year in many areas — saturating plantation zones with an array of new organic compounds whose ecological effects are not yet well understood. Black sigatoka control costs now amount to 25 percent of the gross revenues of the isthmian banana trade. Unlike the original disease, it also afflicts subsistence and domestic-market production of plantains.

While the new epidemic is generally discussed as a distinct event from the first (except for the role of monocultural vulnerability in each), one researcher has postulated that the outbreak of black sigatoka may be an unforeseen consequence of the replacement of bordeaux mixture by oil sprays for control of the original disease. In this scenario, a less virulent variant of the "black" *M. fijienses* fungus may have long been present at very low levels, but unable to dislodge the "yellow" *M. musicola* variant from their mutual ecological niche as long as bordeaux mixture suppressed both. Oil, however, inhibits only the reproductive mechanism favored by the yellow fungus, allowing the unsuppressed *fijienses* to develop a more explosive virulence and replace the original pathogen throughout its domain. If this hypothesis is correct (and it is difficult, if not impossible, to confirm or disprove it), the mid-1970s rampage of black sigatoka across Central America, and the increasing use of toxic chemical combinations to combat it, are delayed consequences of the struggle between United Fruit and the workers of the periquera during the 1940s and 1950s.

Although the role of changing pesticide technology in the black sigatoka epidemic remains speculative, the cumulative and permanent effect of the pericos' labors on soils in the Golfito Division is well established. Central American banana workers sprayed more bordeaux mixture than has ever been applied to any crop: fifty to seventy thousand liters, including 100–150 kilos of copper, per hectare annually. By the late 1950s, banana plants began to uproot spontaneously in widely scattered areas throughout the Palmar Sur district; United's agronomists discovered that inadequate root systems, the result of severe copper toxicity, were to blame. The company abandoned many of the problem areas, selling approximately one thousand hectares over the next fifteen years to small and medium farmers who were not informed of the copper problem. The new growers planted rice on their parcels and found that this crop also failed, unable to take nourishment through stunted roots.

Costa Rican agriculture ministry agronomists ultimately determined that the copper content of all soils planted in bananas between 1940 and 1962 was abnormally high. The effect is not uniform—leaks in piping or areas in which workers took unauthorized rests while continuing to discharge fungicide probably account for some patches of particularly intense contamination. On the whole, however, the most fertile alluvial lands—especially those on which the Terraba River deposited silt in the floods of 1954 and 1955—were most affected, due to copper's tendency to bond with organic matter in soils. Consequently, soil scientists estimate that five to seven thousand hectares in the region are effectively sterilized for most agricultural purposes—unsuitable for any shallow-rooted cultivations, especially cereals. The effect is permanent; no soil amendment has proven capable of neutralizing the bordeaux residues. The copper problem played a role in United's 1985 closure of the entire Golfito banana operation, although a bitter strike, black sigatoka, and market considerations were also involved. Most former plantations are now planted with trees cultivated for wood pulp, or in African oil palms, one of the few tropical crops relatively unaffected by copper toxicity. The "sickness" of former banana lands recalls the vision of the sickened pericos, powerfully evoked in the journalism and memoirs of the bordeaux era. The often-articulated linkage between the ruined bodies of the spray workers and the flourishing crops of the zona bananera is revealed in this light not as an inverse relationship, in which the health of one is sacrificed for the health of the other, but instead as a mutual vulnerability to agrochemical abuse, hidden for a time in the case of the land.

The River of Milk

Environmental and Administrative Tribunal,

Ministry of Energy and the Environment

Does the system work? Costa Rica is among the most legalistic societies in Latin America, and this applies also to environmental regulations. The commitment of state institutions to policing the law is absolute—in theory. Many question the efficacy of the institutions, however, and Costa Rican newspapers are filled with cases of bureaucratic bungling, backsliding, and corruption that have allowed major polluters to go unpunished. Toward the end of the year 2000, neighbors near a large Dos Pinos dairy plant in Alajuela made the astonishing—well-nigh biblical—discovery that the Siquiares River had turned to milk. The river's ecosystem had been choked to death by a fat, creamy scum that the plant kept pumping out day after day. The contamination was denounced to the ministry of the environment. The following judicial decision handed down by the ministry's legal tribunal offers a look at the wheels of Costa Rican environmental justice.

PROVEN FACTS: . . . (5) That the water treatment system of the Dos Pinos, Inc. dairy processing plant discharged into the aeration tanks of the water treatment facilities of the plant an abnormally large batch of skin from milk products that caused an accumulation of cream in the clarifying tank, which resulted in the treatment system not possessing adequate capacity to retain the milk solids, fats, and oils, all of which flowed into the Siquiares River and contaminated it.

(6) That by virtue of official letter UPC-PSF-1609-00 of 4 December 2000, the Director of Permits and Control and Inspection of Complaints of the Ministry of Health, in the face of the contamination of the Siquiares River by Dos Pinos, Inc., issued a sanitary order that within the space of five days Dos Pinos: present a contingency and mitigation plan to avoid the contamination of the river; propose an adequate manner of disposing of the solids that would not

River of Milk

recirculate them through the system; carry out a study that would verify the implementation of the DAF [Dissolved Air Flotation system]; reevaluate the design of the organic load flows; present an Operational Report on the Treatment System; and improve and expand the system of filtration grills. . . .

(7) That on 10 December 2000 employees of the Office for the Protection of the Human Environment and the Specialized Technical Unit of the Ministry of Health carried out an inspection of the dairy processing plant of Dos Pinos, Inc. located in El Coyol of Alajuela, proving that the effluent from the runoff water treatment system was not fulfilling the norms on outflow given an inadequate design of the system for treating that water that stemmed from an overabundant discharge of runoff waters, which created a major concentration of organic bulk that the system had no capacity to assimilate and reduce to the outflow levels established by Executive Decree No. 26042-S-MINAE, published in the official *Gazette* No. 117 of 19 June 1997.

(8) That by virtue of official letter UPC-PSF-0079–01 of 12 January 2001, the Director of Permits and Control and Inspection of Complaints of the Ministry of Health revoked the Sanitary Permit allowing Dos Pinos, Inc. to operate.

(9) That between August of 2000 and 17 February 2001 Dos Pinos, Inc. dumped into the waters of the Siquiares River a Volume of Outflow in excess of 727,842 kilograms of contaminated water. . . .

★ ★ ★

III. IN TERMS OF DAMAGES: From the complete analysis of the evidence received and admitted by this Tribunal, it has been proven that Dos Pinos, Inc. has contaminated the waters of the Siquiares River with its dumping of runoff waters from its treatment plant from August 2000 to the present. These facts are notorious and are admitted by the very representative of the company, Mr. Jorge Pattoni Sáenz, in his declaration. These acts occurred due to a faulty design of the plant, which did not have the capacity to receive the volume of organic contaminant and so could not process it to meet the outflow levels required by the Regulation on Outflow and Reuse of Runoff Waters, which contaminated the Siquiares River, affecting the body of water with the discharge of contaminant which created a thickening of the water and foul odors. . . .

As long as there does not exist a link of Adequate Cause that allows the naming of an individual as the responsible party and determines the content of the obligation of indemnification, no damage can be attributed, even in the manner done by the appraisers in this case, invoking the Principle of Indubio Pronatura [a principle that in case of doubt, one must proceed to legislate in favor of the environment], since this would be putting in jeopardy in a dangerous fashion such Principles as Equity and Innocence and opening dangerous loopholes for the Abuse of the Law of Unjustified Enrichment. Moreover, neither can we accept the calculation of the Cost of the Community Complaint, referring to the costs and expenses incurred by the plaintiff and the community. Some have suggested calculating this as repaying the bills and others as a simple payment of legal fees. Neither are permitted under article 328 of the Law of Public Administration, besides the fact that technically the costs of monitoring the problem are not considered part of the Environmental Damage, and it would do harm to include them, since what causal link is there between costs of this kind and Damage to the Environment?

Finally neither does this Tribunal accept the estimate of Environmental Damage offered by Dos Pinos, Inc., considering that it does not encompass with an exact and real valuation the Environmental Damage caused by the direct contamination of the body of water, and because it is very subjective to recur to a polling method to establish the value of effects on the population that do not necessarily have a causal link with the facts in order to define environmental damage. Considering all this, according to just logic, this Tribunal judges it opportune to value the Environmental Damage done solely under the Equation of Treatment Costs, and charges Dos Pinos, Inc. to pay the sum of (US) $92,189.00 for Environmental Damages. . . . Moreover, given that the assessment done takes into account only the period between August 2000 and 17 February 2001, the Technical Office of National Environment is ordered to make an additional assessment, on the same basis, up to the point when Dos Pinos, Inc. complies with the runoff levels established in the law.

Measures of Mitigation and Stabilization of the Environment: Dos Pinos, Inc. must comply with the Sanitary Orders issued by the Ministry of Health and the Administrative Resolutions issued by the Technical Office of National Environment of the Ministry of Energy and the Environment within the time allotted by those agencies. The Tribunal of Environmental Administration also orders, in conformity with articles 103 and 111 of the Law of the Environment in relation to article 45 of the Law of Biodiversity, the additional fulfillment of the following Measures of Mitigation and Prevention of Environmental Damage:

Within the space of fifteen days from the notification of the current resolution, Dos Pinos, Inc. must present before the Technical Office of National Environment and the Ministry of Health a Plan for suctioning the accumulated sediments and larvae derived from the contamination of the Siquiares riverbed, and the Technical Office of National Environment and Ministry of Health will determine whether or not to approve this plan in accordance with the technical specifications they see fit to apply.

By 1 July 2001 at the latest, Dos Pinos, Inc. will present to the Technical Office of National Environment and the Ministry of Health a plan of environmental management that addresses in integral fashion the handling of solid and liquid wastes.

Handed down on 4 June 2001.

La Loca de Gandoca

Ana Cristina Rossi

Since the beginning of the country's tourism boom in the late 1980s, Costa Rica has seen a great deal of "greenwashing": development that uses the rhetoric of ecological sensitivity to secure approval and community support for projects that in reality devastate the environment. Ana Cristina Rossi's La Loca de Gandoca *(The Mad Woman of Gandoca) has emerged as the country's best-selling novel in recent years. The novel gives a fictionalized account of the author's struggle to defend the coastal wildlife refuge of Gandoca in Limón Province from "ecotourist development," a crusade that exposed her to a great deal of government harassment and a number of death threats. The excerpt looks at the corrupt practices and negligence of state functionaries that pave the way for eco-developers.*

Mariana doesn't understand my sense of urgency about appealing to the Constitutional Tribunal for protection of the refuge. But she is tireless and very intelligent and she has accumulated so many legal acts and pieces of evidence about the failure to act, the negligence, and moronic behavior by the directive body responsible for our natural riches that it turns out to be easy for her to compose a brilliant indictment of the violations perpetrated.

And, in effect, Mariana proves that the Ministry is in violation of articles 6, 23, 24, 45, 50, and 89 of the Constitution of our country, article 18 of the Law on Wilderness Conservation, article 1 of the Decree on the Creation of the Refuge, articles 3, 4, 9, and 10 of the Decree on Rules Concerning the Refuge, the Law on Forests, the Central American Convention on the Environment and Development, the Convention on Protection of the Flora and Fauna and of the Landscape of the Countries of the Americas, the Convention for the Protection of Cultural and Natural Patrimony, the Convention on Wetlands of International Importance, Especially Marine Bird Habitats, and the Convention for the Protection and Development of Marine Areas of the Greater Caribbean. The appeal for an injunction is a document of thirty pages, and Mariana attaches four hundred more pages of evidence and photographs.

She asks me to write an anecdotal summary to bring the case to life for the judges.

* * *

Here, from the Executive Decree creating the Refuge of Gandoca on the basis of the Law of Wilderness Protection and the Law on Forests, from the dark and marvelous swamp, from the unique, extraordinary union of the *yolillo* and the *orey* palm, from the last source of the giant mangrove oyster (*Crasostrea rhizophorea*), and from this tiny warm dimple of sand, I beseech you to shelter me, O great Constitutional Tribunal.

Shelter me from life gone awry and from premature death. Everything here is dying like soldiers breathing deadly gas. Trees are falling before the buzz of chainsaws, the pools and the springs are drying up, and my eyes are drying up with them, O great Constitutional Tribunal. Shelter me from the state authority that accuses me of every crime, when in reality I have committed only one sin: asking that the laws be enforced. O great Constitutional Tribunal, shelter me and issue a binding sentence that defines once and for all whether it is a sin, a crime, a felony, or a virtue to defend beauty. I confess to a long relationship with plant life. My arteries are like vines, and I am convinced that the *majagua* flower is skin. The skin on my hands is wrinkled like the rough surface of wild grape leaves, with their protruding veins a plant passion. And when my hands mind children, they have that leafy, encompassing openness of the great almond trees, their bitter sweetness.

Shelter me from the attitude of those who, designated by the popular will to watch over the natural resources of our people, use the office for their own enrichment. Shelter me from the Ministry that surrenders the coastal rain forests to investors who wear a smile on their face and hold a whisky in their hands, without enforcing the applicable laws on the books. Shelter me from the Minister: when I went to request planning, careful thought, and a plan of operation, he threw me out into the street, fired me from the ad honorem post (no one paid me a penny) in the Ministry that the Deputy Minister and Ana Luisa had given me. The Deputy Minister's advisors, concerned, shook their wise heads and said, "Poor little thing, they threw her out because she is too passionate, too romantic." And I ask you, O great Constitutional Tribunal, "What is romantic about asking that the law be enforced?"

The issue was also that I said to the Minister that it was irresponsible to cut down the Caribbean rain forest to build an ice-skating rink. And the Minister replied, "Don't get involved, my child, don't get in the way of progress, the black folk in this region are so backward, so poor, that we're going to give them the opportunity to train to be speed-skating champions and win all the gold medals in the Winter Olympics, that's how they'll overcome underdevelopment. And anyway we're going ahead with it because it's a totally green skating rink." But are you seriously going to offer ice-skating in this hot, humid land?! "Yes, my child, in fact we've already calculated the value of the vapors, the steam that comes off the nearby forest, the figures on evapotranspiration, condensation, and so on. This natural tropical process is a fabulous source of energy that will move steam turbines to cool the water and transform it into ice." The science sounds alright, I answered, but you are counting on the vapor and steam coming from the forest and the investors ARE GOING TO CUT DOWN THE FOREST. "We have to let them chop down the forest, my child, there's no other way. But inside the Refuge, far away from the coast, there's a stretch of land that's not going to be logged because it was bought for conservation by the Green World organization. We'll bring the energy and the steam from that land. The rest of the Refuge, the part that hasn't been purchased for protection, has to be destroyed if that's what the owners want, my child, because that's the way private property works. It's been ordered by the Constitutional Tribunal."

Is this true, O great Constitutional Tribunal?

Shelter me also from the Deputy Minister who, as an indirect delegate of the people, is the person in charge of protecting natural resources and defending the managed resources from plunder and arbitrary use. Shelter me from this famous conservationist, O great Constitutional Tribunal, since every time I ask him to oppose the cutting of forests and the unlicensed construction of hotels and tourist cabins, he plays deaf. Every time I tell him that Dominique has opened up a beach in the Gandoca Refuge without a permit, opening a deep wound through which sewage and soapy water are going to pour like a river of tears and my children are going to fall sick; every time I tell him that Dominique is going to leave us without water, without quiet, without wildlife, and that she is going to open a dump full of drugs and alcohol behind the tree housing the raccoons and anteaters; every time that I ask him to use the power authorized by the people and his office to protect me, to protect all of us against the disgrace and the pollution going into the sea, the Deputy Minister throws his hands in the air, turns away, and says furiously, "I don't want to hear anything about Frenchwomen!"

Shelter me all-powerful Constitutional Tribunal, from the lawyers and other functionaries of the Forestry Office who laugh lustily at my sadness and rub their hands together every time another tree falls, "one less to protect," they say, "what a relief—let them all fall, what a major drag it is to have to protect them. Let the country perish."

Give me very concrete shelter from the employees of the Forestry Office in

Limón, whom I called many months ago to notify them that the trees on the riverbanks in the Gandoca Refuge were being logged, in the last forest left in the south of the province.

"That's not in our domain," they responded.

"The trees on the banks of the rivers of Limón are in the purview of the Forestry Office of Limón."

"That's odd."

"I have in front of me the law as well as a document saying that national wildlife refuges are the jurisdiction of the Forestry Office."

"Even more strange. . . . Where did you say this logging is going on?"

"In the Gandoca Refuge, south of Limón."

"The thing is, the Gandoca Refuge is really far away. If we went there, we'd get lost."

"It's impossible to get lost, you just follow the highway straight down. All those rivers cross under the highway. The logging is in plain view."

"No, no, believe me, every time we go south, we get lost."

Here, from the tiny warm hole in the sand, hidden from the eyes of the blue herons, the pelicans, and the kingfisher, surrounded by trees of wild sea grapes, with their green and sweet-and-sour bunches hanging so close to the water, here, from my warm little hole in the sand together with the green ocean seaweed, in the double breach of the coral reef, lifted by the waves, weak from waiting, desperate, between the *majaguales* and the *hicacos* and the sunflowers and the wild lilies, drunk with scents that are going to disappear forever, drenched with sun, with rain, I implore you to shelter me, to shelter us, O great Constitutional Tribunal.

The hierarchs charged with looking out for our natural wealth are destroying it or surrendering it in exchange for dollars, and they say it is by your mandate.

Clarify this for me, all-powerful Constitutional Tribunal.

VIII

Tropical Soundings

The past two decades have been momentous ones for Costa Rica. In the 1980s, the country narrowly averted bankruptcy and barely escaped militarization and political disaster during the US counterrevolutionary campaign against Nicaragua. Costa Ricans witnessed the fervent expansion of evangelical Protestantism and watched their national team miraculously reach the second round of the World Cup finals in Italy in 1990. And they saw the sons of the two social democratic titans of their history, Calderón and Figueres, assume the presidency in consecutive terms, only to make a political pact designed to dismantle the welfare state that their fathers had created! In the 1990s, after a decade of strong incentives and pressures from the International Monetary Fund, the World Bank, and the United States Agency for International Development, a thoroughly transformed economy emerged. Coffee and bananas ceased to be the country's largest export earners for the first time in its modern history. More incredible still was that revenues from the entire export agriculture sector were left in the dust by the earnings of the tourism industry and the value of exports produced by a mammoth Intel microchip plant that went up in the heart of the Central Valley. The country's very identity as an agricultural nation found itself in crisis.

This economic overhaul formed part and parcel of an antistatist, free market agenda that swept Latin America in the 1980s and 1990s. Costa Rica has proven something of a test case. Are structural adjustment and the privatization of public institutions possible in a country with still strong social democratic traditions? After some initial victories for the proponents of neoliberal orthodoxy, the popular defense of social democracy has experienced a revival. Gradually, a perception has taken hold that the privatization of state enterprises is allowing members of the politically connected elite to line up at the trough of public wealth. Both the government of Rafael Ángel Calderón Fournier (1990–94) and that of José María Figueres Olsen (1994–98) experienced strong public resistance to key structural reforms early in their presidencies and were eventually forced to abandon "shock therapy" prescriptions for a more gradualist approach to deficit reduction and the privatization of the public sector.

The longest-running and most symbolic of struggles over the future of the social democratic model has revolved around attempts to privatize the Instituto Costarricense de Electricidad (ICE)—the giant, state-owned telephone and electricity company created in 1949 as part of a program to nationalize key industries. The maximum neoliberal agenda, backed by powerful foreign companies, the US government, and the World Trade Organization, has been to break up the monopoly into smaller components for sale (while leaving the un-profitable components under public control); the minimum agenda has been to keep the ICE from control over lucrative new areas of enterprise such as cellular telephony and Internet service. A combative union held the line while the neoliberal momentum ebbed and the disastrous results of similar privati-zation schemes in places like Argentina and California became known. Then, in March and April of 2000, massive popular protests broke out against the so-called Combo ICE, the legislative project to privatize hydroelectric and tele-phone services. Similar mobilizations to defend the ICE and teachers' pensions have continued into 2003.

There was a dire political cost for failing to live up to electoral promises and instead promoting neoliberal economic policies. This became manifest in the dramatic increase in abstentionism between the 1994 presidential elections and those of 2002 when, moreover, the two long-standing parties, National Libera-tion (PLN) and the Social Christians (PUSC), were successfully challenged by the upstart Party of Citizen Action (PAC). The PAC captured an astonishing 26 per-cent of the vote in 2002, just barely missing elbowing out the PLN for second place and forcing a second-round runoff, since neither the PLN nor the PUSC captured the 40 percent of the vote necessary for clear victory in stage one. This political change has taken place in the context of a profound cultural trans-formation that has left national identity in crisis. The image of a white, rural, yeoman farmer, peaceful, and egalitarian Costa Rica—to name the essential components of that identity—has been eroded by rampant urbanization ac-companied by greater violence (especially domestic violence), and, above all, by the consolidation of a class culture. This is visible in the clear division be-tween those who live in private neighborhoods, protected by private security and with access to private medical and educational services, on the one hand, and those who cannot afford any of these things, on the other. In this milieu, Costa Ricans have felt threatened as never before in their history by large-scale Nicaraguan immigration, by the new pressures of the global economy on their jobs or businesses, by corruption, by delinquency, and by the rise of orga-nized crime—whether in the form of drug trafficking, a legacy of the dirty war against the Sandinistas, or in the form of gambling and prostitution (feminine and masculine; adult, juvenile, and child), a legacy of the vertiginous tourist expansion of the 1990s.

Confronted by these changes and threats, Costa Ricans time and again express a deep pessimism in opinion polls — a reflection of the uncertainty with which they see their future. In a number of ways, however, Costa Rica has never been better off than it is right now: the proportion of homes below the poverty line has stabilized at about one in five since 1994 (in the United States, by comparison, the proportion is one in ten), and the 2000 census revealed that virtually every home in the country has access to electricity, while four out of five have a washing machine, a refrigerator, and color television. At the same time, between 1950 and 2000, the proportion of the population of twenty years or older with a secondary education rose from just over 8 percent to almost 40 percent (in the United States, the comparable figure was 83 percent), while the share of the population with postsecondary training rose from only 2 percent to almost 20 percent (33 percent in the United States).

Today, Costa Rica once again finds itself at a Latin American crossroads. This intersection is, however, quite Costa Rican because it can only be reached via a democratic political system open to popular demands, one whose legitimacy rests decisively on the search for social justice. Up to now, this combination has produced a development model in which social, cultural, political, and institutional development have always been a few steps ahead of economic development. Representatives of international financial agencies would say that Ticos have had the luxury of putting into practice a development model that they cannot pay for — one simply not sustainable over the long haul. Nevertheless, one could respond that Costa Rican society discovered a very long time ago that the road combining social development and democracy is the only one worth pursuing. This perseverance and stubbornness introduces some color and hope onto a twenty-first-century world stage that remains, so far, conspicuously without utopias.

Social Development with Limited Resources

Carmelo Mesa-Lago

Carmelo Mesa-Lago, Professor Emeritus of Economics at the University of Pittsburgh, is one of the foremost authorities on social policy in Latin America. The Costa Rican model has long interested him precisely because it offers striking proof that despite relatively scarce resources, a country can achieve social progress higher than its corresponding GDP per capita level. Here he describes the effects of the terrible crisis of the 1980s, analyzes the country's ability to recover quickly from the crisis by the mid-1990s, and optimistically proposes policy reforms that might allow Costa Rica to sustain social development.

In 1993, Costa Rica ranked eighth among the twenty nations of Latin America in terms of per capita Gross Domestic Product (GDP), but it ranked first in terms of social indicators. The life expectancy of its population was the highest in the region, and its poverty incidence and unemployment were the lowest. Costa Rica's social achievements are even more remarkable considering that the country was predominately rural, agricultural, and poor, and that prior to World War II, the nation ranked in the bottom half of the region concerning social indicators. How has Costa Rica been able to attain such a high level of social development in relation to its relatively low ranking in terms of GDP per capita? What are the key components of this successful model? And how was Costa Rica able to undergo economic crisis and reform in the 1980s without sacrificing social development? These are questions of crucial importance to all developing countries.

In spite of the adverse effects of the crisis of the early 1980s, in the early 1990s, Costa Rica ranked first in the region concerning social indicators. Table 1 compares Costa Rica and nine other Latin American countries on fourteen indicators (the remaining ten countries remain well below Costa Rica in terms

Table 1. Comparison of social indicators in Latin America

	GDP per capita (US dollars)	Adult illiteracy (% of age 15+)	School enrollment (as % of age group)[a]		Population (%) with access to:		Daily calorie supply per capita	Infant mortality (per 1000 live births)[b]	Life expect- ancy at birth (years)
			secondary	higher	piped water	sanita- tion			
	1993	1990–92	1990–92		1990	1992	1992	1990–95	1991–95
Argentina	7220	4.1	71	43	92	89[†]	2880	23.2	71.8
Brazil	2930	18.9	39	12	83	73	2824	57.7	66.3
Chile	3170	5.4	72	24	88	83	2583	14.0	74.4
Colombia	1400	13.3	56	15	94	56[†]	2678	37.0	69.2
Costa Rica	2150	5.7	46	28	95	97	2889	13.7	76.3
Cuba	1133	6.0	81	21	98[*]	92	2833	11.8	75.3
Mexico	3610	12.4	53	13	79	66[†]	3181[‡]	35.0	71.5
Panama	2600	11.2	64	24	73	88	2239	25.1	72.9
Uruguay	3830	3.8	83	32	92	82[†]	2750	20.0	72.4
Venezuela	2840	9.6	24	32	81	55[†]	2622	23.2	71.8

[a]   Enrollment in primary education is virtually universal in all countries
[b]   Reported rates; revised in the following countries: Argentina 29%, Chile 17%, Cuba 14%,
      Panama 21%, and Venezuela 33% (PAHO, 1994)
[*]   Figure by PAHO 1994
[†]   UNDP (1995) gives different figures: Argentina 68, Colombia 64, Mexico 50, Uruguay 61, and
      Venezuela 92
[‡]   This figure appears excessively high when compared to other Mexican indicators

of economic and social development). While Costa Rica ranked eighth on GDP
per capita, it ranked first or second in ten of the other thirteen social indicators, and it ranked first overall, based on the unweighted average ranking of
all countries in each of the fourteen indicators. In terms of the United Nations
Human Development Index, which is based on three major indicators—life
expectancy at birth, education (a combination of adult illiteracy and combined
educational enrollment), and adjusted real GDP per capita based on purchasing

Table 1. *Continued*

	Population covered by social security (%)[c]	Unem-ployment rate (% of labor force)	National poverty incidence (% of house-holds)	Average urban income (richest 10% as multiple of poorest 10%)	Military expendi-ture (% of education and health expendi-ture)	Ranking of table variables[d]		Human Develop-ment Index rank[e]	
						Average score	Rank	Among all 174 countries in world	Among 20 countries in Latin America
	1991–93	1995	1992	1992	1990–91				
Argentina	80	18.6	—	8.3	51	4.1	3	30	2
Brazil	—	4.7	43[§]	17.3	23	7.2	9	63	9
Chile	80	5.6	28	11.9	68	4.7	5	33	4
Colombia	16[**]	8.6	—	10.7	57	7.5	10	57	8
Costa Rica	86	4.3[††]	25	6.4	6	2.7	1	28	1
Cuba	100	10–18[‡‡]	—	—	125	4.4	4	72	11
Mexico	59	6.4	36	8.4	5	5.8	6	53	7
Panama	57	14.3	36	10.3	34	6.5	8	49	6
Uruguay	70	10.7	—	4.7	38	3.8	2	32	3
Venezuela	50	10.3	33	6.8	33	6.1	7	47	5

[c] Social insurance health care programs; in Chile, Costa Rica, and Uruguay, coverage is virtually universal when coverage by the ministry of health is considered. Values for Cuba refer to legal coverage by the ministry of health

[d] Arithmetic (unweighted) average ranking of all countries in each variable

[e] All countries are ranked as "high human development" except Cuba, which is ranked "medium"

[§] 1988

[**] 1990

[††] 1992, author's estimates

[‡‡] 1994

power parity rates in US dollars—Costa Rica ranked twenty-eighth among 174 countries in the world, and first among the twenty Latin American countries. It is worth looking most closely at some of these key areas of social development.

In 1994, access to health care was virtually universal. In the same year, the percentage of children below one year immunized against contagious diseases was close to 90 percent. In 1991, 96 percent of all births took place in hospitals and 95 percent of them were attended by a physician or obstetric nurse.

Costa Rica's exceptional health care coverage and facilities, combined with very good nutrition and housing, and above-average income per capita, led to health conditions that ranked among the best two in Latin America. The two most significant indicators of health standards are the infant mortality rate and in life expectancy. In 1993, the infant mortality rate was 13.7 per thousand live births, while life expectancy was 76.3 years.

Overall, the pathological and morbidity profile of Costa Rica in the early 1990s resembled that of developed countries: the four major causes of death were cardiovascular diseases, malignant neoplasms, external causes like traffic accidents and violence, and diseases of the respiratory system. As late as 1975, slightly over half of children under six years of age suffered some degree of malnutrition, most of it mild. By 1992, this figure had declined to 21 percent. Acute diarrhea diseases as a cause of infant death moved from first place in 1970 (27 percent of all deaths) to seventh place in 1993 (3 percent). Contagious and parasitic diseases in 1970 ranked as the leading cause of death (20.5 percent), but ranked tenth in 1991 and were responsible for only 2.8 percent of all deaths. In urban areas, access to potable water was nearly universal by the end of the 1960s, while sewerage access increased from below 30 percent to 100 percent between 1960 and 1983. In rural areas, 86 percent of the population had potable water in 1989, and 94 percent had sewerage and excreta disposal.

Education is central to the Costa Rican model and its ability to hurdle the economic crisis. Enrollment ratios at the preschool level increased between 1985 and 1993 from 52 to 66 percent. The primary school enrollment was essentially 100 percent. The enrollment rate at the secondary level peaked at 53 percent in 1978, but fell slightly during the crisis years and stood at 45 percent in 1993. The higher education enrollment rate increased from 5 percent in 1963–65 to 28 percent in 1991. Higher education was less affected by the crisis than was secondary education, essentially because of a constitutional clause guaranteeing state university funding at a fixed percentage of the national budget and due to the opening of many private universities. As in the case of illiteracy, which stood at a mere 5.7 percent in 1993, there are no significant gender differences in enrollment rates at the different educational levels. Costa Rica's almost equal access to education by gender stands as a remarkable accomplishment in a society predominantly rural until very recently. The figures also suggest that the country had made impressive progress in education until a regression occurred during the 1980s crisis, and that in the 1990s the nation appeared to be on the way to recovering the previous standards. There exist, however, clear disparities in educational achievement between the urban and rural populations.

Costa Rica's social security is virtually unique in Latin America because it combines four key features: almost complete coverage of the entire population, at least on health care; incorporation of social insurance (contributory) and social welfare (noncontributory) programs; integration between most health care services covered by social insurance and the ministry of public health; and almost complete unification in a single institution and standardization of entitlement conditions. The Costa Rican Social Security Fund (ccss or, as Costa Ricans call it, *la Caja*) was created in the 1940s. Legally, all salaried workers (including domestic servants and employees of microenterprises) are mandatorily covered by the ccss, while the self-employed, unpaid family workers, and employers can join voluntarily. The program is financed primarily through payroll taxes. As the formal sector, salaried labor force, public employment, skilled labor, and employment in larger enterprises increase, it is easier to expand coverage. Conversely, the higher the urban informal sector, rural traditional sector, self-employment, unpaid family workers, unskilled laborers, open unemployment, and employment in microenterprises, the harder it is to extend coverage. The expansion of social services has been facilitated in Costa Rica by the fact that the proportion of the economically active population in the urban informal sector was the lowest in the region, while two-thirds of the country's workers were salaried employees. Costa Rica also developed a network of antipoverty programs long before social safety nets became fashionable in Latin America. This network covered practically all social risks and provided social services to almost all the population, even people located in remote rural areas.

One of Costa Rica's major problems has been its high population growth rate, which has made it harder to achieve high GDP per capita growth rates. From 1959 to 1994, nevertheless, Costa Rica's per capita growth rate matched and, from 1991 to 1995, doubled, the regional average. Because Costa Rica has a relatively young population, its ratio of active insured per pensioner has been high, and this has eased Costa Rica's pension burden. The large young segment of Costa Rica's population, however, has increased the nation's health care, education, and other social costs. As the productive age segment expands in the next two decades, the country's dependency ratio will decline and become one of the lowest in the region (the older segment of the population will also expand, but at a much lower rate than the productivity-age segment).

Table 2 summarizes the six most relevant indicators of the crisis of the 1980s and the recovery in Costa Rica compared with those in the other nine countries (the most developed in the region) selected for this study: GDP per capita growth (absolute and per capita), inflation, real minimum wage, urban open unemployment, national poverty incidence, and inequality (Gini coefficient). The data selected illustrate the situation prior to the crisis, at the worst point

Table 2. Socioeconomic impact of the 1980s crisis and the 1990s recovery in Costa Rica and nine other Latin American countries, 1980–1995

	GDP per capita (cumulative %)			Inflation rate (December to December)			Real minimum wage* (1980 = 100)		Urban unemployment (% of labor force)		
	1981–90	1991–95	1981–95	1980	1981–90†	1995	1981–90†	1993	1980	1981–90†	1995
Argentina	−21	24	3	88	4923	2	40	49	3	8	19
Brazil	−5	5	0	78	1864	22	—	—	6	6	5
Chile	12	30	42	31	27	8	69	105§	12	20	5
Colombia	18	13	31	26	32	20	99	106	10	14	9
Costa Rica	−6	10	4	18	27	25	86	113	6	10	4††
Cuba	28‡	−33	−5	4	9	100**	—	—	5	6	10–18††
Mexico	−4	−6	−10	30	159	48	46	42‡‡	4	7	6
Panama	−2	15	13	14	2	1	—	—	10	17	14
Uruguay	−1	15	14	43	83	37	69	51	7	16	11
Venezuela	−19	2	−17	20	81	53	55	61‡‡	7	14	10
Average***	−8	2	−6	56	—	25	—	67	7	—	9

*   Mostly in the capital city or urban areas; national in Argentina and Uruguay
†   At the worst point in the crisis
§   The maximum point was 116 in 1981 and had not been surpassed in 1993
††   1994
‡   If the year 1981 is deleted (its 15.4 percent growth is a matter of controversy), the cumulative rate declines to 10%
**   Based on monetary hangover and black market prices
‡‡   1992
*** Averages from ECLAC, except for wage and unemployment, which were calculated by the author

in the crisis, and in the recovery or latest year available. Costa Rica suffered a decline in cumulative GDP per capita (6 percent) in the period 1981–90; only Argentina and Venezuela suffered a worse decrease. By the time the recovery was well established, in 1991–95, Costa Rica's GDP per capita increased 10 percent, five times the Latin American average. The net outcome of the entire 1980–95 period was modest positive growth of 4 percent. In 1980, Costa Rica's inflation rate (18 percent) was among the lowest of the ten countries and was considerably lower than the regional average (56 percent); in the worst point during the crisis, Costa Rica's inflation reached 27 percent, and in 1995, it was 25 percent, equal to the regional average.

Table 2. *Continued*

	Poverty incidence (% of households)						Gini coefficient (urban households)		
	1980 Urban	Rural	1984–87 Urban	Rural	1991–92 Urban	Rural	1980–81	1986–88	1992
Argentina	7	16	12	17	—	—	0.365	0.406	0.408
Brazil	30	62	34	60	39[§§]	56[§§]	0.493	0.543	—
Chile	—	—	37	45	27	29	—	0.485	0.474
Colombia	36	45	36	42	38	—	0.518	0.455	0.454
Costa Rica	16	28	21	28	25	25	.0328	0.364	0.362
Cuba	—	—	—	—	—	—	—	—	—
Mexico	—	—	28	45	30	46	—	0.321	0.414
Panama	31	45	34	43	34	43	0.399	0.430	0.448
Uruguay	9	21	14	23	8	—	0.379	0.385	0.301
Venezuela	18	35	25	34	32	36	0.306	0.384	0.380
Average***	25	54	30	53	34	53	—	—	—

[§§] 1990

The gradualist approach taken to structural adjustment, and the rapid recovery of social spending, helped to maintain this progress. Costa Rica's response to the crisis was much more gradualist than was that of many other countries in the region. Chile and Argentina, for instance, adopted a so-called shock therapy that was meant to restructure the economy rapidly with little attention paid to adverse social effects (as well as some adverse economic effects). In Chile, unemployment increased tremendously, real wages declined sharply, income distribution became more unequal, and poverty worsened. Costa Rica, on the other hand, took a much more moderate approach to structural adjustment, trying to protect the population from such negative effects—for instance, by maintaining the social safety nets it had in place before the adjustment and by adding some new social programs. Costa Rica's performance in terms of social indicators was considerably better than in terms of economic indicators. For example, the real minimum wage in Costa Rica suffered a relatively modest decline of 14 percent at the worst point in the crisis, and in 1993 had gained 13 percent over 1980, 46 percentage points above the regional average.

Costa Rica's performance in macroeconomic indicators (GDP per capita growth in US dollars, inflation) was fair, better than the regional average (ranking between fifth and eighth). Conversely, Costa Rica was among the two or three countries that suffered the least social costs during the crisis and emerged during the recovery as the best in social development. Social institutions and policies undoubtedly played a key role in Costa Rica's remarkable social performance. The gradualist approach of structural adjustment and the very short period of the transition were additional factors that helped to ameliorate both the economic decline and social costs.

But this positive picture would not be complete unless we go beyond macro indicators and compare the current situation with that prior to the crisis. It is not clear that national poverty incidence was lower in 1992 than in 1980, and most sources estimate that poverty and indigence still are highly concentrated in rural areas and that income distribution worsened. The incidence of at least three out of nine major contagious diseases in the early 1990s was higher than in 1980 and even 1961. The ratio of hospital beds per one thousand inhabitants declined, the ratio of physicians per ten thousand decreased, and immunization rates also fell, leading to serious epidemics in 1990–93. Some of those changes resulted from increased efficiency, but others were due to insufficient resources and suggest a decline in quality. In 1993, CCSS coverage of the contributory program and the real value of pensions were lower than in 1980, and the welfare pension was grossly insufficient to cover basic needs.

Resources allocated to social programs also declined in most cases, or were not adequately distributed according to need. As discussed above, the social share of total public expenditures in 1993 remained below that of 1982: the educational and non-CCSS health shares were smaller, but the CCSS share was bigger. Over this period, curative health care gained resources at the expense of preventive care, and tertiary education gained at the expense of lower levels. Between 1982 and 1990, budgets of antipoverty programs most beneficial to the poorest (nutrition, health, welfare, pensions) were cut from 12 to 35 percent. In 1994, one-third of all resources to fight poverty were allocated to the housing program, which had the least progressive impact.

Available data (on poverty, income distribution, health care, education, so-

cial security) consistently show that there are relatively small groups either excluded from or receiving very low quality social services: the rural population
(particularly outside the Central Valley), the noneducated, the elderly, women
heads of household, agricultural workers (and small farmers), and those in
the urban informal sector (street vendors, domestic servants). Costa Rica has
one of the highest social shares of both GDP and the public budget in the region, and its public social network is impressive, but it has too many agencies
and programs in need of integration, decentralization, improvement in efficiency, participation from below and, above all, better targeting of the small
pockets of disadvantaged groups. The vigorous expansion of public social services has left little space for a private sector role, except in higher education;
and collaboration between the public and private sectors is limited.

Are Costa Rica's social achievements sustainable in the long run and, if so,
how? And what social policy changes are needed to cope with the disadvantaged groups that remain? The country will face serious obstacles to maintain
its most important social programs without further increasing their burden
on GDP, the fiscal budget, and the payroll. In 1992, Costa Rica's social expenditures were 15.6 percent of GDP, much higher than those of the United States
and Japan. Costa Rica's social share of central government expenditures was
67.3 percent in 1992, similar to that of France and more than double that of the
United States. Even without military expenditures, a developing country with
relatively low GDP per capita cannot afford an increase in such burdens, but as
Costa Rica's population ages, its pension program will require increasing resources. The only way out of this dilemma is to reallocate social resources (pri-
oritizing the most important programs and targeting disadvantaged groups)
and improve their efficiency, along the lines recommended below.

Social security (CCSS) expenditures take about half of the social share of both
GDP and the fiscal budget, while education, other health care programs, and
antipoverty expenditures combined take the other half. In spite of the high legal
payroll contribution and state subsidies, the financial and actuarial equilibrium
of the CCSS has deteriorated. Some positive measures taken in the 1990s, including better investment practices and tightening of entitlement conditions,
have improved the financial equilibrium in the medium term, but they will
not be able to correct the actuarial deficit, and increases in contributions are
not advisable. The CCSS, therefore, must become more efficient by reducing its
personnel and generous fringe benefits; further increasing retirement ages (to
sixty-five years for both sexes); pursuing a more productive investment of its reserves; and incorporating and standardizing the independent pension funds of
the legislative and judicial branches. An overall reform of pensions was done at
the end of the 1990s to create a mandatory program that pays a supplementary

pension and in which public and private institutions compete for the insured, but such a reform failed to increase the retirement age in the basic program.

The health care sector also suffers from overlap, waste, and inefficiency due to the separation of the ccss and other state welfare facilities and services. Full integration of institutions is necessary, as is a reallocation of resources in favor of prevention, primary health care, and targeting of the groups in most need, particularly the isolated rural and marginalized urban populations. Hospitals with low occupancy rates should be shut down, and even more emphasis should be placed on rural health posts, health centers, and clinics. The health care infrastructure currently managed by antipoverty state agencies should be given priority for rehabilitation of the physical plant and equipment and maintenance. Consideration should be given to introduction of moderate user fees (exempting those in need) in order to control unnecessary use of services and overprescription of medicine, as well as to increase the revenue of hospitals. Decentralization and integrated services and higher community participation are essential. Collaboration with the private sector should be expanded, based on those programs that have proven effective in reducing costs and raising users' satisfaction. Privatization of nonmedical services such as food catering, cleaning, and so forth should be explored. The gap between paramedic personnel and physicians needs to be closed, and the latter should be compelled to fulfill their duties through a combination of sanctions and incentives. Reforms were introduced in the 1990s to tackle some of these problems, but key steps have not been implemented.

Education has proven to be a determinant factor in access to and quality of health care, social security coverage, employment, income, and poverty reduction. Resources from other public social programs (such as housing and pensions for high-income insured, particularly civil servants) should be transferred to education and, within it, from higher to primary and secondary levels. Targeting of resources is essential, and priority should be given to addressing adult illiteracy and improving rural primary schools and vocational technical schools to enable them to develop skills that meet market demand. New mass education techniques such as TV and video should be expanded. The ministry of education should be reorganized and strengthened; teachers' promotions should be based on merit instead of seniority; supervision and evaluation of teaching must be increased; teachers should be adequately paid and those who are redundant or do not fulfill their duties dismissed. More resources must go to educational materials and maintenance of the infrastructure. Groups with educational deficiencies must be identified and given priority. The constitution should be amended to eliminate (or at least reduce) the budget proportion mandated to universities and fiscal resources transferred from humanities and social sciences to scientific and technical departments, particularly agriculture and business (some of these changes have begun). Free tuition should be granted only to those in need, and the rest of the students should pay proper tuition. Most of the new resources should go to fellowships (including tuition and maintenance) for capable but poor students. Entrance examinations to universities should be tightened to increase quality and improve the student-teacher ratio. Redundant staff should be dismissed and a system of incentives introduced to motivate professors; allocation for research must be increased, as should practical internships and interrelations with foundations, business, and the private sector.

Antipoverty programs should be integrated or highly coordinated, while their administration should be decentralized to allow better targeting of the most disadvantaged groups. Priority should be given to programs that have the greatest impact in helping the poor—nutrition, primary health care, welfare pensions, and skills training—while housing programs should be drastically cut and focused on the rural and urban poor. State welfare agencies should continue transferring funds rather than administering them directly, but not almost exclusively to public agencies. Participation of NGOs, local communities, and nonprofit private institutions should be promoted. Allocation of resources should be based on a clear set of criteria including targeting of the poor, efficiency, and sustainability.

The recommended changes will meet with political difficulties, resistance from the entrenched bureaucracy, and pressure from interest groups adversely affected. But without these reforms, Costa Rica's remarkable social achievements will be in jeopardy, and the foundations of its democracy eroded. A nation that has shown a unique historical commitment to universal access and equity in the social arena should now tackle the transformations needed to sustain its progress, reaffirm its democracy, and forge an even better society.

Visit Beautiful Costa Rica!

Tourism Propaganda of Another Era

In 1931, Costa Rica created the first National Tourism Commission, which became the Costa Rican Tourism Institute (ICT) in 1955. The illustration shows the style of tourist advertising prevalent in the 1930s. Despite the early interest in promoting tourism, the industry did not develop in accelerated fashion until the 1980s — but then it really took off. On Christmas day 1999, the ICT took out a celebratory full-page ad in La Nación, the country's leading newspaper, to announce that, for the first time, one million tourists had visited Costa Rica in a single year (the page included a photo of the lucky millionth visitor from North America, Fay Kruyff, looking rather confused under the weight of an enormous bouquet bestowed on her at the airport). The text accompanying the ad nicely captured the way that Costa Ricans have been mobilized to sustain the tourism industry and have been made aware of it as a new resource. It also shows the somewhat Orwellian, and somewhat apocalyptic, rhetoric of postmodern Costa Rica, with the usual Tico payoff that all this is simply another example of what makes their country so exceptional and wonderful:

As the twentieth century comes to an end, on the verge of a new millennium, for the first time in our history, Costa Rica has received one million tourists. The millionth tourist is right now in Costa Rica enjoying our natural beauties. This is also a beautiful thing for Costa Ricans—and to everyone's credit—because tourism requires constant work and long-term planning, especially by private enterprise and the Costa Rican Tourism Institute. That is why we continue working tenaciously, with our minds fixed on national development and our eyes looking to the future. Because tourism does not just happen; it is harnessed.

A COUNTRY THAT ATTRACTS ONE MILLION TOURISTS MUST BE A COUNTRY OF MARVELS

Visit beautiful Costa Rica
Visualize its romantic past

Orosi's three-hundred-years-old Spanish Mission, as it was left by the Catholic missionaries

Corruption

Alfonso González and Manuel Solís

Structural adjustment involves a rapid and systematic change in The Rules. This makes the perfect scenario for those who would profit by corrupt means. Gray areas and confusion proliferate; new elites appear who seem not to have to answer to the old laws; and nobody is quite sure what the new rules are. Over the past fifteen years, Costa Rican public opinion has been saturated by media reports and rumors of apparently limitless corruption. Social scientists Manuel Solís and Alfonso González took on the difficult task of studying the nature of that corruption and its effects on society.

In the mid-1990s, the frequent practice of bribery and blackmail in the public sector made it seem as though customs and immigration, the public registry, and the state-regulated banking system, among others, had been "taken over" and were governed by rules other than the official ones. With the country in the midst of a great neoliberal reform, corruption started to seem like a singular form of privatization. In 1994, the Banco Anglo Costarricense — the oldest and largest bank in the country — failed as a result of criminal irregularities committed by its publicly appointed directors. When in 1996 government investigators seized documents in the head offices of various banks, it was clearly suggested that a variety of irregular actions were still going on, and the reluctance of the bank boards in question to be inspected and held accountable by the public strengthened this presumption.

Something similar occurred in the public registry. The institution housing the legal documentation that anchors the right of property was also rife with proven irregularities and anomalies. The Office of Judicial Investigation [the national judicial police] discovered the existence of at least nine groups that, altogether, had managed to rob some 50 billion colones in real estate [about a quarter of a billion dollars]. According to press reports, these irregularities were made possible by the complicity of unscrupulous employees of the public registry, the national survey office, customs, and other public agencies. It was also discovered that drug traffickers had become involved, and that their principal interest was in state lands. These were organizations with refined methods that included the hiring of notaries, the disappearance of mortgages, penetration of the registry's data bases, removal of complete rolls of microfilm and of entire files, and their replacement with doctored copies, adulteration of the master files, multiple false powers of attorney, the legal resurrection of dead people, the securing of bank loans to prop up the robberies, and more. The extension and depth of this penetration was such that the national registry evidently could no longer serve as a reliable guardian of property rights. One newspaper editorial recommended that if citizens wanted to rest easy, they would have to check "every day" at the registry to make sure they had not been dispossessed of their real estate. And all this occurred despite the existence within the registry of an internal auditor's office.

In sum, the supposed controls were inoperable; the rights over patrimony had been transformed into an illusion; they were vanishing. A whole series of scandals revealed that this framework of anomalies and irregularities had also reached other public institutions—even those like the Red Cross, which symbolized respect for human life and social solidarity. Everything pointed to a state overflowing and at the same time recreating itself according to other rules. This image of a social fabric perforated on all sides was not simply one created by the media, but one anchored in repeated experiences. Nor was it simply a question of values, as President Figueres Olsen repeated at the outset of his administration in 1994 ("the enormous destructive power of corruption is suffocating the most sacred principles that have given meaning to Costa Rican society throughout our history"). More than principles and values, what appeared corroded were public institutions, the very body of the state. The result was a general sense of apprehension.

And just as the Figueres administration's minister of energy and the environment proposed as a novel strategy of growth the reinvestment of the revenues generated by the exploitation of natural resources in activities associated with these same resources, important "distortions" appeared in tourism and ecological conservation—touted as alternative roads to national development. Particularly scandalous were the territorial concessions in tourist zones in the Golfo de Papagayo. Among the more controversial issues were the size of the territorial concessions (572 hectares that turned out to be considerably more than that); the transfer of exploitation rights via the trading of shares; the nationality of the companies given the concession (Mexican); the business links between a number of national politicians and the principal shareholders of the companies given title; the lowball appraisal of the value of the concessions (a mere $5 million "to be paid in works and over the long term"); the miniscule investment demanded of the companies; the violation of various dispositions of the Law on Maritime and Land Zoning; the special administrative rights over the area given to the company at the expense of the Costa Rican Tourism Institute; and a number of others. Many considered that the social and ecological costs arising from these anomalies were in no way compensated by the positive impact that the development might have on the province of Guanacaste. Sure enough, within a relatively short period of time, the destructive effects on the ecosystem — one of the principal motivations for the investment — began to emerge. With the Papagayo project and the laws that made it possible, Costa Rican society returned to the road it had traveled less than a century earlier with the banana enclaves. Social time seemed to trace a circle that returned the country to an experience already lived, dressed up now in new clothing.

Similar things to those detected and denounced in the tourism industry became visible in other areas, where programs designed to promote economic growth had been converted into a source of multiple methods for defrauding the public treasury. During the second half of the 1980s, the most evident of these were the Certificates of Tax Rebate (CATS). Originally created to provide incentives to entrepreneurs trying to develop nontraditional export industries, CATS were state guarantees that exporters would receive reimbursement for the taxes paid on exports. By 1999, the state was paying out 36 billion colones [US $121 million] a year in CATS — a sum that equaled 4 percent of the annual budget was going to a handful of companies, since of the hundreds of enterprises benefiting from the certificates, almost half the total was handed to twenty-five or thirty companies, some run by people with close connections to the political elites (the complete list of recipient companies remains secret). Two of the most favored companies, one with two employees and another with only six, respectively received 322 and 704 million colones in rebates [roughly US $1.4 and 3 million].

It soon became apparent that these export incentives were being used for corruption and drug trafficking, something that threw into doubt the supposed bonanza that was to accrue from nontraditional exports, not to mention casting suspicion on the principal beneficiaries of the new state policy. The media began reporting cases of companies engaging in millions of dollars worth of phony exports (garbage, rice dust, and ice that were supposedly shark fins; saw dust marked as herbal medicine; vegetable discards sent as heart of palm) and regular cases of artificially increased prices and volumes of exports, as well as exports of products that originally came from other countries. By 1997, the anti-drug police were investigating sixty-three exporting companies under suspicion of laundering money. Though a charge notoriously difficult to prove, it was demonstrated that four of these companies had made fraudulent exports for which they received a total of almost 7 billion colones [some US $29 million] in CATS.

During the twenty-six years in which the CAT incentive plan was in operation, the Costa Rican public had paid out to real, questionable, and bogus exporters a grand total of 300 billion colones [impossible to calculate precisely, but in the billions of dollars]. The amount doled out to CATS between 1984 and 1999 was ten times greater than the total national budget for highway maintenance, equivalent to forty-five bridges over the Tempisque and five total renovations of the Juan Santamaría International Airport. During the last two years of the CAT program, a citizens' action group and certain politicians officially inquired as to whether these incentive rebates were also exempt from income tax. The auditor general's office determined that they were not exempt, though it would not be possible to demand the tax retroactively. The tax decision came rather late, after twenty-five years of existence of a law that had been operating as a potent mechanism for the concentration of wealth, and via multiple irregularities and anomalies that worked against the collective good.

This sorry state of affairs was repeated in other activities that had taken shape as part of the strategies for diversifying production and promoting alternative and sustainable development. What has become clear from all this is not a solid economic startup that runs up against the obstacle of corruption, but rather an economic startup that, to judge from the indexes, relies on an important component of anomalies, irregularities, and corrupt actions, constituted as one dimension of "the road to modernization." Corruption appears over and over again as a mechanism for the privatization of socially created wealth. This even compromises state activities like the power to collect taxes. When in 1996 the government, claiming fiscal need, decreed an increase in the sales tax to 15 percent, it was already calculating into the necessary increase the inevitable fraud that would ensue using Laffer's curve ("the higher the rate, the less the recovery"). In the eyes of some observers, 80 percent of the tax increase has remained in the hands of retailers, which means that this citizens' outlay in the name of the state has actually been destined to the private sector. It begins to seem as though all social activities and spaces have been captured by these new forms of personal enrichment.

The Contemporary

Protest Movement

In 1995, Rafael Ángel Calderón Fournier, the leader of the Partido Unidad Social Cristiana (PUSC) and José María Figueres Olsen, the Liberación Nacional (PLN) president of Costa Rica, signed a pact designed to accelerate a structural adjustment program. It was an extraordinary moment, since these were sons of the two presidents who, although bitterly opposed to one another and on opposite sides of the civil war of 1948, had promoted and consolidated Costa Rica's social reforms from 1940 through the 1970s. Massive protests broke out against the reform of the pension regime for teachers and professors, which were actually protests against the pact in general. One sign reads "No One fulfills their promises: vote for No One." Though government defeated the movement, discontent lingered, and voter turnout for the 1998 presidential elections dropped from 81 to 70 percent.

March against the reform of the Pension Law, 1995 (*Semanario Universidad*)

The Narcotizing of Costa Rican Politics

Mercedes Muñoz Guillén

One of the principal legacies of the Central American crisis of the 1980s was the de-velopment of arms and drug trafficking, an activity fomented by the dirty war waged by the Reagan administration against Sandinista Nicaragua (murky doings that were the basis of the Irangate scandal). The historian Mercedes Muñoz Guillén has special-ized in the theme of the penetration of Costa Rican politics by narco-trafficking. Here we present a brief and provocative extract from her work, one that explores how drug trafficking and money-laundering scandals have given the US new ways to question Costa Rican sovereignty.

When did the issue of narco-trafficking inundate the agenda of Costa Rican politics? Interest in the problem dates back to 1985, when the Mexican narco-trafficker Caro Quintero arrived in the country, and it picked up steam in 1986 with the odd mention in the papers. But it was really the electoral implica-tions of the so-called Alem Case of 1987 that registered the political face of narco-trafficking. This constituted the first proven case of money laundering in the country, and the fact that the stacks of bills came packed and labeled as electoral propaganda for the Party of National Liberation (PLN) candidate-in-waiting, Rolando Araya, sank the presidential aspirations of this noted party leader. His career as a deputy and minister, and the fact that his uncle was Presi-dent Luis Alberto Monge, could not save him, and even the clear demonstra-tion of his innocence could not ultimately erase the negative image. The guilty party in the case, Roberto Alem, was an important PLN campaign strategist and Costa Rican representative of the Central American Integration Bank. The question of the drug cartels' influence in the nation's political sphere would soon begin to monopolize public attention.

Many scandals later—including revelations of secret airports built by the ex–minister of public security for trafficking arms and drugs, and donations by Panamanian dictator Manuel Noriega to the Calderón presidential cam-paign—a legislative commission of inquiry determined in 1989 that "narco-trafficking has penetrated Costa Rica's state powers." The theme of connections to narco-trafficking now became a constant strategy in political campaigning, with information about the questionable connections of candidates held in reserve until the right moment in the race, when the innuendo could be exhumed for maximum mudslinging effect. The same dynamic also came into increasing use within parties to discredit internal contenders for candidacies. Given the embryonic character of the country's intelligence services, the question arises as to the source of the information about Costa Rican activities and connections with narco-trafficking. Without suggesting any conspiracy, it is worth noting that since the arrest by Costa Rican authorities, under US Drug Enforcement Administration guidance, of Alem and some other second-rank political figures engaged in large-scale money laundering, the Drug Enforcement Agency (DEA) and other US intelligence services have undertaken to reconstruct the connections of narco-trafficking with each of the three branches of government in Costa Rica. As a result of their "findings," and of the manner and timing of their presentation, all three of these branches have lost credibility in the eyes of Costa Ricans, at the same time that confidence is lost in the political parties, elites, and democracy itself.

Perhaps most disconcerting is the way that US antidrug agencies have pressured the Costa Rican justice system, specifically the Sala Cuarta [the special constitutional tribunal of the supreme court created in 1989 to defend the constitution as the supreme law of the country]. The US government has repeatedly questioned decisions handed down by the Sala Cuarta concerning rulings that have gone against their interests in detaining, convicting, and extraditing Costa Ricans and foreigners suspected of involvement in drug trafficking. Regardless of the diverse opinions that exist about the possible excesses of the Sala Cuarta, and the obstacle it poses to the implementation of the legislative will, one thing is certain: in that its function is based on the constitutional principle of the sovereignty of the Costa Rican state, and in an unrestricted and indiscriminate defense of human rights, it is evidently on a collision course with the accentuated tendency of the US government to "globalize" justice. The confrontation is an unequal one and, as a result, it has a predictable outcome.

Citizens 2000

March against the Combo ICE

Student protesters against the "Combo ICE" (*Semanario Universidad*)

Costa Rican citizens have repeatedly demonstrated that reports of their demise in the face of globalization have been grossly exaggerated. In March and April of 2000, massive public demonstrations took place against the attempt to privatize the Costa Rican Institute for Electricity (ICE), the large, state-owned hydroelectric and telephone company. Many sectors were involved in the protest, though the participation of youth held fundamental importance for the movement. One young woman in this photo, having just finished, it seems, a soda from Burger King, holds up a sign that asks, "How much is Costa Rica worth?" Protestors nationwide blocked roads and withstood repeated attacks by riot police and tear gas until the privatization initiative was put on permanent hold.

On the Recent Protests against the

Privatization of the Costa Rican

Hydroelectric Company (ICE)

Rodolfo Cerdas

The most unexpected and politically transforming act in recent Costa Rican history was the spontaneous uprising of ordinary people throughout the country in March of 2000 against legislation to privatize the ICE, the publicly controlled hydroelectricity and telephone company. The laws for a combined packet of measures (referred to as the "Combo ICE" in the parlance of the fast-food industry) were drafted and ready for final passage in the legislature, and deputies of both parties were signed on. But despite a decade of concerted government and media propaganda in favor of privatization, the people simply refused to accept it. Blocking roads and staging mass protests in every region of the country, high school and university students, workers, state employees, and the self-employed brought the country to a halt and refused any compromise until political elites agreed to shelve the privatization plan indefinitely. In an op-ed piece, Rodolfo Cerdas, a well-known political scientist and independent critical commentator, reflected on what the mobilization revealed about the growing alienation of the political and business elites from the rest of society.

As the night follows the day, this crisis could be seen coming. Only because many of our politicians are insensitive and incapable of grasping what the ordinary citizen thinks and feels could they have kept themselves in the dark and shown surprise at all this. We cannot resist but parody the already overused expression of Gabriel García Márquez: this is the chronicle of a crisis foretold.

It all started with a democratic disenchantment that the confusion of electoral politics could only screen temporarily. Those who proclaimed the fact were seen as perennial nay-sayers and whiners who needed to be marginalized and silenced. But the worm, like a silent assassin, continued its work of deep rot: electoral participation declined, the legitimacy of those elected was affected by abstentionism, and opinion polls reiterated unprecedented degrees of citizen disbelief and mistrust directed at politicians, parties, parliaments, and government in general.

The politicians were shortsighted, so much so that they did nothing concrete and viable in the face of these warnings. Absolutely nothing. They limited themselves to seeking ways to justify their actions so that they could keep on partying behind the backs of the people. "Everyone here is always talking about a crisis, and nothing ever comes of it," they said, as though it was the same single crisis constantly being invoked, and as though the erosive effects of those left unresolved were not cumulative. "On election day they'll end up voting because they have no other options, you'll see" — as though the opinion poll results and the last elections weren't X-rays demanding surgical intervention rather than simple poultices. "It's just politicians frustrated by being left out who say these things because they haven't been able to adapt to the democratic progress of a two-party system" — as if those who questioned the system were a small group and not the great majority of citizens. As though it wasn't the dual party system and the constant turn to pacts among a tiny group of elites that were being questioned, and as though the cynicism of asking that society participate while denying any meaningful role for citizens had not placed the so-called leaders' dubious capacity to lead on display for all to see.

Now, with the "Combo ICE," the scam is revealed. These elites, who in the face of the people are deaf, blind, and autistic, actually thought that the people were worried about the internal electoral policies of the major parties [an issue among political elites at the time] rather than the politics of privatization and the projects surrounding the ICE. Events showed that the reality was precisely the inverse: the people couldn't care less about internal party voting procedures but they were very interested indeed in the future macroeconomic direction of the country. And that is why it was not enough that the future presidential candidates, some ex-presidents, and the leaders of the parties had all agreed that the project would become law. They ran into an unavoidable stone wall: the "sector" known as citizens. The citizens demanded their right to be heard and taken into account, not as a formality, but as real actors in the making of final decisions. Only the traditional political elites could have thought that the people would not demand a seat at the table. And only the autism that characterizes them could have made them believe that the people, the flesh-and-blood people who had taken to the streets, would cease participation in the process just because they received an invitation to the discussions. . . .

This crisis is not the fault of the president or of this or that politician. It is the result of an objectively verifiable and consistent pattern of secret negotiations, patronage, corruption, manipulation, lies, complicity, and guarantee of impunity among the political ruling class of this country as a group. They have, moreover, been responsible for their own dishonor by incessant mud-slinging against their own and the opposition without understanding that, in the process, they dirty themselves as well. This may be an unjust indictment in some sense, but politically this is what has happened because this is what the great mass of people are thinking about politics and politicians, with an unacceptable price for our democracy. . . .

The urgent changes we need in this society require faith, and instead there is only skepticism. They require confidence, and there is general doubt. There is a need for transparency, and people presuppose the opacity of the system. Credibility and true representation are demanded of those who negotiate on behalf of the people, and there is only incredulity and a crisis of political representation because the representatives appear only to represent the interests of themselves and sectors who do not closely identify with our social reality. And this goes for those who benefit from immobility, thanks to the monopoly of a few so-called labor organizations and union elites, as well as for those who want to privatize everything in order to get in good with transnational corporations. If we were to believe them—that their intentions are sacrosanct and outside any particular interest—then Costa Rica would be a society of angels. Having transparency does not mean hiding or disguising interests; it means justifying them in a clear and acceptable manner. The rest is hypocrisy and lies, which causes rot everywhere, whether in the transparent and healthy or in the hidden and dubious.

The crisis that has come with the "energy combo" could be a curse, especially because up to now there has been a notorious absence of able political leadership in the protest—one capable of proposing creative ways out of the crisis, of taking creative advantage of dialogue to strengthen the viable demands of the popular sectors. And this might turn into frustration, anger, a dead-end street, and violence, something that more than a few people who live in the past are enjoying and more than a few extremists of old and new stripe are trying to foment. This scenario would facilitate an antidemocratic turn that some would like to see emerge from this situation in order to advance without the obstacles of democracy toward a politics of change from above, for those above, and against those below, and against what they consider to be the paralyzing libertinage of democracy.

But this could also be a blessed crisis because it might open the eyes and ears of the more responsible and honest among our political leadership and unite them with a greater political awareness and a more organized participation of the people and the organizations of civil society to strengthen our democracy, broaden popular participation in a positive sense, and speed the transformation of the nation according to a truly modern and sustainable perspective. It could, finally, be the opening onto a political reform not only of the economy and the public sector but also of the regime of political representation and the reach and vitality of our representative democratic system. This is the challenge. And although in some sense we all need to answer the call, it's clear that there are some who need to answer it more than others in accord with the office they hold and the responsibility they have in the social and political life of the country.

Building Your Own Home

Antonio

University of Costa Rica social scientist Carlos Sandoval went to work alongside people in the construction and maquiladora sector to report on their labor conditions, life-styles, and consumer expectations. One construction worker, a Nicaraguan immigrant married to a Costa Rican, explained how he managed to realize the dream of becoming a homeowner in Barrio México, a popular neighborhood in San José's west end.

I lived for two years in a room, and then I got together with a woman, and we lived in Granadilla [on the edge of San José], but we were paying twelve thousand colones [US $90] in rent. Later we moved to Vargas Araya, and for a really tiny house we were paying nine thousand colones. The toilet didn't work properly, and halfway through the month, they were after me for an advance on the next month's rent. So I said to the missus that I was going to build a *rancha* [an improvised hut] in Barrio México. And I did. During some rainstorms I put up some zinc sheets and hooked up the electricity. That week I didn't work, and we moved in on the Thursday. The missus went back to her hometown in Alajuela to see if she could get a few bills for the house. Her pop came and helped us build it. It's just like this building here [gestures, breaks into smile]. Now we have a stove, a fridge, a pressure cooker. My wife used to work in a factory, Farah, up in Lourdes, but since we moved into this house, now she works in the Sylvania, where they make flashlights. It's closer. I'm waiting now for them to pronounce [on their squatters' rights], so I can make the rancha in block. The advantage is that on either side there are already houses of cement block. I would do it with 300,000 colones [US $2,250], in about twenty-two days. So I chanced it and grabbed the lot; the thing is, now you can't buy them. We pay a quota of two hundred colones a week (US $1.50) for the right to occupy the lot.

Men in Crisis?

Sylvia Chant

Masculine identities are changing rapidly in contemporary Costa Rica—and for a variety of reasons. In one instance, the booming tourism industry in northwestern Costa Rica has opened up more employment opportunities for women than for men. This has had a profound impact on gender relations in Guanacaste, an area whose familial patterns have differed from those of the center of Costa Rica. As scholar Sylvia Chant discovered, an already endemic crisis in masculinity stemming from underemployment as agricultural laborers has been deepened by the latest phase of globalization.

If the family is perceived by state and religious bodies to be in "crisis" in Costa Rica, in the northwest province of Guanacaste this is even more so. In a traditionally marginalized region heavily reliant on rural activities and blighted by a high incidence of poverty, un- and underemployment and out-migration, a number of indicators are taken as evidence that *desintegración familiar* (family disintegration) is more marked than in other areas of the country. Formal marriage, for example, has long been less common in Guanacaste than in other parts of Costa Rica. The number of births to adolescent mothers was 21 percent in Guanacaste in 1994, compared with 11 percent nationally, and whereas 42.8 percent of births in 1994 occurred to single women in Costa Rica as a whole, this proportion was 63.7 percent in Guanacaste. On top of these patterns, low-income women and households in the region suffer from significant levels of paternal absence and neglect, with many lone mothers receiving little or no support from the fathers of their children.

If the "family" in Guanacaste has always been a rather fragile entity, however, and certainly a source of stress and struggle for women and children, it is only relatively recently, perhaps, that family instability has come to engender a perceptible sense of crisis among men. Although men have long been rather marginal or peripatetic figures in the typical Guanacastecan household, and have not had to work as hard as women in its daily reproduction, they have nonetheless been guaranteed a place in family units, and often a superior one at that. This derives mainly from their comparative advantage in access to earnings and resources. Currently, however, men's ability to maintain these privileges is on the wane. This is accompanied by a growing sense of alarm about what it means to be a man and how men should respond to the uncertainties around them.

Part of the reason for the historic instability in conjugal and father-child relationships in Guanacaste owes to the fact that the province has traditionally offered little in the way of regular employment. One of the least urbanized areas in Costa Rica, Guanacaste was until recently dominated by cattle ranching, irrigated rice production, and sugar cultivation. Only the last of these activities is labor-intensive, and then only on a seasonal basis, with significant recruitment of workers generally restricted to the harvest period between January and April. For the low-income male population, who form the vast bulk of workers in agriculture and on whom the responsibility for "family breadwinning" has conventionally fallen, this has implied migration to other parts of the country for spells of varying duration to support their families. Although Guanacastecans are commonly found working in the banana plantations on the Caribbean or southern Pacific coast, or clearing pasture in wetter areas such as Puntarenas, work is not always easy to come by (for more than a day at a time at least), besides which prolonged periods of separation place a variety of stresses on couples. It is not uncommon for men to cease sending remittances after time has elapsed, and sometimes not to return home at all. Although this is occasionally because men feel they cannot return to their families with nothing to show for their efforts, more usually it is because they have set up home with other women. For the women left behind, the response has traditionally been to fall back on work in a narrow range of low-wage activities such as domestic service and petty commerce, or to find another partner willing and able to provide.

The tendency for Guanacastecan men to embark on new relationships is by no means an exclusive product of labor migration, but has much to do with the fact that men have often proved themselves as men through engaging in extramarital liaisons and/or having children with a variety of partners. Consonant with a sexual double standard noted for many other parts of the world, these freedoms are nominally denied to women. Although women in Guanacaste are recognized as probably having the same desires and needs as men and, moreover, are rarely legally bound to men by marriage, they are expected to demonstrate restraint and propriety. Reflective of popular discourses on the polarization between male and female sexuality was a statement made by Walberto, a thirty-nine-year-old construction worker, who participated in one of a number of focus-group discussions in my 1997 study: "We have a concept here, OK, that if I go with a lot of women . . . no one will say anything bad, but to a woman, yes." This was echoed by Estanley, a thirty-six-year-old member of the same focus group, who added: "They'll call the man a 'womanizer,' but the woman is a tramp." When having only one girlfriend in life is likely to meet with the accusation of being a *mariconado* (effeminate/gay man), and in light of the kudos attaching to men's ability to "conquer" other women, there has always been a certain acceptance of men moving from one family to another. In many ways, this has acted to overshadow the opprobrium attached to abandoning previous partners and offspring.

Another long-standing marker of masculine identity that has tended to weaken family units is the pressure on men to fraternize with other men and indulge in male-bonding *vicios* (vices) such as drinking. This not only consumes resources that might otherwise be dedicated to men's households but also leads to arguments, conflict, and domestic violence. Although attributed in part to the pressures of toiling in the fields or coping with irregular employment, being seen in the cantina — a male-only drinking place — is also explicitly recognized by men as a means of demonstrating their manliness. Indeed, the three things most commonly stressed in the survey as having made men "feel like men," were getting a job, having their first sexual relations, and experiencing their first taste of *guaro* (slang word for hard alcohol such as locally produced rum).

Drinking often starts in mid- to late adolescence under pressure from peers and older men, and it tends to get heavier if men migrate away to work, such as to the banana plantations, where conditions are grueling and men spend most of their spare time alone or with other male workers. Although men themselves declare that crossing the boundary from being in control to becoming addicted reflects an "unmasculine" weakness, repeated heavy drinking often takes the decision out of men's own hands. Reflecting the extent of the problem, Guanacaste has one of the highest number of Alcoholics Anonymous groups in the country, and the Institute of Alcohol and Drug Dependency has mounted numerous prevention campaigns in schools and communities of the province.

Having identified some aspects of masculine identity which have historically undermined family stability in Guanacaste, it is important to note that these have coexisted with another idealized male role model that emphasizes the importance of financial provision and domestic responsibility, that of the *marido cumplido* (a husband who fulfills his obligations). Although on the surface this might suggest something of a counterweight to the forces that have drawn men away from their families or that have threatened family cohesion, it is important to note that this role does not necessarily preclude men from extra- or antifamilial pursuits, and indeed can even legitimize such behavior. In turn, support of a household is also frequently associated with personal aggrandizement and power. While love, caring, and a sense of responsibility toward dependents genuinely motivates the role of "benevolent patriarch" for some men, male providers also gain from the dependency of others, not least because it secures social approval and endorsement.

Negro, for example, a twenty-six-year-old maintenance man who has had the good fortune to have remained in the same job for five years, claimed in my individual interview with him to feel a great deal of pride when people tell his wife, "You have a good husband, care for him." Like others in his situation, Negro feels his position as breadwinner also justifies a series of personal entitlements arguably not in the best interests of other household members. These include being able to prevent his wife from going out to work, being guaranteed all domestic attentions, and being able to court a girlfriend—with whom he has a child—*a las escondidas* (on the sly). As far as keeping his wife at home is concerned, Negro claims that having *la doña en la casa* (the lady in the house) is good for a man not only because it proves to the outside world that he earns a decent wage but also because it implies that his wife is "honorable" (i.e., her sexuality is exclusively controlled by her husband). Beyond this, depriving a wife of earning her own money maintains the "proper balance" of conjugal power, namely, for the woman to be "a little more submissive," and for the man to have *más volumen en la casa*—literally, "more volume in the home." In some senses, women in the region have been caught in something of a double bind by the situation in which finding a "decent man" (i.e., one prepared to support them) tends to be accompanied by a limited scope for negotiating personal autonomy or household divisions of labor. Nonetheless, this situation has also had its costs for men too, especially given that the majority of them face limited opportunities for well-paid, regular *brete* (slang word for work). This underlines the fact that being a man is not necessarily sufficient in itself to merit "masculine" privileges and power, even if for a long time men's own relationships with the labor market have effectively been the only factor standing in the way.

This leads me to discuss three major findings of a 1997 study I carried out, which are highly relevant to the brewing "crisis of masculinity" in Guanacaste whereby men sense their traditional privileges under threat, namely, the pressure on men to provide, the fundamental importance of family in men's identities, and the need for men to have women around them (on their own terms). Although men are usually the ones to break relationships, women have also tended to look for other companions once they lose the economic support of previous partners. Possibly as a result of women's traditional reliance on male

income, and because repeated bouts of migration weaken affective ties between couples, it seems that women are prone to evaluate men in economic
rather than in emotional terms. Just as many previous studies I had undertaken with women indicated that they could not see much point in being with
a penniless man (expressed by one of my respondents, Layla, as "it's not possible to fall in love with hunger!"), the idea that men's worth is dictated by their
income is felt acutely by men too. Vicente, a thirty-two-year-old bricklayer,
for example, who participated in a focus-group discussion with five other construction workers, commented that, "Here [in Guanacaste], women are very
demanding. . . . Not only do they want *plata* [money] but presents as well." This
was echoed by other members of the group with phrases such as "they like a
lot of luxuries." Men were clearly stressed by the situation in which their pass-
port to a woman's affections had effectively to be bought, and if they wanted to
keep it that way, they needed to continue earning. As it happens, men's money
is probably more important in terms of *entry* than in terms of *endurance* of a relationship, given that women run the risk of losing respectability if they change
sexual partners too frequently.

Despite men's lead role in the abandonment of conjugal relationships, and
despite my original assumption that men were much less tied to their families
than women, when I talked with men in depth, issues of family came up repeatedly in connection with men's psychological well-being and their sense of
masculinity. When men were asked to recount the most important events in
their lives, for example, these were overwhelmingly linked with familial experiences, such as becoming a father, losing a close relative, rejection/acceptance
by a spouse or girlfriend, and so on. Reinforcing this point is the very interesting finding that none of the male respondents lived alone, with those who
were unmarried or who had separated from their spouses generally returning to their parental homes or residing with other family members such as
sisters, aunts, or grown-up daughters. Although the latter is also explicable in
terms of poverty and limited access to housing, "being alone" (for example due
to labor migration or marital dissolution) is frequently deemed an extremely
negative emotional and psychological state by men, and it usually prompts
the rapid formation of a new conjugal household and/or reabsorption within
the homes of natal kin. Some scholars have pointed out the rather paradoxical
situation whereby although home and family are often more explicitly valued
by women, and seen by wider society to be more important for women, it is
actually men who look to reconstitute their families more quickly. In addition,
it is extremely significant that the key person of reference in men's households
is almost always a female family member.

Less of a surprise to me in many ways was that men's primary impetus for attachment to female family members revolved around the notion of being cared for by women, in both affective and practical terms. This was frequently framed with reference to maternal images. Not only do virtually all men identify their mothers as the most important person in their lives but many explain that they got married when their mothers died with a view to their wives as becoming a second mother or *madre-esposa* (mother-wife). Many also reported having married or started cohabiting when they had migrated to work elsewhere in the country and had "no one to look after them." This might also help to explain a common tendency for Guanacastecan men to have their first coresidential relationships with older women. Indeed, among the reasons articulated by respondents for preferring older women was the fact that older women were not so overburdened with childcare and therefore could take better care of their men, and that they would probably have their own family already and thus be unwilling (if not unable) to have another child with the man in question, thereby alleviating some potential pecuniary pressure (they might even have their own resources such as a house and money). Some mentioned that older women were more likely to "give in sexually more easily," that they would be grateful for the men's attentions and so be less demanding, and that they were less likely to run off with another man or be desired by other men.

Although one or two men also stated that older women could be more interesting companions because of their greater experience of life, the basic motivations seemed to revolve around sexual and psychological security and reduced material responsibility. Yet while the majority of women have routinely complied with the notion and practice of caring for men as their part of the patriarchal bargain in Guanacaste, evidence suggests that this is more assured with female blood relatives (particularly mothers) than with female spouses (especially younger ones) and that tensions are mounting in conjugal units over traditional expectations about women servicing men.

Concomitant with this, while links between mothers and children in Guanacaste remain strong and these dyads in natal households are often extremely unified, in conjugal households, relations between spouses, and between fathers and children, appear to be even more vulnerable to dissolution than in the past. Although threats to disunity have always existed, the difference now is that men see the process as driven by women. This goes a long way to explaining the fact that there is a crisis in the making among men. In short, "family crisis" for men has more to do with their loss of power over women than with the breakup of the family per se and the fact that men can no longer necessarily determine if and when to establish or abandon a home.

Major factors accounting for men's sense of crisis about the family in Guanacaste include the erosion of the material and ideological bases of men's identities as husbands and fathers and apparent losses in their command and control over wives. A critical factor underlying these trends is the declining gap between men's and women's access to resources in the region. Although, as we have seen, periods of unemployment and/or temporary labor migration have always punctuated men's working lives in Guanacaste, most women were still kept in financial dependency because even if they did work (usually sporadically during the spells their spouses were away from home, or when they were "between relationships"), men had comparatively greater earning ability, whether locally or as labor migrants. In recent years, however, this has been undermined by women's increased entry into the labor force, with women's recorded rates of economic activity in the region rising from 27.6 to 30.3 percent between 1983 and 1993 alone. This, in turn, has been driven by two main factors. One is the pressure on households to increase their sources of income in light of rising living costs associated with recession and adjustment. The other is the expansion of tourism in the coastal part of the region, in which women are now able to get more regular, higher-paid employment and are often recruited in preference to men. Indeed, whereas in 1994 the national unemployment rate for men (5.3 percent) was much lower than for women (8.3 percent), in Guanacaste the difference was much less, with figures of 7.2 and 8.5 percent, respectively. Similarly, although women's average earnings in the traditionally male-dominated agricultural sector in Guanacaste are only 75 percent of men's, the proportion rises to 90 percent when taking into account nonagricultural activities as well.

Men view women's rising economic participation as threatening. Not only has it encroached on men's terrain within the household and the labor market, but in increasing women's independent access to resources, it has made men feel more vulnerable. Many claim to feel less needed and appreciated by their wives and children and to have less say and authority in the home. A man who is able to keep his wife at home runs less risk of losing control over her, particularly in sexual terms. Once a woman goes out to work, however, she falls prey to numerous possibilities for meeting other men, whether through the journey to work, at the workplace itself, or through going out independently with her female friends. This makes men feel at grave risk of infidelity on the part of their spouses, and even rejection, quite apart from the fact that it is damaging to their self-esteem. As Luis, a thirty-three-year-old waiter put it, for a man who cannot undertake to provide for his wife and children, his self-image and his image in the eyes of others *ya no vale nada* (isn't worth anything).

Women's rising access to income in Guanacaste seems to encourage some men to remain in and/or retreat to the households of their natal kin (especially those of their mothers). In the relatively secure environment of the maternal home, men face less pressure to fulfill functions of (primary) financial provision, they are unlikely to have to bargain or renegotiate gender relations, and they also avoid exposing themselves to the risk of being ousted by their spouses, or, worse still, another man. Since men's major parenting function is defined both by law and by social convention as one of economic support, low-income men whose relationships break up are also likely to have limited access to and/or lose contact with their offspring. Trends toward greater fragility in men's position within conjugal households are widely perceived to have been exacerbated by legislative and policy initiatives in women's interests. In principle, most men claim to be in favor of gender equality and express distaste for what they feel are outmoded *machista* attitudes. Yet they voice considerable concern over the potential "abuse" by women of new entitlements accorded through government programs such as the Law for Social Equality, the Program for Female Heads of Household, the National Plan for the Prevention of Intra-Family Violence, and the Law of Consensual Unions. As one of the construction workers, Walberto, put it, the Law for Social Equality "doesn't work" because it encourages women to think they are superior to men and many women "want to be more than men." This was echoed by don José, who said that although he thought it good that more equality between women and men existed nowadays, he felt that "at times this goes too far, and women tell men off!" He believed that new laws had made it difficult for men to *volar hachas* (wield the axe, meaning to exert control, but with overtones of domestic violence, which has recently become more likely to meet with imprisonment than in the past).

In strengthening women's civil status, legal and labor rights, and access to land and property, these interventions have expanded women's scope to survive independently of men. Yet, coupled with the fact that family-oriented social programs have tended to be directed exclusively at women and to have prioritized women's roles as parents and caregivers, such initiatives can also be seen as reinforcing perceptions of the marginal and/or dependent position of men within households. Government rhetoric on the need to incorporate men in social programs has not so far translated into practice, but it would seem to be vital if greater stability, equality, and security across a wider range of family relations is to be achieved.

Are the Kids Alright?

Osvaldo Orias and Kenneth

Costa Rica experienced few acute social problems associated with urbanization until the 1970s, but since that time the unchecked and unplanned explosion of San José has generated a large urban underclass, extensive marginal neighborhoods, and a familiar cyclical pattern of moral panics about violent, criminal youth gangs followed by vicious police crackdowns on poor kids. This occurs at a time when the demise of utopian goals and the triumph of North American mass consumer culture have left modern youth searching for alternative identities. The following interview with a young graffiti artist from a marginal urban background provides a glimpse of this generation's worldview, an idea of its forms of expression and sociability, and a sense that countercultural and protopolitical sensibility remains on the agenda.

Asprovicruz squatter shanty, south of San José
Interview subject: Kenneth

For me, graffiti is like a thing of protest on social democracy. There is no social assistance. We're mistreated by the law. We protest because of that. I listen to heavy metal that talks about the freedom of youth, Iron Maiden, for example, which is a protest against religion, Guns 'n' Roses, which talks about the lack of affection for sons and daughters. When I hear that stuff, I analyze, and later ideas come. That's what makes me draw graffiti.

Once they evicted us from a property, the police treated us really badly. In reaction against that we started spraying graffiti on the walls. Afterward they came looking for us. We wrote names of artists, like Lennon, and we drew the gringo flag burning. We did all that with chalk and by scraping with rocks.

Another time I was with my friends listening to music on the corner, we were drinking a bit of booze, and we had marihuana and Coke. While we were doing that, we talked about the problems we were living; sex, music, the issue

Graffiti in San José (Solum Donas)

of not being able to hang out after ten at night because the police come by and tell us to leave, that we're not allowed to be there. Later we talked about freedom. We drew a cop and drew an X through him. After that came the influence of metal rock, and we started drawing skulls, cadavers. All for revenge, because the police don't like it.

We drew swastikas because we felt that the police here are like Nazis. Others maybe want to be like Nazis to get back at the police. Nazis are people who are capable of anything.

And we drew the peace sign, too, because peace is tranquility of mind. There are a lot of crazy things. You have to have peace. It's against war. It's against the rich. We poor people are never left in peace. It's loving your brothers. Those who don't have a home to live in. Those who don't have their parents' love. Discriminated against in school for being poor. Graffiti is the only way you can express yourself.

Death. Sometimes you want to be dead. To be that corpse so you don't have to see what's going on in the world. Death would be a break. We all die. Police too.

One time we were smoking up, and later we got the idea of going to a ceme-tery to rob crosses. Anyway, the people there were hypocrites, believers who didn't believe in anything. We jumped the wall of the Workers Cemetery. The guard stopped us. We told him that a guy had attacked us and we were look-ing for him because he had hidden around here. One of my friends gave him a shot of liquor to warm him up, and he started to feel real good.

Meanwhile we were breaking the crosses, and we left with the crosses on our shoulders to the barrio. Afterward there was a national scandal, and they started to invent stories about satanic sects forming in the country, but far from it. Oh ya, the guard we just gave a pack of cigarettes, and that was it. We left graffiti on like three tombs. We made a symbol suggesting that the devil was the one who accompanied you to the grave. That was with spray paint. Of course, we respected the graves of the poor. Later we filled the crosses with graffiti, and my friends put them in the room—upside down. Back then, Lalo was there, now he's a stonemason, Chispa who's gone off, and also Slim and Giova. Doing graffiti is alright.

Costa Rica: A Millennial Profile

Steven Palmer and Iván Molina

Where is this enigmatic social democracy heading as it emerges from the vortex of changes in the 1980s and 1990s?

The Home, the Family, Life, and Things

Proportion of marriages ending in divorce in 1987: 1 out of 11
Proportion ending in divorce in 2001: 4 out of 10

Proportion of female-headed households in 1987: 1 in 6
Proportion in 2001: 1 in 4

Average number of children per family in 1960: 7
Average number in 1997: 2.5

Proportion of Costa Rican children born out of wedlock in 2000: 1 in 2

Percentage of homes beneath the poverty line in 1961: 51
Percentage in 2001: 20

Life expectancy at birth of Costa Ricans in 1927: 41 years
Life expectancy at birth of Costa Rican men in 2001: 75.6 years
Life expectancy at birth of Costa Rican women in 2001: 79.9 years

Costa Rican homes in 2000
with access to electricity: 97 percent
with color televisions and refrigerators: 85 percent
with computers: 14 percent
with international cable television: 12.5 percent
with Internet access: 3.4 percent

Number of Costa Ricans per vehicle in 1985: 11
Number of Costa Ricans per vehicle in 2001: 6

Ratio of public to private high schools in 1975: 7 to 1
Ratio in 2000: 3 to 1

Number of Costa Ricans who had visited a mall in 1982: 0
Number of Costa Ricans who had visited a mall at least once every two
   months in 1997: 1,163,700

Number of advertising agencies in Costa Rica in 1987: 37
Number of advertising agencies in 1994: 60

Costa Ricans who had a credit card in 1996: 27 percent

The Economy

Estimated amount of taxes evaded by political, business, and professional
   elites in 1996: (US) $1.4 billion
Annual interest payments on the Costa Rican foreign debt in 2001: (US) $700
   million
Total Costa Rican foreign debt in 2001: (US) $3.2 billion

Total budget of government of Costa Rica including autonomous agencies
   in 2001: (US) $4.1 billion
Total budget of Yale University in 2001: (US) $1.34 billion

Number of foreign visitors to Costa Rica in 1987: 278,000
Number of foreign visitors in 2000: 1.1 million

Cost of the services of a luxury prostitute in Costa Rica in 2002: (US) $200–
   $300
Cost of the services of an ordinary prostitute: (US) $20–$30
Cost of a tourist package that includes four days and three nights in a five-
   star hotel, transportation, meals, drinks, travel arrangements, and an
   "escort": (US) $1,848.

Politics

53 percent of Costa Ricans had confidence in the justice system in 1996; 76 percent thought that politicians passed laws for their own gain

30 percent of members of both major political parties thought there were no differences between their parties in 1998

Percentage of Costa Ricans who abstained from voting in presidential elections in 1994: 19
Percentage who abstained in 2002: 31

Percentage of Costa Ricans who thought that the state should have more power than private enterprise in 1998: 72

Society and (of course) Soccer

Percentage of Costa Ricans who worked in agriculture and mining in 1950: 55
Percentage who worked in agriculture and mining in 2001: 16

Number of Costa Ricans who have traveled into outer space: 1 (Franklin Chang)

Number of US citizens living in Costa Rica in 2000: 9,511
Number of Costa Ricans living in the United States in 2000: 69,000

Percentage of people polled in San José in 1997 who had been victims of a crime: 5
Percentage who felt they were likely to be victims of a crime in downtown San José: 81

Proportion of Costa Ricans who thought that the country was worse off in 2002 than in 2000: 1 in 2
Proportion who thought they personally and their family were better off: 3 in 4

Rank in 2002 of the Liga Deportiva Alajuelense, the leading Costa Rican soccer team, in the FIFA Club Team World Ranking: 80th
Rank in 2002 of the Costa Rican national soccer team in the FIFA World Ranking: 16th

Demoperfectocracy

Yolanda Oreamuno

Yolanda Oreamuno (1916–56) was a noted Costa Rican writer and a sharp critic of her society. In 1939, probably influenced by Mario Sancho's sarcastic tract, Costa Rica, Switzerland of Central America, *Oreamuno published a piece portraying Costa Rica as a mediocre, provincial, conservative, and self-satisfied society that rather than killing its problematic personalities, simply pulled the rug gently out from under them. In the process, however, the author also identified deep continuities that have allowed—and continue to allow—Costa Rica to be a functional and sustainable polity.*

With open arms hospitable Costa Rica receives the political émigrés of all the Americas, the victims of tyranny X or Y. The news reporters pay them a visit, take their pulse, and if they see that their man is steadfast in his innate rebelliousness, they gently ignore him, and he, too, gently passes into utter anonymity. Great political, literary, revolutionary, demagogic figures have spent periods of exile in Costa Rica, and there is no record of their stays . . . except for their names on customs forms. . . .

And so we come to the "tropical myths." Costa Rica, unlucky Costa Rica violated by the travel agencies, has three things: pretty women, color, and "demoperfectocracy," strictly in that advertising order. The beauty of the women proliferates in the imagination of the Kodak tourist: lovely legs, dark eyes, brown bodies, delicious mouths. . . . For color, or local color, read: Indians who practice strange creole-medieval rituals, permanent sun, zero rain . . . and palm trees, many palm trees . . . , so many, and so visible, that they'd be an easy object for even the most amateur of photographers to snap. Demoperfectocracy is a little more complicated and subtle: the president walks around the streets unguarded, shakes hands with any old anonymous citizen, and makes comments every day for the newspapers without the papers seeing it necessary to print special editions.

Against the travel agencies and the creators of these lucrative tropical myths, I will tell foreigners the truth. In Costa Rica, the women are beautiful, too beautiful . . . (this can continue to be used for advertising). As for Indians, there are about three thousand who live in the interior of the republic; they do not maintain exotic rituals, and although some speak dialect, all speak Spanish. It rains nine months of the year in the most desperate fashion (which, as can be seen, is at odds with the permanent sun and "eternal spring"). There is heat in abundance on the coast and the landscapes are perfect for painters, for post-cards to the family, and for spinsters given to dreaming (these can continue to be used for advertising with the corrections indicated). Perfect democracy we do not have, nor have we ever had (this cannot be used in any way in adver-tisements).

Without attempting a more profound analysis of our "Tico" democracy (which is quite distinct from democracy per se), I will note that there are two conflicting notions of democracy, just as there are two ways of living it. Active democracy, in motion, in evolution, and the passive democracy in the consti-tution of the republic. We have the second. There are also two ways of living democracy: one (and for us so far still in the future), putting it into practice with everyone, without distinction of social, economic, or political categories, and the other, self-applied without reasoning. We live the second, and we sing the first in the national anthem. With the aggravating factor that we frequently proceed as though we lived in an effective democracy, acting with the freedom that this implies, and when we do so, we are treated to a discreet reminder that makes us doubt the constitution of the republic.

This course of action degenerates into an obvious rudeness and into an absolute or almost absolute lack of responsibility. We act for ourselves alone, and frequently we do not have even the simplest thought for our fellows; there is a lack of cohesion . . . a lack of collectivity. The ultimate representative of this nefarious tendency is the type one might call "local talent." "Local talent" is very generous to us, discusses in the hallways, is always engaged in secret and never proven contacts with official sources of political news, is know-it-all, speculator, and gossip. There is something of this in all our great politicians, and a good deal in the soul of the common man. It would be inoffensive if it did not lack, as I've already noted, the simple sense of fellowship and if it did not suffer from the fault of considering our little world, our politics and our economy, centers isolated from the rest of the universe, entities apart floating in the ether, and if it did not carry its virus so far as to contaminate that politics, that world, and that economy making everything little.

Against all this, the reaction is coming; it can be felt pushing uncertainly and taking sometimes puerile paths. . . . By taking the road of struggle against our pathological or acquired inertia, the latter is easily overcome; through an open and simple sensibility, the true shape of the landscape can be grasped, and there in the landscape and in man together with pain and movement the au-tochthonous is calling us. It's a path. There are many with an open perspective.

The errors, the evolutionary and inevitable sins that come with every step forward, ground our nonaggression and the puritan we carry inside, leave us quaking in the face of the capital sin, the fundamental and decisive sin of sur-rendering to the future. Countries are not born with original sin as men are, but they must commit one to move forward.

Costa Rica is reaching puberty, her virgin sex trembles, and the future is calling that she might transform herself into a sinner, authentic and original.

Suggestions for Further Reading

Costa Rica is generating an increasing amount of scholarly and journalistic interest. What follows is a list of where to start reading or surfing if you are interested in a more in-depth look at the country.

General

Barry, Tom. *Costa Rica: A Country Guide.* 3d ed. Albuquerque, N.M.: Inter-Hemispheric Education Resource Center, 1991.

Creedman, Theodore S. *Historical Dictionary of Costa Rica.* 2d ed. Metuchen, N.J.: Scarecrow, 1991.

Molina, Iván, and Steven Palmer. *The History of Costa Rica: Brief, Up-to-Date and Illustrated.* San José, Costa Rica: Editorial de la Universidad de Costa Rica, 1998.

Pérez-Brignoli, Héctor. *A Brief History of Central America.* Translated by Ricardo B. Sawrey A. and Susana Stettri de Sawrey. Berkeley: University of California Press, 1989.

Torres-Rivas, Edelberto. *History and Society in Central America.* Translated by Douglass Sullivan-González. Austin: University of Texas Press, 1993.

Woodward, Ralph Lee, Jr. *Central America: A Nation Divided.* 3d ed. New York: Oxford University Press, 1999.

Web Sites

http://nacion.com/
> La Nación, Costa Rica's most important daily newspaper, with numerous links, a free archive, and an English-language edition

http://www.ticotimes.net/
> Costa Rica's good English language weekly paper

http://www.casapres.go.cr/
> The president of Costa Rica, with links to most government ministries and autonomous state agencies

http://www.tse.go.cr/
> The Supreme Electoral Tribunal, with electoral results and other political data from the 1950s onward

http://www.inec.go.cr/
> National Institute of Statistics and Census of Costa Rica, with free access to important economic, social, and demographic data

http://www.metabase.net/
> METABASE, a site integrating many Central American libraries and library catalogues

http://historia.fcs.ucr.ac.cr/
> The School of History at the Universidad de Costa Rica, with two electronic publications, *Diálogos: Revista Electrónica de Historia* and *Cuadernos Digitales*, and links to other historical and social science research institutes

http://ccp.ucr.ac.cr/
> The Central American Population Center of the Universidad de Costa Rica, with important documents and data bases on Central American and especially Costa Rican demographics

http://www.estadonacion.or.cr/
> The Estado de la Nación (state of the nation) project, updated year by year to provide an analysis of Costa Rica's economic, social, political, cultural, environmental, and gender situation

http://www.flacso.or.cr/
> Information on the work and publications of FLACSO–Costa Rica, the most important independent academic outlet for the state universities

I. Birth of an Exception?

Fernández Guardia, Ricardo. *History of the Discovery and Conquest of Costa Rica.* New York: Gordon, 1978.

Gudmundson, Lowell. *Costa Rica before Coffee: Society and Economy on the Eve of the Export Boom.* Baton Rouge: Louisiana State University Press, 1986.

Karnes, Thomas L. *The Failure of Union: Central America, 1824–1975.* Tempe: Center for Latin American Studies, Arizona State University, 1976.

Lobo, Tatiana. *Assault on Paradise: A Novel.* Translated by Asa Zatz. Willimantic, Conn.: Curbstone, 1998.

MacLeod, Murdo J. *Spanish Central America: A Socioeconomic History, 1520–1720.* Berkeley: University of California Press, 1973.

Stone, Doris. *Pre-Columbian Man in Costa Rica.* Cambridge, Mass.: Peabody Museum Press, 1977.

Stone, Samuel Z. *The Heritage of the Conquistadors: Ruling Classes in Central America from the Conquest to the Sandinistas.* Lincoln: University of Nebraska Press, 1990.

Wortman, Miles L. *Government and Society in Central America, 1680–1840.* New York: Columbia University Press, 1982.

II. Coffee Nation

Bethell, Leslie, ed. *Central America since Independence*. New York: Cambridge University Press, 1991.

Fernández Guardia, Ricardo. *Cuentos Ticos: Short Stories of Costa Rica*. Translated by Gray Casement. 3d ed. Freeport, N.Y.: Books for Libraries Press, 1970.

Gudmundson, Lowell, and Héctor Lindo-Fuentes. *Central America, 1821–1871: Liberalism before Liberal Reform*. Tuscaloosa: University of Alabama Press, 1995.

Hall, Carolyn. *Costa Rica: A Geographical Interpretation in Historical Perspective*. Boulder, Colo.: Westview, 1985.

Roseberry, William, Lowell Gudmundson, and Mario Samper Kutschbach, eds. *Coffee, Society, and Power in Latin America*. Baltimore, Md.: Johns Hopkins University Press, 1995.

Samper, Mario. *Generations of Settlers: Rural Households and Markets on the Costa Rican Frontier, 1850–1935*. Boulder, Colo.: Westview, 1990.

Williams, Robert G. *States and Social Evolution: Coffee and the Rise of National Governments in Central America*. Chapel Hill: University of North Carolina Press, 1994.

III. Popular Culture and Social Policy

Bell, John Patrick. *Crisis in Costa Rica: The 1948 Revolution*. Austin: University of Texas Press, 1971.

González, Luisa. *At the Bottom: A Woman's Life in Central America*. Berkeley, Calif.: New Earth Publications, 1994.

Lyra, Carmen. *The Subversive Voice of Carmen Lyra: Selected Works*. Edited and translated by Elizabeth Rosa Horan. Gainesville: University Press of Florida, 2000.

Miller, Eugene D. *A Holy Alliance? The Church and the Left in Costa Rica, 1932–1948*. Armonk, N.Y.: M. E. Sharpe, 1996.

Palmer, Steven. *From Popular Medicine to Medical Populism: Doctors, Healers and Public Power in Costa Rica, 1800–1940*. Durham, N.C.: Duke University Press, 2003.

IV. Democratic Enigma

Ameringer, Charles D. *Don Pepe: A Political Biography of José Figueres of Costa Rica*. Albuquerque: University of New Mexico Press, 1978.

Booth, John A. *Costa Rica: Quest for Democracy*. Boulder, Colo.: Westview, 1998.

Carey, John M. *Term Limits and Legislative Representation*. New York: Cambridge University Press, 1996.

Lehoucq, Fabrice E., and Iván Molina. *Stuffing the Ballot Box: Fraud, Electoral Reform, and Democratization in Costa Rica*. New York: Cambridge University Press, 2002.

Mahoney, James. *The Legacies of Liberalism: Path Dependence and Political Regimes in Central America*. Baltimore, Md.: Johns Hopkins University Press, 2001.

Paige, Jeffrey M. *Coffee and Power: Revolution and the Rise of Democracy in Central America.* Cambridge, Mass.: Harvard University Press, 1997.

Wilson, Bruce M. *Costa Rica: Politics, Economics, and Democracy.* Boulder, Colo.: Lynne Rienner, 1998.

Yashar, Deborah J. *Demanding Democracy: Reform and Reaction in Costa Rica and Guatemala, 1870s–1950s.* Stanford, Calif.: Stanford University Press, 1997.

V. The Costa Rican Dream

Biesanz, Mavis Hiltunen, Richard Biesanz, and Karen Zubris Biesanz. *The Ticos: Culture and Social Change in Costa Rica.* Boulder, Colo.: Lynne Rienner, 1999.

Bulmer-Thomas, Victor. *The Political Economy of Central America since 1920.* Cambridge: Cambridge University Press, 1987.

Cardona-Hine, Alvaro. *A History of Light: A Memoir.* Santa Fe, N.M.: Sherman Asher, 1997.

Edelman, Marc, and Joanne Kenen, eds. *The Costa Rica Reader.* New York: Grove Weidenfield, 1989.

Honey, Martha. *Hostile Acts: U.S. Policy in Costa Rica in the 1980s.* Gainesville: University Press of Florida, 1994.

Longley, Kyle. *The Sparrow and the Hawk: Costa Rica and the United States during the Rise of José Figueres.* Tuscaloosa: University of Alabama Press, 1997.

Mesa-Lago, Carmelo, et al. *Market, Socialist, and Mixed Economies: Comparative Policy and Performance: Chile, Cuba, and Costa Rica.* Baltimore, Md.: Johns Hopkins University Press, 2000.

VI. Other Cultures and Outer Reaches

Bourgois, Philippe I. *Ethnicity at Work: Divided Labor on a Central American Banana Plantation.* Baltimore, Md.: Johns Hopkins University Press, 1989.

Chomsky, Aviva. *West Indian Workers and the United Fruit Company in Costa Rica, 1870–1940.* Baton Rouge: Louisiana State University Press, 1996.

Edelman, Marc. *The Logic of the Latifundio: The Large Estates of Northwestern Costa Rica since the Late Nineteenth Century.* Stanford, Calif.: Stanford University Press, 1992.

Harpelle, Ronald N. *The West Indians of Costa Rica: Race, Class, and the Integration of an Ethnic Minority.* Montreal, Canada: McGill-Queens University Press, 2001.

Hayden, Bridget A. *Salvadorans in Costa Rica: Displaced Lives.* Tucson: University of Arizona Press, 2003.

Jaramillo Levi, Enrique, ed. *When New Flowers Bloomed: Short Stories by Women Writers from Costa Rica and Panama.* Pittsburgh, Pa.: Latin American Literary Review Press, 1991.

Mosby, Dorothy E. *Place, Language, and Identity in Afro-Costa Rican Literature.* Columbia: University of Missouri Press, 2003.

Palmer, Paula. *"What Happen": A Folk History of Costa Rica's Talamanca Coast.* San
    José, Costa Rica: Editorama, 1993.

Palmer, Paula, Juanita Sánchez, and Gloria Mayorga. *Taking Care of Sibö's Gifts:
    An Environmental Treatise from Costa Rica's KéköLdi Indigenous Reserve.* San
    José, Costa Rica: Asociación de Desarrollo Integral de la Reserva Indígena
    Cocles/KéköLdi, 1993.

Putnam, Lara, *The Company They Kept: Migrants and the Politics of Gender in Caribbean
    Costa Rica, 1870–1960.* Chapel Hill: University of North Carolina Press, 2002.

VII. Working Paradise

Evans, Sterling. *The Green Republic: A Conservation History of Costa Rica.* Austin:
    University of Texas Press, 1999.

Honey, Martha, ed. *Ecotourism and Certification: Setting Standards in Practice.* Washing-
    ton, D.C.: Island, 2002.

McCook, Stuart. *States of Nature: Science, Agriculture, and the Environment in the
    Spanish Caribbean, 1760–1940.* Austin: University of Texas Press, 2002.

Pebley, Anne R., and Luis Rosero-Bixby, eds. *Demographic Diversity and Change in the
    Central American Isthmus.* Santa Monica, Calif.: Rand, 1997.

Savitsky, Basil G., and Thomas E. Lacher Jr., eds. GIS *Methodologies for Developing Con-
    servation Strategies: Tropical Forest Recovery and Wildlife Management in Costa Rica.*
    New York: Columbia University Press, 1998.

Wallace, David Rains. *The Quetzal and the Macaw: The Story of Costa Rica's National
    Parks.* San Francisco: Sierra Club Books, 1992.

VIII. Tropical Soundings

Abshagen Leitinger, Ilse, ed. *The Costa Rican Women's Movement: A Reader.* Pittsburgh,
    Pa.: University of Pittsburgh Press, 1997.

Ai Camp, Roderic. *Citizen Views of Democracy in Latin America.* Pittsburgh, Pa.: Uni-
    versity of Pittsburgh Press, 2001.

Clark, Mary A. *Gradual Economic Reform in Latin America: The Costa Rican Experience.*
    Albany: State University of New York Press, 2001.

Edelman, Marc. *Peasants against Globalization: Rural Social Movements in Costa Rica.*
    Stanford, Calif.: Stanford University Press, 1999.

Helmuth, Chalene. *Culture and Customs of Costa Rica.* Westport, Conn.: Greenwood,
    2000.

Schifter, Jacobo. *From Toads to Queens: Transvestism in a Latin American Setting.* New
    York: Harrington Park, 1999.

Steigenga, Timothy J. *The Politics of the Spirit: The Political Implications of Pente-
    costalized Religion in Costa Rica and Guatemala.* Lanham, Md.: Lexington Books,
    2001.

Acknowledgment of Copyrights

Index

STEVEN PALMER is an Assistant Professor in the
Department of History at the University of Windsor,
Canada. He is the author of *From Popular Medicine to
Medical Populism: Doctors, Healers, and Public Power in
Costa Rica, 1800–1940*. IVÁN MOLINA is a Professor of
History at the Escuela de Historia and a Researcher at
the Centro de Investigación en Identidad y Cultura
Latinoamericanas (CIICLA), both at the Universidad de
Costa Rica. Among his many books are *Costa Rica
(1800–1850): El legado colonial y la génesis del capitalismo*;
La miel de los mudos y otros cuentos ticos de ciencia ficción;
and *La estela de la pluma: Cultura impresa e intelectuales
en Centroamérica durante los siglos XIX y XX*. Palmer and
Molina are coauthors of *Educando a Costa Rica:
Alfabetización popular, formación docente y género, 1880–
1950*; *Historia de Costa Rica: Breve, actualizada y con
ilustraciones*; and *La voluntad radiante: Cultura impresa,
magia y medicina en Costa Rica, 1897–1932*. They have
coedited *El paso del cometa: Estado, política social y
culturas populares en Costa Rica (1800–1950)*; and *Héroes al
gusto y libros de moda: Sociedad y cambio cultural en Costa
Rica, 1750–1900*.

Library of Congress Cataloging-in-Publication Data
The Costa Rica reader : history, culture, politics /
edited by Steven Palmer and Iván Molina.
p. cm. — (Latin America readers)
Includes index.
ISBN 0-8223-3386-4 (cloth : alk. paper) —
ISBN 0-8223-3372-4 (pbk. : alk. paper)
1. Costa Rica—History.   2. Costa Rica—Social
conditions.   3. Costa Rica—Economic conditions.
I. Palmer, Steven Paul.   II. Molina Jiménez, Iván.
III. Series.
F1546.C765   2004
972.86—dc22   2004004078